Social Comparison and Social Psychology

Much of our knowledge about ourselves, and about the world in which we live, is based on a process of social comparison. Our tendency to appraise events, objects, people, and social groups by making comparisons has captured the interest of social psychologists for over half a century. This volume provides an up-to-date synthesis of the latest theoretical and empirical developments in social psychology through research on social comparison processes. With chapters by leading theorists and internationally renowned researchers, it provides invaluable information on the role of this process of comparison as it occurs within a single individual over time, between individuals, and between social groups. It also features an original international study testing the universality of the effects of social comparison on the self. This book will appeal to scholars and students alike and will serve as an important reference for the study of cognition, intergroup relations, and culture.

SERGE GUIMOND is Professor of Psychology at the Université Blaise Pascal in Clermont-Ferrand, France.

Social Comparison and Social Psychology

Understanding Cognition, Intergroup Relations, and Culture

edited by

Serge Guimond

CAMBRIDGE
UNIVERSITY PRESS

CAMBRIDGE UNIVERSITY PRESS
Cambridge, New York, Melbourne, Madrid, Cape Town, Singapore, São Paulo

CAMBRIDGE UNIVERSITY PRESS
The Edinburgh Building, Cambridge CB2 2RU, UK

Published in the United States of America by Cambridge University Press,
New York

www.cambridge.org
Information on this title: www.cambridge.org/9780521608442

First published 2006

Printed in the United Kingdom at the University Press, Cambridge

A catalogue record for this book is available from the British Library

ISBN-13 978-0-521-84593-9 hardback
ISBN-10 0-521-84593-9 hardback
ISBN-13 978-0-521-60844-2 paperback
ISBN-10 0-521-60844-9 paperback

Cambridge University Press has no responsibility for
the persistence or accuracy of URLs for external or
third-party internet websites referred to in this book,
and does not guarantee that any content on such
websites is, or will remain, accurate or appropriate.

Contents

List of figures	*page* viii
List of tables	x
List of contributors	xi
Preface	xv

Introduction: social comparison processes and levels of analysis   1
SERGE GUIMOND

Part 1 Cognition: comparison processes within and between individuals   13

1 Social comparison orientation: a new perspective on those who do and those who don't compare with others   15
ABRAHAM P. BUUNK AND FREDERICK X. GIBBONS

2 The why, who, and how of social comparison: a social-cognition perspective   33
THOMAS MUSSWEILER, KATJA RÜTER, AND KAI EPSTUDE

3 Autobiographical memory, the self, and comparison processes   55
RASYID BO SANITIOSO, MARTIN A. CONWAY, AND SOPHIE BRUNOT

4 Comparing oneself over time: the temporal dimension in social comparison   76
SANDRINE REDERSDORFF AND SERGE GUIMOND

Part 2 Intergroup relations: comparison processes within and between groups   97

5 Predicting comparison choices in intergroup settings: a new look   99
HANNA ZAGEFKA AND RUPERT BROWN

6   The variable impact of upward and downward social
    comparisons on self-esteem: when the level
    of analysis matters   127
    DELPHINE MARTINOT AND SANDRINE REDERSDORFF

7   Attitudes toward redistributive social policies: the effects
    of social comparisons and policy experience   151
    DONNA M. GARCIA, NYLA R. BRANSCOMBE,
    SERGE DESMARAIS, AND STEPHANIE S. GEE

8   Social comparison and group-based emotions   174
    VINCENT YZERBYT, MURIEL DUMONT,
    BERNARD MATHIEU, ERNESTINE GORDIJN,
    AND DANIEL WIGBOLDUS

9   The counter-intuitive effect of relative gratification
    on intergroup attitudes: ecological validity, moderators
    and mediators   206
    MICHAËL DAMBRUN, SERGE GUIMOND,
    AND DONALD M. TAYLOR

10 Social comparison and the personal group discrimination
    discrepancy   228
    MURIEL DUMONT, ELÉONORE SERON,
    VINCENT YZERBYT, AND TOM POSTMES

**Part 3   Culture: comparison processes within and
across cultures**   247

11 Stereotype content across cultures as a function of
    group status   249
    SUSAN T. FISKE AND AMY J. C. CUDDY

12 The cultural norm of individualism and group status:
    implications for social comparisons   264
    FABIO LORENZI-CIOLDI AND ARMAND CHATARD

13 Ambivalent sexism, power distance, and gender
    inequality across cultures   283
    PETER GLICK

14 Social comparisons across cultures I: Gender
    stereotypes in high and low power
    distance cultures   303
    MICHEL DÉSERT AND JACQUES-PHILIPPE LEYENS

15 Social comparisons across cultures II: Change and stability
    in self-views – experimental evidence   318
    S. GUIMOND, A. CHATARD, N. R. BRANSCOMBE,
    S. BRUNOT, A. P. BUUNK, M. A. CONWAY, R. J. CRISP,
    M. DAMBRUN, M. DÉSERT, D. M. GARCIA, S. HAQUE,
    J.-P. LEYENS, F. LORENZI-CIOLDI, D. MARTINOT,
    S. REDERSDORFF, AND V. YZERBYT

Author index   345
Subject index   348

Figures

2.1 The selective accessibility mechanism (from
    Mussweiler, 2003a)   *page* 42
2.2 Self-evaluations of adjustment to college after
    comparison with a high versus low standard
    by similarity versus dissimilarity focus (from
    Mussweiler, 2001)   45
3.1 The autobiographical memory knowledge base   59
5.1 Mean Comparison Interest in different targets   106
6.1 State self-esteem in women by social comparison
    direction, and group membership of comparison
    target   135
6.2 Identification with women by social comparison
    direction, and comparison group   135
6.3 State self-esteem in both men and women by group
    status, social comparison direction, and comparison
    group   141
6.4 Perceived informativeness of the comparison target,
    by group status and group membership of target   144
7.1 Mean responses on the perceptions of meritocracy
    inventory   165
7.2 Mean responses on the neosexism measures   165
7.3 Adjusted mean responses for support of affirmative
    action after controlling for participants' age, education,
    political orientation, and education × political
    orientation   166
7.4 Adjusted mean responses for support of comparable
    worth after controlling for participants' age, education,
    political orientation, and education × political orientation   167
9.1 The effect of intelligence RG on different ethnic targets   212
9.2 Effect of RG on different student targets   213
9.3 Linear and quadratic relationships between the RG-RD
    continuum and prejudice towards immigrants   216

9.4	Affective and cognitive components of RG as potentials mediators	219
9.5	Ethnic identification and SDO as two independent mediators of the effect of RG on prejudice and right-wing political attitudes	222
10.1	Perceived personal and group discrimination as a function of threat	235
11.1	Status-competence correlation in EU nations' average ratings of each other	257
11.2	Status-competence correlation in Hong Kong sample	258
12.1	Principal components analysis of "What confers prestige to a goods"	268
12.2	Principal components analysis of the descriptions of one's own car	269
12.3	Self-perception of male and female college students according to the gender vs. cultural prime: individual and collective norms	272
12.4	Self-descriptions as a function of participant sex and comparative context	276
14.1	Means of attributions of agentic/independent characteristics to men and women, as a function of culture	309
14.2	Means of attributions of gift in math and science to men and women, as a function of culture	310
15.1	Mean scores on the measure of power distance beliefs	328
15.2	Mean scores on the Social Comparison Orientation scale	330
15.3	Gender by culture interaction on relational self-construal in the control condition	334
15.4	Sex by culture interaction on agency in the intergroup comparison condition	336

Tables

4.1	Distinguishing different levels of temporal comparisons	*page* 78
5.1	Comparison motives	109
5.2	Effect of RD on comparison interest, Study 3	112
5.3	Identification and comparison interest in different targets	117
6.1	Effects of intergroup comparisons on self-esteem as a function of group status, direction of comparison and group of comparison target	129
7.1	The effects of the presence or absence of redistributive policies in organizational settings on self perception, perceptions of structural inequality, and policy support	162
11.1	Scales	254
11.2	Status-competence correlations, all studies	256
13.1	National means on power distance, gender ideologies, and gender equality	293
13.2	Correlations of ambivalent gender ideologies with power distance and gender equality	294
13.3	Correlations of gender gaps in ASI/AMI scores with power distance and gender equality	298
14.1	Means for attribution of the relational/interdependent dimension to men and women, as a function of participants' gender	308
14.2	Means for attribution of the relational/interdependent dimension to men and women, as a function of culture and participants' gender	308

Contributors

NYLA R. BRANSCOMBE	Department of Psychology, University of Kansas, USA
RUPERT BROWN	Department of Psychology, University of Sussex, England
SOPHIE BRUNOT	Département de Psychologie, Université Rennes 2, Rennes, France
ABRAHAM P. BUUNK	Unit of Social and Organisational Psychology, University of Groningen, The Netherlands
ARMAND CHATARD	Université de Genève, FPSE, Genève, Switzerland
MARTIN A. CONWAY	Institute of Psychological Sciences, The University of Leeds, England
RICHARD J. CRISP	School of Psychology, The University of Birmingham, Birmingham, England
AMY J. C. CUDDY	Department of Psychology, Princeton University, USA
MICHAËL DAMBRUN	Laboratoire de Psychologie Sociale et Cognitive (CNRS), Université Blaise Pascal, Clermont-Ferrand, France
MICHEL DÉSERT	Laboratoire de Psychologie Sociale et Cognitive (CNRS), Université Blaise Pascal, Clermont-Ferrand, France
SERGE DESMARAIS	Department of Psychology, University of Guelph, Canada
MURIEL DUMONT	Catholic University of Louvain, Department of Psychology, Louvain-la-Neuve, Belgium
KAI EPSTUDE	Psychologie II Universitaet Wuerzburg, Wuerzburg, Germany
SUSAN T. FISKE	Department of Psychology, Princeton University, USA

DONNA M. GARCIA	Department of Psychology, University of Kansas, USA
STEPHANIE S. GEE	University of Windsor, Windsor, Canada
FREDERICK X. GIBBONS	Department of Psychology, Iowa State University, USA
PETER GLICK	Psychology Department, Lawrence University, USA
ERNESTINE GORDIJN	Department of Psychology, University of Groningen, The Netherlands
SERGE GUIMOND	Laboratoire de Psychologie Sociale et Cognitive (CNRS), Université Blaise Pascal, Clermont-Ferrand, France
SHAMSUL HAQUE	Department of Psychology, International Islamic University Malaysia, Kuala Lumpur, Malaysia
JACQUES-PHILIPPE LEYENS	Catholic University of Louvain, Department of Psychology, Louvain-la-Neuve, Belgium
FABIO LORENZI-CIOLDI	Université de Genève, FPSE, Genève, Switzerland
DELPHINE MARTINOT	Laboratoire de Psychologie Sociale et Cognitive (CNRS), Université Blaise Pascal, Clermont-Ferrand, France
BERNARD MATHIEU	Catholic University of Louvain, Department of Psychology, Louvain-la-Neuve, Belgium
THOMAS MUSSWEILER	Psychologie II Universitaet Wuerzburg, Wuerzburg, Germany
TOM POSTMES	Department of Psychology, University of Exeter, England
SANDRINE REDERSDORFF	Laboratoire de Psychologie Sociale et Cognitive (CNRS), Université Blaise Pascal, Clermont-Ferrand, France
KATJA RÜTER	Psychologie II Universitaet Wuerzburg, Wuerzburg, Germany
RASYID BO SANITIOSO	Université Paris V and Laboratoire de Psychologie Sociale et Cognitive (CNRS), Clermont-Ferrand, France
ELÉONORE SERON	Catholic University of Louvain, Department of Psychology, Louvain-la-Neuve, Belgium
DONALD M. TAYLOR	Department of Psychology, McGill University, Montreal, Québec, Canada

DANIËL WIGBOLDUS   Department of Social Psychology, Radboud
                          University Nijmegen, Nijmegen,
                          The Netherlands
VINCENT YZERBYT   Catholic University of Louvain, Department
                          of Psychology, Louvain-la-Neuve, Belgium
HANNA ZAGEFKA   Department of Psychology, School of Life
                          Sciences, University of Sussex, England

Preface

The idea for this book derives from a research project developed by a group of social psychologists from the Social and Cognitive Psychology Laboratory (LAPSCO-CNRS) of the Université Blaise Pascal in Clermont-Ferrand, France. It is a great pleasure for me to acknowledge the material and financial support received for this project from our laboratory and its staff, and from the ACI-Cognitique Program of the French Government in the form of a research grant. Most of the people that have contributed to this volume were associated with this project from very early on. Indeed, one of the stated objectives of the project was to develop research on social comparison processes through international collaborations. To this end, a first meeting was held in July 2002 in San Sebastian, Spain involving American, British, Belgian, Dutch, and French social psychologists, and a second meeting was held in Clermont-Ferrand in January 2004, involving American, Dutch, French, German, and Swiss social psychologists. These meetings provided unique opportunities to discuss theoretical and research issues, and these discussions were important to develop many ideas covered in this book.

I would like to thank all the contributors to this volume who have agreed to participate in this project. Their dedication and goodwill helped to turn hard work into nice times. I am grateful to Sandra Duarte and Magali Villate for their precious help during various phases of this project, to Jean-Léon Beauvois, Jean-Pierre Deconchy, Nicole Dubois, Gérard Lemaine, Jean-Marc Monteil, and Donald Taylor for inspiring discussions, and to Sarah Caro, Elizabeth Davey, and Laura Hemming from Cambridge University Press for their enthusiasm, professionalism, and support. A special thanks is due to Kate Reynolds and John Turner for providing the opportunities to share some ideas related to the preparation of this book at a memorable meeting hosted by the Australian National University. Last but not least, I want to express my love to my family, Caroline, Antoine and Marité, who have contributed immensely to this volume by their comments and questions, and to my parents, Gilda and Camille, who are truly "incomparable."

S. G., CLERMONT-FERRAND,
February 2005

xv

Introduction: social comparison processes and levels of analysis

Serge Guimond

"I do not know how far I differ from other people. That is another memoir writer's difficulty. Yet to describe oneself truly one must have some standard of comparison; was I clever, stupid, good looking, ugly, passionate, cold – ? Owing partly to the fact that I was never at school, never competed in any way with children of my own age, I have never been able to compare my gifts and defects with other people's"

(Virginia Woolf, A sketch of the past, autobiographical writings of 1939)

Fifty years ago, Festinger (1954) published a *Theory of social comparison processes*. Today, thirty-five social and cognitive psychologists who share a common interest in comparison processes combined their efforts to make this new book on the same topic a reality. Few theories in social psychology have stood the test of time as successfully as the theory of social comparison. Even today, major theoretical and empirical papers on social comparison processes are being published in the best scientific journals (for example, Buunk and Ybema, 2003; Markman and McMullen, 2003; Mugny, Butera, Quiamzade, Dragulescu and Tomei, 2003; Mussweiler, 2003; Spears, Gordijn, Dijksterhuis and Stapel, 2004; Stapel and Suls, 2004 and many others). How can one explain the tremendous amount of research that continues to investigate the psychological role of social comparison? What makes social comparison so important? These questions will be answered in the following chapters.

However, this book is not "only" about social comparison. It is also about social psychology. Social psychology is devoted to understanding and explaining the behavior of individuals. Social psychologists are interested in cognition, how people think and behave. But what makes social psychology a distinctive scientific discipline is its concern with how individual behavior and cognition are shaped by the social context (Monteil, 1998; Monteil and Huguet, 1999). Human beings do not live as isolated individuals. The laboratory situation of a sole individual working on a cognitive task is far from the social reality of individuals constantly interacting with one another at home, at school, at work or at play. Thus, social psychology deals with how we think, feel and behave by

1

taking into account the influence of the social environment in which we live. The process of social comparison turned out to be extremely useful in this venture (Turner, Oakes, Haslam, and McGarty, 1994). Indeed, this uniquely social-psychological process arises precisely because we are constantly surrounded by the physical, symbolic or imaginary presence of others. As a result, we can relate to others, we can psychologically compare ourselves to others. Writing in 1939, Virginia Woolf understood amazingly well the power of social comparison, although at that time very little research had been conducted on the topic. There is now a strong body of evidence showing that social comparison processes shape the way we think, feel, and react. The mere fact that we compare ourselves to X rather than to Y has the power to transform our thinking, our emotions, and our behaviour. Thus, a first major reason for the persistent importance of social comparison in social psychology is that it allows for a better explanation of social behaviors and provides invaluable insights into the complexities of human social interactions.

Another reason for the striking and continuing influence of social comparison processes in social psychology may be found in the work of Jerry Suls. In addition to several other related publications, three major books on social comparison were edited by Jerry Suls and colleagues, in 1977 (Suls and Miller), in 1991 (Suls and Wills), and in 2000 (Suls and Wheeler). In every instance, the work represented a substantial contribution to theory and research on social comparison. The major influence of these books undoubtedly helps explain the sustaining interest for social comparison in social psychology. Each time, however, this work was also largely focused on social comparisons occurring at the individual level of analysis, not at the group level.

In a paper published in French, Tajfel (1972) argued that it might be useful to think about social comparison occurring not only between individuals but also between groups. These ideas were published in a more expanded version in English in 1974 and formed the basis of one of the most influential theories in social psychology, now known as Social Identity Theory (Tajfel and Turner, 1986). Around that time, Lemaine (1974) was also showing how social comparison can lead to differentiation and the creation of new dimensions of comparison in a search for originality. A year later, an important theoretical paper by Turner (1975) was entitled: "Social comparison and social identity: some prospects for intergroup behaviour." This work, as shown by the title, was devoted to an elaborate discussion of social comparison processes. Yet, even superficial references to Tajfel, Lemaine, Turner, or the topic of intergroup social comparisons cannot be found in Suls and Miller (1977). One has to read eighteen chapters of the *Handbook of social comparison* (Suls and

Wheeler, 2000) before coming to Part IV of the handbook, entitled "Applications," to find, in Chapter 19 by Hogg, an analysis of the relations between intergroup social comparisons and social identity. This does not reflect the simple fact that social comparison theory and research in and of themselves have nothing to do with social groups. To the contrary, Forsyth (2000) points out that "social comparison theory is as much a theory about group dynamics as it is a theory about individual's perceptions of their opinions and abilities." (p. 98)

If we examine research dealing with Social Identity Theory, or the related work on the more recent Self-Categorization Theory, a similar state of affairs can be found. Oakes, Haslam, and Turner (1994) do not consider in any substantial manner traditional social comparison research even though their theoretical perspectives highlight the importance of comparative context. Ellemers, Spears, and Doosje's book (1999) entitled *Social identity* generally confirms this trend. Indeed, Hogg (2000) concluded his chapter by noting that: "Although the cornerstone of social identity theory is the comparative relations that exist between groups and the comparative nature of the social categorization process that underpins social identity phenomena, there is remarkably little systematic attention paid by social identity theorists to social comparison theory." (p. 415) Overall, it seems fair to state that within social psychology, two major traditions of research both dealing with the psychology of social comparison, albeit each in distinctive ways, have ignored each other.

However, there are some significant exceptions to this general trend. Research by Brewer and Weber (1994), Redersdorff and Martinot (2003), Schmitt, Silvia, and Branscombe (2000), and Taylor, Moghaddam, and Bellerose (1989) has endeavored to integrate social comparison processes as they occur both at the individual level and at the group level of analysis. This empirical work strongly confirms one assumption of the present volume: each tradition of research has something of importance to contribute to the other. The nature of our comparative activity, and its role in social life, may be better understood by sharing insights. It is, in part, to address this theoretical gap that the present book was produced. At the intersection of a concern for both the individual person and the social group, theories in social psychology can emphasize one level of analysis (i.e., the individual level) or another (i.e., the group level). One long-term goal is to combine and integrate these various levels of explanation into a better and more thorough theoretical account of human behavior (Doise, 1986). With this goal in mind, the present book is unique in bringing together leading researchers and theorists, many of whom think about social comparison mainly from the individual level of analysis whereas others consider primarily the group level of analysis. As such, this work represents the first concerted attempt at fostering the integration of research on social comparison processes occurring at different levels of analysis.

Structure and content: overview of present work

This book is structured in three parts. Part One deals with social comparison within and between individuals. Part Two is dedicated to social comparison within and between groups, and Part Three examines social comparison processes at the cultural level of analysis. Together, all three sections of this book are necessary to grasp the insights that looking at social comparison processes from different levels of analysis has to offer.

Part One. Cognition

The four chapters in the first part are devoted to theory and research relevant to comparative processes occurring within and between individuals. In Chapter 1, Buunk and Gibbons present an overview of their program of research on the cognitive and affective impact of upward and downward social comparisons. They approach this topic by considering that whereas everyone will engage in social comparisons from time to time, some people are likely to be more concerned than others by social comparison. The scale of Social Comparison Orientation was developed to measure this varying degree of concern. As very few attempts have been made to study individual differences in social comparison (Wheeler, 2000), the use of this scale by Buunk and Gibbons, in a large variety of contexts and with a wide range of people, to study the impact of social comparison information provides the basis for a refreshing new look at key issues that have dominated traditional social comparison theory and research.

In Chapter 2, Mussweiler, Rüter, and Epstude also deal with key issues emanating directly from Festinger (1954) but from a social cognition perspective. There is no doubt that the social cognition movement has been a driving force behind the theoretical and methodological advances over the last twenty years. It paved the way for a better understanding of the ways in which basic cognitive processes such as memory, attention, and categorization, enter into the construction of social thinking. It led to important innovations in the measurement of traditional psychological concepts such as attitudes, self-esteem, and stereotypes. It raised new issues about automaticity, unconscious cognitions, and the extent to which our behavior is under a certain amount of cognitive control.

It also brought a renewed concern with the extent to which cognitive activity can be impacted by contextual variables. The work of Mussweiler and colleagues reflects these important developments and not only suggests how they may be fruitfully integrated within social comparison theory and research, but also provides strong empirical support for this new approach.

Continuing this emphasis on cognition, Sanitioso, Conway, and Brunot discuss in Chapter 3 the possible connections between social comparison and autobiographical memory. They present some fascinating evidence of variations in memories as a function of the self and the social context. However, contrary to Mussweiler, Rüter, and Epstude, they attribute a fundamental role to motivation. They consider that much of our social and temporal comparison activities, and their reflections in our autobiographical memories, are driven by the motivation for a positive self-concept. In Chapter 4, Redersdorff and Guimond focus on the issues that Sanitioso, Conway, and Brunot raised at the end of their chapter in relation to temporal-self comparison. They review evidence from studies involving comparison with the past and comparison with the future, using social comparison theory and relative deprivation theory as conceptual frameworks, and note emerging trends that are found when the temporal dimension is considered. They suggest that cognitive factors such as how the past and the future are mentally represented, as well as implicit theories of intelligence, may be as important as motivational factors in order to understand the role of temporal-self comparisons. This is an area where new research is being undertaken and this chapter plays a useful role in trying to specify what is known and what needs to be looked at in the future.

Part Two. Intergroup relations

Social psychologists have always been interested in cognition (Zajonc, 1980). However, they have also shown a longstanding interest in the psychological aspects of intergroup rivalry and conflict (Sherif and Wilson, 1953). In recent years, the field of intergroup relations took center stage in social psychology largely through the influence of European social psychologists such as Tajfel, Doise, and Moscovici (Moreland, Hogg, and Hains, 1994). From being relatively minor in the 1960s and 1970s, the social psychology of intergroup relations has become one of the most active and influential domains of research within the discipline. Even though social comparison processes between groups were at the very basis of the theoretical explanation of intergroup behavior (Tajfel, 1974; Turner, 1975), this work has not been considered as part of the typical research on social comparison processes. In an attempt to foster integrative thinking in this area, the six chapters in Part Two are devoted to theory and research on social comparison within and between groups. The issues raised in these chapters have clear implications for any theory that uses the concept of social comparison. In Chapter 5, Hanna Zagefka and Rupert Brown systematically assess, in a series of ten studies, the factors that have been hypothesized as determinants of social comparison choices in intergroup relations. Their findings are extremely informative in terms of the frequency with which people engage in various types of social comparison in naturalistic settings, and also about the reasons why people do so. As the results are quite consistent from one study to the next, they offer a solid contribution to the literature on social comparison.

The remaining chapters in Part Two are mainly concerned with the effects of social comparison, which represent, with the topic of comparison choices, the defining issues of social comparison research. In Chapter 6, Martinot and Redersdorff present an overview of their experimental research on the effects of ingroup versus outgroup comparisons on self-esteem. The issue of self-esteem is central to both individual-level research and intergroup research on social comparison (see Crocker and Major, 1989; Long and Spears, 1997). One of the main points to emerge from the research of Martinot and Redersdorff is that the effects of social comparison on self-esteem vary in systematic and predictable ways as a function of the level of analysis. In Chapter 7, Garcia, Branscombe, Desmarais, and Gee look at similar issues but in a naturalistic setting. They develop the theoretical implications of Self-Categorization Theory (Turner, Hogg, Oakes, Reicher, and Wetherell, 1987) for an understanding of women and men's attitudes toward gender-based redistributive policies in employment settings. Their findings suggest that these social policies may have some unsuspected effects among those who have experienced them, effects which can be predicted on the basis of the role of intra versus intergroup social comparisons. In Chapter 8, Yzerbyt, Dumont, Mathieu, Gordijn, and Wigboldus argue for the role of social comparison processes in the emergence of group-based emotions. The idea that individuals can experience emotions as group members was developed theoretically by Smith (1993) and led to several studies documenting various facets of these "intergroup emotions." This chapter, however, is the first to reveal the striking impact of contrasting social comparisons on group-based emotions, and to specify the ways in which these comparisons can generate distinctly different emotions.

In Chapter 9, Dambrun, Guimond, and Taylor discuss recent research related to the concept of relative gratification. As Pettigrew (2002) noted: "relative deprivation has been studied for half a century but not its reverse – relative gratification. What are the consequences of making comparisons for yourself and your group that reveal your advantaged position?" (p. 354) The aim of the research discussed by Dambrun and colleagues is precisely to investigate the effects of comparing favorably to others. The results are quite clear: people become more prejudiced against low status targets in these conditions. The chapter explores the role of several variables moderating and/or mediating the effects of relative gratification. In Chapter 10, Dumont, Seron, Yzerbyt, and Postmes examine the personal-group discrimination discrepancy from a social comparison perspective. They show that underlying this phenomenon, which has generated numerous studies, are some striking demonstrations of the ways in which social comparisons at the individual level and social comparisons at the group level are both needed to understand people's behavior. Their research identifies conditions under which people are more likely to engage in self-ingroup contrastive social comparisons, distancing themselves psychologically from their ingroup, and as a result, claim that their ingroup is discriminated against, but not themselves.

Part Three. Culture

The chapters in Part Three address the cultural level of analysis. Culture is a major construct in social sciences and probably the most recent one to become part of mainstream social psychology. Cross-cultural psychologists have long been arguing that in order to develop truly general principles of human behavior, psychological phenomena need to be studied across cultures and not only within cultures. These arguments were often dismissed as being irrelevant to a "proper" scientific approach. There are now definite signs that this is changing. It is becoming more and more frequent to find, in mainstream journals, studies of similarities and differences between people in various cultures. Books have been written about a cross-cultural social psychology (Moghaddam, Taylor, and Wright, 1993; Smith and Bond, 1999) and leading experimental social psychologists have devoted entire research programs to the study of cultural differences (e.g., Nisbett, 2003). Perhaps even more important, there are now indications that social comparison processes have vital methodological as well as theoretical implications for understanding the role of culture (see Heine, Lehman, Peng, and Greenholtz, 2002). Thus, the third and last part of this book is particularly innovative in providing detailed theoretical and empirical analyses of the link between comparative processes and the study of cultures.

In Chapter 11, Fiske and Cuddy discuss the development of the Stereotype Content Model on the basis of a series of international studies.

They highlight the role of perceived group status which implies a comparative judgment on a dimension of prestige, social standing, or power. Evidence of pancultural uniformity in stereotype content is found among fourteen nations representing diverse cultures and, presumably, various modes of thinking. This raises the question of whether thinking about relative group status could reflect a potentially universal process of social comparison. In Chapter 12, Lorenzi-Cioldi and Chatard also discuss the role of group status and cultural norms but in an entirely different perspective. On the basis of several studies, they suggest that dominant groups are those who embody the dominant cultural norms, such as the norm of individualism in western societies. This implies that subordinate groups are somewhat at variance with such norms. They draw out the implications of this analysis for the operation of social comparison processes and find support for their thinking in studies of gender groups. As such, this chapter explains why women and men can react quite differently to the same social comparison information.

In Chapter 13, Peter Glick presents a cross-cultural analysis of ambivalent gender ideologies based on data from twenty-five nations. He discusses the relations between cross-gender social comparisons and gender inequality, and argues that cultural ideologies can influence such social comparisons. Using the United Nations' index of "objective" gender inequality across nations, he documents how gender ideologies may not simply result from, but may also contribute to, these inequalities. The cultural dimension of power distance (Hofstede and McCrae, 2004) proved to be one important element in providing support for this analysis. In Chapter 14, Michel Désert and Jacques-Philippe Leyens also look at cultures differing on the dimension of power distance but with data from individual participants in a study of gender stereotypes (Part Two of this study is discussed in Chapter 15). Consistent with previous research, they find that beliefs about the attributes of women and men are widely shared across gender and across cultures. However, they report some intriguing interactions, involving gender and cultures, which suggest that there are definite variations in these stereotypic beliefs as a function of power distance. This leads them to point out a number of difficulties in some current theoretical perspectives, such as System Justification Theory (Jost and Banaji, 1994). Indeed, their discussion highlights that gender stereotypes can fulfill many different functions and serve different purposes for dominant as opposed to subordinate groups, and that the system-justifying function is only one of them.

The concluding chapter is the result of a collaborative effort on the part of several authors of this book. It discusses the findings of one of the first cross-cultural studies of the effects of social comparison. Using the Social Comparison Orientation scale (Gibbons and Buunk, 1999), the chapter reports on cultural variations in the propensity to engage in interpersonal social comparisons. As Suls (1986) argued, "Different eras and different cultures may encourage or discourage comparisons with dissimilar others." (p. 111) Consistent with this claim, we do find some remarkable cultural differences in social comparison orientation. Furthermore, manipulating within and between-gender social comparisons, the study explores the extent to which the effects of these comparisons on self-construal vary across cultures. Overall, the findings provide strong support for the idea that social comparison processes at the individual level and at the group level can be useful to understand cultural similarities and differences. This is one way in which social comparison can be used to link together research on cognition, intergroup relations, and culture.

References

Brewer, M. B. and Weber, J. G. (1994). Self-evaluation effects of interpersonal versus intergroup social comparison. *Journal of Personality and Social Psychology*, 66, 268–275.

Buunk, B. P. and Ybema, J. F. (2003). Feeling bad, but satisfied: The effects of upward and downward comparison upon mood and marital satisfaction. *British Journal of Social Psychology*, 42, 613–628.

Crocker, J. and Major, B. (1989). Social stigma and self-esteem: The self protective properties of stigma. *Psychological Review*, 96, 608–630.

Doise, W. (1986). *Levels of explanation in social psychology*. Cambridge: Cambridge University Press.

Ellemers, N., Spears, R., and Doosje, B. (eds.) (1999). *Social identity*. Oxford: Blackwell.

Festinger, L. (1954). A theory of social comparison processes. *Human Relations*, 7, 117–140.

Forsyth, D. R. (2000). Social comparison and influence in groups. In J. Suls and L. Wheeler (eds.), *Handbook of social comparison: Theory and research* (pp. 81–104). New York: Kluwer Academic/Plenum Publishers.

Gibbons, F. X. and Buunk, B. P. (1999). Individual differences in social comparison: Development and validation of a measure of social comparison orientation. *Journal of Personality and Social Psychology*, 76, 129–142.

Heine, S. J., Lehman, D. R., Peng, K., and Greenholtz, J. (2002). What's wrong with cross-cultural comparisons of subjective likert scales? The reference-group effect. *Journal of Personality and Social Psychology*, 82, 903–918.

Hofstede, G. and McCrae, R. R. (2004). Personality and culture revisited: Linking traits and dimensions of culture. *Cross-cultural Research*, 38, 52–88.

Hogg, M. A. (2000). Social identity and social comparison. In J. Suls and L. Wheeler (eds.), *Handbook of social comparison: Theory and research* (pp. 401–422). New York: Kluwer Academic/Plenum Publishers.

Jost, J.T. and Banaji, M.R. (1994). The role of stereotyping in system-justification and the production of false consciousness. *British Journal of Social Psychology, 33*, 1–27.

Lemaine, G. (1974). Social differentiation and social originality. *European Journal of Social Psychology, 4*, 17–52.

Long, K. and Spears, R. (1997). The self-esteem hypothesis revisited: Differentiation and the disaffected. In R. Spears, P.J. Oakes, N. Ellemers, and S.A. Haslam (eds.), *The social psychology of stereotyping and group life* (pp. 296–317). Oxford: Blackwell.

Markman, K.D. and McMullen, M.N. (2003). A reflection and evaluation model of comparative thinking. *Personality and Social Psychology Review, 7*, 244–267.

Moghaddam, F.M., Taylor, D.M., and Wright, S.C. (1993). *Social psychology in cross-cultural perspective.* New York: W.H. Freeman.

Monteil, J.-M., (1998). Contexte social et performances scolaires: Vers une théorie du feed-back de comparaison sociale. In J.-L. Beauvois, R.-V. Joule, and J.-M. Monteil (eds.), *20 ans de psychologie sociale expérimentale francophone* (pp. 151–187). Grenoble: Presses Universitaires de Grenoble.

Monteil, J.-M. and Huguet, P. (1999). *Social context and cognitive performance: Towards a social psychology of cognition.* London: Psychology Press.

Moreland, R.L., Hogg, M.A., and Hairns, S.C. (1994). Back to the future: Social psychological research on groups. *Journal of Experimental Social Psychology, 30*, 527–555.

Mugny, G., Butera, F., Quiamzade, A., Dragulescu, A., and Tomei, A. (2003). Comparaisons sociales des compétences et dynamique d'influence sociale dans les tâches d'aptitudes. *L'Année Psychologique, 104*, 469–496.

Mussweiler, T. (2003). Comparison processes and social judgment: Mechanisms and consequences. *Psychological Review, 110*, 472–489.

Nisbett, R.E. (2003). *The geography of thought: How Asians and Westerners think differently and why.* London: Nicholas Brealey Publishing.

Oakes, P.J., Haslam, S., and Turner, J.C. (1994). *Stereotyping and social reality.* Malden, MA: Blackwell Publishers.

Pettigrew, T.F. (2002). Summing up: Relative deprivation as a key social psychological concept. In I. Walker and H.J. Smith (eds.), *Relative deprivation: Specification, development and integration* (pp. 351–373). Cambridge: Cambridge University Press.

Redersdorff, S. and Martinot, D. (2003). Impact des comparaisons ascendantes et descendantes sur l'estime de soi: importance de l'identité mise en jeu. *L'Année Psychologique, 104*, 411–444.

Schmitt, M.T., Silvia, P.J., and Branscombe, N. (2000). The intersection of self-evaluation maintenance and social identity theories: Intragroup judgment in interpersonal and intergroup contexts. *Personality and Social Psychology Bulletin, 26*, 1598–1606.

Sherif, M. and Wilson, M.O. (eds.) (1953). *Group relations at the crossroads.* New York: Harper and Brothers.

Smith, E.R. (1993). Social identity and social emotions: Towards new conceptualizations of prejudice. In D. Mackie and D. Hamilton (eds.), *Affect, cognition and stereotyping* (pp. 297–315). San Diego, CA: Academic Press.

Smith, P. B. and Bond, M. H. (1999). *Social psychology across cultures.* New York: Allyn and Bacon.

Spears, R., Gordijn, E., Dijksterhuis, A., and Stapel, D. A. (2004). Reaction in action: Intergroup contrast in automatic behavior. *Personality and Social Psychology Bulletin, 30,* 605–616.

Stapel, D. A. and Suls, J. (2004). Method matters: Effects of explicit versus implicit social comparisons on activation, behavior, and self-views. *Journal of Personality and Social Psychology, 87,* 860–875.

Suls, J. (1986). Comparison processes in relative deprivation: A life-span analysis. In J. M. Olson, C. P. Herman, and M. P. Zanna (eds.), *Relative deprivation and social comparison: The Ontario Symposium* (pp. 95–116), Volume IV. Hillsdale, NJ: Erlbaum.

Suls, J. M. and Miller, R. (eds.) (1977). *Social comparison processes: Theoretical and empirical perspectives.* Washington, DC: Hemisphere.

Suls, J., and Wheeler, L. (eds.) (2000). *Handbook of social comparison: Theory and research.* New York: Kluwer Academic/Plenum Publishers.

Suls, J. M. and Wills, T. A. (eds.) (1991). *Social comparison. Contemporary theory and research.* Hillsdale, NJ: Erlbaum.

Tajfel, H. (1972). La catégorisation sociale. In S. Moscovici (ed.), *Introduction à la psychologie sociale* (Volume I). Paris: Larousse.

(1974). Social identity and intergroup behavior. *Social Science Information, 13,* 65–93.

Tajfel, H. and Turner, J. C. (1986). The social identity theory of intergroup behaviour. In S. Worchel and W. G. Austin (eds.), *Psychology of intergroup relations* (pp. 7–24). Chicago: Nelson-Hall.

Taylor, D. M., Moghaddam, F. M., and Bellerose, J. (1989). Social comparison in an intergoup context. *The Journal of Social Psychology, 129,* 499–515.

Turner, J. C. (1975). Social comparison and social identity: some prospects for intergroup behaviour. *European Journal of Social Psychology, 5,* 5–34.

Turner, J. C., Hogg, M. A., Oakes, P. J., Reicher, S. D., and Wetherell, M. S. (1987). *Rediscovering the social group: A self-categorization theory.* Oxford: Blackwell.

Turner, J. C., Oakes, P. J., Haslam, S. A., and McGarty, C. (1994). Self and collective: Cognition and social context. *Personality and Social Psychology Bulletin, 20,* 454–463.

Wheeler, L. (2000). Individual differences in social comparison. In J. Suls and L. Wheeler (eds.), *Handbook of social comparison: Theory and research* (pp. 141–158). New York: Kluwer Academic/Plenum Publishers.

Woolf, V. (1976). A sketch of the past. In J. Schulkind (ed.), *Virginia Woolf–Moments of beings. Unpublished autobiographical writings* (pp. 64–137). New York: Harcourt Brace Jovanovich.

Zajonc, B. (1980). Cognition and social cognition: A historical perspective. In L. Festinger (ed.), *Retrospections on social psychology* (pp. 180–204). New York: Oxford University Press.

Part One

Cognition: comparison processes within
and between individuals

1   Social comparison orientation: a new perspective on those who do and those who don't compare with others

Abraham P. Buunk and Frederick X. Gibbons

Social comparison as an individual difference characteristic

Social comparison – how we use others to make sense of ourselves and our social world – is a focal human concern. Indeed, scholars have long recognized the importance of social comparison for human adaptation and survival. As Suls and Wheeler (2000) have noted, theorizing and research on social comparison can be traced to some of the classic contributions to western philosophy and to pivotal work in social psychology and sociology, including work on the self, adaptation level, reference groups, and social influence. In many respects, it is a fundamental human social interaction process.

Nevertheless, it was not until Festinger's (1954) classic paper that the term *social comparison* was proposed. According to Festinger, "There exists, in the human organism, a drive to evaluate his opinions and abilities." (p. 117) Although they generally do not like the term "drive," most social psychologists would probably agree that the desire to learn about the self through comparison with others is a universal characteristic of humans. As P. Gilbert, Price, and Allan (1995) noted, social comparison is phylogenetically very old, biologically very powerful, and is recognizable in many species. Indeed, it has been suggested that the process of social comparison has an evolutionary basis, and stems from the need to assess one's power and strength compared to that of one's competitors. In the course of evolution, this tendency to compare oneself with others has undoubtedly increased as humans came to live in larger groups. According to Beach and Tesser (2000), as *Homo sapiens* began to emerge as a distinct species, there was a shift toward more specialization within groups, and this required the ability to assess the domains in which one could specialize – in order to enhance one's status and reproductive opportunities. Social comparison facilitates such an assessment.

Although the tendency to engage in social comparison would appear to be a universal human characteristic, it has been observed by various authors that many individuals are reluctant to admit to engaging in social comparison (Brickman and Bulman, 1977; Helgeson and Taylor, 1993; Hemphill and Lehman, 1991; Schoeneman, 1981). Many cancer patients in the classic work by Wood, Taylor, and Lichtman (1985) who made statements that reflected some kind of self-other comparison, initially denied engaging in social comparison with other cancer patients. In a series of studies, Wilson and Ross (2000) found that in open-ended descriptions, social comparisons were much less frequently used to characterize oneself than were comparisons with one's own self in the past (i.e., temporal comparisons, see Chapters 3 and 4, this volume). The fact that individuals frequently do not acknowledge their own social comparison activities may indicate that because comparisons can occur automatically, people are often unaware of the fact that they have made or make comparisons (Brickman and Bulman, 1977). Indeed, as D. Gilbert, Giesler, and Morris (1995) suggested, the process of social comparison is "spontaneous, effortless, and unintentional" and it is "relatively automatic." As such, it may not always be salient or memorable (see Chapter 2, this volume).

Although many comparisons may occur automatically, we would suggest that some individuals *do* indeed seldom engage in social comparison. In fact, several researchers have theorized that people may differ in their disposition to compare themselves with others. For instance, Diener and Fujita (1997) suggested, "... making any comparisons at all, may often be a function of one's personality." (p. 349) Hemphill and Lehman (1991) mentioned "the need for researchers to include measures of social comparison that acknowledge the fact that people may not wish to compare with others to an equal extent." (p. 390) Thus, when research participants explain their difficulties with social comparison questionnaires and claim that they seldom compare themselves with others, this may mean that they truly lack an interest in social comparison information, and thus are indeed not disposed to assess their own situation vis à vis that of others. We believe that the *extent* to which, and the *frequency* with which people compare themselves with others varies from one individual to the next. That belief led to our efforts to develop a scale assessing individual differences in what we labeled social comparison orientation (Gibbons and Buunk, 1999). Our measure of *social comparison orientation* (SCO), the English version of which is described in Gibbons and Buunk (1999), explicitly assesses individual differences in the inclination to compare one's accomplishments, one's situation, and one's experiences with those of others. In this chapter, we summarize some of the findings with this measure. After presenting the basic psychometric properties of the scale and looking at how it relates to other relevant psychological measures, we present an overview of our program of research documenting the role of social comparison orientation with respect to a variety of social behaviors.

The Social Comparison Orientation Measure

The scale for SCO that we developed was labeled the Iowa-Netherlands Comparison Orientation Measure (INCOM). It contains eleven items that produced corrected item-total correlations that were all >.36; elimination of any item reduced the alpha. Examples of items are "I often compare how my loved ones (boy or girlfriend, family members, etc.) are doing with how others are doing," "I always like to know what others in a similar situation would do" and "I often compare myself with others with respect to what I have accomplished in life." In a representative sample of Dutch citizens in all age groups, the scale had a normal distribution with a skewness of −.18. The mean ($M = 32.7$) as well as the median ($Md = 33$) were both virtually identical to the scale midpoint (33), which suggests that there are as many high comparers as there are low comparers. The standard deviation was $SD = 7.84$, which indicates that the lowest (11) as well as the highest (55) possible scores were less than 3 SDs from the mean. The alpha was very consistent across a variety of samples, ranging from .78 to .85 in the US and the Netherlands. Test-rest correlations have ranged from .71 for 3–4 weeks, to .60 for a year in the US and Spain, to .72 for 7.5 months, in the Netherlands (Buunk, Zurriaga, Peiró, Nauta, and Gosalvez, 2005; Gibbons and Buunk, 1999). This level of stability is reasonable, but not as high as some measures, which is to be expected given that the construct is sensitive to situational factors, and therefore would be expected to change somewhat over time (see Kelly and McGrath, 1988).

Previous researchers have suggested the existence of normative sanctions against acknowledging or admitting social comparison (Hemphill and Lehman, 1991; Wood, 1996). Thus, there was some reason to expect a negative relation between the INCOM and measures of social desirability. In fact, these correlations were small. The correlation with the Marlowe-Crowne scale was nonsignificant in The Netherlands (−.14) and weak in the US ($r = −.12, p < .05$). The correlation with the Eysenck lie scale (Eysenck and Eysenck, 1975) was also nonsignificant (.08). Thus, concerns that responses on the INCOM might be strongly influenced by social desirability motives appear unfounded.

Personality and SCO: looking for the typical comparer

Many personality characteristics have been shown to correlate with SCO. On the basis of these findings, we would conclude that the "typical" comparer is characterized by three features. First, those high in SCO seem to have a high chronic activation of the self. Evidence of this is the fact that SCO is quite strongly related to public and private self-consciousness (Gibbons and Buunk, 1999); in fact, these are among the strongest correlates of SCO, varying from $r = .38$ to $.49$. Thus, those high in SCO tend to be particularly aware of themselves in the presence of others and tend to engage in reflection upon their own thoughts and feelings. In line with this, an experiment by Stapel and Tesser (2001) showed that those high in SCO have a more chronically activated self, as apparent from their tendency to mention more first-person nouns when trying to guess the correct translation of twenty pronouns from an unknown language.

Second, individuals high in SCO are also characterized by a strong interest in what others feel, a strong empathy for others, and a general sensitivity to the needs of others. This may at first sight seem odd, because, as suggested by Gardner, Gabriel, and Hochschild (2002), social comparison would seem to be associated with a sense of independence that is oriented toward differentiating oneself in a competitive way from others. However, the evidence suggests that SCO is different from competition, and refers more to a prosocial orientation and to an interdependent self. Indeed, in addition to self-consciousness, one of the strongest correlates of SCO is interpersonal orientation ($r = .45$, $p < .001$), a construct that includes an interest in what makes people tick, as well as a tendency to be influenced by the moods and criticism of others, and an interest in mutual self-disclosure – all aspects that are characteristic of individuals with a high interdependent self (Swap and Rubin, 1983). In a similar vein, SCO is also correlated moderately ($r = .31$, $p < .001$) with Clark *et al.*'s (1987) Communal Orientation Scale, which measures a sensitivity to the needs of others and a willingness to help others in need. As would be expected from individuals with an interdependent self, there is also a negative correlation ($r = -.35$, $p < .001$) between SCO and the Big Five trait intellectual autonomy (or openness to experience as it is sometimes called; Gibbons and Buunk, 1999). This means that those high in SCO are generally somewhat lower in independent and creative thinking, or, put differently, higher in conformity.

A third main feature of SCO is its relation with negative affectivity and uncertainty of the self, including low self-esteem and neuroticism, although the correlations with these variables vary, and are lower than those with self-consciousness and interpersonal orientation. Low correlations ($r < .25$) have been found of SCO with depression and anxiety. Self-esteem is consistently negatively correlated with SCO, with an average correlation in American samples of $-.18$ and in Dutch samples of $-.35$. Thus, people prone to compare themselves with others tend to have a less positive view of themselves. Neuroticism is related in a similar, but somewhat stronger fashion with SCO, with an average correlation of .31, suggesting that those who tend to compare themselves with others more often experience mood swings and negative emotions. To summarize, these findings suggest that those with high SCO are characterized by a combination of a high accessibility and awareness of the self, an interest in what others feel and think, and some degree of negative affectivity and self-uncertainty.

Social comparison behavior in a variety of contexts

An increasing number of studies in a variety of contexts have shown that those high in SCO do indeed compare themselves more, and are more affected by such comparisons. As we will describe below, those high in SCO seek out more comparisons, spend more time engaging in comparisons, experience more reactions (feelings) from comparing themselves with others, base their personal risk perceptions (more) on comparisons with others, and assess their own relational future on the basis of comparisons with others.

Seeking out social comparison

Gibbons and Buunk (1999) showed that after a (bogus) test in which participants thought they had done well, those high in SCO spent more time reading information about how others had done, and were more interested in discussing their score with others. In a study by Van der Zee, Oldersma, Buunk, and Bos (1998), cancer patients were offered a computer program that contained twenty-four interviews with other cancer patients, each of which was announced by a line like "My illness caused a lot of strain in my marriage." Half of the interviews contained upward comparison information, the other half downward comparison information. Patients could select as many interviews as they wanted. Those high in SCO selected more interviews, spent more time reading the interviews, and appeared to be more affected by them, as they reported more positive and more negative affects after reading these comparisons. In a study among physicians working in health care centers, those high in SCO reported that they compared themselves relatively more often upward, i.e. with colleagues performing better than they did ($r = .23$, $p < .01$), as well as downward, i.e. with colleagues performing worse than they did ($r = .39$, $p < .01$) (Buunk *et al.*, 2005). Thus, those high in SCO engaged in upward comparisons nearly as often as in downward comparisons. This was also found in a related study among nurses, in which the correlations were even higher; SCO correlated $r = .40$, $p < .01$, with the frequency of upward comparisons, and $r = .42$, $p < .01$, with the frequency of down-ward comparisons (Buunk, Zurriaga, Gonzalez-Roma, and Subirats, 2003). Although the results of these last two studies are based on self-reports, they provide converging evidence that those high in SCO do engage more often in social comparisons, whether this comparison is upward or downward.

Establishing one's risk

It has been suggested that one way in which individuals (especially young ones) assess whether a particular risky behavior, such as heavy drinking or unprotected sex, is risky for them *personally* is through social comparison with others (Klein and Weinstein, 1997). Although the reasoning is intuitive, there have been surprisingly few empirical demonstrations of this type of cognitive mediation. In one study, Gibbons, Lane, Gerrard, Pomery, and Lautrup (2002) asked college students how risky they thought drinking and driving was and also how common it was among their friends and peers. As might be expected, the more common students thought the behavior was among their comrades, the less risk they ascribed to it (e.g., "people do it all the time and get away with it"). Moreover, the lower the perceived risk, the more drunk driving the students engaged in subsequently. This entire mediational sequence, however, was significant only among those who were high in SCO. For students low in SCO, the perception of what others were doing was not related to their inferences about their own risk and these inferences were not related to their actual behavior.

In a more recent study, Stock, Gibbons, and Gerrard (2004) presented relatively high-risk college students (who had had several sexual partners and admitted not using protection regularly) with a bogus social compari-son target who reported that she or he had contracted a sexually trans-mitted disease. For half the participants, this "victim" reported that he or she had engaged in relatively low-risk sex (only one partner, condom used most of the time); the other half heard about someone who had engaged in very risky behavior (with multiple partners and infrequent condom use). The authors found evidence of a type of "absent–exempt" effect (Weinstein, 1982); the idea being that, if I haven't gotten caught (infected) by now, I must be immune – it's not going to happen to me. Specifically, those high-risk students who compared with a low-risk – but nonetheless infected target – reported less personal risk, and this lower perceived risk was associated with greater willingness to engage in future risky sex. The authors suggested that this "optimistic bias" (Weinstein, 1980), or sense of personal immunity, was a more-or-less logical deduction of the high-risk students who had "gotten away with" repeated episodes of unhealthy behavior. This additional example of cognitive mediation of risky behavior was again moderated by SCO – in fact, it was significant only among those students who had reported earlier that they were high in SCO (and therefore more likely to infer their own risk levels from others).

Assessing one's relational future

In a laboratory experiment by Buunk (in press), it was assumed that individuals high in SCO would engage in a relatively more extensive and elaborate consideration of their own situation vis à vis that of a target and of the implications of the fate of the target for their own future. Participants were exposed to a scenario in which a target talked about his or her romantic relationship that was characterized by either a high degree of autonomy, independence, and mutual freedom, or by a high degree of commitment, intimacy, and togetherness. It was expected that when the situation of the other was viewed as a desirable state in the future, high SCO individuals would experience more positive affects and when such a situation was viewed as an undesirable state, they would experience more negative affects. On the basis of various theories, particularly the model proposed by Cross and Madson (1997), it was predicted that for men the relationship with a high level of freedom and autonomy would be viewed as a more desirable future, and for women a relationship with a high level of closeness and commitment would be viewed more favorably. Indeed, only when they were high in SCO did men view the autonomy scenario as a more desirable future for themselves than women, and respond with less negative affect to this scenario. Among women, only those high in SCO saw the commitment scenario as a more desirable future for themselves than men, and responded with less negative affect to this scenario.

Comparing oneself with a depressed target

In a study by Buunk and Brenninkmeijer (2001), it was assumed that nondepressed individuals would respond more positively to a target who had put a high degree of effort into getting over his or her depression, than to a target who had got over his or her depression relatively easily. The primary rationale for this prediction was that exposure to others who manage to overcome their depression by taking an active stance supports one's sense of controllability. However, this should only occur when individuals relate the situation of the target in some way to their own situation, in other words, when they are high in SCO. In contrast, given the typical outlook of depressed individuals – the sense of defeat, the lack of control, and the helplessness – every act can be a struggle (cf. Hammen, 1997; Seligman, 1975). Therefore, it might be threatening for them to learn that overcoming depression involves a great deal of effort, whereas it might be much more reassuring, given their own passivity, to learn that someone recovered from his or her depression without having to do much. Again, this process should be much more likely among individuals high in SCO. In this study, clinically depressed and nondepressed individuals were exposed to a description of a target who got over his or her depression. As predicted, this study found that among the nondepressed participants, with increasing levels of SCO, a high effort target evoked a relatively more positive mood change and a low-effort target evoked a relatively more negative mood change. In contrast, among the depressed, with increasing levels of SCO, a low-effort target evoked a relatively more positive mood change and a high-effort target evoked a relatively more negative mood change. To conclude then, those high in SCO clearly tend to relate what happens to others to themselves, even when the situation of the comparison target might seem a quite remote possibility for oneself.

Social comparison in work-related contexts

Although we originally assumed that SCO would only lead to more comparison of the self with others and enhance the impact of social comparisons, our research thus far clearly suggests that the reality is more complex. For example, given the high uncertainty and accessibility of the self, one might expect that high SCO persons working in teams would benefit from social comparisons. Indeed, a general tenet in the social comparison literature is that social comparisons fulfill an adaptive function by reducing uncertainty and by facilitating adjustment to threat. Festinger (1954) assumed that social comparisons would assist individuals in obtaining accurate knowledge of their opinions and abilities. Similarly, in his downward comparison theory, Wills (1981) also emphasized the adaptive function of downward social comparisons among individuals facing a threat to their well-being. Nevertheless, many theorists have also pointed to the potential downside of social comparisons. For example, Baron and Kreps (1999) noted that in organizational contexts, the more people work closely together, the more opportunities they have to compare themselves with others, which may have negative consequences, such as feelings of injustice or jealousy when perceiving that colleagues having the same jobs earn more, or competitive attitudes when striving to outperform one's colleagues. In addition, downward comparisons may instill negative feelings for a variety of reasons, including annoyance, because one believes that group members are free riding; resentment, because one feels that one is working so much harder; or anxiety, because one views the fate of the other as a potential future for oneself (e.g., Buunk, Ybema, Van der Zee, Schaufeli, and Gibbons, 2001).

Our work so far suggests that in performance and work-related contexts, social comparisons often fulfill a negative rather than an adaptive function for individuals high in SCO. Whereas Buunk *et al.* (2005) found that physicians high in SCO tended to experience negative affect from upward comparisons ($r = .18$, $p < .01$), but not from downward comparisons ($r = .02$, *ns*), in the study by Buunk *et al.* (2003) among nurses, SCO correlated significantly with deriving negative affect from both upward comparison ($r = .43$, $p < .001$) and downward comparison ($r = .22$, $p < .05$). In a study among 653 undergraduate business students, Buunk, Nauta, and Molleman (2004) provided less direct, but quite strong evidence for the negative effects of social comparison among those high in SCO. This study examined the impact on satisfaction with one's educational group of SCO and affiliation orientation, i.e. the preference for doing things together and in groups versus a preference for doing things alone. A multi-level analysis showed that individual level variance in group satisfaction was explained by an interaction between affiliation orientation and SCO: a high level of affiliation orientation was associated with high group satisfaction of individual group members only among those low in SCO. Among those high in SCO, a high level of affiliation orientation was actually negatively associated, though not very strongly, with group satisfaction. These effects held up when simultaneously controlling for all "Big Five" personality dimensions. Thus, those high in SCO seem to focus on the negative implications of social comparisons for themselves, which can make working in groups a painful experience, especially for those high in affiliation orientation, i.e. those who want to be in groups. In contrast, it seems that those low in SCO who are high in affiliation orientation succeed relatively better in avoiding such negative feelings by not comparing themselves with others, which makes working in groups a more rewarding experience. In sum, at least in work and performance related contexts, and according to the measures used in these studies, those high in SCO seem to focus more on the negative implications of social comparisons.

The negative impact of downward comparisons

There is evidence from a number of studies that individuals high in SCO tend not to respond indiscriminately in a negative way to social comparisons, but primarily to exposure to others who are worse off than they are. So far, this has been found in studies using an induced comparison procedure in which participants were first presented with an alleged interview with someone in a similar situation who talks about his or her experiences, and then were asked how reading this interview made them feel. In this paradigm, upward comparisons tend to evoke more positive affect than downward comparisons, and downward comparisons tend to evoke more negative affect than upward comparisons. SCO seems to influence negative, but not positive responses to downward comparisons. For example, Buunk, Ybema, Gibbons and Ipenburg (2001) presented sociotherapists with a bogus interview with someone involved in the same profession who was either very successful (upward comparison) or very unsuccessful (downward comparison). SCO did not affect the feelings evoked by the upward comparison. However, the higher the level of burnout, the more negative affect evoked by the description of the downward comparison target, but only among individuals high in SCO. This pattern of results suggests that those high in comparison orientation do relate the failure of a colleague to their own performance, and feel particularly threatened by this failure when they are high in burnout themselves. In a similar study by Buunk, Van der Zee, and Van Yperen (2001), a sample of nurses was exposed to either a downward or an upward target. The higher individuals were in SCO, the more negative affect they reported following exposure to the downward comparison target. Interestingly, this effect stayed the same when controlling for neuroticism. Also in this study, SCO did not affect the feelings evoked by upward comparison, but neuroticism did: the higher the level of neuroticism, the less positive affect upward comparison evoked. All effects were also obtained when perceived direction of comparison (i.e., other relative to self) was used as a predictor instead of the experimentally manipulated direction. The findings of this study are important not only because they demonstrate once again, that SCO negatively affects the feelings evoked by downward comparison and not by upward comparison, but also because they show that this effect cannot be explained as the result of neuroticism. Thus, although SCO is associated with neuroticism and although neuroticism tends to be related to negative outcomes of social comparison (e.g., Van der Zee, Buunk, and Sanderman, 1998), SCO tends to affect the responses to social comparison independently from neuroticism. Our interpretation of the role of SCO in moderating the impact of social comparison, is that those high in SCO are more likely to identify with the downward target, and therefore are concerned they may end up like that target.

In a study with a somewhat different perspective from those described here, evidence was also found that those high in SCO tend to respond particularly negatively to downward comparisons. This study was conducted among lesbian women (Buunk and Dijkstra, 2001). Participants were presented with a scenario in which they were asked to imagine that their partner was flirting with another woman. These women reported more jealousy when they were exposed to a physically attractive rival as compared to one who was unattractive. However, although SCO did not affect jealousy in response to an attractive rival, high SCO women responded with more jealousy to the unattractive rival. These findings suggest that women high in SCO tended to reason that the fact that their partner was interested in a non-attractive other woman, said something about their own attractiveness, i.e. that they are at the same level as the non-attractive rival.

The fact that those high in SCO tend to respond more negatively to downward comparisons may be interpreted as indicating that they view the situation of comparison targets as reflecting upon their own situation, and that they are concerned that they may be like, or may become like, low status targets. As the study by Buunk *et al.* (2001) suggested, this tendency seems to be manifest especially among those under stress. This seems to contradict Wills's (1981) downward comparison theory, which suggests that those facing stress may enhance their well-being by engaging in downward comparisons. However, we believe these findings are actually quite compatible with Wills's theory. That is, as individuals facing some type of threat may be concerned about evaluating themselves unfavorably, they may respond negatively to confrontation with worse-off others, who function as a sort of "dark mirror". At the same time, they may counteract this concern by cognitively distancing themselves from such others. Thus, we would suggest that downward comparison under stress often seems to involve an active, motivated cognitive process rather than a quest for others who are doing worse (e.g., Buunk, 1994, Taylor and Lobel, 1989). For example, studies among victimized populations suggest that they use different *cognitive* downward comparison strategies, such as imagining others with whom they look better in comparison, or thinking about dimensions on which they think they are better off than others, or simply (cognitively) creating worse-off comparison targets (e.g. Buunk and Ybema, 1995, 1997; Gibbons and Gerrard, 1997; Taylor, Wood, and Lichtman, 1983; Van der Zee, Buunk, and Sanderman, 1995; Wills, 1997). Taylor *et al.* (1983), for example, discussed a tendency for husbands of women with breast cancer to engage in social comparison with an image they maintained of husbands who were coping poorly with their wife's illness. Downward comparison with these "mythical men," as

Taylor *et al.* called them, appeared to allow these men to feel better about themselves and about the way they were dealing with their wife's illness. This type of downward comparison seems to have an effortful and possibly even intentional character (Tennen and Affleck, 1997) that is directed at making the perception of one's situation more acceptable by adopting a different standard of evaluation. Moreover, there is some suggestive evidence that such a strategy may indeed contribute to a more favorable perception of one's situation among individuals facing distress (e.g., Van der Zee *et al.*, 1995). For instance, Jensen and Karoly (1992) found that chronic pain patients who showed a stronger tendency to use downward comparison experienced lower levels of depression.

In line with this reasoning, in a series of studies, we examined if individuals high in SCO who face relational distress may, through engaging in a process of cognitive downward comparison, enhance the evaluation of their relationship and conclude that it is "not so bad after all" (Buunk, Oldersma, and de Dreu, 2001). In these experiments, we used a thought-generating task in which participants were asked to generate features of their relationship that they considered to be better than those of most others (downward comparison condition) versus features that they simply considered to be good (no-comparison condition). We included this latter category to demonstrate that the possible effect of cognitive downward comparison was not due to bringing to mind the positive features of one's relationship. Indeed, we found clear evidence that for those facing distress in their relationship – both dating and marital – downward comparison resulted in more relationship satisfaction than merely generating good qualities of the relationship, but only for those high in SCO. Moreover, after downward comparison, individuals had relatively shorter response latencies when answering questions about their relationship, suggesting that the comparison task made attitudes toward their own relationship cognitively more accessible. The differential effect in both conditions was not due to the fact that relatively more features were generated in the comparison condition, or that these features were relatively more positive. Thus, only those high in SCO experiencing distress in their close relationships reported greater satisfaction after focusing on the features in which their relationship was better than that of others.

A similar process of distancing oneself from others who are doing worse is found in a series of studies that examined the impact that downward comparison with health images has on health behavior (see Gibbons and Gerrard, 1997, for a review). The idea that individuals may use downward comparison with images of others as a means of facilitating coping led to the development of the prototype/willingness model of adolescent health behavior (Gibbons and Gerrard, 1997; Gibbons, Gerrard, and Lane, 2003). According to the model, people maintain health images (e.g., the "typical smoker," or the "drug addict") that influence their decisions to engage or not engage in the relevant behavior. An adolescent who has an unfavorable image of smokers, for example, is less likely to smoke when given the opportunity. The model postulates that this prototype influence occurs via a social comparison process of the self with the image. In support of this contention, a number of studies have now been conducted that have shown that health images have more impact on the health behavior of individuals who are prone to socially compare – i.e., those high in SCO.

An early example of this research is a study by Gibbons and Gerrard (1995) that used a shorter version of the INCOM. This study found a positive relation between prototype favorability and college students' health risk behavior (e.g., risky sex, reckless driving). As expected, this relation was moderated by social comparison tendencies: the higher the students were in SCO, the stronger the relation between their social image and their subsequent behavior. Following up on this, Ouellette, Hessling, Gibbons, Reis-Bergan, and Gerrard (in press) asked college students to think about the typical person of their age who does or does not regularly engage in exercise. Actual exercise behavior was assessed at the start of the session and then again several weeks later. As expected, image (prototype) contemplation had significantly more of an impact on students' subsequent behavior if they were high in SCO.

The potential benefits of upward comparisons

It is less clear how SCO is related to responses to upward comparisons. When presented with bogus upward comparison interviews, responses usually do not differ between those high and low in SCO. In two studies, however, it was found that those high in SCO indicated that they had relatively more often experienced negative feelings from upward comparisons (Buunk et al., 2003, 2005). There is also some evidence that responses to upward comparisons may depend on the attributions made for the situation of the upward target. In a study among marital couples, Buunk and Oldersma (2001) examined the role of attributions for the happy marital state of a comparison target. It was assumed that upward comparisons are more likely to result in positive feelings when the state of the target is seen as within reach of being achieved by the subject. In general, a high degree of control by the target seems to lead to more positive affective responses to upward comparisons (e.g., Lockwood and Kunda, 1997; Testa and Major, 1990; Ybema and Buunk, 1995). Moreover, it is easier to interpret the very happy state of another marriage as less threatening when a very high level of effort is put into the marriage. This implies that upward comparisons will evoke more positive affect when the marital state of the target is attributed to the fact that the targets have put a high degree of effort into their relationship. To test these assumptions, marital couples were presented with an upward comparison in the form of a story about another marital couple with a successful relationship that was said to be the result of either high or low effort. The higher the SCO, the more positive affect confrontation with the high effort couple evoked, and the less positive affect confrontation with the low effort couple evoked. Apparently, for those high in SCO, the idea that another couple enjoyed a happy relationship without much effort was threatening, whereas the notion that this happy state can be attained by high effort was particularly stimulating. Additional analyses showed that in this latter condition, the degree of positive affect was completely mediated by the fact that those high in SCO and marital satisfaction identified with the couple. That is, happily married individuals high in SCO identified more with the happily married targets who worked hard on the relationship, and therefore responded more positively to this target. In contrast, individuals high in SCO did not identify with the couple who appeared to have a happy marriage without having to exert much effort and so they responded directly and negatively to this target. This response occurred independently of the effect of identification and marital quality.

Conclusion

Social comparison is a ubiquitous social phenomenon. Virtually everyone does it from time to time, mostly because it can serve a very fundamental purpose: providing useful information about where one stands in one's social world. At the same time, research described in this chapter indicates that people do vary on this important dimension quite a bit. Furthermore, it appears from data presented in Chapter 15 of this volume that people from different cultures may differ in their propensity to compare with others as measured by SCO. Thus, some people seem very attuned to the ways in which they and their behavior differ from and resemble others and their behavior, whereas some people don't seem to be very concerned about this at all. Moreover, high SCO individuals are not only more interested in the comparison process, they also appear to be more affected by it as well. This is especially true when the comparison involves others who are not doing well, apparently because of the threat such comparisons pose ("I might become like them"). At the same time, focussing on the fact that one is better off than others, may affect especially those high in SCO. More is to be learned about the response of those high in SCO to upward comparisons, but it seems that those high in SCO respond especially positively to upward comparison information when the situation of the target is within reach. The scale for SCO is now available in various languages and may be useful in future research in this area. More generally, we would argue that information about individuals' comparison tendencies has considerable utility, because it can facilitate understanding and prediction of many different types of social behavior – how adolescents respond to competition, for example, or how couples determine the health of their relationship, how young people decide what their own level of risk is when contemplating a risky behavior, or how employees react to their assessment of the relative status of their colleagues. Such reactions are at the core of the human social experience and therefore of interest to psychologists and other social scientists as well.

References

Baron, J. N. and Kreps, D. M. (1999). *Strategic human resources. Frameworks for general managers.* NY: Wiley.

Beach, S. R. and Tesser, A. (2000). Self-evaluation maintenance and evolution: Some speculative notes. In L. Wheeler and J. Suls (eds.), *Handbook of social comparison: Theory and research* (pp. 123–140). Dordrecht, Netherlands: Kluwer Academic Publishers.

Brickman, P. and Bulman, R. J. (1977). Pleasure and pain in social comparison. In J. Suls and R. L. Miller (eds.), *Social comparison processes: Theoretical and empirical perspectives.* Washington, DC: Hemisphere.

Buunk, B. P. (in press). How do people respond to others with high levels of commitment or autonomy in their relationships? Effects of gender and social comparison orientation. *Journal of Social and Personal Relationships.*

(1994). Social comparison processes under stress: Towards an integration of classic and recent perspectives. In W. Stroebe and M. Hewstone (eds.), *European Review of Social Psychology* (Vol. v, pp. 211–241). Chichester, England: John Wiley and Sons Ltd.

Buunk, B. P. and Brenninkmeijer, V. (2001). When individuals dislike exposure to an actively coping role model: Mood change as related to depression and social comparison orientation. *European Journal of Social Psychology, 31,* 537–548.

Buunk, B. P. and Dijkstra, P. (2001). Evidence from a homosexual sample for a sexspecific rival-oriented mechanism: Jealousy as a function of a rival's physical attractiveness and dominance. *Personal Relationships, 8,* 391–406.

Buunk, B. P, Nauta, A., and Molleman, E. (2004). In search of the true group animal: the effects of affiliation orientation and social comparison orientation upon group satisfaction. *European Journal of Personality, 18,* 1–13.

Buunk, B. P. and Oldersma, F. L. (2001). Social comparison and close relationships. In M. S. Clark and G. J. O. Fletcher (eds.), *Blackwell handbook in social psychology.* (Vol. II, pp. 388–408). *Interpersonal processes.* Oxford: Blackwell.

Buunk, B. P., Oldersma, F. L., and De Dreu, K. W. (2001). Enhancing satisfaction through downward comparison: the role of relational discontent and individual differences in social comparison orientation. *Journal of Experimental Social Psychology, 37*, 452–467.

Buunk, B. P., van der Zee, K. I., and van Yperen, N. W. (2001). Neuroticism and social comparison orientation as moderators of affective responses to social comparison at work. *Journal of Personality, 69*, 745–763.

Buunk, B. P. and Ybema, J. F. (1995). Selective evaluation and coping with stress: Making one's situation cognitively more livable. *Journal of Applied Social Psychology, 25*, 1499–1517.

Buunk, B. P. and Ybema, J. F. (1997). Social comparisons and occupational stress: The identification-contrast model. In B. P. Buunk and F. X. Gibbons (eds.), *Health, coping, and well-being: Perspectives from social comparison theory* (pp. 359–388). Mahwah, NJ: Lawrence Erlbaum Associates.

Buunk, B. P., Ybema, J. F., Gibbons, F. X., and Ipenburg, M. L. (2001). The affective consequences of social comparison as related to professional burnout and social comparison orientation. *European Journal of Social Psychology, 31*, 337–351.

Buunk, B. P., Ybema, J. F., Van der Zee, K., Schaufeli, W. B., and Gibbons, F. X. (2001). Affect generated by social comparisons among nurses high and low in burnout. *Journal of Applied Social Psychology, 31*, 1500–1520.

Buunk, B. P., Zurriaga, R., Gonzalez-Roma, V., and Subirats, M. (2003). Engaging in upward and downward comparisons as a determinant of relative deprivation at work: A longitudinal study. *Journal of Vocational Behavior, 62*, 370–388.

Buunk, B. P., Zurriaga, R., Peiró, J. M., Nauta, A., and Gosalvez, I. (2005). Social comparisons at work as related to a cooperative social climate and to individual differences in social comparison orientation. *Applied Psychology: An International Review, 54*, 61–80.

Clark, M. S., Ouellette, R., Powell, M. C., and Milberg, S. (1987). Recipient's mood, relationship type, and helping. *Journal of Personality and Social Psychology, 53*, 94–103.

Cross, S. E. and Madson, L. (1997). Models of the self: Self-construals and gender. *Psychological Bulletin, 122*, 5–37.

Diener, E. and Fujita, F. (1997). Social comparisons and subjective well-being. In B. P. Buunk and F. X. Gibbons (eds.), *Health, coping, and well-being: Perspectives from social comparison theory* (pp. 329–358). Mahwah, NJ: Lawrence Erlbaum Associates.

Eysenck, H. I. and Eysenck, S. B. G. (1975). *Eysenck personality inventory manual.* London: Hodder and Stoughton.

Festinger, L. (1954). A theory of social comparison processes. *Human Relations, 7*, 117–140.

Gardner, W. L., Gabriel, S., and Hochschild, L. (2002). When you and I are "we," you are not threatening: The role of self-expansion in social comparison. *Journal of Personality and Social Psychology, 82*, 239–251.

Gibbons, F. X. and Buunk, B. P. (1999). Individual differences in social comparison: Development of a scale of social comparison orientation. *Journal of Personality and Social Psychology, 76*, 129–142.

Gibbons, F. X. and Gerrard, M. (1995). Predicting young adults' health risk behavior. *Journal of Personality and Social Psychology*, *69*, 505–517.

(1997). Health images and their effects on health behavior. In B. P. Buunk and F. X. Gibbons (eds.), *Health, coping, and well-being: Perspectives from social comparison theory* (pp. 63–94). Mahwah, NJ: Lawrence Erlbaum Associates.

Gibbons, F. X., Gerrard, M., and Lane, D. J. (2003). A social reaction model of adolescent health risk. In K. A. Wallston and J. Suls (eds.), *Social psychological foundations of health and illness* (pp. 107–136). Malden, MA: Blackwell Publishers.

Gibbons, F. X., Lane, D. J., Gerrard M., Pomery, E. A., and Lautrup, C. I. (2002). Drinking and driving: A prospective assessment of the relation between risk cognitions and risk behavior. *Risk Decision and Policy*, *7*, 267–283.

Gilbert, D. T., Giesler, R. B., and Morris, K. A. (1995). When comparisons arise. *Journal of Personality and Social Psychology*, *69*, 227–236.

Gilbert, D., Price, J., and Allan, S. (1995). Social comparison, social attractiveness and evolution: How might they be related? *New Ideas in Psychology*, *13*, 149–165.

Hammen, C. (1997). *Depression*. Hove: Psychology Press.

Helgeson, V. S. and Taylor, S. E. (1993). Social comparisons and adjustment among cardiac patients. *Journal of Applied Social Psychology*, *23*, 1171–1195.

Hemphill, K. J. and Lehman, D. R. (1991). Social comparisons and their affective consequences: The importance of comparison dimension and individual difference variables. *Journal of Social and Clinical Psychology*, *10*, 372–394.

Jensen, M. P. and Karoly, P. (1992). Comparative self-evaluation and depressive affect among chronic pain patients: An examination of selective evaluation theory. *Cognitive Therapy and Research*, *16*, 297–308.

Kelly, J. R. and McGrath, J. E. (1988). *On time and method*. Beverly Hills, CA: Sage.

Lockwood, P. and Kunda, Z. (1997). Superstars and me: Predicting the image of role models on the self. *Journal of Personality and Social Psychology*, *73*, 91–103.

Ouellette, J. A., Hessling, R., Gibbons, F. X., Reis-Bergan, M. J., and Gerrard, M. (in press). Using images to increase exercise behavior: Prototypes vs. possible selves. *Personality and Social Psychology Bulletin*.

Schoeneman, T. J. (1981). Reports of the sources of self-knowledge. *Journal of Personality*, *49*, 284–294.

Seligman, M. E. P. (1975). *Helplessness: On depression, development, and death*. San Francisco: Freeman.

Stapel, D. A. and Tesser, A. (2001). Self-activation increases social comparison. *Journal of Personality and Social Psychology*, *81*, 742–750.

Stock, M. L., Gibbons, F. X., and Gerrard, M. *When low risk information promotes high risk behavior: Absent – exempt bias as a reaction to downward comparison.* Manuscript in preparation.

Suls, J. and Wheeler, L. (2000). A selective history of classic and neo-social comparison theory. In *Handbook of social comparison: Theory and research* (pp. 3–22). Dordrecht, Netherlands: Kluwer Academic Publishers.

Swap, W. C. and Rubin, J. Z. (1983). Measurement of interpersonal orientation. *Journal of Personality and Social Psychology, 44*, 208–219.

Taylor, S. E. and Lobel, M. (1989). Social comparison activity under threat: Downward evaluation and upward contacts. *Psychological Review, 96*, 569–575.

Taylor, S. E., Wood, J. V., and Lichtman, R. R. (1983). It could be worse: Selective evaluation as a response to victimization. *Journal of Social Issues, 39*, 19–40.

Tennen, H. and Affleck, G. (1997). Social comparison as a coping process: A critical review and application to chronic pain disorders. In F. X. Gibbons and B. P. Buunk (eds.), *Health, coping, and well-being: Perspectives from social comparison theory* (pp. 263–298). Mahwah, NJ: Lawrence Erlbaum Associates.

Testa, M. and Major, B. (1990). The impact of social comparisons after failure: The moderating effects of perceived control. *Basic and Applied Social Psychology, 11*, 205–218.

Van der Zee, K., Buunk, B. P., and Sanderman, R. (1995). Social comparison as a mediator between health problems and subjective health evaluations. *British Journal of Social Psychology, 34*, 53–65.

 (1998). Neuroticism and reactions to social comparison information among cancer patients. *Journal of Personality, 66*, 175–194.

Van der Zee, K. I., Oldersma, F. L., Buunk, B. P., and Bos, D. A. J. (1998). Social comparison preferences among cancer patients as related to neuroticism and social comparison orientation. *Journal of Personality and Social Psychology, 75*, 801–810.

Weinstein, N. D. (1980). Unrealistic optimism about future events. *Journal of Personality and Social Psychology, 39*, 806–820.

 (1982). Unrealistic optimism about susceptibility to health problems. *Journal of Behavioral Medicine, 5*, 441–460.

Wills, T. A. (1997). Modes and families of coping: An analysis of social comparison in the structure of other cognitive and behavioral mechanisms. In B. P. Buunk and F. X. Gibbons (eds.), *Health, coping, and well-being: Perspectives from social comparison theory* (pp. 167–194). Mahwah, NJ: Lawrence Erlbaum Associates.

 (1981). Downward comparison principles in social psychology. *Psychological Bulletin, 90*, 245–271.

Wilson, A. E. and Ross, M. (2000). The frequency of temporal-self and social comparisons in people's personal appraisals. *Journal of Personality and Social Psychology, 78*, 928–942.

Wood, J. V. (1996). What is social comparison and how should we study it? *Personality and Social Psychology Bulletin, 22*, 520–537.

Wood, J. V., Taylor, S. E., and Lichtman, R. R. (1985). Social comparison in adjustment to breast cancer. *Journal of Personality and Social Psychology, 49*, 1169–1183.

Ybema, J. F. and Buunk, B. P. (1995). Affective responses to social comparison: A study among disabled individuals. *British Journal of Social Psychology, 34*, 279–292.

2 The why, who, and how of social comparison: a social-cognition perspective

Thomas Mussweiler, Katja Rüter, and Kai Epstude

People frequently engage in social comparisons. Whenever they are confronted with information about how others are, what others can and cannot do, or what others have achieved and have failed to achieve, they relate this information to themselves. And, whenever they try to determine how they themselves are or what they themselves can and cannot do, they do so by comparing their own characteristics, fortunes, and weaknesses to those of others. In fact, such social comparisons are so deeply engraved into our psyche that they are even engaged with others who are unlikely to yield relevant information concerning the self (Gilbert, Giesler, and Morris, 1995). Social comparisons are also engaged with others who – phenomenologically – are not even there, because they were perceived outside of conscious awareness (Mussweiler, Rüter, and Epstude, 2004a). In this respect, comparisons with others appear to be one of the most fundamental, ubiquitous, and robust human proclivities.

The proclivity to compare, however, goes much further. People not only compare themselves to others, they pretty much compare any target to a pertinent standard. This is apparent in psychophysical as well as social judgments. To evaluate how heavy a target weight is, for example, judges compare it to a given standard weight (Brown, 1953; Coren and Enns, 1993). Similarly, to evaluate how aggressive a target person is, judges compare him or her to an accessible standard (Herr, 1986). This essential relativity of human judgment has played a particularly prominent role in the domain of social cognition research. Here, it has been demonstrated that comparisons play a core role in areas as diverse as stereotyping (Biernat, 2003; Biernat and Manis, 1994), attitudes (Sherif and Hovland, 1961), person perception (Herr, 1986; Higgins and Lurie, 1983), and affect (Higgins, 1987). Taken together, this research suggests that people engage in comparison whenever they process information about or evaluate a given target.

Social comparison thus appears to be one instantiation of a general leaning towards comparative information processing. In light of this generality, it seems surprising that for a long time social comparison research has thrived in relative isolation from these other research domains in which comparative processing assumes such a prominent role (Suls and Wheeler, 2000). In the present chapter, we will attempt to help overcome this relative isolation and will apply basic social cognition principles to social comparison processes (for similar approaches see, Blanton, 2001; Mussweiler and Strack, 2000a, 2000b). If social comparison is but one instantiation of a fundamental psychological mechanism that is as broad and ubiquitous as the accumulated evidence suggests (for a review, see Mussweiler, 2003a), then the principles that guide this mechanism should be consistent with those principles that guide human information processing in general. Following this rationale, we will apply what are arguably the two core principles of social cognition research to the domain of social comparison, namely the principles of cognitive efficiency and knowledge accessibility. Applying these principles may help answer three fundamental questions in social comparison research. *Why* do people engage in social comparison? *Who* do they select for comparison? And, *how* do comparisons shape self-perception and self-evaluation?

Cognitive efficiency in social comparison

People as cognitive misers (Taylor, 1981) have to be efficient in the use of their scarce cognitive resources. To fulfill this requirement, they rely, for instance, on heuristics in decision making (e.g., Tversky and Kahneman, 1973, 1974), apply stereotypes in person perception (e.g., Macrae, Milne, and Bodenhausen, 1994), and fall back upon habits in their own actions (e.g., Aarts and Dijksterhuis, 2000). In all of these domains, a more elaborate route of information processing may appear more rational and appropriate. It may appear to be wiser to weigh up and average out all the pros and cons before making a decision or taking action. It may appear to be more appropriate to pay attention to individuating information about a person before making an inference. However, such visions of optimal information processing often conflict with reality (Gigerenzer and Todd, 1999) and do not take into account human's "bounded rationality" (Simon, 1956). Simon (1956) stressed in his work that the human mind is limited in time, knowledge, attention, and cognitive resources. People are often not able to calculate the optimal solution to a decision problem (Klein, 2001; Nisbett and Ross, 1980). Instead of optimizing their decision, they rather "satisfice" and rely on a satisfactory alternative (Simon, 1956). Thus, even though people may wish to reach an optimal solution or make an accurate judgment, they cannot ignore the effort involved in such a process. Especially when processes are conducted frequently (and therefore processing time and resources are limited), the need for efficiency is high (Bargh, 1997; Smith, 1994; Taylor, 1981).

Social comparison certainly is such an often-conducted process. First, it is one case of the essential relativity of human judgment and information processing. Furthermore, social comparison enables people to satisfy fundamental needs such as feeling good about oneself and knowing who one is, what one can and cannot do (see Baumeister, 1998, for a review). Therefore it is not surprising that self-reflective thoughts make up a large portion of people's mental activity. Csikszentmihalyi and Figurski (1982), for example, found that their participants spent about 8 percent of all thoughts in the course of the day on the self. Many of these thoughts are likely to be comparative in nature (Festinger, 1954; Mussweiler, 2003b; see also Masters and Keil, 1987). In light of this striking necessity and frequency of social comparison activities, their automatic and capacity-saving qualities are essential to ensure our psychological functioning. If we do indeed engage in social comparisons so frequently, then we cannot afford to allocate too many resources to them. Social comparison instead has to be a highly efficient process that requires little cognitive capacity and can easily be carried out even under suboptimal conditions.

Despite the growing evidence of the importance of efficiency in cognitive processes, however, the integration of this insight in social comparison theory can still not be taken for granted. On the contrary, social comparisons are typically portrayed as strategic processes, which are executed to satisfy specific motives or goals. In particular, social comparison is mostly understood as a process which is engaged to fulfill fundamental needs like self-evaluation, self-enhancement, and self-improvement (Kruglanski and Mayeless, 1990; Suls, Martin, and Wheeler, 2002; Wood and Taylor, 1991). To be able to satisfy these varying motives, social comparisons have to be carefully crafted. Arduous processes like a strategic standard selection seem to be indispensable (for a different view see Mussweiler and Rüter, 2003). Since different standards are required for self-enhancement, self-evaluation, or self-improvement (Wood and Taylor, 1991) comparers can only guarantee that the comparison will lead to the desired outcome by strategically selecting an appropriate comparison standard. However, trying to select the most suitable standard will bring with it a high price.

Take as an example a standard selection process based on similarity in the critical dimension itself (Festinger, 1954) or on attributes that are related to this dimension (Goethals and Darley, 1977) (for a discussion of the limitations of both notions, see Miller and Prentice, 1996).

Similarity is typically seen as the driving force behind standard selection, because comparisons with dissimilar others may not have clear implications for self-evaluation. Such a comparison may be of limited diagnostic value, because it would be unclear whether the comparison outcome is due to one's personal qualities or to the difference on an important related attribute. This normative perspective on standard selection is supported by considerable empirical evidence (e.g., Gruder, 1971; Suls, Gastorf, and Lawhon, 1978; Wheeler, 1966; Zanna, Goethals, and Hill, 1975). At the same time, however, the efficiency of these arduous processes and thus their practicability is typically not taken into account. Finding a standard which is similar on the critical dimension or on related attributes is an elaborate process in which different dimensions, different potential standards, and different criteria have to be considered (Festinger, 1954; Goethals and Darley, 1977; Wood and Taylor, 1991). Oftentimes, there seem to be too many choices and too little time. In principle, people may satisfy their different motives via arduous standard selection processes, but oftentimes they may lack the extensive processing capacities these processes require.

In this respect, applying the basic social cognition principle of cognitive efficiency to the realm of social comparison research, suggests a novel perspective on why, with whom and how people compare. In addition to asking how people reach a certain goal by comparing with others, one may wonder how people manage to do so *in spite of* their limited cognitive resources.

The *why* of social comparison: efficiency advantages of comparative information processing

The need to process information in an efficient manner may not only be seen as a constraint of comparison processes. In fact, efficiency in comparison processes may well be the reason why comparisons are so frequently engaged in the first place. The ubiquity of comparative information processing appears to be one of the more striking characteristics of human judgment. As we have pointed out before, people not only compare with others when evaluating the self, they pretty much compare any object with a pertinent standard when evaluating this object. Why may this be the case? Why do comparisons play such a ubiquitous role in human information processing? We have recently suggested that comparisons are so ubiquitous because they allow us to process information in a more efficient manner than more absolute modes of information processing (Mussweiler and Epstude, 2005). This may be the case, because comparisons limit the range of information that has to be considered to evaluate or judge a given object.

Assume, for example, that you were to evaluate your athletic abilities. To do so in an absolute manner, i.e., with little use of comparisons, you would have to consider all the different aspects of athletic ability and retrieve all the information you have available about these aspects. Thus, in principle, you would have to consider all the information that applies to your abilities as a runner, a swimmer, a basketball player, a soccer player, etc. Clearly, considering all this information has the potential to become an endless task. In marked contrast, evaluating your athletic abilities in a comparative manner, for example by comparing yourself with your best friend Bob, seems considerably easy. Instead of considering all the information that has some implications concerning your athletic abilities, you would merely have to consider the particular information that is relevant for the comparison with Bob. If Bob does not play soccer at all, for example, your abilities as a soccer player do not have any relevance for the comparison and thus do not have to be considered. Social comparison may thus allow you to focus on a small subset of all the information that is potentially relevant for a given self-evaluation. This informational focusing effect of comparisons may render comparative information processing relatively efficient in the realm of social comparison – and beyond.

Consistent with this reasoning, a series of our own studies has recently demonstrated that comparative information processing does indeed have efficiency advantages (Mussweiler and Epstude, 2005). Comparisons appear to facilitate human judgment and to save cognitive resources. In these studies, we induced participants to process information in either a more comparative or a more absolute manner with the help of a procedural priming task (Smith, 1994). To do so, participants were given a pair of pictures and were either asked to compare or to describe them before they received the critical judgment task. Previous research has demonstrated that a processing mode that is induced in such a priming task carries over to a subsequent task (Mussweiler, 2001). Thus, participants who compared the two pictures are likely to rely more heavily on comparisons in the subsequent critical judgment task than participants who described the two pictures. In this critical judgment task, participants were asked to judge a fictitious city on several dimensions (e.g., number of inhabitants, number of students). If comparative processing is indeed more efficient, then participants who were induced to make these judgments in a more comparative manner should be faster in making the critical judgments. Furthermore, they should require less cognitive resources so that they have more resources available for the processing of a secondary task (e.g. Macrae et al., 1994). Our results were consistent with these implications. Participants who were primed to rely more heavily on comparisons during the critical judgments made faster decisions about the target city and performed better on a secondary task. This indicates that comparative information processing does indeed hold valuable efficiency advantages.

These studies illustrate that comparisons, not only in a social context, are an efficient tool in human judgment. Applying these insights to the domain of social comparison suggests that comparisons with others may play such a central role in our mental lives because they save scarce cognitive resources. Determining who we are, what we can and cannot do requires less processing capacity if we do so in comparison to others. Social comparison may thus help to fulfill one of the most fundamental requirements of any psychological process, namely cognitive efficiency.

The *who* of social comparison: efficiency advantages of routine standard use

Cognitive efficiency, however, may not only determine why we compare with others. It is also likely to shape the process of social comparison itself. Specifically, who is selected for comparison is also likely to depend on efficiency considerations. In traditional research on social comparison (see Suls and Wheeler, 2000) much evidence has accumulated that such standard selection processes are often influenced by strategic considerations based on motives like self-enhancement, self-improvement, and self-evaluation (Kruglanski and Mayeless, 1990; Suls *et al.*, 2002; Wood and Taylor, 1991). Surprisingly little is said, however, about the role of efficiency in standard selection. This relative neglect stands in marked contrast to the core role efficiency considerations play in the literature on human judgment and decision making.

One of the main tools that is applied to simplify complex decisions and to consequently make them more efficient is the application of routines (e.g., Aarts and Dijksterhuis, 2000; Betsch, Haberstroh, Glöckner, Haar, and Fiedler, 2001; Verplanken, Aarts, van Knippenberg, and van Knippenberg, 1994). Betsch, Haberstroh, and Höhle (2002) define a routine as an "option that comes to mind as a solution when the decision maker recognizes a particular decision problem." In other words, a routine is based on a strong association between a decision problem and a particular solution to this problem. Frequently pursuing the same choice in a decision process strengthens the association between the problem and the solution (Aarts and Dijksterhuis, 2000; Bargh, 1990). Thus, instead of repeatedly solving the decision problem anew, one simply falls back on the solution most closely associated with the problem (Aarts and Dijksterhuis, 2000). The efficiency advantage of such a routine application is, for example, apparent in the fact that people resort more readily to their decision routines under suboptimal conditions (Betsch, Fiedler, and Brinkmann, 1998).

In much the same way, one could also apply routines in the standard selection process during social comparison. In a strategic standard selection process (e.g., Festinger, 1954; Goethals and Darley, 1977), the comparer, as any decision maker, is expected to choose the best alternative out of a set of applicable options. However, if one were to exhaustively consider all alternatives plus their possible consequences before making a decision, one would soon be overwhelmed (Selten, 2001). Applying the concepts of routines to social comparison may provide a more efficient alternative to such a strategic standard selection process. Instead of engaging in the arduous and often impossible task of finding the most diagnostic standard, one may simply compare with those standards that one routinely uses for comparison. The development of such a routine would thereby depend on the frequency of prior use of the routine standard. The more often a particular standard has been used, the more strongly it would be associated with the self-evaluation task and the more likely one engages in further comparisons with this standard. In this respect, routine standards enable people to skip a standard selection process altogether and still engage in comparative self-evaluation.

To demonstrate the use of routine standards in social comparison we conducted a series of studies (Mussweiler and Rüter, 2003) in which we demonstrated a preference either for naturally occurring routine standards (e.g. the best friend) or for experimentally created routine standards (based on frequent previous comparisons) in social comparison. In one of these studies (Study 1), for example, we demonstrated that subsequent to a series of self-evaluative judgments (compared to a series of evaluations of another person), participants were faster in recognizing the name of their best friend (i.e., the routine standard) than the name of an exfriend (i.e., the control standard) in a lexical decision task. Because these response latencies depend on the accessibility of the persons identified with the names, this data pattern confirmed our hypothesis that people activate their best friends as a natural routine standard during self-evaluations. More importantly, in another study (Study 3) we were able to show that the routine standard is indeed preferred to a strategically more suitable standard. Even if participants perceived their best friend as very dissimilar to themselves (which indicates the standard's low diagnosticity for self-evaluation), participants were still faster in judging their dissimilar best friend than in judging their similar acquaintance on the dimension on which they had previously evaluated themselves. This suggests that participants had activated information about the best friend's standing on the judgmental dimension during self-evaluation.

Thus, people seem to use the routine standard even though this person is not an adequate standard from a strategic point of view. These findings indicate that our participants skipped the elaborate standard selection process altogether and instead fell back on a standard with which they are used to compare themselves.

Skipping an elaborate standard selection process, however, is just one efficiency advantage of routine standards – the advantages may go even further. Given that a routine standard is created by repeatedly comparing with the same standard, this comparison is also highly practiced. Thus, the comparison process itself may profit from the use of routine standards and become more efficient. In another series of studies we (Rüter and Mussweiler, 2005) showed that comparisons between the self and a routine standard (e.g., the best friend) are conducted faster than comparisons between the self and other standards (e.g., exfriends) (Study 1). Furthermore, this result could be replicated for routine standards established in the experiment by repeated comparisons with the self (Study 2). The mere practice of comparing a person with the self repeatedly facilitates further comparisons with the same standard even if the control standard was used equally often in comparisons previously (but not with the self) and the subsequent comparisons take place on new, unrelated dimensions. Thus, practice effects (see also Smith, 1989; Smith and Lerner, 1986; and Smith, Branscombe, and Bormann, 1988 for practice effects in social judgments in general) may be the second base for the efficiency of routine standards during self-evaluations.

Taken together this research indicates that efficiency considerations play an important role in social comparison. The fundamental need to process information in an efficient manner and to thus save scarce cognitive resources seems as important for social comparisons processes as for other psychological processes. A cognitive miser perspective (Taylor, 1981) not only helps to explain *why* comparisons are conducted so frequently, it is also useful to understand *who* is selected as comparison standard.

Accessibility in social comparison

The second hallmark principle of social cognition research that can be fruitfully applied to the domain of social comparison is the accessibility principle. Abundant research (for reviews see Higgins, 1996; Wyer and Srull, 1989) has demonstrated that judges typically do not use all the information that is potentially relevant for a given judgment. In fact, such an exhaustive use of judgment-relevant knowledge would stand in marked contrast to the efficiency principle described above. To make judgments in an efficient manner, judges have to be selective in the use of knowledge. Knowledge accessibility is one core feature that helps judges to fulfill their need for selectivity in knowledge use. In most situations, judges focus on the judgment-relevant knowledge that is particularly accessible at the time the judgment is made. Knowledge may become accessible either because it has recently been used and activated (Higgins, Rholes and Jones, 1977; Srull and Wyer, 1979) or because it has been frequently used in the past (Bargh, Bond, Lombardi, and Tota, 1986; Higgins, King, and Mavin, 1982). We have applied this fundamental accessibility principle to conceptualize how social comparisons influence self-perception and self-evaluation. Specifically, we assume that comparison consequences are produced by mechanisms of selective accessibility.

The how of social comparison: mechanisms of selective accessibility

The core assumption of this perspective is that to understand how social comparisons influence the self, one has to examine how they change the accessibility of self knowledge (for a more detailed discussion of the model, see Mussweiler, 2003a). As with any judgment, post-comparison self-evaluations are based on the implications of the judgment relevant knowledge that is accessible at the time the judgment is made (for an overview, see Higgins, 1996). Thus, social comparisons may effect self-evaluations because they influence what knowledge is rendered accessible and is consequently used as a basis for target evaluation. From this perspective, understanding what knowledge is sought and activated during the comparison and is consequently rendered accessible is crucial to understand their self-evaluative consequences. The main process that we assume underlies the search for and activation of judgment-relevant knowledge during a comparison is the selective accessibility mechanism (see Figure 2.1).

To carry out a social comparison, judges have to obtain specific judgment-relevant information about the self and the standard, which allows them to evaluate both persons relative to one another. To determine whether oneself or one's best friend is more athletic, for example, one has to activate knowledge about the athletic abilities of both persons. This specific knowledge is best obtained by an active search for judgment-relevant information through processes of hypothesis-testing (Trope and Liberman, 1996). Such hypothesis-testing processes are often selective in that they focus on one single hypothesis that is then evaluated against a specific criterion (Sanbonmatsu, Posavac, Kardes, and Mantel, 1998; see also, Klayman and Ha, 1987; Trope and Liberman, 1996). Rather than engaging in an exhaustive comparative test of all plausible hypotheses,

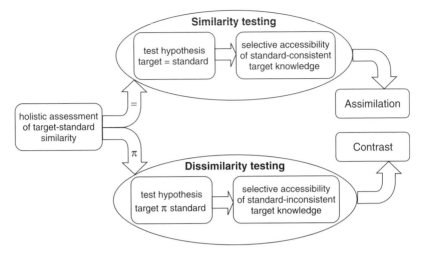

Figure 2.1. The selective accessibility mechanism (from Mussweiler, 2003a)

judges follow the efficiency principle and limit themselves to the test of a single focal hypothesis. In light of this tendency toward selective hypothesis-testing, the critical question is which concrete hypothesis will be tested. In principle, two hypotheses can be distinguished. Judges can either test the possibility that the self is similar to the standard or they can test the possibility that the self is dissimilar from the standard. When comparing one's athletic abilities to those of one's best friend, for example, one may either assume that both are about equally athletic, or that one is clearly more athletic.

Which of these hypotheses is tested, depends on the overall perceived similarity of the self and the standard. As an initial step in the selective accessibility mechanism, judges engage in a quick holistic assessment of the self and the standard (Smith, Shoben, and Rips, 1974) in which they briefly consider a small number of features (e.g., category membership, salient characteristics) to determine whether both are generally similar or dissimilar. The outcome of this initial screening is a broad assessment of perceived similarity. If, for example, one's best friend belongs to a category that clearly sets him apart with respect to athletic abilities (e.g., he is a pro athlete), then the initial holistic assessment of similarity is likely to indicate that self and standard are generally dissimilar with respect to the critical dimension. In the absence of such clear indications of dissimilarity, however, this assessment is likely to indicate that self and standard are generally similar. Although such a broad assessment is by itself too general to be used as the basis for self-evaluation, it is sufficient to determine the specific nature of the hypothesis that is then tested in more detail. The hypothesis-testing mechanism is thus assumed to focus on the possibility that is suggested by the initial holistic assessment. If this assessment indicates that the self is generally similar to the standard, judges will engage in a process of similarity testing and test the hypothesis that the self is similar to the standard. If the initial assessment indicates that the self is dissimilar from the standard, however, judges will engage in a process of dissimilarity testing and test the hypothesis that the self is dissimilar from the standard.

Notably, because judges typically select standards that are similar to a given target (Festinger, 1954) and because they initially establish a common ground against which they compare target and standard (Gentner and Markman, 1994), similarity testing constitutes the default comparison mechanism. In fact, comparisons are often characterized by an initial focus on similarities (Chapman and Johnson, 1999; Lockwood and Kunda, 1997) so that dissimilarity testing appears to be more of an exception that is primarily carried out when salient characteristics clearly indicate dissimilarity between the self and the standard.

The critical initial assessment of self-standard similarity is conceptualized as a quick holistic screening of features that are salient, easy to process and have immediate implications for target-standard similarity. Two features which fulfill these criteria are category membership and standard extremity. Similarity testing, for example, is more likely to be engaged for standards that belong to the same category as the standard (Mussweiler and Bodenhausen, 2002) and whose standing on the judgmental dimension is moderate rather than extreme (Mussweiler, Rüter, and Epstude, 2004b). In addition, the motivational underpinnings of the comparison situation may influence the outcome of this initial assessment. For example, if judges are motivated to preserve a positive self-image when confronted with a low standard they may focus more on the ways in which they are different from this standard and consequently engage in dissimilarity testing.

The literature on hypothesis-testing further suggests that once a hypothesis is selected, it is often tested by focusing on hypothesis-consistent evidence (Klayman and Ha, 1987; Snyder and Swann, 1978; Trope and Bassok, 1982; Trope and Liberman, 1996). Applied to the case of hypothesis-testing in social comparison, this suggests that judges selectively generate information that is consistent with the focal hypothesis of the comparison. If judges test the hypothesis that the self is similar to the standard, for example, they will do so by selectively searching for standard-consistent self-knowledge – evidence indicating that the self is indeed similar to the standard with respect to the judgmental dimension. Judges, who engage in similarity testing when comparing their athletic abilities to those of their best friend, may thus focus on those aspects of their self-knowledge which indicate that they are both similarly athletic. For example, these judges may bring to mind, that they and their friend often work out together, that their tennis matches are typically fairly close, and that they keep up with one another on their daily five kilometer runs. By the same token, if judges test the hypothesis that the self is dissimilar from the standard, they do so by selectively searching for standard-inconsistent self-knowledge – evidence indicating that the self is different from the standard. In our example, judges may thus bring to mind, that they always lose table-tennis matches against their best friend and that they swim like a stone whereas their friend was on the university swimming team. This selectivity in the acquisition of judgment-relevant self-knowledge has clear consequences for the accessibility of self-knowledge. The mechanism of similarity testing selectively increases the accessibility of standard-consistent self-knowledge, whereas dissimilarity testing selectively increases the accessibility of standard-inconsistent self-knowledge.

To the extent that judges use the self-knowledge that became accessible during the comparison as a basis for target evaluations, their subsequent judgment will reflect the implications of this knowledge. Basing self-evaluations on the implications of standard-consistent knowledge indicating that the self's standing on the judgmental dimension is similar to that of the standard will thus move evaluations closer to the standard. Basing target evaluations on the implications of standard-inconsistent knowledge indicating that the self's standing on the judgmental dimension is dissimilar from that of the standard, on the other hand, will move evaluations further away from the standard. This suggests that the default evaluative consequence of similarity testing is assimilation, whereas dissimilarity testing typically leads to contrast.

Empirical support for selective accessibility From this perspective, whether judges engage in the alternative comparison processes of similarity or dissimilarity testing critically determines the self-evaluative consequences of social comparisons. The informational focus judges take during the comparison – whether they focus on similarities or differences – critically determines whether target evaluations are assimilated towards or contrasted away from the standard.

Direct support for the critical role that judges' informational focus on similarities versus differences plays for the direction of comparison consequences stems from a social comparison study in which we manipulated

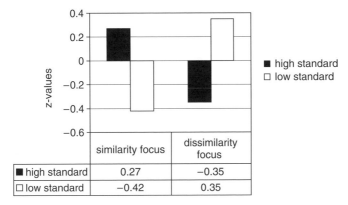

Figure 2.2. Self-evaluations of adjustment to college after comparison with a high versus low standard by similarity versus dissimilarity focus (from Mussweiler, 2001)

participants' informational focus. In particular, we used a procedural priming task to manipulate whether judges focus on similarities to or differences from the standard (Mussweiler, 2001). Prior to a social comparison, participants worked on an unrelated task in which they compared sketches of two scenes. About half of the participants were asked to list all the similarities between the two scenes they could find. The other half were asked to list all the differences they could find. In both cases, the respective informational focus on similarities or differences should become procedur-alized (Smith, 1994) and carry over to the subsequent comparison. That is, searching for similarities or differences in the two scenes should set participants' minds on either processing style and should induce them to search for the same kind of evidence in the subsequent social comparison. Pretesting revealed that this is indeed the case.

Subsequent to the procedural priming task, participants compared themselves with a social standard which was either high or low on the critical dimension of adjustment to college. They then evaluated their own adjustment to college. Consistent with a selective accessibility perspective on comparison consequences, subsequent self-evaluations critically depended on whether participants were induced to focus on similarities or differences (see Figure 2.2). Judges who were primed to focus on similarities and to thus engage in similarity testing assimilated self-evaluations towards the standard. These judges evaluated their own adjustment to college to be better after a comparison with a high rather than a low standard. Judges who were primed to focus on differences and to thus engage in dissimilarity testing, on the other hand, contrasted self-evaluations away from the standard. These judges evaluated their own adjustment to college to be worse after a comparison with a high rather than a low standard. How a comparison influenced target evaluations thus critically depended on whether judges focussed on similarities or differences during the comparison process.

Furthermore, recent evidence (Mussweiler *et al.*, 2004b) suggests that assimilative and contrastive social comparison consequences are often accompanied by traces of the two alternative selective accessibility mechanisms of similarity and dissimilarity testing. In one study, for example, participants compared themselves with either moderate or extreme comparison standards of athletic ability before evaluating their own athletic ability. For example, participants were asked to compare their athletic ability either with the moderately low standard Bill Clinton or with the extremely low standard Pope John Paul. They then evaluated a number of core athletic abilities, such as the number of sit-ups they can perform and the time they need to run 100 meters. Consistent with evidence in the social judgment literature (Herr, 1986), participants assimilated their self-evaluations to the moderate standards and contrasted them away from the extreme standards. Subsequent to these self-evaluations, participants were given the same pictures that we had previously used to induce the alternative informational foci on similarities versus dissimilarities (Mussweiler, 2001). This time we used these pictures to assess these respective foci subsequent to assimilative and contrastive comparisons. Specifically, participants were asked to compare these two pictures and to indicate how similar they are. If assimilative comparison consequences are indeed produced by an informational focus on similarities and contrastive consequences result from a focus on dissimilarities, then these respective foci should carry over to the picture comparison task. Participants who assimilated self-evaluations towards the moderate standards because they selectively focussed on similarities to these standards should also focus on similarities between the two pictures. Participants who contrasted self-evaluations away from extreme standards because they selectively focussed on dissimilarities, should also focus on dissimilarities between the two pictures. Consistent with these expectations, our results demonstrate that participants rated both pictures to be more similar after comparing themselves with a moderate rather than an extreme social comparison standard. This finding suggests that the alternative informational foci on similarities versus dissimilarities do indeed underlie assimilative and contrastive comparison consequences.

From a selective accessibility perspective, these varying social comparison consequences are produced by differences in the accessibility of self-knowledge. Specifically, similarity testing increases the accessibility of self-knowledge indicating that self and standard are similar on the critical dimension. Dissimilarity testing, however, selectively increases the accessibility of self-knowledge, which indicates that self and standard are dissimilar on the critical dimension. Consistent with this assumption, some of our recent evidence demonstrates that social comparisons that involve similarity versus dissimilarity testing have diverging effects on the accessibility of self-knowledge. In these studies (Mussweiler and Bodenhausen, 2002), we made use of the fact that similarity testing is more likely to occur if the self and the standard belong to the same social category, whereas dissimilarity testing is more likely if both belong to different categories. As a consequence, social comparisons with intracategorical versus extracategorcial standards should render divergent sets of self-knowledge accessible. Social comparison with an ingroup standard, on the one hand, should involve similarity testing so that standard-consistent self-knowledge is rendered accessible. Comparisons with an outgroup standard, on the other hand, should involve dissimilarity testing so that standard-inconsistent self-knowledge is rendered accessible. To test this assumption, we had male participants engage in a spontaneous comparison with a standard person who was described as very tidy and clean. This standard either belonged to the same or the opposite gender category to our participants. Subsequent to the comparison, we assessed the accessibility of standard-consistent versus standard-inconsistent self-knowledge with the use of a special type of lexical decision task (Dijksterhuis *et al.*, 1998). We found standard-consistent self-knowledge to be more accessible after a spontaneous comparison with an ingroup member than after a comparison with an outgroup member. This finding suggests that under conditions that promote similarity testing, the accessibility of standard-consistent target knowledge is increased. Under conditions that promote dissimilarity testing, however, standard-inconsistent knowledge becomes more accessible. Further studies (Mussweiler and Bodenhausen, 2002) demonstrated that social comparisons with ingroup standards typically lead to assimilation whereas comparisons with outgroup standards lead to contrast (see also Chapter 6, this volume). Taken together, these findings suggest that changes in the accessibility of self-knowledge do indeed play a core role in the genesis of social comparison consequences.

In this respect, the accessibility principle can be fruitfully applied to specify the psychological mechanisms that underlie the influences comparisons with others have on how we see and evaluate ourselves. Social comparison shapes self-evaluations in multiple and variable ways (for reviews see, Blanton, 2001; Collins, 1996; Mussweiler, 2003a, 2003b; Mussweiler and Strack, 2000b; Taylor, Wayment and Carrillo, 1996; Wood, 1989). Sometimes the self is assimilated towards a given standard (e.g., Lockwood and Kunda, 1997; Mussweiler and Strack, 2000a; Pelham and Wachsmuth, 1995). At other times the self is contrasted away from the given standard (e.g., Morse and Gergen, 1970). Which of these opposing evaluative consequences prevails depends on a host of moderators such as psychological closeness (Lockwood and Kunda, 1997; Pelham and Wachsmuth, 1995; Tesser, Miller, and Moore, 1988), self-esteem (e.g., Aspinwall and Taylor, 1993; Buunk, Collins, Taylor, Van Yperen, and Dakof, 1990) and category membership (e.g., Blanton, Crocker, and Miller, 2000; Mussweiler and Bodenhausen, 2002; Mussweiler, Gabriel, and Bodenhausen, 2000). At first sight, these moderators have little in common so that the literature on social comparison consequences appears like a disintegrated puzzle. From a social cognition perspective, all of these factors can be related to changes in the accessibility of self-knowledge (for a more elaborate discussion see, Mussweiler, 2003a). If a social comparison involves a focus on the ways in which self and standard are similar, then the accessibility of standard-consistent self-knowledge is increased so that self-evaluations are assimilated towards the standard. If a social comparison involves a focus on the ways in which self and standard are different, then the accessibility of standard-inconsistent knowledge is increased so that self-evaluations are contrasted away from the standard. Changes in the accessibility of self-knowledge may thus be the critical mechanism that drives the effects social comparisons have on the self.

Conclusion

Social comparison constitutes a basic psychological process that appears to be engaged whenever information about the self (Mussweiler and Rüter, 2003) or others (Dunning and Hayes, 1996; Mussweiler, 2003c; Mussweiler and Bodenhausen, 2002) is processed. A process that is characterized by such ubiquity necessarily has to follow the general principles that guide human information processing in general. In the present chapter, we have examined how social comparisons are shaped by what are arguably the two most fundamental principles of social information processing, namely the principles of cognitive efficiency and knowledge accessibility. We have suggested that both principles have important implications for core questions in social comparison research. In fact, they may help us understand *why* social comparisons are engaged, *who* is selected as a comparison standard, and *how* a social comparison influences the self.

The answers to these questions that we have derived from a social cognition perspective do at times deviate from the classic answers that have been given by social comparison researchers. For example, it is traditionally assumed that social comparisons are primarily carried out to obtain diagnostic information about the self (Festinger, 1954). A social cognition perspective, however, suggests that social comparisons may be engaged to process information about the self or others in a more efficient manner. Furthermore, social comparison theory traditionally assumes that standard selection is primarily guided by similarity between the self and the standard (Festinger, 1954; Goethals and Darley, 1977). People primarily select standards that are similar to themselves (e.g., Gruder, 1971; Suls *et al.*, 1978; Wheeler, 1966; Zanna *et al.*, 1975). A social cognition perspective, however, suggests that oftentimes people may simply compare with those whom they routinely use as comparison standards (Mussweiler and Rüter, 2003). This tendency saves scarce cognitive resources and is thus again consistent with the cognitive efficiency principle (Rüter and Mussweiler, 2005).

In this way, a social cognition perspective suggests novel answers to classic questions. Examining the social-cognitive underpinnings of social comparison processes may thus prove to be a fruitful path that promises to shed new light on the *why*, *who*, and *how* of social comparison.

Author note

Our research described in this chapter was supported by a grant from the German Research Foundation (DFG). We would like to thank the members of the Würzburg Social Cognition Group for stimulating discussions of this work.

References

Aarts, H. and Dijksterhuis, A. (2000). Habits as knowledge structures: Automaticity in goal directed behavior. *Journal of Personality and Social Psychology, 78*, 53–63.

Aspinwall, L. G. and Taylor, S. E. (1993). Effects of social comparison direction, threat, and self-esteem on affect, self-evaluation, and expected success. *Journal of Personality and Social Psychology, 64*, 708–722.

Bargh, J. A. (1990). Auto-motives – Preconscious determinants of social interaction. In E. T. Higgins and R. M. Sorrentino (eds.), *Handbook of motivation and cognition* (pp. 93–130). New York: Guilford Press.

(1997). The automaticity of everyday life. In R. S. Wyer (ed.), *Advances in social cognition* (Vol. x). Hillsdale, NJ: Erlbaum.

Bargh, J. A., Bond, R. N., Lombardi, W. J., and Tota, M. E. (1986). The additive nature of chronic and temporary sources of construct accessibility. *Journal of Personality and Social Psychology, 50*, 869–878.

Baumeister, R. F. (1998). The self. In D. T. Gilbert, S. T. Fiske, and G. Lindzey (eds.), *The handbook of social psychology* (Vol. i, pp. 680–740). New York: McGraw-Hill.

Betsch, T., Fiedler, K., and Brinkmann, J. (1998). Behavioral routines in decision making: The effects of novelty in task presentation and time pressure on routine maintenance and deviation. *European Journal of Social Psychology*, *28*, 861–878.

Betsch, T., Haberstroh, S., Glöckner, A., Haar, T., and Fiedler, K. (2001). The effects of routine strength on adaptation and information search in recurrent decision making. *Organizational Behavior and Human Decision Processes*, *84*, 23–53.

Betsch, T., Haberstroh, S., and Höhle, C. (2002). Explaining routinized decision making – A review of theories and models. *Theory and Psychology*, *12*, 453–488.

Biernat, M. (2003). Toward a broader view of social stereotyping. *American Psychologist*, *58*, 1019–1027.

Biernat, M. and Manis, M. (1994). Shifting standards and stereotype-based judgments. *Journal of Personality and Social Psychology*, *66*, 5–20.

Blanton, H. (2001). Evaluating the self in the context of another: The three-selves model of social comparison assimilation and contrast. In G. B. Moskowitz (ed.), *Cognitive social psychology: The Princeton Symposium on the legacy and future of social cognition* (pp. 75–87). Mahwah, NJ: Erlbaum.

Blanton, H., Crocker, J., and Miller, D. T. (2000). The effects of in-group versus out-group social comparison on self-esteem in the *Context* of a negative stereotype. *Journal of Experimental Social Psychology*, *36*, 519–530.

Brown, D. R. (1953). Stimulus-similarity and the anchoring of subjective scales. *American Journal of Psychology*, *66*, 199–214.

Buunk, B. P., Collins, R. L., Taylor, S. E., VanYperen, N. W., and Dakof, G. A. (1990). The affective consequences of social comparison: Either direction has its ups and downs. *Journal of Personality and Social Psychology*, *59*, 1238–1249.

Chapman, G. B. and Johnson, E. J. (1999). Anchoring, activation, and the construction of values. *Organizational Behavior and Human Decision Processes*, *79*, 1–39.

Collins, R. L. (1996). For better or worse: The impact of upward social comparison on self-evaluations. *Psychological Bulletin*, *119*, 51–69.

Coren, S. and Enns, J. T. (1993). Size contrast as a function of conceptual similarity between test and inducers. *Perception and Psychophysics*, *54*, 579–588.

Csikszentmihalyi, M. and Figurski, T. J. (1982). Self-awareness and aversive experience in everyday life. *Journal of Personality*, *50*, 15–28.

Dijksterhuis, A., Spears, R., Postmes, T., Stapel, D. A., Koomen, W., van Knippenberg, A., and Scheepers, D. (1998). Seeing one thing and doing another: Contrast effects in automatic behavior. *Journal of Personality and Social Psychology*, *75*, 862–871.

Dunning, D. and Hayes, A. F. (1996). Evidence of egocentric comparison in social judgment. *Journal of Personality and Social Psychology*, *71*, 213–229.

Festinger, L. (1954). A theory of social comparison processes. *Human Relations*, *7*, 117–140.

Gentner, D. and Markman, A. B. (1994). Structural alignment in comparison: No difference without similarity. *Psychological Science*, *5*, 152–158.

Gigerenzer, G. and Todd, P. M. (1999). Fast and frugal heuristics: The adaptive toolbox. In G. Gigerenzer, P. M. Todd, and the ABC Research Group (eds.), *Simple heuristics that make us smart* (pp. 3–36). New York: Oxford University Press.

Gilbert, D. T., Giesler, R. B., and Morris, K. A. (1995). When comparisons arise. *Journal of Personality and Social Psychology*, 69, 227–236.

Goethals, G. R. and Darley, J. M. (1977). Social comparison theory: An attributional approach. In J. M. Suls and R. L. Miller (eds.), *Social comparison processes: Theoretical and empirical perspectives* (pp. 259–278). Washington, DC: Hemisphere.

Gruder, C. L. (1971). Determinants of social comparison choices. *Journal of Experimental Social Psychology*, 7, 473–489.

Herr, P. M. (1986). Consequences of priming: Judgment and behavior. *Journal of Personality and Social Psychology*, 51, 1106–1115.

Higgins, E. T. (1987). Self-discrepancy: A theory relating self and affect. *Psychological Review*, 94, 319–340.

(1996). Knowledge activation: Accessibility, applicability, and salience. In E. T. Higgins and A. W. Kruglanski (eds.), *Social psychology: Handbook of basic principles* (pp. 133–168). New York: Guilford Press.

Higgins, E. T., King, G. A., and Mavin, G. H. (1982). Individual construct accessibility and subjective impressions and recall. *Journal of Personality and Social Psychology*, 43, 35–47.

Higgins, E. T. and Lurie, L. (1983). Context, categorization and recall: The "change-of-standard" effect. *Cognitive Psychology*, 15, 525–547.

Higgins, E. T., Rholes, W. S., and Jones, C. R. (1977). Category accessibility and impression formation. *Journal of Experimental Social Psychology*, 13, 141–154.

Klayman, J. and Ha, Y.-W. (1987). Confirmation, disconfirmation, and information in hypotheses testing. *Psychological Review*, 94, 211–228.

Klein, G. (2001). The fiction of optimization. In G. Gigerenzer and R. Selten (eds.), *Bounded rationality: The adaptive toolbox* (pp. 103–122). Cambridge, MA: The MIT Press.

Kruglanski, A. W. and Mayseless, O. (1990). Classic and current social comparison research: Expanding the perspective. *Psychological Bulletin*, 108, 195–208.

Lockwood, P. and Kunda, Z. (1997). Superstars and me: Predicting the impact of role models on the self. *Journal of Personality and Social Psychology*, 73(1), 91–103.

Macrae, C. N., Milne, A. B., and Bodenhausen, G. V. (1994). Stereotypes as energy-saving devices: A peek inside the cognitive toolbox. *Journal of Personality and Social Psychology*, 66, 37–47.

Masters, J. C. and Keil, L. J. (1987). Generic comparison processes in human judgment and behavior. In J. C. Masters and W. P. Smith (eds.), *Social comparison, social justice, and relative deprivation. Theoretical, empirical, and policy perspective* (pp. 11–54). Hillsdale, NJ: Erlbaum.

Miller, D. T. and Prentice, D. A. (1996). The construction of social norms and standards. In E. T. Higgins and A. W. Kruglanski (eds.), *Social psychology: handbook of basic principles* (pp. 799–829). New York: Guilford.

Morse, S. and Gergen, K. J. (1970). Social comparison, self-consistency, and the concept of self. *Journal of Personality and Social Psychology*, *16*(1), 148–156.

Mussweiler, T. (2001). "Seek and Ye shall find": Antecedents of assimilation and contrast in social comparison. *European Journal of Social Psychology*, *31*, 499–509.

(2003a). Comparison processes in social judgment: Mechanisms and consequences. *Psychological Review*, *110*, 472–489.

(2003b). 'Everything is relative': Comparison processes in social judgment. *European Journal of Social Psychology*, *33*, 719–733.

(2003c). When egocentrism breeds distinctness: Comparison processes in social prediction. *Psychological Review*, *110*, 581–584.

Mussweiler, T. and Bodenhausen, G. (2002). I know you are but what am I? Self-evaluative consequences of judging ingroup and outgroup members. *Journal of Personality and Social Psychology*, *82*, 19–32.

Mussweiler, T. and Epstude, K. (2005). *Relatively fast! Efficiency advantages of comparative information processing*. Manuscript submitted for publication.

Mussweiler, T., Gabriel, S., and Bodenhausen, G. V. (2000). Shifting social identities as a strategy for deflecting threatening social comparisons. *Journal of Personality and Social Psychology*, *79*, 398–409.

Mussweiler, T. and Rüter, K. (2003). What friends are for! The use of routine standards in social comparison. *Journal of Personality and Social Psychology*, *85*, 467–481.

Mussweiler, T., Rüter, K., and Epstude, K. (2004a). The man who wasn't there: Subliminal social comparison standards influence self-evaluation. *Journal of Experimental Social Psychology*, *40*, 689–696.

(2004b). The ups and downs of social comparison: Mechanisms of assimilation and contrast. *Journal of Personality and Social Psychology*, *87*, 832–844.

Mussweiler, T. and Strack, F. (2000a). The "relative self": Informational and judgmental consequences of comparative self-evaluation. *Journal of Personality and Social Psychology*, *79*, 23–38.

(2000b). Consequences of social comparison: Selective accessibility, assimilation, and contrast. In J. Suls and L. Wheeler (eds.), *Handbook of social comparison: Theory and research* (pp. 253–270). New York: Plenum.

Nisbett, R. E. and Ross, L. (1980). *Human inferences: Strategies and shortcomings of social judgment*. Englewood Cliffs: Prentice Hall.

Pelham, B. W. and Wachsmuth, J. O. (1995). The waxing and waning of the social self: Assimilation and contrast in social comparison. *Journal of Personality and Social Psychology*, *69*(5), 825–838.

Rüter, K. and Mussweiler, T. (2005). *The efficiency of routine standards in social comparison*. Manuscript submitted for publication.

Sanbonmatsu, D. M., Posavac, S. S., Kardes, F. R., and Mantel, S. P. (1998). Selective hypothesis testing. *Psychonomic Bulletin and Review*, *5*, 197–220.

Selten, R. (2001). What is bounded rationality? In G. Gigerenzer and R. Selten (eds.), *Bounded rationality: The adaptive toolbox* (pp. 13–36). Cambridge, MA: The MIT Press.

Sherif, M. and Hovland, C. I. (1961). *Social judgment: Assimilation and contrast effects in communication and attitude change*. New Haven, CT: Yale University Press.

Simon, H. A. (1956). Rational choice and the structure of the environment. *Psychological Review*, *63*, 129–138.

Smith, E. R. (1989). Procedural efficiency: General and specific components and effects on social judgment. *Journal of Experimental Social Psychology*, *25*, 500–523.

(1994). Procedural knowledge and processing strategies in social cognition. In R. S. Wyer and T. K. Srull (eds.), *Handbook of social cognition* (2nd ed., Vol. I, pp. 99–152). Hillsdale, NJ: Erlbaum.

Smith, E. R., Branscombe, N. R., and Bormann, C. (1988). Generality of the effects of practice on social judgment tasks. *Journal of Personality and Social Psychology*, *54*, 385–395.

Smith, E. R. and Lerner, M. (1986). Development of automatism of social judgments. *Journal of Personality and Social Psychology*, *50*, 246–259.

Smith, E. E., Shoben, E. J., and Rips, L. J. (1974). Structure and process in semantic memory: A featural model for semantic decisions. *Psychological Review*, *81*, 214–241.

Snyder, M. and Swann, W. B. (1978). Hypothesis-testing processes in social interaction. *Journal of Personality and Social Psychology*, *36*, 1202–1212.

Srull, T. K. and Wyer, R. S. (1979). The role of category accessibility in the interpretation of information about persons: Some determinants and implications. *Journal of Personality and Social Psychology*, *37*, 1660–1672.

Suls, J., Gastorf, J. W., and Lawhon, J. (1978). Social comparison choices for evaluating a sex- and age-related ability. *Personality and Social Psychology Bulletin*, *4*, 102–105.

Suls, J., Martin, R., and Wheeler, L. (2002). Social comparison: why, with whom, and with what effect? *Current Directions in Psychological Science*, *11*, 159–163.

Suls, J. and Wheeler, L. (2000). A selective history of classic and neo-social comparison theory. In J. Suls and L. Wheeler (eds.), *Handbook of social comparison: Theory and research*. New York: Kluwer Academic.

Taylor, S. E. (1981). The interface of cognitive and social psychology. In J. Harvey (ed.), *Cognition, social behavior, and the environment* (pp. 182–211). Hillsdale, NJ: Erlbaum.

Taylor, S. E., Wayment, H. A., and Carrillo, M. (1996). Social comparison, self-regulation, and motivation. In R. M. Sorrentino and E. T. Higgins (eds.), *Handbook of motivation and cognition*. (pp. 3–27). New York: Guilford Press.

Tesser, A., Miller, M., and Moore, J. (1988). Some affective consequences of social comparison and reflection processes: The pain and pleasure of being close. *Journal of Personality and Social Psychology*, *54*, 49–61.

Trope, Y. and Bassok, M. (1982). Confirmatory and diagnostic strategies in social information gathering. *Journal of Personality and Social Psychology*, *43*, 22–34.

Trope, Y. and Liberman, A. (1996). Social hypothesis testing: Cognitive and motivational factors. In E. T. Higgins and A. W. Kruglanski (eds.), *Social psychology: Handbook of basic principles* (pp. 239–270). New York: Guilford Press.

Tversky, A. and Kahneman, D. (1973). *Judgment under uncertainty: Heuristics and biases* (Vol. XIII). Oxford: Oregon Research Institute.

(1974). Judgment under uncertainty: Heuristics and biases. *Science, 185,* 1124–1130.

Verplanken, B., Aarts, H., van Knippenberg, A., and van Knippenberg, C. (1994). Attitude versus general habit: Antecedents of travel mode choice. *Journal of Applied Social Psychology, 24,* 285–300.

Wheeler, L. (1966). Motivation as a determinant of upward comparison. *Journal of Experimental Social Psychology, 2* (Suppl. 1), 27–31.

Wood, J. V. (1989). Theory and research concerning social comparisons of personal attributes. *Psychological Bulletin, 106*(2), 231–248.

Wood, J. V. and Taylor, K. L. (1991). Serving self-relevant goals through social comparison. In J. Suls and T. A. Wills (eds.), *Social comparison: Contemporary theory and research* (pp. 23–49). Hillsdale, NJ: Erlbaum.

Wyer, R. S. and Srull, T. K. (1989). *Memory and cognition in its social context.* Hillsdale, NJ: Erlbaum.

Zanna, M. P., Goethals, G. R., and Hill, J. F. (1975). Evaluating a sex-related ability: Social comparison with similar others and standard setters. *Journal of Experimental Social Psychology, 11,* 86–93.

3 Autobiographical memory, the self, and comparison processes

Rasyid Bo Sanitioso, Martin A. Conway, and Sophie Brunot

The theory of social comparison as proposed by Festinger (1954) states that people seek to compare themselves to others to obtain accurate information about themselves. For example, when a person is uncertain about an aspect of themselves, e.g. their intelligence, social comparisons with similar others might be used for the purposes of self assessment. In contrast, social comparisons may serve a hedonic or pleasurable purpose as when a person makes, for instance, a downward social comparison (Wills, 1981). Such hedonic comparisons may help maintain a positive view of the self (Kunda, 1990; Woods, 1989). We suggest that, in general, the purpose of comparison is to support and develop the coherence of the self (cf. Conway, Singer, and Tagini, 2004). That is, comparisons provide information that further the integrity of the self and its effectiveness in operating on the world – especially the social world. In this view, one of the key effects of comparisons is motivational, where they drive the individual to generate new goals and pursue new lines of action. Within this general "self-coherence/motivational" view of social comparison, a greatly overlooked source of comparisons are those that arise from comparisons of the current self with past (remembered) selves and with future (imagined) selves. Indeed, autobiographical memory – memories of the events and facts of our lives – has been viewed as a major part of the self-system, a part that grounds the current self in a remembered reality and in so doing constrains the universe of plausible possible selves and, consequently, the range of possible self comparisons (Conway and Pleydell-Pearce, 2000).

This chapter incorporates current research on the self in social comparison. Specifically, we incorporate the idea that the self is a complex knowledge structure that includes not only past autobiographical memories but also future aspirations. The role of motivation in the recall of autobiographical memories and in the construction of images of the self will be presented and linked to the motives in social comparison. In what follows, we will review research on motivational influence on momentary self-perception and its consequences on perceived similarity to another as a potential standard of comparison. We also discuss internal standards of comparison comprising possible and "actual" selves (see ahead for our conception of "actual selves"). The "Self-Memory System" (SMS) proposal of Conway and Pleydell-Pearce (2000) is used as a theoretical framework to integrate motives thought to drive social comparison and the directive use of self-images, past and future. It is to the SMS model that we turn first.

Motivational influence on self-perception and autobiographical memory

In this section, we present autobiographical remembering and self-perception as two interlinked processes driven by active self-goals. Specifically, we emphasize that the search process in autobiographical memory is strongly determined by a need for coherence between current active aspects of the self and autobiographical memories.

Autobiographical memory: coherence, correspondence, and "actual selves"

One of the great tensions in humans is that between correspondence and coherence: to be of value memories must correspond to reality, to at least some degree, but memories should also be consistent with the self, that is they should be self-coherent and not self contradictory or cause self-incoherence. Memories that contradict the self are costly because they require change. Conveniently forgetting a memory that undermines aspects of self avoids the need for change and the emotional, cognitive, behavioral, and social costs associated with changes to the self. Distorting a memory to fit better the current nature of the self is also a way in which to avoid costly change. In some cases distortions can be extreme. Consider, for example, the following memory of a witness to the 9/11 terrorist attack on the World Trade Center:

> He had a powerful distorted image flashback in which he saw himself high above the ground observing the collision of plane and building. The scene is very peaceful and there is no noise. Whenever this, clearly false image, intruded into consciousness he felt intense, destabilizing, guilt.

In fact this person suffered from post-traumatic stress disorder (PTSD) and the cognitive-behavioral therapy treatment program which he subsequently underwent successfully focussed on reinstating memories that were more realistic, which included his original perspective and which allowed him to recall the intensely negative feelings he had at the time (see Conway, Meares, and Standart, in press, for a more detailed account of this and several related cases). Clearly, PTSD memories are at the extreme end of the spectrum of memory disorders. Nonetheless, they do highlight how memories can be distorted to avoid change and, perhaps, indicate how this might happen more frequently in everyday life. Details might be forgotten, misremembered in some way and distorted in favor of the self, or thoughts and fantasies may be recalled as reality.

Despite the strong need for self-coherence in memory there is an equally strong need for memories to correspond to reality with some degree of accuracy. A person with a completely fantasized past would hardly be able to operate effectively upon the world and especially in social interactions. Indeed one of the hallmarks of psychological illness is when memories no longer constrain beliefs. Thus, for instance, a young schizophrenic man believed himself to be a world famous rock guitarist even though he knew he could not play the guitar; another patient had a persistent memory of having an intense row with his father the previous evening even though he could simultaneously recall attending his father's funeral some years previously. These and other cases, such as "as if" personalities, dysfunctional attachment styles, etc., are frequently found to have memories that very strikingly contradict, or which have been distorted to be consistent with, powerful self-beliefs which are as a consequence deluded beliefs (for reviews see Conway and Pleydell-Pearce, 2000; Conway, Singer, and Tagini, 2004; Fotopoulou and Conway, 2004; Fotopoulou, Conway, and Cassidy, 2005). It is then mainly in psychological illness that coherence takes precedence over correspondence. Under normal circumstances the trade off between coherence and correspondence is in favor of correspondence. Although, of course, a memory is the product of a self interacting with a mental representation of its world and it is to this that it corresponds rather than to some objective reality (Conway, Singer, and Tagini, 2004). The veridicality of memories is determined by the nature of the interaction the self has with the world and, of course, this usually should be an interaction which in large measure deals with a more or less accurate representation of reality.

The meaning that is placed on this "more or less accurate representation of reality" is quite another issue. Aspects of reality might be remembered with a high degree of accuracy but the meaning ascribed to the memory is determined solely by the self, at the time of experience and later in constructive recall. It is perfectly possible for details of an experience to be accurately remembered but be associated with a meaning or interpretation that was not generated at the time and which is a misinterpretation in the service of the self or a new interpretation arising from new knowledge and/or reappraisal. All of this underscores the fact that autobiographical remembering is a highly complex process. Conway and Pleydell-Pearce (2000) proposed that memories were dynamic mental constructions of the *Self-Memory-System* (SMS). The SMS is conceived of as a virtual memory system with two major parts: the working self and the autobiographical knowledge base. The working self consists primarily of a complex hierarchy of goals through which memories are encoded and later constructed. Working-self goals are thought of as "processes" and as such cannot themselves enter consciousness. Derivatives from self-goal, such as emotions, images, memories, thoughts, and verbal statements, can enter consciousness and provide certain types of consciously appraisable knowledge about progress with goal processing. It is the goal structure which is resistant to change and in which change is so costly. More recently, this conception of the working self has been extended to include a domain called the Conceptual Self that stores enduring beliefs, images of, and appraisals, of the current working self (see Conway *et al.*, 2004).

The working self modulates access to the autobiographical knowledge. Although working self processes cannot directly influence search processes in the knowledge base they can indirectly influence these by determining which cues are to be used to initiate a search. For example, in an individual with agentic self focus, working self processes might shape cues to access autobiographical knowledge about periods, events, and specific episodic memories in which issues of power featured (see Woike, 1995). Conway and Holmes (2003) refer to this raised accessibility of working self congruent memories as the "accessibility principle" and suggest that it operates across the life span rendering memories consonant with current existential concerns highly accessible. The working self then powerfully influences what types of memories most readily come to mind. It cannot, however, readily influence the content of memories. In the SMS model, knowledge in the knowledge base is linked together by cues that form complex knowledge structures (see Figure 3.1) that channel patterns of activation through the networks in which autobiographical knowledge is represented (see Conway and Pleydell-Pearce, 2000, for a more detailed account of this). A specific memory is considered to be brought to mind when a stable pattern of activation is established over indices in the knowledge base and this should encompass both conceptual autobiographical knowledge (I had a holiday in Greece last year, I went to the University of London, etc.) as well as episodic memories of specific experiences (Conway, 2001). This scheme of the

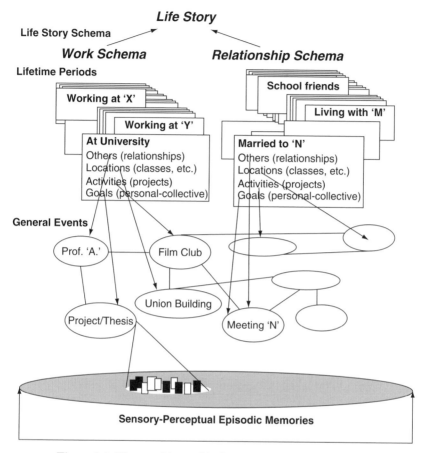

Figure 3.1. The autobiographical memory knowledge base

organization of autobiographical knowledge is illustrated in Figure 3.1 and discussed extensively in Conway and Pleydell-Pearce (2000).

Autobiographical memories are then complicated mental constructions intimately bound up with active, current, aspects of the self – the working self. Every memory, however, was originally formed by a self and as such each memory is a representative of a self. Memories imply or even directly reinstate a previous self or part of a previous self-system. Memories then, despite their errors, distortions, and other biases in favor of coherence, represent *actual selves* to which they correspond. They stand then in contrast to more hypothetical self representations often referred to as "possible selves" (Markus and Nurius, 1986). They have permanence in long-term memory that many, but by no means all, possible selves do not have and, moreover, they can be used in the construction of transitory selves.

The bias to recall self-congruent memories

Memory self-congruency bias was originally demonstrated in a seminal paper by Markus (1977) who found that people with a marked self-schema relating to the dependent-independent dimension showed pre-ferential access to memories of experiences in which they had behaved in dependent or independent ways. In contrast, individuals in whom the dependent-independent schema was not especially marked did not have this memory bias.

These types of self-memory congruency effects have since been observed in several studies and most especially in the work of McAdams (1982, 1985, 2001; McAdams, Diamond, de St. Aubin, and Mansfield, 1997) on power, intimacy, and generativity. McAdams (1982), using the Thematic Apperception Test (TAT), (Murray, 1938, 1943) considered to assess non-conscious aspects of personality (McClelland, Koestner, and Weinberger, 1989), categorized individuals (on the basis of their TAT responses) into those with a strong intimacy motivation or, in contrast, with a distinctive power motivation. Content analysis of subsequently free recalled memories of "peak" and other experiences found that the intimacy motivation group recalled peak experiences with a preponderance of intimacy themes compared with individuals who scored lower on this motivation, who in turn showed no memory bias. Similarly, the power motivation group recalled peak experiences with strong themes of power and satisfaction. Interestingly, neither group showed biases in memories for more mundane, less emo-tional, less self-defining, memories. These striking biases in memory availability by dominant motive type suggest that the goal structure of the working self makes highly available those aspects of the knowledge base that relate most directly to currently active goals. In more recent work, McAdams *et al.*, (1997) have examined the influence of the Eriksonian notion of "generativity" on the life stories of middle-aged adults (Erikson, 1950). Generativity refers to nurturing and caring for those things, products, and people that have the potential to outlast the self. Those individuals who were judged high in generativity i.e. who had a "commitment" life story, were found to recall a preponderance of events highly related to aspects of generativity. In contrast, those partici-pants who were not identified as holding a commitment story showed no such bias.

Work by Woike and her colleagues has further established the connection between personality and self-congruent memories (Woike, 1995; Woike, Gershkovich, Piorkowski, and Polo, 1999). In the tradition of personality research deriving from Murray (1938) and McClelland (e.g. McClelland et al., 1989), Woike identified implicit and explicit motives in a group of people who then recorded memorable events over a period of sixty days. According to McClelland et al., (1989) implicit motives are evident in preferences for certain types of affective experience such as "doing well" for achievement and "feeling close" for intimacy whereas explicit motives are present in social values and aspects of the self that can be introspected. A corollary of this view is that affective experiences should give rise to memories associated with implicit motives. Explicit motives, on the other hand, should lead to memories of less affective, routine, experiences more closely associated with self description than with measures of implicit motives, i.e. TAT performance. This was exactly Woike's finding in both a diary study and in a laboratory-based autobiographical memory retrieval implicit/explicit motive priming experiment. In a subsequent study, Woike et al. (1999) investigated groups of individuals classified as "agentic" (concerned with personal power, achievement, and independence) or as "communion" (concerned with relationships, interdependence, and others). Agentic personality types are considered to structure knowledge in terms of "differentiation" (the emphasis is on differences, separateness, and independence) whereas communal individuals, in contrast, structure knowledge in terms of "integration" (the emphasis is on similarity, congruity, and interdependence). Across a series of studies people with agentic self-focus were found to consistently recall emotional memories of events that involved issues of agency (mastery, humiliation) with their content structured in terms of differentiation. People with communal self-focus recalled emotion memories featuring others, often significant others, in acts of love and friendship, with the memory content structured in terms of integration. These findings clearly implicate the working self (particularly the focus of the working self) in determining recall and lend further weight to the suggestion that the working self influences access to sets of goal-congruent memories.

The working self may make available self-congruent memories and simultaneously act to suppress working self incongruent memories because of the dissonant comparisons and associated negative affects that would result. However, working self incongruent memories may not always result in negative emotion, despite being dissonance arousing. Robinson (1986) pointed out that autobiographical memories may act as a resource of the self, a resource that can help the self through difficult times perhaps by providing dissonant but positive comparisons. That is, they provide comparisons that demonstrate at least the possibility of a more secure self. We close this section then with some lines from the First World War poet Rupert Brooke, which exemplify the use of dissonant but positive autobiographical memories of his childhood in Grantchester (a small village near Cambridge, England). The lines are from *The Old Vicarage, Grantchester* and were written while Brooke was ill in Germany in 1912:

Stands the Church clock at ten to three?
And is there honey still for tea? (Brooke, 1915)

Autobiographical memories and the actual selves they derive from offer a resource that working self can use to create momentary or transitory selves – in the example from Rupert Brooke, the transitory self is one that takes afternoon tea in a peaceful English village. In general, however, events that map on to important working self goals can activate those goals in ways that influence subsequent judgments about oneself.

Self-perception and motivation

Kunda and Sanitioso (1989) demonstrated that motivation to see oneself positively influences momentary self-perception. In their studies, participants were first induced to believe that either extroversion or introversion is conducive to success. Next, in a supposedly separate experiment, participants had to complete a self-evaluation task. The findings showed that participants who were led to believe that extroversion is conducive of success subsequently perceived themselves as more extroverted and less introverted compared to those who were led to believe the opposite.

Autobiographical memories play a key role in motivated self-perception, consistent with the SMS model presented earlier. According to Kunda and colleagues, motives direct recall of autobiographical memories which subsequently leads to or justifies changes in momentary self-perception. That is, motives lead to increased accessibility of motive-consistent memories relative to motive-inconsistent memories. The accessed memories subsequently lead to (or justify) a self-definition consistent with the motivation (see Bluck, 2003; Conway, 2003). For example, when motivated to see themselves as extroverted, an individual may recall more easily past events reflecting extroversion such as the jokes he or she told at a dinner party, the long phone calls to friends and less easily past events reflecting introversion such as feeling nervous about giving a presentation to colleagues for a project, or that she or he did not dare initiate a conversation with a person she or he finds attractive at the public swimming pool.

In a number of studies, Sanitioso, Kunda, and Fong (1990) measured the type of memories that people tend to recall first as well as the reaction time with which people recall different memories, following an induction of beliefs relating a given trait to success. Participants who were led to believe that extroversion is conducive of success showed the tendency to recall past extroverted memory first, whereas those led to believe the opposite tend to recall past introverted memory first. In another study, participants who were led to believe that extroversion leads to success recalled extroverted memories faster and introverted memories slower, compared to those led to believe the opposite. Thus, how individuals see themselves at any given time is influenced by their motivation to see themselves positively, and this is possible because people selectively recall past events that support their desired self at that time. Brunot and Sanitioso (2004) subsequently showed that in addition to the type of memories likely to be recalled, motives also influence the quality of the memories. That is, people are more likely to recall abstract or general memories related to a desired trait compared to an undesired trait. Abstract or general memories have indeed been shown to have more impact on one's self-definition compared to specific memories that could be thought of as aberrations or exceptions.

The above studies thus demonstrate that motivation influences how one perceives oneself at any one time or momentary self-perception. They also show that motives lead to increased accessibility of autobiographical memories likely to justify or confirm a desired self compared to memories that may disconfirm it. To draw a parallel with the SMS model, the congruence between generated memories and the self concerns, in this case, motivated self or how one desires to see oneself at that time. In the next part, we argue that these motivational and memory processes are involved in social and temporal-self comparison situations and that they help to understand the effects of comparisons on self-perception.

Comparison processes and motivated self-perception

Two kinds of comparison will be considered: comparison with others and comparison with past or future selves. For each (type of comparison), we will evoke the role of motivation and autobiographical memories in the impact of the comparison on momentary self-perception. Finally, we will argue that preferences for social and temporal-self comparisons are also driven by self-goals and involve autobiographical knowledge.

Social comparison and self-perception

In his theory of social comparison, Festinger (1954) proposed that the more an individual thinks he or she is similar to a standard, the more likely social comparison is to take place and be considered as informative and valid. However, the concept of similarity itself was never explicitly detailed in the (original) theory. Goethals and Darley (1977) subsequently proposed precision of how people may determine this similarity, namely via an analysis of related attributes. That is, people may judge their similarity to a standard on attributes they consider as relevant. The integration of research on the self and autobiographical memories, specifically related to the malleable self as described above, emphasizes that this perceived similarity may be influenced by motives activated in the social comparison situations, such as the motives to perceive oneself positively or to protect one's positive self-image.

The motive to see oneself positively may influence the perceived similarity between oneself and a potential standard of comparison. People may see themselves as similar to desirable standards (see Lockwood and Kunda, 1997; Kunda and Sanitioso, 1989). On the other hand, when the comparison may be detrimental to one's self, the individual may attempt to distance themselves from the standard to invalidate the comparison (Mussweiler, Gabriel, and Bodenhausen, 2000; see Collins, 1996). This thus emphasizes the effects of social comparison on momentary self, either to bring it closer to, or further away from, a standard. In other words, changes in an individual's momentary self may underlie assimilation (perceived similarity) or contrast (perceived dissimilarity) between the self and the standard (see, Mussweiler, 2003).

Kunda and Sanitioso (1989, Study 2) assessed similarity judgment among their participants to a person who was described as extroverted or introverted, and as either successful or unsuccessful in university. Subsequently, participants perceived more similarity between themselves and the successful other and less similarity with the unsuccessful other. Furthermore, the results suggested that the perceived similarity was mediated by changes in the participants' self-perception as more or less extroverted (or introverted) in line with the characteristic of the successful other (i.e., the other's perceived level of extroversion). Selective accessibility appears to underlie these changes in self-perception aiming to be more or less similar to the other person (see, Sanitioso *et al.*, 1990).

Selective activation of autobiographical knowledge in the service of the motivation to maintain a positive self is also illustrated in a series of studies conducted by Mussweiler *et al.* (2000). In their studies, participants were first exposed to another person who did better or worse than they on a test. Results showed that when participants were exposed to another who did better on the test and thus found themselves in a potentially threatening comparison situation, they tended to activate self-knowledge that renders them dissimilar to, and thus invalidate any social comparison with, the standard.

The studies of Kunda and Sanitioso (1989) and of Mussweiler *et al.* (2000) demonstrated the effects of the same motivation, namely to see oneself positively, on momentary self. However, whereas Kunda and Sanitioso showed increased similarity to a desirable standard (see also, Lockwood and Kunda, 1997), Mussweiler *et al.* showed instead increased dissimilarity between the self and the better standard (to invalidate social comparison that can have disastrous consequences on the individual's self-evaluation). Mussweiler *et al.*'s findings are thus more consistent with the downward social comparison literature as documented by Wills (1981). It should be noted that whereas the studies of Kunda and Sanitioso (1989, see also Lockwood and Kunda, 1997) used personality dimensions or abilities that in principle could change with time (or at the very least one can imagine acquiring these traits and abilities in the future) and may include autobiographical memories that are rich and varied, the studies of Mussweiler *et al.* concerned self-characteristics that are immutable (e.g., ethnicity and gender). Complexity of autobiographical memory system may thus be important in one's ability to perceive similarity between oneself and a desirable standard (Linville, 1985), as this allows the individual to construct a momentary self that is similar to the standard or to generate motive-congruent memories.

Thus, incorporating empirical research on the self and autobiographical memories allows us to address a fundamental question in social comparison, namely the judgment of similarity between the self and a standard of social comparison. This focusses on the possible changes in momentary self, via selective accessibility of autobiographical memories or information about the self, in the service of the motivation to see oneself positively. These changes may underlie contrast (increased dissimilarity) or assimilation (increased perceived similarity) of the self to a standard in a comparison situation. Whether exposure to a desirable standard leads to contrast or assimilation may thus be determined by the motivation activated at the time of comparison (in this case, we can assume the motivation to maintain a positive self) and the complexity of autobiographical knowledge that an individual can generate to construct a momentary self that approaches the desirable standard.

In the section that follows, we address another issue in social comparison, namely temporal comparison between actual and past or future selves. The inclusion of these concepts also sheds light on why, under certain conditions, comparison with a better standard actually leads to more positive self-evaluation and perceived similarity between the self and the standard. In their study, Lockwood and Kunda (1997) found that participants exposed to another person who is brilliant and clearly better off actually came to see themselves more positively than those not exposed. Lockwood and Kunda (1997) interpreted the positive effects among their participants following exposure to the desirable standard via possible selves that the participants might have constructed or activated as inspired by the brilliant standard. Temporal aspects of the self and comparisons emanating from past and future selves constitute the next issue we address.

Comparison with past or future selves and self-perception

Autobiographical memories and their self-defining characteristics can be, and are, used as standards against which the current working self can be compared. Reconstruction and evaluation of past selves thus represent a key question in the comparison between present and past selves.

How individuals think of themselves in the past has been the subject of numerous studies (e.g., Karney and Coombs, 2000; Mcfarland and Ross, 1987; Ross, 1989; Wilson and Ross, 2001). Current self-perception, as detailed previously, can be influenced by recalled past behavior or information. On the other hand, current self may also influence recall of past behavior, signifying a bi-directional relationship between the self and the recall of autobiographical memories (Wilson and Ross, 2003). So far, we have emphasized how the past may be assimilated into the current self. This is especially true when people evaluate themselves vis à vis the past on attributes that they think are stable. Contrasts, on the other hand, are observed when people believe that the attributes are unstable or when changes or development are expected. Wilson and Ross, for instance, found that people who had completed a given course tend to underestimate their previous abilities on the dimension, probably because they assumed that their abilities must have improved after the course. People in general also tend to have theory of (age-related) decline concerning memories, and they thus tend to overestimate their past memory/recall capabilities. Thus the past may at times be contrasted or assimilated to the present. The motivation to see oneself positively has been shown to lead people to recall or construct past selves that are worse off than they are now and should thus, by contrast, lead to positive evaluation of their current self. However, people may also evoke positive past selves to boost evaluation of their current self, signifying assimilation of past selves to the present. People may indeed evoke a past self that is worse off than the present when they wish to emphasize change (or more precisely, improvement) and that this past self is no longer part of the current or future self. On the other hand, positive past selves that contribute additively to the current self may be evoked when people emphasize stability of the self and this past self may still be part of the present or can become part of the future self.

Contrast or assimilation of past selves may be reflected in how people recall autobiographical memories. People tend to recall past events and behaviors (from which inferences about past selves may be made) that they consider to be true of their current self from a first person perspective (i.e., as if they were reliving the experience). On the other hand, past events that are not (or no longer) considered true of the self and provide a past self against which the current self is contrasted tend to be recalled from a third person perspective (i.e., as if they were observing someone else behave, see Libby and Eibach, 2002). To maintain a positive self-perception, people may thus recall past positive events using first person perspective and negative event using a third person perspective to feel good about their current self. Psychological distance perceived between the present and the past may also contribute to the likelihood that past self or past information is contrasted or assimilated to the present self (Ross and Wilson, 2002). A past event, regardless of when it actually took place in the past, may be perceived as distant (e.g., It feels like such a long time ago) or recent (e.g., It feels like it was yesterday) as a function of the motives activated or implicit theories that people have about the stability/change of their self. In three studies, Ross and Wilson (2002) found that participants reported feeling closer to past selves and experiences that are enhancing to the present self, than to those that are unfavorable.

Future selves represent another standard against which actual self may be compared. Possible selves or images of the self that one would like to have or would like to avoid in the future (Markus and Nurius, 1986) represent such future self standards. According to Markus and Nurius (1986) possible selves are cognitive representations of motivations and represent what one wishes to realize in the future such as "Me as a successful professor," "the thin and rich Me," "Me as a good parent," as well as future selves to be avoided such as "Me as a bag lady," "unemployed me" etc. One function of possible selves stated by Markus and Nurius is directly related to social comparison, namely that possible selves serve as contexts of evaluation for current self and behaviors. That is, possible selves are standards with which the current or past self may be compared. The discrepancy perceived between possible and actual selves provides thus the incentive for individuals to bring their actual self closer to the possible self (if the possible self is positive) or to ensure that the possible self never becomes a reality (if the possible self is negative). In general, possible selves contribute additively to current self-evaluation (i.e., assimilation) and thus directly impact current self-perception. That is, positive possible selves lead to a more positive current self, and negative possible selves impact the current self negatively.

As concrete and personalized goals, the construction of possible selves always involves autobiographical memories to a significant degree. First, possible selves may actually be past selves that an individual wishes to recapture or to avoid. An individual may have a possible self as happy and thin in the past, for instance, which may not be the case in his or her current situation. The same individual may remember himself or herself as an insecure person in the past and this represents a possible self to be avoided in the future. Autobiographical memories, involved in the construction of possible selves, provide thus continuity between past or current self with the imagined future selves (Markus and Nurius, 1986; see also Conway, 2003). Possible selves contain behavioral strategies and means by which goals may be realized and as such provide a vehicle for mental rehearsals and selection of past behaviors that correspond to the goals (and suppression of those not corresponding to the goals) embodied in these future images. That is, people recruit pertinent knowledge about themselves to create a concrete possible self embodying a specific goal, allowing them to formulate and rehearse the necessary actions to attain (or to avoid) the possible self. Autobiographical memories thus have a regulatory function in dealing with anticipated situations pertinent to a goal.

Positive possible selves contribute additively to the actual well-being or current self-perception of individuals. This may be attributed to the fact that despite the perceived discrepancy, there is continuity or sufficient similarity (that appears to be the inevitable consequence of personalization of abstract goals) between the current or past self with the future self, increasing the perceived possibility of attaining the desired or future self (Lockwood and Kunda, 1997; Conway, 2003), via regulation of current behaviors to bring one closer to the distant self (or further away from negative possible selves). Ruvolo and Markus (1992), for instance, showed that participants who had imagined themselves as successful persisted on a task more than those who had not imagined (or activated) the successful possible self. Positive reactions to highly desirable standards in a social comparison situation also appear to be mediated by the individuals' ability to generate a possible self that approaches the standard (i.e., that the individual may in the future be like the standard, see Lockwood and Kunda, 1997 described earlier, see also Buunk and Breeninkmeijer, 2001). Though possible selves can be negative, most studies show that they are mostly positive (Markus and Nurius, 1986). Their assimilation contributes thus to a more positive current self-evaluation.

Other future selves as standards of comparison include ideal selves as proposed by Higgins (1987). Ideal selves represent one's aspirations, hopes, and desires or what one wishes to be. Research conducted by Higgins and colleagues (e.g., Higgins, Bond, Klein, and Strauman, 1986; Strauman and Higgins, 1987) have focused on the emotional consequences that result from perceiving a discrepancy between actual and ought or ideal selves. Specifically, people may experience depression-related emotions when the discrepancy between their ideal and actual selves is or becomes salient. Autobiographical memories may aid in the reduction of the perceived discrepancy in two ways, namely via changes in momentary self (related to the self function of autobiographical memories) and via behavioral regulation (related to the directive function of autobiographical memories). At the level of the momentary self, individuals may recruit past selves and information coherent with the ideal self. This may indeed result in an actual self-perception that is closer to the ideal. However, existing autobiographical memories may constrain people's ability to conjure up images of their current self that "match" their ideal self (and in theory, this discrepancy will always exist). That is, the individual lacks autobiographical memories that are coherent with the ideal self. These constraints of existing autobiographical memories have indeed been observed in research on motivated self-perception (see Sanitioso et al., 1990). Another means to overcome limitations imposed by existing memory system is to reduce the discrepancy in the long term, via behavioral regulation. That is, people may put into place plans that would bring them closer to the ideal self via gradual changes in behaviors. Concept such as Life Tasks (see, Cantor, Norem, Langston, and Zirkel, 1991) may be considered as part of these behavioral regulations to reduce discrepancy between actual self and self-guides. Past behaviors that may be consistent with the goal may be repeated and those that may be contradictory suppressed. New behaviors may, on the other hand, be simulated and rehearsed mentally. These regulatory behaviors related to a goal may be embodied in, among others, one's possible selves. The activation of ideal selves may indeed lead to dissonance via the contrast perceived between actual and the wished for selves. However, they nonetheless evoke the possibilities of more positive future selves that may attenuate the negative emotional consequences of the dissonance (Robinson, 1986).

Thus, temporal self comparison as well as social comparison involve self-goals activation that influence self-perception (e.g., increasing similarity to a desirable standard) via increased accessibility of motive-consistent memories. In other words, motives (such as the motivation to see oneself positively) and recall processes determine the effects of comparison on the self. Next, we argue that preferences for social or temporal-self comparisons are also driven by motivations.

Motivation and preference for social and temporal-self comparisons

Several factors appear to influence the choice of social or temporal-self comparisons. First, people engage in temporal-self comparison when comparison with others is not possible due to absence of external standards or information concerning others. Second, others may be thought of as inappropriate standards of comparison (see Levine and Moreland, 1987). Finally, people may also use internal standards of comparison when historical development of the self is a better index of one's abilities and growth or progress towards a personal goal, than comparison to others that may have a different personal history altogether (see Albert, 1977, for a related discussion). The latter may be motivated by the need to maintain a sense in the stability of the self, especially in periods of changes (Albert, 1977). Research also points to motivational influences in the choice of social or temporal-self comparisons.

Wilson and Ross (2000) found that young adults are more likely to use comparison with their past selves when they wish to enhance themselves and to use social comparison when they wish to evaluate themselves accurately. Among participants of this population, past selves are less likely to impose a threat (such as the perception of decline over time as may be the case with older adults). The motivation to see oneself positively may also favor use of comparison with future selves. As future selves are by definition imagined selves, they can be constructed with fewer reality constraints (than past selves or others as standards) and therefore be relatively more malleable to fit the motive and risk-free. Indeed, correlational studies conducted among people of disadvantaged groups (i.e., disabled students in a study of Dif, Guimond, Martinot, and Redersdorff, 2001; unemployed people in a study of Brunot, 2004) reveal a strong link between the use of comparisons with future selves and self-esteem. These results suggest that optimistic comparison with future selves may be used as a strategy to protect self-esteem. Furthermore, a study by Frye and Karney (2002) on marital satisfaction showed that temporal comparisons with future selves are likely to be used when self-esteem is threatened. These researchers found that, in cases of severe problems, spouses are likely to use favorable comparison with future selves (i.e., thinking that those problems will improve over time) rather than favorable social comparisons (i.e., perceiving themselves as better off than other couples). The same authors also found that levels of abstraction of threats may drive the choice of the different types of comparison. When threat is perceived at a general level, people may compare themselves against others as they can select the dimensions on which they are superior (compared to others) to use as the bases of comparison. On the other hand, when the comparison is on a specific dimension, people may compare themselves against their past selves which represent a less constrained standard than others.

Conclusion

The present chapter integrates research on autobiographical memories and the self in social and temporal-self comparison processes. In our view, access to autobiographical knowledge and memories is driven by the working self which itself is made up of a hierarchy of goals. Once activated, memories and autobiographical knowledge influence momentary self-perception. In this framework, we suggest that the effects of social or temporal-self comparison on self-perception may depend on the goal activated at that time. For example, the motives to maintain a positive self-perception may lead individuals to activate self-knowledge that increases similarity with a desirable standard and decreases similarity with an undesirable standard. Thus, in social or temporal-self comparison situations, autobiographical memories may be involved especially in changes in momentary self following exposure to a standard or activation of past selves. Furthermore, motivation also appears to influence the choice of social or temporal-self comparison.

Experimental studies directly investigating the role of autobiographical knowledge and memories in social comparison processes are currently lacking. Future studies should thus be geared towards providing a direct empirical test of the effects of comparison contexts on the recall of autobiographical memories and its subsequent impact on changes in the self and perceived similarity between the self and a comparison target. How motives influence preferences for temporal or social comparison also needs to be investigated in future studies.

Author note

Preparation of this chapter was made possible by the Cognitique grant from Le Ministère de l'Education Nationale (France), attributed to Serge Guimond. The idea for the chapter arose following a meeting organized by Serge Guimond and supported by the same grant and LAPSCO.

Martin A. Conway was supported by the award of a Professorial Fellowship from the Economic and Social Research Council of the United Kingdom.

References

Albert, S. (1977). Temporal comparison theory. *Psychological Review*, *84*, 485–503.

Bluck, S. (2003). Autobiographical memory: Exploring its functions in everyday life. *Memory*, *11*, 113–123.

Brooke, R. (1915). *The Old Vicarage, Grantchester*. In Poetry Please! J. M. Dent Everyman: London.

Brunot, S. (2004). L'estime de soi et les comportements de recherche d'emploi chez des chômeurs de longue durée: Le rôle des comparaisons sociales et interpersonnelles. *Actes du V° Congrès International de Psychologie Sociale en Langue Française*, Lausanne, Switzerland, pp. 327–328.

Brunot, S. and Sanitioso, R. (2004). Motivational influence on the quality of memories: Recall of general autobiographical memories related to desired attributes. *European Journal of Social Psychology*, *34*, 627–635.

Buunk, B. P. and Brenninkmeijer, V. (2001). When individuals dislike exposure to an actively coping role model: Mood change as related to depression and social comparison orientation. *European Journal of Social Psychology*, *31*, 537–548.

Cantor, N., Norem, J., Langston, C., and Zirkel, S. (1991). Life tasks and daily life experience. *Journal of Personality*, *59*, 425–451.

Collins, R. L. (1996). For better or worse: the impact of upward social comparison on self-evaluations. *Psychological Bulletin*, *119*, 51–69.

Conway, M. A. (2001). Repression revisited. *Nature*, *410*, 319–320.

(2003). Cognitive-affective mechanisms and processes in autobiographical memory. *Memory*, *11*, 217–224.

Conway, M. A. and Holmes, E. (2003). *Autobiographical memory*. In press with the Open University (publisher yet to be announced).

Conway, M. A., Meares, K., and Standart, S. (in press). Images and goals. *Memory*.

Conway, M. A. and Pleydell-Pearce, C. W. (2000). The construction of autobiographical memories in the self memory system. *Psychological Review*, *107*, 261–288.

Conway, M. A., Singer, J. A., and Tagini, A. (2004). The self and autobiographical memory: correspondence and coherence. *Social Cognition*, *22*, 491–529.

Dif, S., Guimond, S., Martinot, D., and Redersdorff, S. (2001). La théorie de la privation relative et les réactions au handicap: le rôle des comparaisons intrapersonnelles dans la gestion de l'estime de soi. *Journal International de Psychologie*, *36*, 314–328.

Erikson, E. H. (1950). *Childhood and society*. New York: W. W. Norton and Company.

Festinger, L. (1954). A theory of social comparisons processes. *Human Relations*, *7*, 117–140.

Fotopoulou, A. and Conway, M. A. (2004). Confabulation, pleasant and unpleasant. *Neuro-Psychoanalysis*, 6(1), 26–33.

Fotopoulou, A., Conway, M. A., and Cassidy, T. (2005) Confabulation and anosognosia following right-hemisphere damage: the fragmented self and negative emotions, under review.

Frye, N. E. and Karney, B. R. (2002). Being better or getting better? Social and temporal comparisons as coping mechanisms in close relationships. *Personality and Social Psychology Bulletin*, 28, 1287–1299.

Goethals, G. R. and Darley, J. (1977). Social comparison theory: An attributional approach. In J. Suls and R. I. Miller (eds.), *Social comparison processes: Theoretical and empirical perspectives* (pp. 259–278). Washington DC: Hemisphere Publishing.

Higgins, E. T. (1987). Self-discrepancy: A theory relating self and affect. *Psychological Review*, 94, 319–340.

Higgins, E. T., Bond, R. N., Klein, R., and Strauman, T. (1986). Self-discrepancies and emotional vulnerability : How magnitude, accessibility and type of discrepancy influence affect. *Journal of Personality and Social Psychology*, 51, 5–15.

Karney, B. R. and Coombs, R. H. (2000). Memory bias in long-term close relationships: Consistency or improvement? *Personality and Social Psychology Bulletin*, 26, 959–970.

Kühnen, U. and Hannover, B. (2000). Assimilation and contrast in social comparisons as a consequence of self-construal activation. *European Journal of Social Psychology*, 30, 799–811.

Kunda, Z. (1990). The case for motivated reasoning. *Psychological Bulletin*, 108, 480–498.

Kunda, Z. and Sanitioso, R. (1989). Motivated changes in the self-concept. *Journal of Experimental Social Psychology*, 25, 272–285.

Levine, J. M. and Moreland, R. L. (1987). Social comparison and outcome evaluation in group contexts. In J. C. Masters and W. P. Smith (eds.), *Social comparison, social justice and relative deprivation: Theoretical, empirical and policy perspectives* (pp. 105–127). Hillsdale, NJ: Erlbaum.

Libby, L. K. and Eibach, R. P. (2002). Looking back in time: Self-concept change affects visual perspective in autobiographical memory. *Journal of Personality and Social Psychology*, 82, 167–179.

Linville, P. W. (1985). Self-complexity and affective extremity: Don't put all your eggs in one cognitive basket. *Social Cognition*, 3, 94–120.

Lockwood, P. and Kunda, Z. (1997). Superstars and me: Predicting the impact of role models on the self. *Journal of Personality and Social Psychology*, 73, 91–103.

Markus, H. R. (1977). Self-schemata and processing information about the self. *Journal of Personality and Social Psychology*, 35, 63–78.

Markus, H. R. and Kunda, Z. (1986). Stability and malleability of the self-concept. *Journal of Personality and Social Psychology*, 51, 858–866.

Markus, H. R. and Nurius, P. (1986). Possible selves. *American Psychologist*, 41, 954–969.

McAdams, D. P. (1982). Experiences of intimacy and power: Relationships between social motives and autobiographical memory. *Journal of Personality and Social Psychology*, 42, 292–302.

(1985). *Power, intimacy, and the life story: Personological inquiries into identity.* New York: Guilford Press.

(2001). The psychology of life stories. *Review of General Psychology*, 5, 100–122.

McAdams, D. P., Diamond, A., de St. Aubin, E., and Mansfield, E. (1997). Stories of commitment: The psychosocial construction of generative lives. *Journal of Personality and Social Psychology*, 72, 678–694.

McClelland, D. C., Koestner, R., and Weinberger, J. (1989). How do self-attributed and implicit motives differ? *Psychological Review*, 96, 690–702.

McFarland, C. and Ross, M. (1987a). The relation between current impressions and memories of self and dating partner. *Personality and Social Psychology Bulletin*, 13, 228–238.

(1987b). Memories in the self memory system. *Psychological Review*, 107, 261–288.

Murray, H. A. (1938). *Explorations in personality.* New York: Oxford University Press.

(1943). *The thematic aperception test: manual.* Cambridge, MA: Harvard University Press.

Mussweiler, T. (2003). "Everything is relative": Comparison processes in social judgment: The 2002 Jaspars Lecture. *European Journal of Social Psychology*, 33, 719–733.

Mussweiler, T., Gabriel, S., and Bodenhausen, G. V. (2000). Shifting social identities as a strategy for deflecting threatening social comparisons. *Journal of Personality and Social Psychology*, 79, 398–409.

Robinson, J. A. (1986). Autobiographical memory: A historical prologue. In D. C. Rubin (ed.), *Autobiographical memory* (pp. 19–24). Cambridge: Cambridge University Press.

Ross, M. (1989). Relation of implicit theories to the construction of personal histories. *Psychological Review*, 96, 341–357.

Ross, M. and Wilson, A. E. (2002). It feels like yesterday: Self-esteem, valence of personal past experiences, and judgments of subjective distance. *Journal of Personality and Social Psychology*, 82, 792–803.

Ruvolo, A. P. and Markus, H. R. (1992). Possibles selves and performance: The power of self-relevance imagery. *Social Cognition*, 10, 95–124.

Sanitioso, R., Kunda, Z., and Fong, G. T. (1990). Motivated recruitment of auto-biographical memories. *Journal of Personality and Social Psychology*, 44, 229–241.

Strauman, T. and Higgins, E. T. (1987). Automatic activation of self-discrepancies and emotional syndromes: When cognitive structures influence affect. *Journal of Personality and Social Psychology*, 53, 1004–1014.

Wills, T. A. (1981). Downward comparison principles in social psychology. *Psychological Bulletin*, 90, 245–271.

Wilson, A. E. and Ross, M. (2000). The frequency of temporal-self comparisons in people's personal appraisals. *Journal of Personality and Social Psychology*, 78, 928–942.

(2001). From chump to champ: People's appraisals of their earlier and current selves. *Journal of Personality and Social Psychology*, 80, 572–584.

(2003). The identity function of autobiographical memory: time is on our side. *Memory*, 11, 137–149.

Woike, B. (1995). Most-memorable experiences: Evidence for a link between implicit and explicit motives and social cognitive processes in everyday life. *Journal of Personality and Social Psychology*, *68*, 1081–1091.

Woike, B., Gershkovich, I., Piorkowski, R., and Polo, M. (1999). The role of motives in the content and structure of autobiographical memory. *Journal of Personality and Social Psychology*, *76*, 600–612.

Woods, J. V. (1989). Theory and research concerning social comparisons of personal attributes. *Psychological Bulletin*, *106*, 231–248.

4 Comparing oneself over time: the temporal dimension in social comparison

Sandrine Redersdorff and Serge Guimond

"The knowledge of some other part of the stream, past or future, near or remote, is always mixed in with our knowledge of the present"

James (1890/1950)

The temporal dimension of our life, as suggested by James (1890), appears to be an important key to understand and examine the present. Nonetheless, in presenting his theory, Festinger (1954) described the process of social comparison without taking into account the temporal dimension. Several years later, Albert (1977) pointed out that a theory of temporal comparison could be developed along the same line as that developed on social comparison. Albert's (1977) theory of comparison processes is a temporal translation of social comparison theory, in which processes that occur between different individuals at one point in time are assumed to apply to a single person comparing himself or herself at various points in time. The role of temporal comparison has received far less empirical attention than that of social comparison (Wedell and Parducci, 2000). Yet, recent research suggests that temporal comparison may often be more important psychologically than social comparison. Is it really the case? Is it possible to distinguish empirically processes of temporal and social comparisons, or are they always inter-related? What type of temporal comparisons are important, comparisons with the past or comparisons with the future? In order to start answering these questions, this chapter provides an overview of existing research on temporal-self comparison. We begin with the problem of defining a process of temporal comparison. We then examine research on the frequency with which people engage in temporal-self comparison over the life-span. Finally, we discuss the findings of research that point to a role of temporal-self comparisons in three main areas: self-evaluation, self-esteem, and socio-political attitudes and behaviors.

What is temporal comparison?

Following Albert (1977), many researchers and theorists use the concept of temporal comparison to refer to "a process of comparison that goes on only within a single individual." (p. 485) Thus, one can distinguish interpersonal comparison, i.e. the process of social comparison as defined by Festinger (1954), from intrapersonal comparison, i.e. Albert's (1977) process of temporal comparison. However, this does not appear to be entirely satisfactory since a temporal dimension may also be involved at the interpersonal level (e.g., Frye and Karney, 2002). Furthermore, many researchers studying intergroup comparisons have also used the concept of temporal comparison (e.g., Blanz, Mummendey, Mielke, and Klink, 1998). Indeed, as shown in Table 4.1, if we distinguish between four main levels of analysis, the comparative activity at each level can involve a temporal dimension (see also Levine and Moreland, 1987). We can compare ourselves over time, as individuals: this represents the intrapersonal level. But in our interpersonal relations, we may keep track of where we stand over time compared to one of our friends (interpersonal level). Finally, we can compare ourselves as group members and keep track of the evolution of our own group over time (intragroup level) or compare the standing of our own group relative to that of another group at different points in time (intergroup level).

This suggests that the global concept of temporal comparison is probably too broad whereas that of intrapersonal comparison may be too narrow. Table 4.1 suggests some alternative and more precise labeling of temporal comparisons occurring at each level of analysis. Thus, when the comparison concerns the status of a single group over time (intragroup level), the concept of *temporal-group comparison* is proposed, and so on. Because the focus of the present chapter is on comparisons occurring within individuals, we will use the concept of *temporal-self comparison* (cf. Wilson and Ross, 2000) in what follows, rather than simply temporal comparison. As such, temporal-self comparisons can be defined as anytime an individual relates his or her attributes, or what goes on in his life, to a timeframe. Two main types of temporal-self comparisons may be distinguished: temporal-past comparisons when the past is compared to the present, and temporal-future comparisons when the present is compared to the future. Do people often engage in such temporal-self comparisons? If so, which kind of temporal-self comparison is more frequent and why?

Frequencies of temporal comparisons: Do people use social or temporal-self comparisons more often?

Comparing outcomes with those of others (social comparison) and comparing outcomes over time (temporal-self comparison) are both relevant to self-appraisal (Suls, Marco, and Tobin, 1991; Suls and Mullen, 1982;

Table 4.1. *Distinguishing different levels of temporal comparisons*

	With the past	With the future
Intrapersonal level: *Temporal-self comparison*	Comparing the current self to past selves (Wilson and Ross, 2003) Comparing past selves to the current self (Wilson and Ross, 2001)	Do I expect my position to improve or to deteriorate in the future? (Dif, Guimond, Martinot, and Redersdorff, 2001)
Interpersonal level: *Temporal self-other comparison*	Over the last five years, I have been better off/worse off compared to this person (Pettigrew and Meertens, 1995)	Do I expect that my position compared to this person will change for the better or for the worse in the future? (deCarufel, 1986)
Intragroup level: *Temporal-group comparison*	Comparing the current status of one's group to its past status (Hinkle and Brown, 1990)	Comparisons of the current status of one group to its predicted or anticipated future status (Hinkle and Brown, 1990)
Intergroup level: *Intergroup temporal comparison*	Over the last five years, my ingroup has been better off/worse off than the outgroup (Pettigrew and Meertens, 1995)?	Will the position of my group compared to a relevant outgroup improve or deteriorate in the future? (Ouwerkerk, Ellemers, Smith, and van Knippenberg, 2005)?

Rickabaugh and Tomlinson-Keasey, 1997). The concept of temporal-self comparison has been primarily examined from a developmental perspective, across the life-span, or in relation to important changes in one's personal life. There is evidence to suggest that temporal-self comparisons are used more often than social comparisons when coping with illness. For example, people with arthritis made more favorable temporal-self comparisons with the past than social comparisons, reflecting the fact that they thought of themselves as better at present than before (Affleck and Tennen, 1991). Elderly people more frequently made unfavorable temporal-self comparisons regarding their health status, expressing as one would expect that their health was worse at present than in the past (Suls, Marco, and Tobin, 1991).

Suls and Mullen (1982), in their life-span model, have proposed a theory of personal development which, at different stages of life, corresponds to different comparison processes. They proposed, in line with Albert (1977), that temporal comparisons play an important role when objective standards of comparison are unavailable. According to the life-span model, during the first and second stage of life (from one to three years and from four to eight years), children evaluate their performance first by physical comparisons, and later by temporal comparisons. Children start to make social comparison only during the second stage. Young children may engage in temporal-self comparison for appraisal purposes because they have acquired the concept of *more or less than*. Moreover, teachers, parents, and educational environments emphasize skill acquisition, which is best assessed over time, rather than achievement relative to others, which may be assessed by social comparison. Thus, temporal-self comparison may emerge at a younger age than social comparison because the former is cognitively simpler than the latter, and does not reflect a choice on the part of children (e.g., Dweck and Elliot, 1983; Higgins and Parsons, 1983; Stipek and MacIver, 1989; Suls and Mullen, 1982). This argument is consistent with Albert's theory (1977) concerning the greater importance of temporal-self comparison relative to social comparison in times of rapid learning. Thus, research suggests that beginner tennis players are more likely to value temporal comparisons and advanced tennis players are more likely to value social comparisons (Sheldon, 2003). As soon as people have acquired a certain level of skills, they tend to use social comparisons increasingly. Indeed, as argued by Ruble and Frey (1991), "a lack of rapid changes lessens the need for temporal comparison." (p. 112) In sum, according to Suls and Mullen (1982), when children have the required abilities, they use predominantly social comparisons and this preference for social comparison lasts until old age. During the third (from eight to forty years) and fourth stage of life (from forty to sixty-five years), people make mainly social comparisons. It is only during the last stage of life (sixty-five and more) that the use of social comparisons decreases and temporal comparisons become more frequent. Suls (1986) provides evidence from a survey that is consistent with several aspects of the life-span model.

However, other research suggests that the relative balance between social and temporal-self comparisons during the life course may be more complex. For example, at the group level, Brown and Middendorf (1996) found that temporal-group comparison was preferred to social comparison at the group level in every age group (the authors focused on three different age groups: 18–39 years, 40–64 years and 65–87 years). Indeed, the use of temporal-group comparisons increased with age, whereas the use of non-temporal group comparison remained stable over life-span. Unfortunately, Brown and Middendorf (1996) did not assess temporal-self comparisons. Further research is needed to test whether similar or different principles underlie the use of temporal-self versus temporal-group comparisons. At the moment, the two seem to follow quite distinct patterns. Smith and Leach (2004) conducted a study to determine whether people use temporal, interpersonal or intergroup comparisons, and the frequency of each. Their results, obtained among students (hence young adults), showed that people make more interpersonal social comparisons than intergroup comparisons or temporal-self comparisons (past and future combined). These latter comparisons represented less than 6 percent of all comparisons. Nonetheless, looking at the way Smith and Leach (2004) have presented their research, this result may not be too surprising. When outlining what they meant by comparison, Smith and Leach (2004) apparently provided mainly examples of social comparison to their participants which could account, in part, for their findings.

In contrast, Wilson and Ross (2000) report that when young adults are asked to provide a general description of themselves in an open-ended format (Study 1), when they are asked to describe themselves in relation to three specific attributes (Study 2), or when looking at comments that celebrities make about themselves in popular magazines (Study 3), one finds evidence of a high frequency of temporal-self comparisons, as high as social comparison. In fact, in all three studies, the results suggest that temporal-past comparisons are more frequently used than social comparisons or temporal-future comparisons.

All in all, research so far suggests that the process of temporal-self comparison deserves greater attention (see also Zagefka and Brown, this volume). As discussed below, deciding which is the most important between temporal-self and social comparison processes may actually be beside the point. However, at this stage of the research, the fact that across a variety of samples, there is clear evidence that people engage in temporal-self comparisons, sometimes as often as they do social comparison, is an important fact. We need to examine why they do so and with what consequences. After looking at the relations between temporal-self comparison and self-evaluation, we will consider research suggesting that this type of comparison activity may have an impact on self-esteem and well-being, as well as on one's socio-political attitudes and behaviors.

Temporal-self comparison and self-evaluation

For both individuals and groups, the past is constantly altered and reconstructed in light of one's current interests (Bartlett, 1932). According to Albert's theory (1977), individuals favor temporal over social comparisons in situations of change and adjustments reflecting the need to perceive one's self as continuous through time. Temporal self-appraisal theory (Wilson and Ross, 2001) suggests that a number of psychological factors lead people to retrospectively revise their evaluations of past selves (Ross and Wilson, 2000). Wilson and Ross (2003) demonstrated that people's current self-views influence their recollections and appraisals of former selves (for a more detailed review of research on autobiographical memory, see Sanitioso, Conway and Brunot, this volume). In order to appear consistent and to self-enhance, people may disparage earlier selves (Ross and Wilson, 2000; Wilson and Ross, 2001). However, former selves may also influence the present self. Indeed, evaluations of the present self can be influenced by the recall of past information (McFarland and Ross, 1987; Wilson and Ross, 2001).

The selective accessibility model of social comparison developed by Mussweiler (2003) may be useful to understand the process of temporal-self comparisons. According to this model, comparison with a similar other leads to an assimilative effect whereas comparison with a dissimilar other leads to a contrast effect (for more details, see Mussweiler, Rüter, and Epstude, this volume). Thus, the presence of a negative past self makes one feel good about the present self by comparison (a contrast effect). This view of the comparison between a past and a present self leading to a contrast effect has been called the incongruence approach (for a detailed review of this approach to temporal-self comparison, see Beike and Niedenthal, 1996). People increase the distance between their current-self and their past-self, stressing dissimilarities, and thus are able to benefit from a contrast effect in favor of their current self. However, assimilation effects may also occur. For example, Beike and Niedenthal (1998) have shown that past selves can have a congruent impact on self-evaluation. Negative information about the past sometimes has a negative effect on current self-evaluations, and conversely, positive information about the past sometimes enhances current self-evaluations. In short, there is a bi-directional influence between the past and present selves.

Wilson and Ross (2000) suggested that temporal and social comparisons might serve different goals. Whereas people use social comparison in order to self-evaluate, temporal-past comparisons may serve a self-enhancement purpose. In two experiments, Wilson and Ross (2000) induced explicitly (Study 4) or primed (Study 5) a self-enhancement goal or a self-evaluative goal. Temporal-past comparisons were more frequent in the self-enhancement condition and social comparisons more prevalent in the self-evaluation condition. More specifically, the participants reported more upward social comparisons when the goal was a self-evaluative one rather than a self-enhancement one. In contrast, participants reported more downward social comparisons when they had a self-enhancement goal rather than a self-evaluative one.

This goal-oriented preference for temporal-self and social comparisons was also studied by Butler (2000a) in a very interesting set of research. The author asked junior high-school students to solve the water jar problem. The research was presented to one half of the students with a mastery goal (e.g., a goal which leads learners to strive to improve over time), and to the other half with an ability goal (e.g., which leads learners to display high ability by outperforming others). Students also filled out a measure of perceived math competence. Students were told that they would receive a global objective feedback on their performance for the different exercises but they could also ask to get their percentile score relative to other students (social comparison information) or their own score for each of the exercises (temporal comparison information), or they could ask not to be given any comparative information whatsoever. There were differences between the ability and mastery conditions. In the ability condition, students asked for social comparison information more than in temporal comparison information. But students with a low perceived math competence chose not to receive any comparative feedback. In the mastery goal condition, most students asked for additional comparison information, and especially temporal comparisons. These results are consistent with the idea that temporal comparisons are more directed toward self-enhancement and social comparisons are thus used more often for self-evaluation purposes (Wilson and Ross, 2000).

In addition, Butler (2000b) examined the potential moderating role of intelligence theories. Dweck and Legget (1988) made a distinction between incremental and entity theorists. The former are oriented towards acquiring and developing competence, whereas the latter are oriented to documenting their ability. In other words, incremental theorists perceive intelligence and competence as malleable whereas entity theorists tend to perceive them as stable. Based on this distinction, Butler (2000b) argued that incremental and entity theorists should respond in a different way to social and temporal comparison information. People who believe that intelligence and abilities are stable (entity theorists) should be more influenced by social comparison. For them, abilities do not change over time and therefore, temporal-self comparisons may not be perceived as very informative. Rather, entity theorists were expected to base their self-evaluations more on social comparison than incremental theorists. The opposite was expected in terms of the effect of ascending versus descending temporal feedback. This type of feedback, involving a process of temporal-self comparison, was expected to have a greater impact on the self-evaluation of incremental theorists who believe that abilities can change over time, compared to entity theorists who believe that this is not so. The results strongly confirmed these predictions. Entity theorists based their self-appraisals on the first social comparison feedback they received, and did not take into account their improvement or their decline over time. They did not consider temporal-self comparisons to be relevant for self-appraisals. On the other hand, incremental theorists based their self-appraisals essentially on their performance over time: when their performance increased, their self-appraisal was better than when their performance decreased. But incremental theorists did not differ in their self-appraisal following social comparison feedback. In other words, the relevance of temporal-self and social comparisons for self-appraisals is highly dependent on the perceived malleability or stability of abilities.

The effects of temporal and social comparison information may also depend on the context, as suggested by Levine and Green (1984). They have provided convincing evidence suggesting that the type of social comparison that people seek may depend on the overall context of comparison. They showed that when elementary school pupils learned that their performance improved over time, they were oriented toward both downward and upward social comparisons. But when they learned that their own performance decreased over time, they sought downward social comparisons only. Thus, when temporal-self comparisons lead to negative self-evaluation, pupils are more likely to look for a positive social comparison (a downward social comparison). One may argue that this "need" to seek downward social comparison following a negative temporal-self comparison is a self-protective strategy. Indeed, there is evidence to suggest that in addition to social comparisons, temporal-self comparisons can also have an important bearing on global self-esteem and general feelings of well-being.

Temporal-self comparison, self-esteem, and well-being

People are generally motivated to protect their self-esteem and to have a positive image of themselves. In the previous chapter, Sanitioso, Conway, and Brunot have discussed how this motivation may direct the strategic selection of social versus temporal-self comparisons and noted a number of studies in support of this view. Over and above this motivational aspect, our focus here will be more cognitive in nature. There is evidence that the mental representations of the past and the future may be quite distinct. As such, the impact of temporal-past comparison on self-esteem and well-being would be expected to differ relative to the impact of a comparison with the future. However, from a motivational standpoint, there is very little reason to expect such a difference. People should use temporal-self comparisons to protect and/or enhance their self-image and the fact that the past or the future is involved should make little difference. It is true, as our colleagues argue, that people can sometimes invent a future more easily than they can reconstruct their past. In other words, because the future can be distorted more easily than the past, temporal-future comparisons would be preferred in order to protect and enhance our self-esteem. However, there are a number of problems with this argument. First, there is strong evidence, as mentioned above, that people can and do reconstruct and distort the past. It is simply not the case that one's own past is there for all to see.

In discussing bias in recall, Ross (1989) notes that following a self-improvement program that promises more than it delivers, participants can believe the promises and construct evidence in support of that claim in one of two ways: "People can distort their post program standing or revise their impressions of how they were before the program began." (p. 348) Further, he argues that it may often be *easier* for people to modify their impressions of their past status than to enhance their present standing. Conway and Ross (1984) found support for this hypothesis: participants in a study skills program overestimated their improvement because they exaggerated how poorly off they were *before* the program started. Thus, if motivation accounts for this type of bias related to the past, there is little reason why it should impel people to distort the future more than the past.

In contrast, when we look at how people conceptualize the past and the future, in and of themselves, we find some rather distinct cognitive processes. Concerning the past, Schwarz, Wänke and Bless (1994) point out that comparing the present and the past is not so simple. To engage in such a comparison, we need to define the past and we need to define the present. Figuring out how far the past extends (two days, one year, five years?) and where the present begins can be surprisingly tricky. Yet, how the past and the present are cognitively represented can be expected to have an important bearing on the outcome of a temporal-past comparison. This was demonstrated by Strack, Schwarz, and Gschneiger (1985) in a study of judgments of well-being and life satisfaction. They asked participants to report three positive and three negative events that happened to them either recently or at least five years ago. Thus, in one case, the past is defined as "recent" whereas in the other, it is defined as "five years ago." This definition had an impact on subsequent judgments. When participants reported three recent events, they indicated higher current life satisfaction when the events were positive rather than negative (assimilation effect). However, in the "five years ago" condition, they reported lower current life satisfaction when positive events were brought to mind than when negative events were considered (contrast effect). Clearly, cognitive factors are involved here, not motivational ones.

In a series of investigations, Newby-Clark and Ross (2003) found that people spontaneously conceive the past as affectively mixed, with both "highs" and "lows," but that they uniformly conceive the future in positive terms. Furthermore, they showed that positive events in the future come to mind more quickly: participants in several experiments were faster in generating future positive than negative events. No such cognitive bias was observed concerning the past. Participants reported negative past events with the same rapidity as positive past events. If this is the case, if people define the future as positive and the past as mixed, then one can predict the following: when asking participants to think about the future and to make a temporal comparison, this should relate to more positive affect, and perhaps higher self-esteem, then if they are asked to think about their past. There is strong support for this hypothesis.

Using relative deprivation theory as a conceptual framework, Dif, Guimond, Martinot, and Redersdorff (2001) have developed measures of temporal-self Relative Deprivation/Relative Gratification (RD/RG) with the past and with the future. These measures assessed both the cognitive (perceived change over time) and the affective (affect associated with this perception) components of RD/RG (Cook, Crosby, and Hennigan, 1977; Guimond and Dubé-Simard, 1983). In the first study, 581 university students filled out a questionnaire containing a measure of self-esteem (Rosenberg, 1965) and the measures of temporal-self RD/RG. More specifically, students were asked to think about the past and to indicate using seven-point scales: first, if they thought that things had improved for themselves over time or had become worse (cognitive component); and second, they were asked to rate the feelings that they experienced when comparing their current situation to what it was in the past (1 = negative feelings; 7 = positive feelings). As expected, these ratings were positively and strongly correlated. They were averaged to form an index of temporal-self RD/RG with the past. A similar procedure was used to measure temporal-self RD/RG with the future. Students were asked to think about the future and to rate the extent to which they thought things would improve for themselves and the feelings they experienced when comparing their current situation with their likely future one.

Simple bivariate correlational analyses revealed that temporal-self RD/RG with the past was correlated positively ($r = .31$, $p < .001$) with the same measure framed in terms of the future and both were positively and significantly correlated with self-esteem. However, when using multiple regression analysis, only temporal-self RD/RG with the future remained significantly predictive of self-esteem. In other words, consistent with the hypothesis proposed above, the results showed that future relative gratification has a greater impact on self-esteem than past relative gratification. Apparently, people use mainly temporal-self comparison with the future to bolster their self-esteem, not comparison with the past. A second study, this time among university students with and without a physical disability replicated the previous results and suggested, as expected, that students with a disability were more likely than others to anticipate improvements in the future and to feel good about this. In fact, students with a disability displayed significantly higher levels of self-esteem and there was evidence that this difference in self-esteem between students with and without a disability was mediated by temporal self-RD/RG with the future, but not by temporal-self RD/RG with the past. In other words, the results suggested that the self-esteem of members of a stigmatized social group can be similar, or even higher, than that of members of a non-stigmatized social group because of the greater use of temporal-self comparison with the future. Adding importance to this role of temporal-future comparisons, Dif *et al.* (2001) also assessed, in the same study, the cognitive and affective components of interpersonal social comparisons (self with similar others), and the cognitive and affective components of intergroup social comparisons (handicapped vs non-handicapped). None of these measures were important predictors of self-esteem as temporal-future comparisons were.

Using slightly different measures, with an entirely different population of long-term unemployed persons, Brunot (2004) made very similar observations to those reported by Dif *et al.* (2001). Unemployed people were asked to rate the frequency with which they made temporal-self comparison with the past and with the future, intragroup and intergroup comparisons. Using multiple regression analysis with all the different kinds of comparison as predictors, temporal-self comparison with the future was again found to be the single most important predictor of self-esteem. Thus, supporting Dif and colleagues' data, these results suggest that temporal-self comparison with the future relates more strongly to self-esteem than interpersonal social comparison or intergroup social comparison of a non-temporal nature. Moreover, in Brunot's (2004) experiment, the more unemployed people made temporal-self comparisons with the future, the more they were involved in job prospecting. This result is important. It suggests that temporal-future comparisons function as expectations about the future rather than mere fantasies.

The distinction between "expectations" and "fantasies" as different ways of thinking about the future has been underlined by Oettingen and Mayer (2002). They define expectations as a way of thinking about the future that involves beliefs assessing the probability of occurrence. However, fantasies represent a different way of thinking about the future that is more akin to wishful thinking or daydreaming. Fantasies would involve images, rather than beliefs, containing future events as they appear in the stream of thought. In four experiments, Oettingen and Mayer (2002) have shown that positive expectations predicted high effort and performance in various domains. In contrast, positive fantasies predicted low effort and performance. In this perspective, Brunot's (2004) research showing that temporal-future comparison predicts high effort among the unemployed is illuminating. It means that this type of comparison probably corresponds to a realistic view of the future, not to wishful thinking.

Taylor and Brown (1988), in a classic study, proposed that positive illusions promote psychological well-being as well as higher motivation, greater persistence, more effective performance and ultimately greater success. However, Robins and Beer (2001) argued that positive illusions (i.e., a self-enhancement bias) might have positive short-term benefits but long-term costs. Having too many positive illusions or fantasies does not appear beneficial for individuals, and thus, temporal-self comparison with the future needs to be realistic and attainable. This argument can also be related to the work of Lockwood and Kunda (1997) on the role of models in interpersonal contexts.

Overall then, studies of the relations between temporal-self comparisons and self-esteem are very consistent with the results of Wilson and Ross (2000) and their hypothesis according to which temporal-self comparisons are part of a self-enhancement dynamic. However, the fact that the future is spontaneously conceived in more positive terms than the past, and the fact that it is temporal-self comparison with the future, not with the past, that relates more strongly to self-esteem, is not necessarily supportive of a motivational explanation. A cognitive explanation, as we have argued, is also plausible. Existing studies do not allow definite conclusions in this regard. Further research is needed to examine more closely the cognitive and motivational factors involved in temporal-self comparisons and their relations with self-esteem.

In their review of the relations between social stigma and self-esteem, Crocker and Major (1989) highlighted the fact that members of stigmatized social groups do not generally display lower levels of self-esteem than non-stigmatized group members, as many theoretical perspectives in psychology would expect. They argued that social comparison processes may account for this finding but neglected to consider the role of temporal-self comparisons. The research above shows that temporal-self comparison is highly relevant to an explanation of the behavior of members of stigmatized social groups. This is consistent with several studies related to relative deprivation theory which point to the political role of temporal-self comparisons.

Temporal-self comparison, relative deprivation and socio-political attitudes

As Walker and Smith (2002) state: "Social comparisons between people (as individuals or as groups) are at the heart of relative deprivation." (p. 4) Indeed, research taking into consideration the distinction proposed by Runciman (1966) between egoistic (or personal) RD and fraternal (or group) RD has shown that the latter is more important than the former to explain involvement in social movements seeking social change (Abeles, 1976; Guimond, 2003; Guimond and Dubé-Simard, 1983; Tougas, Dubé, and Veilleux, 1987; Vanneman and Pettigrew, 1972). The focus on this distinction has been productive and theoretically useful. However, it led to the neglect of a third major type of RD involving temporal-self comparisons (Guimond and Tougas, 1994). Indeed, much of the early work related to the concept of relative deprivation stressed the importance of the temporal dimension. Alexis de Tocqueville's (1856) analysis of the French Revolution, which inspired Davies' (1962) famous theory of revolutions, did not mention social comparison but temporal comparison. More specifically, Tocqueville's main finding, and one of the crucial paradoxes at the basis of theorizing on RD, was that the areas in France where people were the most involved in the revolution were precisely those where the greatest economic progress had been achieved. How can that be? Tocqueville argued that "Le mal qu'on souffrait patiemment comme inévitable semble insupportable dès qu'on conçoit l'idée de s'y soustraire (p. 278; in English, "Evils which are patiently endured when

they seem inevitable become intolerable once the idea of escape from
them is suggested," our translation). In other words, when things get
better, people may nevertheless be less satisfied. They may feel a greater
need for change because they can construct "cognitive alternatives" to the
status quo (Tajfel and Turner, 1986). Social psychologists were successful in demonstrating this phenomenon in carefully controlled laboratory
situations (see deCarufel, 1986; Folger, 1977). People working on a task
and experiencing *increases* in their outcome level over time felt more
deprived than those experiencing a constant level of outcome. These
findings suggest that people compare their own outcome over time and
that this process explains their reactions. When outcomes improve,
people start forming expectations that things will keep improving.
When this does not occur totally as expected, it makes them angry. In
contrast, if things do not change much, then there is no reason to expect
more in the future, and no feelings of deprivation develop. Early theorists
were dealing with such a process, not with social comparison-based
deprivation. Davies (1962) spoke about "rising expectations" whereas
Gurr (1970) distinguished between aspirational, decremental, and pro-
gressive relative deprivation all implying a temporal dimension.

The results of several field studies are consistent with these theoretical
perspectives. A study by Grofman and Muller (1973) among 503 respondents from Waterloo, Iowa in the United States showed that the
perceived change in one's outcome over time was a reliable predictor of
involvement in political protest (see Dambrun, Guimond, and Taylor,
this volume, for more details about this study). In Canada, Krahn and
Harrison (1992) found that "self-referenced relative deprivation" was
important in explaining variations in political attitudes. Finally, Dif
et al.'s study (2001) mentioned previously, carried out in France among
disabled and non-disabled university students, also confirmed the
political implications of temporal-self comparisons. As a measure of
militancy, students were asked to indicate their willingness to take part
in collective actions in favor of the handicapped, using a four-item scale
referring to various types of action. Consistent with previous research,
measures of group relative deprivation involving feelings of discontent
and injustice (at the ways in which handicapped people were treated
compared to non-handicapped people) were found to be predictive
of militancy. However, as mentioned above, this study also contained
measures of various social comparison-based and temporal-self based
comparison/deprivation. Consistent with Grofman and Muller (1973),
multiple regression analysis revealed that perceiving an improvement in
one's own outcome over time (and the feelings associated with this
perception) was an additional predictor of militancy, independent of

the role of group relative deprivation. This, and other results reported by Dif *et al.* (2001), confirm that measures involving temporal-self comparisons can be empirically distinguished from both, measures involving interpersonal comparison (self with others) and measures involving intergroup comparisons.

Concerning the explanation of socio-political attitudes and behaviors, this relation between a perceived improvement in the future and the willingness to take action is consistent with the idea that a feeling of empowerment, rather than powerlessness, may be needed for participation in collective action to occur (Simon, Loewy, Stürmer, Weber, Freytag, and Habig, 1998). Finally, temporal-self comparison with the past may also be politically powerful. Guimond (1996) tested the relative importance of this type of comparison in a study of 200 young university graduates in Canada, five years after they had entered the job market. As a measure of social comparison, these graduates were asked: "Compared to other people of similar age and background, do you feel that overall you are better off than them?" Ratings were made on a five-point scale from "much worse off than others" to "much better off." As a measure of temporal-self comparison, they were asked: "Considering your life and career achievements, would you say that your situation has improved or worsened compared to what it was five years ago?" with higher scores on this measure indicating a perceived improvement. Answers to these two questions were found to be positively correlated ($r = .37$, $p < .001$). However, when predicting satisfaction with one's current financial situation, the temporal comparison item was found to add significantly to the prediction over and above the variance explained by the social comparison item (which was also significant). Furthermore, there was evidence that a perceived improvement was more important than social comparison to predict attitudes toward political groups and voting patterns. Those who reported voting for the conservative party (right-wing) were more likely to consider that their outcomes had improved over time compared to those who reported voting for a left-wing party (liberals or NDPs) but they were not more likely to think of themselves as better-off than others. In short, there are a variety of studies suggesting that temporal-self comparison has not only considerable psychological importance but also social and political significance.

Conclusion

In the present chapter, we have argued that the concept of temporal comparison is a very broad one that can relate to many distinct levels of analysis. In fact, the concept is so broad that inappropriate inferences may be drawn as a result of this lack of specificity. For example, we have reviewed Suls and Mullen's (1982) life-span model that suggests that social comparison is predominant in all life stages except among very young children and the elderly where "temporal comparisons" would be more frequent. However, in a study of "temporal comparisons," Brown and Middendorf (1996) report higher frequency of temporal than social comparisons among all age groups. Nevertheless, the conclusion that this study is not consistent with Suls and Mullen (1982) does not follow because, for Suls and Mullen, temporal comparisons mean comparisons of self over time whereas for Brown and Middendorf, it means comparisons of a social group over time. These two types of temporal comparisons may simply vary according to different principles, something that should be looked at in the future. To prevent this kind of confusion, we have argued that the concept of temporal-self comparison be used to refer to the intrapersonal level, when the individual compares himself or herself over time, and temporal-group comparisons, when the target of temporal comparison is a social group.

Although research on temporal-self comparison has been sparse, a number of important findings have been reviewed in the present chapter. For example, temporal-self appraisal theory (Wilson and Ross, 2001) suggests that comparisons to past selves can make people feel positively about their current self. Indeed, much evidence suggests that the motivation to maintain and/or enhance a positive self-regard can lead us to derogate our past and to distance ourselves from our failures. We have argued, however, that cognitive principles could also account for existing evidence. Recent research looking at both temporal-past and temporal-future comparisons within the framework of relative deprivation theory seems to support this view (see Dif et al., 2001). However, no definite conclusion can be reached in this regard on the basis of existing evidence. Thus, Haddock (2004) found support for a motivational hypothesis but he must acknowledge that the data can also be interpreted in cognitive terms. Similarly, Sanna, Chang, and Carter (2004) suggest that both motivational and cognitive factors may account for the subjective distance bias proposed within temporal-self appraisal theory. Thus, more research is needed on the relative importance of cognitive and motivational factors in accounting for the selection, and the effects, of temporal-self comparisons.

Finally, we have examined research suggesting that temporal-self comparisons may also be related to important social and political outcomes. This is to be expected given that the temporal dimension means bringing into focus the historical side of issues and events. Perceiving improvements or deteriorations in one's life ought to make a difference to one's attitudes, beliefs, and behaviors. Furthermore, while our focus was on temporal-self comparisons, this is not to suggest that studying the temporal dimension of other types of social comparison may not be worthwhile. On the contrary, we strongly believe that perceiving an improvement or a decline in one's ingroup status can have even more serious social and political consequences (see Dambrun, Guimond, and Taylor, this volume). Indeed, there is growing evidence that the temporal dimension may also be central in research on intergroup comparisons (Blanz *et al.*, 1998; Mummendey, Kessler, Klink, and Mielke, 1999; Niens, Cairns, Finchilescu, and Tredoux, 2003; Ouwerkerk, Ellemers, Smith, and Van Knippenberg, 2005; Tougas, de la Sablonnière, Lagacé, and Kocum, 2003). We hope this chapter will be helpful to the development of research on the temporal dimension of social comparison at all levels of analysis.

References

Abeles, R. P. (1976). Relative deprivation, rising expectations, and black militancy. *Journal of Social Issues, 32*: 119–137.

Affleck, G. and Tennen, H. (1991). Social comparison and coping with major medical problems. In J. Suls and T. A. Wills (eds.), *Social comparison: Contemporary theory and research* (pp. 369–411). Hillsdale, NJ: Lawrence Erlbaum Associates.

Albert, S. (1977). Temporal comparison theory. *Psychological Review, 84*, 485–503.

Bartlett, F. C. (1932). *Remembering: An experimental and social study.* Cambridge: Cambridge University Press.

Beike, D. R. and Niedenthal, P. M. (1998). Processes of temporal self-comparison in self-evaluation and life satisfaction. In P. T. P. Wong and P. S. Fry (eds.), *The human quest for meaning: A handbook of psychological research and clinical applications* (pp. 71–89). Hillsdale, NJ: Lawrence Erlbaum Associates.

Blanz, M., Mummendey, A., Mielke, R., and Klink, A. (1998). Responding to negative social identity: A taxonomy of identity management strategies. *European Journal of Social Psychology, 28*, 697–729.

Brown, R. J. and Middendorf, J. (1996). The underestimated role of temporal comparison: a test of the life-span model. *Journal of Social Psychology, 136*, 325–331.

Brunot, S. (2004). L'estime de soi et les comportements de recherché d'emploi chez les chômeurs de longue durée: le role des comparaisons socials et intrapersonnelles. *5e Congrès International de Psychologie Sociale en langue française.* Lausanne, Switzerland, 1–4 septembre.

Butler, R. (2000a). What learners want to know: The role of achievement goals in shaping information seeking, learning, and interest. In C. Sansone and J. M. Harackiewicz (eds.), *Intrinsic and extrinsic motivation: The search for optimal motivation and performance* (pp. 161–193). San Diego: Academic Press.

(2000b). Making judgments about ability: The role of implicit theories of ability in moderating inferences from temporal and social comparison information. *Journal of Personality and Social Psychology*, *78*, 965–978.

Conway, M. and Ross, M. (1984). Getting what you want by revising what you had. *Journal of Personality and Social Psychology*, *47*, 738–748.

Cook, T. D., Crosby, F. E., and Hennigan, K. M. (1977). The construct validity of relative deprivation. In J. M. Suls and R. L. Miller (eds.), *Social comparison processes: theoretical and empirical perspectives*. Washington, DC: Hemisphere.

Crocker, J. and Major, B. (1989). Social stigma and self-esteem: The self-protective properties of stigma. *Psychological Review*, *26*, 608–630.

Davies, J. (1962). Toward a theory of revolution. *American Sociological Review*, *27*, 5–19.

De Carufel, A. (1986). Pay secrecy, social comparison and relative deprivation in organizations. In Olson, J. M., C. P. Herman, and M. P. Zanna, (eds.), *Relative deprivation and comparison: The Ontario symposium* (pp. 181–200). Hillsdale, NJ: Lawrence Erlbaum Associates.

Dif, S., Guimond, S., Martinot, D., and Redersdorff, S. (2001). La théorie de la privation relative et les reactions au handicap: le role des comparaisons intrapersonnelles dans la gestion de l'estime de soi. *International Journal of Psychology*, *36*, 314–328.

Dweck, C. S. and Elliot, E. S. (1983). Achievement motivation. In P. H. Mussen (ed.), *Handbook of child psychology*, (Vol. IV, 4th ed). New York: Wiley.

Dweck, C. S. and Leggett, E. L. (1988). A social-cognitive approach to motivation and personality, *Psychological Review*, *95*, 256–273.

Festinger, L. (1954). A theory of social comparison processes. *Human Relations*, *7*, 117–140.

Folger, R. (1977). Distributive and procedural justice: Combined impact of "voice" and improvement on experienced inequity, *Journal of Personality and Social Psychology*, *35*, 108–119.

Frye, N. E. and Karney, B. R. (2002). Being better or getting better? Social and temporal comparisons as coping mechanisms in close relationships. *Personality and Social Psychology Bulletin*, *28*, 1287–1299.

Grofman, B. N. and Muller, E. (1973). The strange case of relative gratification and potential for political violence: The V-curve. *American Political Science Review*, *67*, 514–539.

Guimond, S. (1996). Privation relative, problème d'emploi et attitudes politiques. Communication présentée au *Premier Congrès International de Psychologie Sociale en Langue Française*, Montréal, Québec.

(2003). Stigmatisation et mouvements sociaux. In J.-C. Croizet and J.-P. Leyens (eds.), *Mauvaises réputations* (pp. 257–281). Paris: Armand Colin.

Guimond, S. and Dubé-Simard, L. (1983). Relative deprivation theory and the Quebec nationalist movement: The cognition-emotion distinction and the personal-group deprivation issue. *Journal of Personality and Social Psychology*, *44*, 526–535.

Guimond, S. and Tougas, F. (1994). Sentiments d'injustice et actions collectives: La privation relative. In R. Y. Bourhis and J. Ph. Leyens (eds.), *Stéréotypes, discrimination, et relations intergroupes* (pp. 201–231). Liège, Belgium: Mardaga.

Gurr, T. R. (1970). *Why men rebel*. Princeton, NJ: Princeton University Press.

Haddock, G. (2004). Temporal-self appraisal and attributional focus. *Journal of Experimental Social Psychology, 40,* 787–794.

Higgins, E. T. and Parsons, J. E. (1983). Social cognition and the social life of the child: Stages as sub-cultures. In E. T. Higgins, D. N. Ruble, and W. W. Hartup, (eds.), *Social cognition and social development* (pp. 15–62). Cambridge, MA: Cambridge University Press.

Hinkle, S. and Brown, R. (1990). Intergroup comparisons and social identity: Some links and lacunae. In D. Abrams and M. A. Hogg (eds.), *Social identity theory: Constructive and critical advances* (pp. 48–70). Hemel Hempstead: Harvester Wheatsheaf.

James, W. (1890). *The principles of psychology*. New York: Holt, Rinehart and Winston.

Krahn, H. and Harrison, T. (1992). "Self-referenced" relative deprivation and economic beliefs: The effects of the recession in Alberta. *Canadian Review of Sociology and Anthropology, 29,* 191–209.

Levine, J. M. and Green, S. M. (1984). Acquisition of relative performance information: The roles of intrapersonal and interpersonal information. *Personality and Social Psychology Bulletin, 10,* 385–393.

Levine, J. M. and Moreland, R. L. (1987). Social comparison and outcome evaluation in group contexts. In J. C. Masters and W. P. Smith (eds.), *Social comparison, social justice, and relative deprivation: Theoretical, empirical, and policy perspectives* (pp. 105–127). Hillsdale, NJ: Lawrence Erlbaum Associates.

Lockwood, P. and Kunda, Z. (1997). Superstars and me: Predicting the impact of role models on the self. *Journal of Personality and Social Psychology, 73*(1), 91–103.

McFarland, C. and Ross, M. (1987). The relation between current impressions and memories of self and dating partners. *Personality and Social Psychology Bulletin, 13,* 228–238.

Mummendey, A., Kessler, T., Klink, A., and Mielke, R. (1999). Strategies to cope with negative social identity: Predictions by social identity and relative deprivation theory. *Journal of Personality and Social Psychology, 76,* 229–245.

Mussweiler, T. (2003). Comparison processes in social judgment: mechanisms and consequences. *Psychological Review, 110,* 472–489.

Newby-Clark, I. R. and Ross, M. (2003). Conceiving the past and future. *Personality and Social Psychology Bulletin, 29,* 807–818.

Niens, U., Cairns, E., Finchilescu, G., Foster, D., and Tredoux, C. (2003). Social identity theory and the authoritarian personality theory in South Africa, *South African Journal of Psychology, 33*(2), 109–117.

Oettingen, G. and Mayer, D. (2002). The motivating function of thinking about the future: Expectations versus fantasies. *Journal of Personality and Social Psychology, 83,* 1198–1212.

Ouwerkerk, J., Ellemers, N., Smith, H. J., and van Kinppenberg, A. (2005). Giving groups a past and a future: Affective and motivational consequences of intergroup comparisons in a dynamic situation. Manuscript submitted for publication.

Pettigrew, T. F. and Meertens, R. W. (1995). Subtle and blatant prejudice in western Europe. *European Journal of Social Psychology*, *25*, 57–75.

Rickabaugh, C. A. and Tomlinson-Keasey, C. (1997). Social and temporal comparisons in adjustment to aging. *Basic and Applied Social Psychology*, *19*, 307–328.

Robins, R. W. and Beer, J. S. (2001). Positive illusions about the self: Short-term benefits and long-term costs. *Journal of Personality and Social Psychology*, *80*, 340–352.

Rosenberg, M. (1965). *Society and the adolescent self-image*. Princeton, NJ: Princeton University Press.

Ross, M. (1989). Relation of implicit theories to the construction of personal histories. *Psychological Review*, *96*, 341–357.

Ross, M. and Wilson, A. E. (2000). Constructing and appraising past selves. In D. L. Schatcher and E. Scarry (eds.), *Memory, brain and belief* (pp. 231–258). Cambridge, MA: Harvard University Press.

Ruble, D. N. and Frey, K. S. (1991). Changing patterns of behavior as skills are acquired: A functional model of self-evaluation. In J. Suls and T. A. Wills (eds.), *Social comparison: contemporary theory and research* (pp. 79–113). Hillsdale, NJ: Lawrence Erlbaum Associates.

Runciman, W. G. (1966). *Relative deprivation and social justice*, London: Routledge.

Sanna, L. J., Chang, E. C., and Carter, S. E. (2004). All our troubles seem so far away: Temporal pattern to accessible alternatives and retrospective team appraisal. *Personality and Social Psychology Bulletin*, *30*, 1359–1371.

Schwarz, N., Wänke, M., and Bless, H. (1994). Subjective assessments and evaluations of change: Some lessons from social cognition research. *European Review of Social Psychology*, *5*, 181–210.

Sheldon, J. P. (2003). Self-evaluation of competence by adult athletes: Its relation to skill level and personal importance. *The Sport Psychologist*, *17*, 426–443.

Simon, B., Loewy, M., Stürmer, S., Weber, U., Freytag, P., and Habig, C. (1998). Collective identification and social movement participation. *Journal of Personality and Social Psychology*, *74*, 646–658.

Smith, H. J. and Leach, C. W. (2004). Group membership and everyday social comparison experiences. *European Journal of Social Psychology*, *34*, 297–308.

Stipek, D. J. and MacIver, D. (1989). Developmental change in children's assessment of intellectual competence. *Child Development*, *60*, 521–538.

Strack, F., Schwarz, N., and Gschneiger, E. (1985). Happiness and reminiscing: The role of time perspective, mood, and modes of thinking. *Journal of Personality and Social Psychology*, *49*, 1460–1469.

Suls, J. (1986). Comparison processes in relative deprivation. In J. Olson, M. Zanna, and C. P. Herman (eds.), *Relative deprivation and social comparison: The Ontario Symposium* (Vol. IV). Hillsdale, NJ: Lawrence Erlbaum Associates.

Suls, J., Marco, C., and Tobin, S. (1991). The role of temporal comparison, social comparison and direct appraisal in self-evaluations of health in the elderly. *Journal of Applied Social Psychology*, *21*, 1125–1144.

Suls, J. and Mullen, B. (1982). From the cradle to the grave: Comparison and self-evaluation across the life-span. In J. Suls (ed.), *Psychological perspectives on the self* (Vol. I). Hillsdale, NJ: Lawrence Erlbaum Associates.

Tajfel, H. and Turner, J. C. (1986). The social identity theory of intergroup behaviour. In S. Worchel and W. G. Austin (eds.), *Psychology of intergroup relations*. Chicago: Nelson-Hall.

Taylor, S. E. and Brown, J. D. (1988). Illusion and well-being: A social psychological perspective on mental health. *Psychological Bulletin, 103*, 193–210.

De Tocqueville, A. (1857). *L'ancien régime et la Révolution*. Paris: Lévy (3rd edition).

Tougas, F., de la Sablonnière, R., Lagacé, M., and Kocum, L. (2003). Intrusiveness of minorities: Growing pains for the majority group? *Journal of Applied Social Psychology, 33*, 283–298.

Tougas, F., Veilleux, F., and Dubé, L. (1987). Privation relative et programmes d'action positive. *Canadian Journal of Behavioral Science, 19*, 167–176.

Vanneman, R. D. and Pettigrew, T. (1972). Race and relative deprivation in the urban United States, *Race, 13*, 461–486.

Walker, I. and Smith, H. J. (2002). Fifty years of relative deprivation research. In I. Walker and H. J. Smith (eds.), *Relative deprivation theory: Specification, development, and integration* (pp. 1–9). New York: Cambridge University Press.

Wedell, D. H. and Parducci, A. (2000). Social comparison: lessons from basic research on judgment. In J. Suls and L. Wheeler (eds.), *Handbook of social comparison: theory and research.* (pp. 223–252). New York: Kluwer Academic/ Plenum Publishers.

Wilson, A. E. and Ross, M. (2000). The frequency of temporal-self and social comparisons in people's personal appraisals. *Journal of Personality and Social Psychology, 78*, 928–942.

(2001). From chump to champ: People's appraisals of their earlier and current selves. *Journal of Personality and Social Psychology, 80*, 572–584.

(2003). The identity function of autobiographical memory: Time is on our side. *Memory: Special Issue Exploring the Functions of Autobiographical Memory, 11*, 137–149.

Part Two

Intergroup relations: comparison processes
within and between groups

Predicting comparison choices in intergroup
settings: a new look

Hanna Zagefka and Rupert Brown

The question of which comparisons members of social groups make is a
fascinating one, not least because a preference or aversion for certain
types of comparisons will have a number of important implications. For
example, comparison choices may determine whether people perceive
existing discrimination, whether they feel deprived, and whether they are
satisfied with their own or their group's outcomes. Comparison choices
might also affect perceptions of entitlement and they might raise or lower
people's aspirations. Not surprisingly, then, comparisons play a central
role in several social psychological theories of intergroup relations, such
as Social Identity Theory (Tajfel and Turner, 1986) and Relative
Deprivation Theory (Runciman, 1966).

In this chapter, we will briefly review some predictions about comparison choices that can be derived from one of the most important theories of
intergroup relations, namely Social Identity Theory (SIT). Then, we will
discuss some other theories and research which suggest that some additional mechanisms are at play which are neglected in the original SIT
conception. Synthesizing the insights from these two sections, the research
questions can be summarized in four themes: the effect on comparison
choices of (a) comparison motives, (b) status/deprivation relative to a
target, (c) structural variables (stability, permeability, and legitimacy),
and (d) identification. To address these four themes, we will review some
empirical evidence we have obtained from three surveys among members
of different ethnic groups and seven studies that used different methodologies and focussed on different intergroup contexts. Finally, some general
conclusions are drawn and directions for future research are discussed.

Social identity theory: predictions regarding comparison choices

The basic premise of SIT is that people derive part of their self-concept
and self-esteem from their group memberships. Further, it is assumed

99

that people have a need for a positive social identity and that they therefore strive to distinguish their ingroup positively from relevant outgroups.
Hence, people compare their ingroup with outgroups (intergroup comparison) in order to construe their group as both different from and
superior to other groups. Implicit in this hypothesis is an assumption
which will be of relevance in the present context: SIT assumes that
comparisons will mainly be motivated by "*enhancement,*" i.e. by a desire
to see the ingroup as comparatively better. By inference, this should mean
that people will avoid comparing with upward social targets which are
doing better than the ingroup and which are further up in the social
hierarchy (Hogg, 2000; see also Buunk and Oldersma, 2001; Wills,
1981, for evidence of this mechanism from the interpersonal domain).

However, in naturalistic settings there is often a wealth of potential
downward targets available (Taylor, Moghaddam, and Bellerose, 1989),
comparisons with many of which might be fit to fulfil the enhancement
motive. Therefore, there is a need for some more specific predictions
about which one of those comparators will be chosen in any given context. SIT suggests that "similarity, proximity, and situational salience are
among the variables that determine outgroup comparability" (Tajfel and
Turner, 1986, p. 17) – i.e., that make comparisons with a given group
more likely. The role of similarity and proximity has also been acknowledged by other theorists, mainly in the interpersonal research domain and
has yielded largely supportive findings (Festinger, 1954; Gartrell, 2002;
Goethals and Darley, 1977; Runciman, 1966; Wheeler, 1966; Zagefka
and Brown, 2005).

However, SIT also posits that certain socio-structural conditions might
render previously incomparable groups comparable (Tajfel, 1978; see
also Hogg, 2000; Hogg and Abrams, 1988): in situations in which the
social stratifications appear illegitimate and/or unstable, the psychological possibility arises that the stratifications might (be) change(d), and
people might start comparing with quite dissimilar outgroups, such as
privileged groups at the very top of the social hierarchy or deprived groups
at its lower end. Another socio-structural variable of importance is the
permeability of group boundaries. SIT predicts that the default strategy
of members of low status groups for obtaining a positive social identity is
"individual mobility" (i.e. leaving the group). Only under conditions
where this is not an option will people resort to other means of obtaining
a positive social identity (Ellemers, 1993; Wright, 1997), such as selectively adjusting their comparison preferences.

Another variable important in SIT research which might influence
comparison choices is the strength of people's ingroup identification.
Identification is thought to be associated with a person's readiness to

use social categories for self-definition (Turner, 1999), and it should therefore also influence comparisons that are based on these social categories. High identifiers should furthermore be more motivated to distinguish their ingroup positively from relevant outgroups. Since positive distinctiveness is thought to be achieved mainly by means of intergroup comparisons, it follows that one might expect high identifiers to be more interested in *intergroup* comparisons than low identifiers. This prediction is echoed by the theorizing of other scholars also (Crocker, Major, and Steele, 1998; Major, 1994).

The predictions that can be derived from SIT regarding factors that influence comparison choices can now be summarized. First, comparisons are mainly motivated by "enhancement", i.e. by a desire to see the self and the ingroup in a positive light. Hence, comparisons with upward targets should be avoided and downward targets should be preferred. Second, perceived similarity with, proximity to and frequency of contact with a given outgroup should make comparisons with this group more likely. Third, impermeability of the group boundaries and perceived illegitimacy and instability of the social stratifications will impact on comparison choices to render previously incomparable targets comparable. Fourth, ingroup identification should be positively related to interest in comparing with outgroups.

We were particularly interested to test the first, third, and fourth of these predictions (for evidence regarding the second, see Zagefka and Brown, 2005). While much research has investigated the *consequences* of comparisons in intergroup settings (e.g. Guimond, Dif, and Aupy, 2002; Hewstone, Rubin, and Willlis, 2002; Mullen, Brown, and Smith, 1992), to date surprisingly little work has assessed comparison choices themselves (Brown, 2000; see Brown and Haeger, 1999, Smith and Leach, 2004; Taylor *et al.*, 1989, for exceptions) or even tested the predictions regarding comparisons that might be derived from SIT. The program of work presented here set out to do precisely that. However, our research was not only guided by SIT, but also influenced by some more recent insights yielded in other fields of social psychology. These will now be reviewed.

Other theories and research

Motives other than enhancement. While SIT postulates the primacy of an *"enhancement"* motive guiding comparisons, the existence of other motives has long been acknowledged. In his seminal paper on social comparison, Festinger (1954) highlighted a motivation to accurately *"evaluate"* the position of the self. Also of importance might be *"equity"* and justice concerns (Tyler, 2001), whereby people are motivated to point out, draw attention to, and ultimately rectify social injustices (either against themselves or against the comparison Other) by means of comparisons (Haeger, Mummendey, Mielke, Blanz, and Kanning, 1996; Levine and Moreland, 1987; Van Knippenberg and Van Oers, 1984). Equity was also identified as an important motive in a study by Taylor and colleagues (1989) who tested the effects of the motives of "equity appeal," "reality testing" and "group enhancement" on intergroup comparisons in Quebec. Another important motive is "improvement," a desire to seek out information on how to ameliorate the position of the self (Collins, 1996; Huguet, Dumas, Monteil, and Genestoux, 2001). A host of other motives has also been suggested, such as the motive to establish psychological closeness and a "common bond" with the comparison target through the comparison activity (Hegelson and Mickelson, 1995). However, it is beyond the scope of this chapter to review all those. Apart from "enhancement," "evaluation" and "equity" are without doubt the motives that are cited most frequently in the literature. Hence, we were interested to test their effects on comparison choices in intergroup settings.

Primacy of the ingroup? As outlined above, on the basis of SIT one could expect identification to be positively correlated with intergroup comparison interest. However, some alternative scenarios are conceivable. Going back to Allport's classic *The nature of prejudice* (1954), in Chapter 3 he clearly states that ingroup attachment and the preference of ingroups over outgroups might often be a more primary concern of group members than hostilities against outgroups (see also Brewer, 1999). Indeed, following this thinking, people's group identities need not necessarily be sustained in relation to other groups. If this was true, one might expect identification to be positively related to a heightened *intra*group – rather than *inter*group – focus, and therefore identification might be positively related to intragroup comparisons (i.e. comparisons *within* the group, with other ingroup members), rather than intergroup comparisons. We were interested to test these two hypotheses against each other.

Other types of comparisons. As should be clear from the review above, SIT is concerned with intergroup comparisons, i.e. with people comparing their ingroup with relevant outgroups (we will call this comparison type "*intergroup comparisons on the group level*"). However, many other types of comparisons also exist (for taxonomies, see Haeger *et al.*, 1996; Levine and Moreland, 1987). Here, we are concerned with three additional types; those are what we label "*intergroup comparisons on the group membership level*," "*intragroup comparisons*," and "*temporal comparisons*."

Intergroup comparisons can be sub-divided into two categories: comparing the entire ingroup with some outgroup (what we call "intergroup comparisons on the group level"), or comparing the individual self with members of outgroups while group memberships are salient, i.e. while the comparison subject is aware of the respective group memberships (what we call "intergroup comparisons on the group membership level"). We argue that these two types are conceptually and empirically distinct. Intergroup comparisons on the group membership level are particularly relevant to Stigma Theory. Crocker and Major (1989) propose three strategies by which members of low-status stigmatized groups protect themselves from the adverse effects of holding a negatively evaluated social identity. One of these strategies is the "intragroup comparison bias." The theory proposes that members of stigmatized groups will compare their outcomes to those of other ingroup members, rather than to those of privileged outgroup members, in order to protect their self-esteem. In other words, they might elect to be "cognitively blind" to their comparatively bad outcomes, because they avoid any information that reflects negatively on the self. This notion, which has generated some empirical support (Deaux and Martin, 2001; Finlay and Lyons, 2000), is reminiscent of the SIT hypothesis that people are motivated by "enhancement" considerations to avoid comparisons with superior outgroup targets. The two theoretical approaches differ, however, in that SIT concerns itself with intergroup comparisons on the group level (i.e. ingroup-outgroup comparisons), whereas Stigma Theory is concerned with the relative frequency of "intergroup comparisons on the group membership level" and "intragroup comparisons" (i.e. individual self-outgroup member comparisons, or individual self-ingroup member comparisons). The present research attended to all these comparison types. One advantage of focussing on the individual self in intergroup comparisons is that – in line with Crocker and Major's (1989) suggestions – the self-expressed interest in comparing the self with outgroup members (intergroup comparison on the group membership level) can be compared to the interest of the same person in comparing the self with *ingroup* members (intragroup comparison). We will elaborate on this below.

Another important type of comparison that does not feature in SIT is *temporal* comparison (Albert, 1977, see Chapter 4, this volume), in which people compare either themselves or their entire ingroup with the same target at some point in the past or the future.[1] Recently some evidence has emerged showing that this type of comparison might be more important than previously thought (Brown and Haeger, 1999; Brown and Middendorf, 1996; Wilson and Ross, 2000). Importantly, research suggests that temporal comparisons might be particularly amenable to self-gratifying cognitive distortions that result in a favorable comparative outcome (McFarland and Alvaro, 2000). Hence, they might be particularly suited to fulfil the "enhancement" motive emphasized by SIT (Brown and Haeger, 1999; Blanz, Mummendey, Mielke, and Klink, 1998). For these reasons, the present research focussed simultaneously on social comparisons (with other people or groups) and temporal comparisons (with the self/ingroup in the past).

Synthesizing the insights gained from the original formulation of SIT and related theories and research, the following questions guided our program of work: first of all, we were interested to see which comparisons members of a naturalistic group do and do not engage in. Then, we were concerned with predicting comparison choices, particularly to investigate the effects of variables that have heretofore been unduly neglected. These are (a) comparison motives, (b) status/deprivation relative to a target, (c) structural variables (stability, permeability, and legitimacy), and (d) identification.

Comparisons in ethnic minority settings

Much of our research was concerned with ethnic minority and majority members in two European countries. These groups were chosen because we wanted to investigate comparisons in a naturalistic setting where comparison choices have potentially important practical consequences, rather than using artificial laboratory groups, which have already been frequently employed by research in the SIT tradition. Ethnic groups as a social category also easily lend themselves for testing some of the predictions central to SIT, as many of the variables important to the theory (identification, comparison motives, permeability, legitimacy, etc) should be of great subjective relevance to the actors in these settings.

We chose "economic standing" as the comparison dimension. Although we acknowledge that patterns that emerge for one comparison dimension might not necessarily generalize to other dimensions (e.g. members of ethnic groups might choose different comparison targets when thinking about their economic situation than they would when thinking about their moral values or military power), restricting the research to one dimension was necessary for practical reasons. Again, "economic standing" was chosen because many of the variables of interest to us can easily be conceived to be of importance for this topic (e.g., thinking about one's financial situation might be affected by enhancement motives, or equity concerns, etc). Three hitherto unpublished surveys among ethnic minority and majority members will provide the empirical "backbone" for the rest of the chapter. However, for each hypothesis, we also review some evidence generated by research that focussed on other types of groups and that used different methodologies.

To get a handle on which comparisons members of ethnic groups are interested in out of a wealth of possibilities, three surveys were conducted. The first one comprised 300 ethnic majority members in Germany (i.e. Germans), the second comprised ethnic majority and minority members in Germany (116 Germans, 166 minority members of mainly Turkish descent), and the third comprised 221 minority members in England (mainly of Asian and African descent). The third study had a longitudinal design: 118 of the participants filled out the same questionnaire at a second point in time approximately two weeks later. Participants in all studies were adolescent secondary school students.

Participants were asked to indicate on five-point Likert scales how important it was for them to compare with several targets when thinking or talking about their economic situation (1 = not at all to, 5 = very). Options were "ingroup members" (intragroup target), "people in the country where you and/or your parents are from" (origin target, for minority participants only), "your own situation in the past" (temporal target), "majority members" (majority target, for minority participants only), "people in the developing world" (developing world target), "members of other minorities in your country of residence" (for minority participants only) or "members of minorities" (for majority participants), "Americans" (American target), and "Asylum seekers" (Asylum target, this option was not included in Study 3). Participants also completed some other measures (e.g. ingroup identification). Those will be discussed later.

For each sample, an ANOVA was conducted with "Target" as a repeated measures factor, testing for differences in comparison interest in those targets. All analyses yielded significant main effects for Target. As is apparent from Figure 5.1, participants in both majority member samples (Studies 1 and 2) were most interested in the intragroup, temporal, and developing world targets. Participants in both minority member samples (Studies 2 and 3) were most interested in the intragroup, temporal, and origin targets. We have obtained similar results in two other surveys among members of ethnic groups (Zagefka and Brown, 2005), where results also showed that participants were primarily interested in comparing with other ingroup members or with themselves at a point in the past.

Two points are worth noting. The fact that mean comparison interest for some of the targets was below the midpoint of the scale does mean that it was not particularly high for those targets. However, this does not impair the conclusions drawn here, since we were mainly concerned with *relative*,

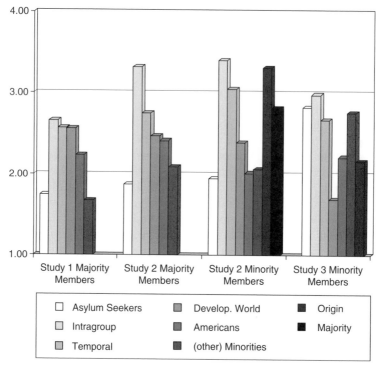

Figure 5.1. Mean Comparison Interest in different targets

rather than *absolute*, comparison interest. Second, in retrospect it is unclear whether the "origin" target was perceived to be an ingroup or outgroup target for minority members. Quite possibly, interest in this target was so high precisely because many minority participants perceived this to be an intragroup comparison. Results for this target are not easily interpretable without further data. Nonetheless, overall, the findings have a number of important implications: they provide some preliminary evidence that the emphasis SIT puts on intergroup comparisons might have to be revised or at least qualified: intragroup and temporal comparisons seem to be more common than intergroup comparisons, at least for the groups and contexts investigated here. Our findings support the idea of the "primacy of the ingroup" (i.e. people are more concerned with their ingroup and less with other groups and intergroup comparisons). They also underscore the importance of focussing simultaneously on intragroup and intergroup comparisons, a perspective that is in line with Stigma Theory, but not SIT. Further, our findings emphasize the importance of attending not only to social comparisons, but to temporal comparisons also.

The next task is to explain why the targets that generate the modal comparison interest are so attractive. Which factors cause the high interest in intragroup and temporal comparisons? Why are majority members also interested in the developing world target and why are minority members also interested in the origin target? The literature reviewed above suggests a variety of factors that might drive the pattern of results. Considering the potential effects of "motives," intragroup and temporal comparisons might have been particularly attractive because they best satisfy "enhancement" desires. Furthermore, majority members might have compared with people in the third world because of equity concerns on behalf of the comparison Other, and minority members might compare with people in their country of origin because of a desire to affiliate and feel close to this category of people. But, of course, "motives" are not the only factor that might have driven the responses. In the next section, we will explore the effects on comparison choices of comparison motives, status/deprivation relative to a target, structural variables (stability, permeability, and legitimacy), and identification.

(a)   Comparison motives

As outlined above, comparisons can be made for different reasons. In other words, they can be differentially motivated. This rationale is what we had in mind when we asked the participants of Studies 1 and 2 to indicate which factors motivate their interest in comparing with different targets. Specifically, we were interested in "enhancement," "equity," and "evaluation." The following predictions were made: (H1a) in line with findings from the interpersonal comparison literature, "evaluation" was expected to be a consistently important motivator of comparisons. (H1b) in line with the "intragroup comparison bias" hypothesis of Stigma Theory and with the finding that temporal comparisons might be particularly self-servingly amenable, it was expected that intragroup and temporal comparisons would be motivated by "enhancement" rather than "equity" concerns. (H1c) In line with the assertion that "equity" motives will be particularly important in ethnic intergroup settings due to the prevailing popular discourse and media coverage, it was expected that intergroup comparisons would be motivated primarily by "equity" rather than "enhancement" (as would be expected on the basis of SIT).

Participants indicated *why* they compare themselves with ingroup members, with themselves in the past, and with members of the majority (for minority participants) or members of ethnic minorities (for majority participants). They indicated on five-point Likert scales how much they compared with each target (a) in order to show that they are treated unfairly and get less than they deserve (equity own motive), (b) in order to show that members of other groups are treated unfairly and get less than they deserve (equity other motive), (c) in order to evaluate their situation as correctly and accurately as possible (evaluation motive), and (d) in order to feel good about themselves (enhancement motive). Note that the "equity other" motive was not assessed in relation to the temporal target. In Study 1, all participants responded to all four motives when comparing with each of the three targets. In Study 2, "Target" was a between subjects factor: each participant responded to each of the four motives only with regard to *one* of the three targets. ANOVAs were conducted to assess the importance of different motives when comparing with different types of targets. Results are displayed in Table 5.1.

As is apparent in the table, the results were in line with our predictions: "evaluation" was an important motive consistently across "comparison targets" and across samples; temporal comparisons were motivated more by "enhancement" than by "equity" concerns; intragroup comparisons were motivated more by "enhancement" than by "equity" concerns (although "equity other" was also important for the participants of Study 1); and comparisons with outgroup members were motivated more by "equity" concerns than by "enhancement" (more precisely, by "equity other" in Study 1, and "equity own" in the other two samples).

Some further evidence that "motives" causally affect comparison preferences was yielded by Study 3. Here "motives" were assessed in a more general manner (i.e., not specifically tied to comparison targets): two scales assessed participants' general motivation to point out and rectify injustices that their ingroup suffers ("equity own"), and to see the ingroup in a positive light and ignore everything that reflects negatively on the ingroup ("enhancement"). A comparison bias (i.e. a preference to compare with intragroup and temporal targets rather than with intergroup targets) was regressed longitudinally from these two motives (controlling for the DV at time 1). The overall model was significant and both motives were significant predictors. In line with H1b and H1c, low "equity" motives and high "enhancement" motives causally predicted a preference for intragroup and temporal, rather than intergroup, comparisons.

Evidence from other intergroup settings. An effect of "motives" on comparisons was also obtained in some other studies, focussing on other types of groups and employing other research designs. In line with some previous findings from the interpersonal comparison domain (Wood, 1989), it was expected that "evaluation" would generally lead to a heightened interest in upward social targets, and that "enhancement" would generally lead to more interest in downward social targets (H1d). In one experiment (Study 4, Brown and Zagefka, 2004), work groups of psychology students

Table 5.1. *Comparison motives*

Majority members (Study 1) N = 300

Motives	Past target (Temporal comparison) N = 279	Ingroup target (Intragroup comparison) N = 279	Outgroup target (Intergroup comparison) N = 279
Enhancement	2.19 b (1.15)	2.09 c (1.12)	1.77 b (1.04)
Evaluation	3.05 a (1.23)	3.07 a (1.23)	2.78 a (1.26)
System blame/Equity own	1.57 c (0.92)	1.75 d (1.08)	1.61 b (1.02)
Equity other	n/a	2.35 b (1.19)	2.91 a (1.31)

Majority members (Study 2) N = 116

Motives	Past target N = 35	Ingroup target N = 35	Outgroup target N = 39
Enhancement	3.20 a (1.41)	2.66 ab (1.35)	2.67 b (1.54)
Evaluation	3.37 a (1.40)	3.03 a (1.29)	3.21 a (1.24)
System blame/Equity own	2.17 b (1.20)	2.20 b (1.26)	2.87 ab (1.43)
Equity other	n/a	2.17 b (1.07)	2.46 b (1.10)

Minority members (Study 2) N = 166

Motives	Past target N = 54	Ingroup target N = 53	Outgroup target N = 52
Enhancement	3.31 a (1.24)	2.74 b (1.35)	2.44 bc (1.32)
Evaluation	3.33 a (1.05)	3.11 a (1.29)	2.92 a (1.31)
System blame/Equity own	2.52 b (1.28)	2.32 b (1.34)	2.52 ab (1.42)
Equity other	n/a	2.43 b (1.26)	1.98 c (1.11)

Note: Different subscripts denote significant differences between means according to pairwise comparisons with Bonferroni adjusted alpha levels per column at $p < .05$. Standard deviations in parentheses.

($N = 115$) were given (fake) feedback about the performance of their group compared to other work groups in the class. They were asked to indicate how interested they were in comparing their result with several social targets (e.g. the group that did best/worst, just a bit better/worse than their own group) and with the performance of their own group at a different point in time. Their "motives" for comparing were manipulated: participants were asked to choose those targets that would either help them to "evaluate" their result, that would help them to "enhance" (i.e. feel good about their result), or they were given no specific instructions (control condition). As expected, participants in "Evaluate" were significantly more interested in social upward comparisons (reflected in a higher interest in comparing with the "best" group, and in an overall higher rank of the outgroups chosen for comparative purposes) than participants in "Enhance."

In another study (Study 5), school students ($N = 207$) were given (fake) feedback about the average IQ of the students in their school. They were asked how interested they were in comparing this result to the result of (a) the best school in town, (b) the worst school in town, and (c) the average result of their school last year. Some students were asked to indicate their choices with an "evaluation" motive in mind, and others with an "enhancement" motive in mind. Controlling for initial comparison interest, instructions to compare in order to "enhance" led to a significant decline in interest in comparing with the best school.

In another study (Study 6) with school students, participants ($N = 164$) were given (fake) feedback about the average IQ of students at their school. They were asked to indicate on Likert scales how interested they were in comparing this result to the result of (a) the best school in town, (b) the worst school in town, (c) a school similar to theirs, and (d) the result of their school in the past. This time, evaluation and enhancement motives were measured, rather than manipulated. Regression analyses revealed that students attributed greater importance to comparisons with the best and worst schools the more they were motivated by "evaluation," and greater importance to comparisons with the temporal and similar targets the more they were motivated by "enhancement."

Another study (Study 7) that found an effect of "motives" on comparison choices was a survey we conducted among academic staff at a mid-ranking British university ($N = 199$) (Brown and Zagefka, 2004). In the UK, all universities are regularly evaluated for their teaching and research and their relative merits are published in national league tables. Participants were asked to indicate which comparators they look for in the league tables in order to assess the performance of their institution. Since participants were from a mid-ranking university, there were plenty of both upward and downward social comparison options. Participants' interest in comparing the current performance of their university with the performance in the past was also assessed. Comparison interest in each of the targets was measured on a Likert-scale. In addition, half the participants indicated their choices in a hypothetical scenario in which "enhancement" motives would be present, and the other half in a scenario where this would not be the case (control). As expected, this manipulation significantly affected participants' comparison choices. Compared to the control condition, participants in the enhancement condition were significantly less interested in making social upward choices, and more interested in making social downward choices.

In sum, and supporting some previous theorizing and research (see above), we find converging evidence that people engage in social comparisons in a strategic way. Comparisons are motivated and people will seek out that comparison target which best promises to match their goal and prevalent motive at the time. In general, it seems to be that social upward targets satisfy particularly an "evaluation" motive, temporal, intragroup, and social downward targets seem mainly to lend themselves to the fulfilment of "enhancement" motives, and comparisons with members of outgroups are often motivated by "equity" concerns, be it on behalf of the self or on behalf of the comparison Other.

(b)   Relative status/deprivation of the target

Implicit in SIT is the hypothesis that the status of the self compared to a target, and the relative deprivation (RD, Gurr, 1970; Runciman, 1966) of the self vis-à-vis the target, should also affect interest in comparing with it. On the basis of the primary enhancement motive postulated by SIT, one could expect comparisons with upward targets to be avoided, because such comparisons will reflect negatively on the self (negative effect of RD on comparison interest). The same prediction is made by Stigma Theory, which also assumes that "enhancement" will be the factor driving the comparisons of members of stigmatized groups. Yet, at the same time, SIT proposes that under some circumstances targets that are disparate from the self/ingroup on the status hierarchy become "comparable." This is expected to be the case when status hierarchies are perceived as illegitimate and unstable. Under these conditions, people might elect to compare with superior targets relative to which they are deprived in order to challenge the social stratifications (positive effect of RD on comparison interest).[2] As we have seen above, such a positive effect might also be expected if "equity" concerns – stressed in the Equity and Justice Literature – are strong. In sum then, we expected RD vis-à-vis a target

Table 5.2. *Effect of RD on comparison interest, Study 3*

DV: Interest in comparing with …	Overall R^2	Individual βs		
		DV at time 1	Cognitive RD	Affective RD
Ingroup members (Intragroup comparison)	.29***	.48***	−.16*	−.04
Origin	.35***	.53***	−.12	−.09
Past target (Temporal comparison)	.26***	.36***	−.03	−.24**
Majority members (Intergroup comparison)	.34***	.51***	.11	.21**
Developing world (Intergroup comparison)	.33***	.54***	−.12	−.03
Members of (other) minorities (Intergroup comparison)	.17***	.42***	.008	.05
Americans (Intergroup comparison)	.27***	.52***	−.04	.04

Note: *$p < .05$, **$p < .01$, ***$p < .001$.

to negatively impact on comparison interest if enhancement motives are prevalent (H2a). In contrast, we expected RD to positively impact on comparison interest if equity motives are prevalent (H2b).

Study 3 (i.e. the longitudinal study among ethnic minority members, see above) included interval measures of affective and cognitive deprivation perceived relative to each of the comparison targets. Items were adapted from Tropp and Wright (1999; see also Wright and Tropp, 2002). The measures were used to predict longitudinally the comparison interest in each target (controlling for comparison interest at time 1). Results are displayed in Table 5.2. As is apparent, affective RD positively predicts comparison interest for the majority target, affective RD negatively predicts comparison interest for the temporal target, and cognitive RD negatively predicts comparison interest for the intragroup target. Given what we have already seen about the differential motives that guide comparisons with these targets, this pattern is in line with H2a and b: the effect or RD on comparison interest is moderated by prevalent motives. If ethnic minority members compare with majority members mainly out of equity concerns and to point out injustices against their group, we would expect such a positive effect of RD. If, on the other hand, ethnic minority members compare with temporal and intragroup targets mainly for enhancement reasons, we would expect such negative effects of RD.

Evidence from other intergroup settings. Although the positive effect of RD on comparison interest for the intergroup target makes sense for ethnic minority members in situations where equity concerns are important, those concerns need not be *necessarily* always the most prevalent ones in intergroup settings. It is self-evident that in settings where the hierarchy is not conceived of as unfair, members of inferior groups will not be concerned about unfairness against their group. We reasoned that while inequality and fairness is likely to be important for ethnic minorities in any given European country (due to the current prevailing media coverage and discourse regarding institutionalized discrimination), thus giving rise to equity concerns, such issues will be of less significance when people compare the economic situation of their country with that of other European countries. In this instance, equity concerns might be pushed aside by stronger "enhancement" motives. In line with H2a, under prevalent "enhancement" motive conditions a negative effect of perceived relative deprivation of the ingroup vis-à-vis a given target on interest in comparing with this target might be expected. With this in mind, an experiment was conducted (Study 8, Zagefka, 2004) which manipulated perceived deprivation of Italian students ($N = 52$) vis-à-vis English students. Participants read fake newspaper articles which led half the sample to believe that Italian students are very deprived compared to English students, or that they are not deprived compared to this target for the other half. Then, participants' interest in comparing with English students in general, their personal situation with that of English students, and the situation of Italian students as a whole with that of English students was assessed. As expected, the manipulation significantly affected comparison interest. In line with the predictions, comparison interest on all three indices was lower in the "high deprivation" condition than it was in the "no deprivation" condition.

However, a slightly more complicated state of affairs might be underlying the effect of RD on comparison preferences. As we have seen above, there is considerable merit in assessing simultaneously intragroup and intergroup comparison interest. Further, "enhancement" motives are suggested to be prevalent in inter-nation settings (causing the negative effect of RD on comparison interest). It is conceivable that participants prefer intra- over intergroup comparisons (and *vice versa*) *only* if such a comparisons bias is conducive to the fulfilment of the "enhancement" motive. More specifically, one could expect participants to prefer intragroup over intergroup comparisons if they are group but not personally deprived (i.e., deprived vis-à-vis members of a higher status outgroup, but not deprived vis-à-vis ingroup members; Runciman, 1966; Vanneman and Pettigrew, 1972; see also Dubé and Guimond, 1986; Smith, Spears, and Hamstra, 1999). In contrast, one could expect participants to prefer intergroup over intragroup comparisons if they are personally but not group deprived. Such a pattern would be in line with "enhancement" motivated comparisons: people always prefer the type of comparison with the most self-flattering result. Intragroup comparisons should be particularly flattering for those who feel group but not personally deprived (PD), and intergroup comparisons should be particularly flattering for those who feel personally but not group deprived (GD).

An experiment was conducted to test this prediction (Study 9, Zagefka, 2004). We manipulated both the perceived personal and the perceived group deprivation of Italian students ($N = 76$) by having them read fake newspaper articles. Participants were led to believe that they are either deprived or not deprived personally compared to other Italian students. This experimental factor was crossed orthogonally with the experimental "group deprivation" factor: students were led to believe that Italian students as a whole are either deprived or not deprived vis-à-vis students in other European countries. Then, their intragroup and intergroup comparison interest was measured by participants' indicating on Likert scales how much they would like to "read more" about the situation of other Italian students and about the situation of students in other European countries, respectively. Analysis of the ratings yielded the predicted pattern of means: those in the high PD/ low GD condition showed a preference for intergroup over intragroup comparisons, while those in the low PD/ high GD condition did not.

In sum, clear evidence was found that perceived deprivation relative to a target affects interest in comparing with this target. The effect will be negative if "enhancement" is strong and it will be positive if "equity" concerns are strong. In addition, Study 9 showed that a preference for one type of comparison over another is influenced by the standing of the self relative to *both* comparison targets. Again, this result underscores the considerable merit of focussing simultaneously on both intra- and inter-group processes (see also Tyler, Degoey, and Smith, 2001).

(c)   Structural variables: legitimacy, stability, and permeability

As we have seen, SIT proposes that stability, illegitimacy, and permeability will impact on comparison choices. However, predictions that can be derived are very vague. At a most basic level, perceived instability and illegitimacy of the social stratifications will increase the interest in comparing with targets that were previously incomparable because they were too different from the self referent. What might this mean concretely? This might mean that people will start comparing with targets at the very top of the social hierarchy (for ethnic minority members, which can be conceived of as being quite far down this index), or that members of mid-ranking groups will start comparing with targets at both the very top and bottom of the hierarchy. Predictions about the effects of permeability are even harder to derive. We therefore tested the effects of the structural variables in a more exploratory manner.

One study fit to answer questions about the effect of permeability and stability is Study 3 (the longitudinal study with ethnic minority members, see above). Participants of this study had completed measures to indicate how easy they thought it was to transcend ethnic group boundaries (e.g. "It is easy for members of ethnic minority groups to be considered British") and how stable they perceived the social stratifications of ethnic groups in Britain to be in terms of status and economic standing. Interest in comparing with majority members, ingroup members, and the temporal target were regressed, in turn, from permeability, stability, and their interaction.

Cross-sectionally, temporal comparison interest was predicted by both stability and permeability. Stability and permeability did not significantly predict comparisons with majority members and ingroup members. Longitudinally, intragroup comparison interest was predicted by permeability (but not stability). Stability and permeability did not have any longitudinal effects on temporal comparisons and comparisons with majority members.

Evidence from other intergroup settings. Another study that yielded data regarding the effects of structural variables on comparison choices is the staff survey already mentioned above (Study 7). In addition to an assessment of the participants' interest in comparing with a wealth of social and temporal targets, this survey had also included some measures of how legitimate and how stable the league table hierarchy was perceived to be. Interest in comparing with each target was assessed from these two variables across the experimental conditions mentioned above (their interaction and some other predictors that are not of relevance here were also included in the analyses). Results showed that perceived illegitimacy increased the likelihood of participants' comparing with targets that were very different in their position relative to the mid-ranking ingroup, i.e. with targets at the very top and bottom of the league table hierarchy. Stability did not have any significant effects.

The evidence yielded for the SIT predictions with regards to the effects of legitimacy, permeability, and stability on intergroup comparisons can be summarized briefly. As would be expected according to SIT, perceived illegitimacy of the social hierarchy does indeed seem to render previously incomparable targets (at the very bottom and top of the hierarchy) comparable (for additional evidence on this issue, see Chapter 15, this volume). However, the other two variables fare less well: no evidence was found that perceived instability affects comparisons with social outgroup targets at all. If anything, it seems to affect comparisons with temporal targets. Further, no evidence was found that perceived permeability affects comparisons with social outgroup targets. If anything, this variable seems to affect comparisons with intragroup and temporal targets.

(d)   Ingroup identification

A final concern was to assess the effect of identification on comparison choices. Specifically, we were interested in testing whether identification is positively related to intergroup comparison interest, as might be expected on the basis of SIT, or whether it is positively related to intragroup and temporal comparisons, as might be expected on the basis of the "primacy of the ingroup" hypothesis outlined above.

As indicated earlier, Studies 1–3 (the studies among ethnic minority and majority participants, see above) also included a measure of ingroup identification, based on the scales of Brown *et al.* (1986) and Ellemers, Kortekaas, and Ouwerkerk (1999). Example items are "I see myself as a member of my group" and "I am glad to be a member of my group." For each sample, identification was regressed from the interest in comparing with the different targets. Although we conceive of identification as an antecedent of comparison choices, it was entered into the cross-sectional regressions as a DV for practical reasons. Results are displayed in Table 5.3. As is apparent, the three studies yielded converging evidence that identification is positively related to intragroup and temporal comparison interest, but not to intergroup comparison interest.

We have found this effect also with some other samples of members of ethnic groups (Zagefka and Brown, 2005, Study 2): When regressing identification from interest in comparing with intragroup, temporal, and various intergroup targets in a sample of ethnic minority members and in a sample of ethnic majority members in Germany, both regressions yielded significant overall R^2s. However, for the minority sample, only the β for the temporal target was significant: identification was positively related to interest in comparing with the past. Interest in comparing with majority members or members of other minorities was unrelated to identification. For the majority sample, only the β for the intragroup target was significant: identification was positively related to interest in comparing with other ingroup members. Identification was unrelated to interest in comparing with members of outgroups.

However, one question that remains open from these cross-sectional surveys is whether the effect of identification on comparisons is indeed causal. Luckily, the longitudinal design of Study 3 helps to illuminate this issue. When regressing the interest in comparing with the intragroup

Table 5.3. *Identification and comparison interest in different targets*

		Majority members (Study 1)	Majority members (Study 2)	Minority members (Study 2)	Minority members (Study 3)
Overall model	R^2	.10	.18	.07	.15
	F	5.35 (5,288)***	3.48 (6,103)**	1.32 (8,141)	4.92 (7,191)***
Individual βs	Ingroup members (Intragroup comparison)	.31***	.34**	.09	.22*
	Origin	n/a	n/a	.02	−.08
	Past target (Temporal comparison)	−.06	−.05	.07	.18*
	Majority members (Intergroup comparison)	n/a	n/a	−.05	−.06
	Developing world (Intergroup comparison)	−.11	−.17	−.13	.09
	Members of (other) minorities (Intergroup comparison)	.11	.03	.16	.07
	Americans (Intergroup comparison)	−.02	.15	−.08	.04
	Asylum seekers (Intergroup comparison)	.01	−.08	.17	n/a

Note: *p < .05, **p < .01, ***p < .001. *Df* in parentheses.

and temporal targets at time 2, respectively, from identification at time 1 (controlling for comparison interest in these items at time 1), identification was not a significant predictor (however, it should be noted that comparison interest had a very high test-retest reliability, possibly making it difficult to pick up existing effects). When regressing the interest in comparing with outgroup targets (majority members, members of other minorities) at time 2 from identification at time 1 (controlling for the DV at time 1), identification was a *negative* significant predictor. Thus, identification caused a *lowered* interest in intergroup comparisons.

Evidence from other intergroup settings. Evidence for identification affecting comparison preferences was also yielded in some other studies, using other types of groups and other paradigms. One of those studies is already mentioned above (Study 4). Recall that in this study work groups of psychology students were given (fake) feedback about the performance of their group compared to other work groups in the class. They were asked to indicate on Likert-scales how interested they were in comparing their result with several social targets and with the performance of their own group at a different point in time. Regressing identification from interest in the different targets included in the design (across experimental conditions), identification was positively related to comparison interest in the temporal target, but it was unrelated to interest in comparing with any of the social outgroup targets. Hence, once again identification was positively related to temporal comparison interest, and unrelated to intergroup comparison interest.

A similar finding emerged in another experiment already mentioned above (Study 5). When regressing identification from interest in comparing with the three comparison targets of this study (across experimental conditions), the overall model was significant. However, only the β for the temporal target was significant.

In yet another study (Study 10) – using a computer-paradigm previously employed in the interpersonal domain (Gibbons and Buunk, 1999) – university students ($N = 85$) had the opportunity to evaluate the performance of their university compared to other universities in the country and compared to the performance of their own university in the past (information was based on national league tables). We measured the time students spent reading information about upward social comparison targets, information about downward social targets, and temporal information. When regressing identification with the university from these three predictors, the overall model was significant. Interest in the temporal target was a positive predictor, interest in social downward targets was a *negative* predictor, and interest in social upward targets was unrelated to identification. Yet again, this finding underscores that identification is positively related to interest in temporal comparisons, and that it is either unrelated or *negatively* related to intergroup comparisons.

In sum, it seems that identification leads to more interest in comparing within other ingroup members or in comparing with temporal targets. Identification seems to be either unrelated to intergroup comparisons (see also Deaux, Reid, Mizrahi, and Cotting, 1999, for similar findings), or even *negatively* related to this comparison type. These results are not in line with the hypotheses we derived from SIT.

Conclusion

The most important results of the research reviewed here can be briefly summarized. We found evidence that members of ethnic groups who compare their economic situation with that of several reference standards place more emphasis on intragroup and temporal targets than on inter-group targets. At a general level, this finding is more in line with Stigma theory's "self-protection hypothesis" and with Allport's "primacy of the ingroup hypothesis" than it is with what might be expected on the basis of SIT. We also investigated the effect of antecedents of comparison choices, namely comparison motives, status/deprivation relative to a target, structural variables (stability, permeability, and legitimacy), and identification. In the following, we will for each of these variables briefly review the main findings, their implications, and directions for future research.

Comparison motives. First, we have yielded clear evidence that "motives" affect comparison choices, and that different comparison targets are chosen *precisely because* they fulfil different motives. In general, in our data social upward comparisons satisfied particularly "evaluation" motives, temporal, intragroup, and social downward comparisons satisfied mainly "enhancement" motives, and comparisons with members of out-groups were often motivated by "equity" concerns.

While comparison motives have received some attention in the inter-personal research domain, they have been largely neglected in intergroup research (with some notable exceptions mentioned above, e.g. Taylor *et al.*, 1989). However, our findings suggest that intergroup research could benefit from widening its scope and attending to this variable. Directions for future empirical work are plentiful. For instance, future research should supplement the traditional emphasis put on SIT's "enhancement" motive by some attention to several other motives, like the ones included in our research or yet other ones. Future research might also investigate prevalent motives for different types of social groups and contexts since it is becoming clear that social identity processes and their underlying functions do not operate similarly in all groups. Several recent studies have provided converging evidence for the diversity of psychological affiliations to human groups (Aharpour and Brown, 2002; Deaux, Reid, Mizrahi, and Cotting, 1999; Lickel, Hamilton, Wieczorkowska, Lewis, Sherman, and Uhles, 2000). Most importantly, a fruitful endeavor would be to take one step back, and not only investigate the effects of motives on comparisons, but also investigate the factors that *give rise* to one motive or another in any given situation. Knowing under which conditions members of stigmatized groups will be motivated by "enhancement" and cognitively blind to discrimination against their group, and when they will instead be motivated by "equity" and a desire to rectify social injustices, would not only be theoretically interesting, but would also have tremendous applied value.

Status/deprivation relative to a target. Second, we have demonstrated that the relative status and perceived deprivation of the self/ingroup vis-à-vis some target impacts on interest in comparing with it. Whether the effect of RD is positive or negative depends on the specific situation, and the "motives" that are prevalent within it. To our knowledge, this is the first time that this effect has been demonstrated for members of ethnic groups in Europe and also reverses the conventional assumption that comparisons always *precede* perceptions of deprivation. Again, therefore, there are several issues that future research might follow up.

The impact of RD on comparisons in ethnic groups could be investigated experimentally (recall that our experiments used a different social category, i.e. national groups), or the impact of other variables related to RD, like for instance political deprivation and discrimination, might be explored. Again, such work would have potentially important practical implications. It would yield information on the conditions that lead to (dis)functional comparison and identity management strategies employed by members of social groups, in the sense of strategies that serve to perpetuate unfair social stratifications. Such research would readily connect with work in the "system justification" tradition in helping to clarify when subordinate groups tolerate or even ignore manifest inequalities in the social structure (Jost and Banaji, 1994). Such an approach might even shed some light, therefore, on how more psychologically and socially desirable strategies can be encouraged.

Structural variables (stability, permeability, and legitimacy) Third, we found some initial evidence supporting the SIT hypothesis that a perceived illegitimacy of the social hierarchy might render previously incomparable targets comparable. However, no evidence was found for the SIT prediction that instability or impermeability affects comparisons with social outgroup targets. Rather, those two predictors were related more to intragroup and temporal comparisons.

To our knowledge, to date very little other evidence has been gathered regarding the effects of SIT's socio-structural variables on comparisons. Given their central position in the SIT theorizing, this seems surprising, and the fact that one of the first attempts to yield evidence for the predicted effects was not successful is potentially bad news for the theory. Further research is urgently needed, which should ascertain which role exactly those variables play (or not), and, indeed, to discover what factors are most likely to generate perceptions of illegitimacy and instability in the first place.

Identification. Fourth, our results show that identification leads to more interest in comparing within other ingroup members or in comparing with temporal targets. Identification was either unrelated to intergroup comparisons, or even *negatively* related to this comparison type.

These results are more in line with the "primacy of the ingroup" hypothesis than they are with the predictions we derived from SIT. We also have considerable faith in the pattern, since we obtained similar results across a range of different studies and methodologies. Again, however, we are unaware of other research that has addressed the same question, and a replication of our findings by others might be necessary before too strong an implication should be drawn. Still, our findings clearly suggest that SIT's traditional emphasis on *intergroup* processes should be supplemented with a simultaneous focus on *intragroup* processes (see also Tyler, Degoey, and Smith, 2001). From our point of view, future research would be well advised to advance in this direction, as clearly a full account of group processes has to take into account both types of processes and their interplay.

Finally, some limitations to the present work should be acknowledged. First of all, one might question whether questions about the economic situation were of relevance to the adolescent participants of Studies 1–3. On the basis of qualitative data collected from the participants, we would argue that they were. However, at the same time one should be cautious about extrapolating from the present findings to the mechanisms that will be at play in samples of adults. Although "age" did not have any significant main effects and did not qualify any of the relationships described above, in order to be sure that the findings presented here will generalize to older samples the studies would have to be replicated to those types of samples.

Second, the self-report measures employed by the present research assume that comparison preferences are conscious. In this, our work follows in the footsteps of much previous work (e.g. Wheeler, 1966). We assume that although people are not necessarily always aware of the comparisons they make, they can *be made* aware of them, e.g. by being asked about which comparisons they made. The fact that participants' responses to our comparison items produced a non-random pattern of results can be read as support for this assumption. Note also that our assumption does not contradict work that shows the automaticity of comparisons (Gilbert, Giesler, and Morris, 1995): automaticity and consciousness can plausibly be assumed to be independent of each other. What is true, however, is that we can only draw conclusions about variables we asked about. That is, there might be a wealth of other comparisons, motives, and so on which have a major psychological impact. Naturally, we could not assess all of these, and so there is an abundance of issues left to explore in future work.

Notes

1 Obviously, other types of temporal comparisons are also possible. For instance, people might compare themselves with another person in the past (for instance with their mother when she was the same age). However, here we are not concerned with those types of comparisons. In the present context, "temporal comparisons" refer to "self-self in the past" or "ingroup-ingroup in the past" comparisons.
2 Note that in the RD research tradition, deprivation is often conceived of as a *consequence* of comparisons, rather than an antecedent. However, as we have seen, on the basis of both SIT and Stigma theory, RD might usefully be employed as an independent variable also.

References

Aharpour, S. and Brown, R. (2002). Functions of group identification: an exploratory analysis. *Revue Internationale de Psychologie Sociale*, 15, 157–186.
Albert, S. (1977). Temporal comparison theory. *Psychological Review*, 84, 485–503.
Allport, G. W. (1954). *The nature of prejudice*. Reading, MA.: Addison-Wesley.
Blanz, M., Mummendey, A., Mielke, R., and Klink, A. (1998). Responding to negative social identity: A taxonomy of identity management strategies. *European Journal of Social Psychology*, 28, 697–730.
Brewer, M. B. (1999). The psychology of prejudice: Ingroup love or outgroup hate? *Journal of Social Issues*, 55, 429–444.
Brown, R. (2000). Social identity theory: Past achievements, current problems and future challenges. *European Journal of Social Psychology*, 30, 745–778.
Brown, R., Condor, S., Matthews, A., Wade, G., and Williams, J. A. (1986). Explaining intergroup differentiation in an industrial organisation. *Journal of Occupational Psychology*, 59, 273–286.
Brown, R. and Haeger, G. (1999). Compared to what?": Comparison choice in an international context. *European Journal of Social Psychology*, 29, 31–42.

Brown, R. and Middendorf, J. (1996). The underestimated role of temporal comparison: A test of the life-span model. *Journal of Social Psychology, 136,* 325–331.

Brown, R. and Zagefka, H. (2004) Choice of comparisons in intergroup settings: Temporal information, comparison motives and group identification. *MS under review.*

Buunk, B. P. and Oldersma, F. L. (2001). Enhancing satisfaction through downward comparison: The role of relational discontent and individual differences in social comparison orientation. *Journal of Experimental Social Psychology, 37,* 452–467.

Collins, R. L. (1996). For better or worse: The impact of upward social comparisons on self-evaluations. *Psychological Bulletin, 119,* 51–69.

Crocker, J. and Major, B. (1989). Social stigma and self-esteem: The self-protective properties of stigma. *Psychological Review, 96,* 608–630.

Crocker, J., Major, B., and Steele, C. (1998). Social stigma. In D. T. Gilbert, S. T. Fiske, and G. Lindzey (eds.), *The handbook of social psychology* (4th edn., Vol. II, pp. 504–553).

Deaux, K. and Martin, D. (2001). *Which context? Specifying levels of context in identity processes.* Indiana Conference on Identity Theory, Bloomington.

Deaux, K., Reid, A., Mizrahi, K., and Cotting, D. (1999). Connecting the person to the social: The functions of social identification. In T. R. Tyler, R. Kramer, and O. John (eds.), *The psychology of the social self.* Mahwah, NJ: Lawrence Erlbaum Associates.

Dubé, L. and Guimond, S. (1986). Relative deprivation and social protest: The personal-group issue. In J. M. Olson, C. P. Herman, and M. P. Zanna (eds.), *Relative deprivation and social comparison: The Ontario Symposium* (Vol. IV). London: Lawrence Erlbaum Associates.

Ellemers, N. (1993). The influence of socio-structural variables as identity management strategies. In W. H. Stroebe and M. Hewstone (eds.) *European Review of Social Psychology, 4* (pp. 27–58). Chichester: Wiley.

Ellemers, N., Kortekaas, P., and Ouwerkerk, J. K. (1999). Self-categorisation, commitment to the group and group self-esteem as related but distinct aspects of social identity. *European Journal of Social Psychology, 29,* 371–389.

Festinger, L. (1954). A theory of social comparison processes. *Human Relations, 7,* 117–140.

Finlay, W. M. L. and Lyons, E. (2000). Social categorizations, social comparisons and stigma: Presentations of self in people with learning difficulties. *British Journal of Social Psychology, 39,* 129–146.

Gartrell, C. D. (2002). The embeddedness of social comparison. In I. Walker and H. Smith (eds.), *Relative deprivation. Specification, development, integration* (pp. 164–184). Cambridge: Cambridge University Press.

Gibbons, F. X. and Buunk, B. P. (1999). Individual differences in social comparison: Development of a scale of social comparison orientation. *Journal of Personality and Social Psychology, 76,* 129–142.

Gilbert, D. T., Giesler, R. B., and Morris, K. A. (1995). When comparisons arise. *Journal of Personality and Social Psychology, 69,* 227–236.

Goethals, G. R. and Darley, J. M. (1977). Social comparison theory: An attributional approach. In J. Suls and R. L. Miller (eds.), *Social Comparison processes:
theoretical and empirical perspectives*. Washington: Hemisphere.
Guimond, S., Dif, S., and Aupy, A. (2002). Social identity, relative group status
and intergroup attitudes: When favourable outcomes change intergroup rela-
tions . . . for the worse. *European Journal of Social Psychology*, *32*, 739–760.
Gurr, T. (1970). *Why Men Rebel*. Princeton, NJ: Princeton University Press.
Haeger, G., Mummendey, A., Mielke, R., Blanz, M., and Kanning, U. (1996).
Zum Zusammenhang von negativer sozialer Identität und Vergleichen
zwischen Personen und Gruppen: Eine Felduntersuchung in Ost – und
Westdeutschland. *Zeitschrift für Sozialpsychologie*, *27*, 259–277.
Hegelson, V. S. and Mickelson, K. D. (1995). Motives for social comparison.
Psychology Bulletin, *21*, 1200–1210.
Hewstone, M., Rubin, M., and Willis, H. (2002) Intergroup bias. *Annual Review
of Psychology*, *53*, 575–604.
Hogg, M. A. (2000). Social identity and social comparison. In J. Suls and
L. Wheeler (eds.), *Handbook of social comparison: theory and research*
(pp. 401–421). Dordrecht: Kluwer Academic Publishers.
Hogg, M. A. and Abrams, D. (1988). *Social identifications. A social psychology of
intergroup relations and group processes*. London: Routledge.
Huguet, P., Dumas, F., Monteil, J. M., and Genestoux, N. (2001). Social com-
parison choices in the classroom: Further evidence for students' upward
comparison tendency and its beneficial impact on performance. *European
Journal of Social Psychology*, *31*, 557–578.
Jost, J. T. and Banaji, M. R. (1994). The role of stereotyping in system justifica-
tion and the production of false consciousness. *British Journal of Social
Psychology*, *33*, 1–27.
Levine, J. M. and Moreland, R. L. (1987). Social comparison and outcome
evaluation in group contexts. In J. C. Masters and W. P. Smith (eds.), *Social
comparison, social justice, and relative deprivation. Theoretical, empirical and
policy perspectives*. London: Lawrence Erlbaum Associates.
Lickel, B., Hamilton, D., Wieczorkowska, G., Lewis, A., Sherman, S. J., and
Uhles, A. N. (2000). Varieties of groups and the perception of group entita-
tivity. *Journal of Personality and Social Psychology*, *78*, 223–246.
Major, B. (1994). From social inequality to personal entitlement: The role of
social comparisons, legitimacy appraisals, and group membership. *Advances
in Experimental Social Psychology*, *26*, 293–353.
McFarland, C. and Alvaro, C. (2000). The impact of motivation on temporal
comparisons: Coping with traumatic events by perceiving personal growth.
Journal of Personality and Social Psychology, *79*, 327–343.
Mullen, B., Brown, R., and Smith, C. (1992). Ingroup bias as a function of
salience, relevance, and status: An integration. *European Journal of Social
Psychology*, *22*, 103–122.
Runciman, W. G. (1966). *Relative deprivation and social justice. A study of attitudes
to social inequality in twentieth century England*. London: Routledge and
Kegan Paul.

Smith, H. and Leach, C.W. (2004) Group membership and everyday social comparison experiences. *European Journal of Social Psychology*, *34*, 297–308.

Smith, H. J., Spears, R., and Hamstra, I. (1999). Social identity and the context of relative deprivation. In N. Ellemers, R. Spears, and B. Doosje (eds.). *Social identity*. Oxford: Blackwell (pp. 205–229).

Tajfel, H. (1978). Social categorisation, social identity and social comparison. In H. Tajfel (ed.), *Differentiation between social groups: studies in the social psychology of intergroup relations*. London: Academic Press.

Tajfel, H. and Turner, J. C. (1986). The social identity theory of intergroup behavior. In S. Worchel and W. G. Austin (eds.), *Psychology of intergroup relations* (pp. 7–24). Chicago: Nelson Hall.

Taylor, D. M., Moghaddam, F. M., and Bellerose, J. (1989). Social comparison in an intergroup context. *Journal of Social Psychology*, *129*, 499–515.

Tropp, L. R. and Wright, S. C. (1999). Ingroup identification and relative deprivation: An examination across multiple social comparisons. *European Journal of Social Psychology*, *29*, 707–724.

Turner, J. C. (1999). Some current issues in research on social identity and self-categorization theories. In N. Ellemers, R. Spears, and B. Doosje (eds.). *Social Identity*. Oxford: Blackwell, (pp. 6–34).

Tyler, T. R. (2001). Social justice. In R. Brown and S. Gaertner (eds.), *Blackwell handbook of social psychology: intergroup processes* (pp. 344–366). Oxford: Blackwell.

Tyler, T. R., Degoey, P., and Smith, H. (2001). Understanding why the justice of group procedures matters: A test of the psychological dynamics of the group-value model. In M. A. Hogg and D. Abrams (eds.), *Intergroup relations. Key reading in social psychology*. Hove: Taylor and Francis.

Van Knippenberg, A. and Van Oers, H. (1984). Social identity and equity concerns in intergroup perceptions. *British Journal of Social Psychology*, *23*, 351–361.

Vanneman, R. and Pettigrew, T. F. (1972). Race and relative deprivation in the urban United States. *Race*, *13*, 461–486.

Wheeler, L. (1966). Motivation as a determinant of upward comparison. *Journal of Experimental Social Psychology*, *2*, 27–39.

Wills, T. A. (1981). Downward comparison principles in social psychology. *Psychological Bulletin*, *90*, 245–271.

Wilson, A. E. and Ross, M. (2000). The frequency of temporal – self and social comparisons in people's personal appraisals. *Journal of Personality and Social Psychology*, *78*, 928–942.

Wood, J. V. (1989). Theory and research concerning social comparisons of personal attributes. *Psychological Bulletin*, *106*, 231–248.

Wright, S. C. (1997). Ambiguity, social influence, and collective action: Generating collective protest in response to tokenism. *Personality and Social Psychology Bulletin*, *23*, 1277–1290.

Wright, S. C. and Tropp, L. R. (2002). Collective action in response to disadvantage: Intergroup perceptions, social identification, and social change. In

I. Walker and H. Smith (eds.), *Relative deprivation. Specification, development, and integration* (pp. 200–236). Cambridge: Cambridge University Press.

Zagefka, H. (2004) *Comparisons and deprivation in ethnic minority settings.* Unpublished PhD dissertation, University of Kent.

Zagefka, H. and Brown, R. (2005). Comparisons and perceived deprivation in ethnic minority settings. *Personality and Social Psychology Bulletin, 31,* 467–482.

6 The variable impact of upward and downward social comparisons on self-esteem: when the level of analysis matters

Delphine Martinot and Sandrine Redersdorff

One of the main concerns stemming directly from research related to Festinger's theory of social comparison processes (1954) involves understanding the relations between upward comparisons, downward comparisons, and self-esteem (e.g., Blanton, 2001). Do we feel better about ourselves when we compare with more successful others (upward comparison), or when we compare with less successful others (downward comparison), and why? Given the crucial role played by self-esteem in social adaptation and cognitive functioning (e.g., Greenberg, Solomon, Pyszcynski, Rosenblatt, Burling, Lyon, Simon, and Pinel, 1992; Steele, 1988; Taylor and Brown, 1988; Tesser and Campbell, 1983), the striking determination and persistence that researchers have shown in studying this issue is readily understood (for reviews see Part One, this volume; Markman and McMullen, 2003; Mussweiler, 2003). It is much less obvious, however, why, up until quite recently, most of this research was designed without taking into consideration the level of analysis at which social comparisons occur.

Some thirty years ago, Tajfel (1972, 1974) and Turner (1975), suggested that social comparisons could take place at the individual level as in Festinger's theory, but also at the group level. Furthermore, as shown in Social Identity Theory (Tajfel and Turner, 1979), social comparisons at the group level are likely to have a significant bearing on self-esteem (see Long and Spears, 1997). Therefore, taking into account the level of analysis immediately raises new questions about the impact of social comparison on self-esteem. Some of these questions have less than trivial implications such as whether the findings of past research carried out strictly at the individual level of analysis (e.g. Morse and Gergen, 1970; Suls and Miller, 1977) can be generalized to situations where group membership, and a group level of analysis, may be important. This chapter focuses on this issue and reviews recent evidence, including several studies from our own laboratory, showing that indeed the impact of social comparison on self-esteem varies in a predictable manner as a function of the level of analysis. Furthermore, we will argue that taking into account the role of relative group status is central to a better understanding of the many and diverse findings in the area.

A conceptual framework

Members of a complex society belong to a range of social groups, the significance of which may vary from one person to the other. Positive or negative connotations are also linked to these groups and play a role in an individual's social identity. According to social identity theory (Tajfel and Turner, 1979, 1986), the value of a social group membership is determined by group-level social comparisons between the ingroup and relevant outgroups. These comparisons occur in terms of attributes or value-laden characteristics. Social identity takes on meaning from the vantage point of both intergroup social comparisons and the dynamics of social group relations.

To understand this dynamic in theoretically relevant ways, social psychologists distinguish between dominant or high status groups, those who enjoy material and symbolic privileges, and subordinate or low status groups, those who receive relatively less favorable outcomes and are often the target of negative stereotypes and prejudice (Crocker, Major, and Steele, 1998; Jost and Banaji, 1994; Sidanius and Pratto, 1999; Tajfel and Turner, 1979). Thus, a first variable that needs to be taken into account in order to understand the effect of social comparison on self-esteem is relative group status, which involves adopting an intergroup level of analysis. A second variable, relevant to both high or low status group members, is the well-known distinction within social comparison research between upward and downward comparisons (Collins, 2000). Finally, should we adopt an intergroup level of analysis, then one must consider that individuals can make this upward or downward comparison with other ingroup members (within group or intragroup social comparisons) or with outgroup members (between groups or intergroup social comparisons). As shown in Table 6.1, this framework provides eight cells or eight basic situations of social comparison. If the direction of comparison (e.g. upward vs. downward) is the only variable that makes a difference in self-esteem), then it may be concluded that the level of analysis is essentially irrelevant. But, if the fact that comparisons occur with ingroup or outgroup members, from a dominant or a subordinate group, can also make a difference, then the level of analysis needs to be considered.

Upward social comparison with ingroup members

First, let us consider evidence relating to comparison with ingroup members. Many social psychologists assume that people usually compare

Table 6.1. *Effects of intergroup comparisons on self-esteem as a function of group status, direction of comparison and group of comparison target*

		With ingroup	With outgroup
Dominant status group	Upward comparison	**Cell 1** *Negative effect on self-esteem* Target is perceived as self-informative but comparison information is processed at interpersonal level	**Cell 2** *No negative effect on self-esteem* Target is not perceived as self-informative because of difference in group membership
	Downward comparison	**Cell 3** *No negative effect on self-esteem* Emphasis on personal identity	**Cell 4** *No negative effect on self-esteem* Emphasis on personal identity
Subordinate status group	Upward comparison	**Cell 5** *No negative effect on self-esteem* Individuals assimilate their self-esteem with the positive performance of superior ingroup members. Ingroup identification mediates effect of comparison on self-esteem	**Cell 6** *Negative effect on self-esteem* Comparison target is perceived as self-informative because of his/her dominant group status
	Downward comparison	**Cell 7** *No negative effect on self-esteem* Emphasis on personal identity	**Cell 8** *No negative effect on self-esteem* Emphasis on personal identity

themselves with other ingroup members. For members of stigmatized social groups, Crocker and Major (1989) have suggested that social comparison with other ingroup members, and similarly stigmatized individuals, is more likely because comparing with more favored outgroup members would be too painful. Indeed, they suggested that the tendency to compare only with ingroup members would be one explanation for the fact that stigmatized group members do not generally show evidence of lower self-esteem than members of higher status groups (see Redersdorff and Guimond, this volume). The literature in the field of interpersonal comparison widely concurs with this hypothesis. Festinger's (1954) contribution has shown that we prefer comparing ourselves with individuals perceived as similar to us. Several researches show that individuals prefer comparisons with same-sex individuals, although they are aware that gender is not a relevant attribute for the dimension of comparison (e.g., Major and Forcey, 1985; Suls, Gaes, and Gastorf, 1979) and even when more relevant information is available (Tesser and Campbell, 1983). Similar preferences were shown for comparisons with people close in age or race (Tesser, 1986).

Several explanations have been advanced to justify the preference for comparison targets with whom one shares group membership (Miller and Prentice, 1996; Wood, 1989). The identity put forward seems to play a significant role. Basing themselves on reference groups theory (Merton and Kitt, 1950), Miller, Turnbull, and McFarland (1988) have shown that individuals often choose standards that help them determine their position within their personal frame of reference. In this context, gender and ethnic groups appear highly significant, to such an extent that individuals would ignore the standards provided by the outgroup, basing their self-evaluation on the position they hold within their own group (Major, 1994). The abilities of the members of the ingroup are perceived as relevant standards for the self because of this shared group membership. Gardner, Gabriel, and Hochschild (2002) found that upward comparisons lead to more positive affect and higher estimations of one's own performance when the other person was construed as a part of the self, compared to when the self and other were categorized as separate individuals. Thus, if same group membership actually increases the perception of a similarity between self and a member of the ingroup, it would be expected that social comparisons with ingroup members are likely to induce an assimilation effect. Indeed, expectations of similarity between the self and another person increase the probability of assimilating the characteristics of this person (e.g., Manis, Biernat, and Nelson, 1991). In other words, upward comparisons with members of the ingroup i.e. more successful peers, appear to generate an assimilation of the self-evaluations with the good performances of the ingroup and should translate into a positive effect on self-esteem. Conversely, downward comparisons with members of the ingroup, i.e. with less successful peers, are likely to generate an assimilation of the self-evaluations with poor performances of the ingroup translating into a negative effect on self-esteem. However, the results pertaining to the effects of ingroup social comparisons on self-esteem are not always consistent with this type of theoretical reasoning. Certain experimental results concur with this reasoning while others invalidate it.

When ingroup success reflects positively on self-esteem:
the assimilation process

Mackie (1984) has highlighted the self-protective aspect of upward comparisons with members of the ingroup. She observed that children from minority ethnic groups preferred upward comparisons with members of the ingroup in cases where these comparisons related to evaluative dimensions making more salient a negative stereotype linked to their group. According to Mackie (1984), by favoring comparisons with more successful peers, children from minority ethnic groups are seeking proof of the excellence of their group so as to dispel or "dismiss" negative stereotypes about them. In the same way, Blanton, Crocker, and Miller (2000) have shown that the self-esteem of female African-American participants, compared to other female African-Americans in an intergroup context potentially threatening for the social identity, is higher in an upward rather than a downward comparison. These authors conclude that when ingroup upward comparisons occur in an intergroup context threatening for the social identity, the good performances of members of the ingroup serve to invalidate negative stereotypes about this group. Individuals would appear to favor the positive information concerning their own group and would compensate their own personal failure through a process of assimilation (Brewer and Weber, 1994; Lockwood and Kunda, 1997) whereby one's self-evaluations are assimilated with the good performance of members of one's own group (see also, Mussweiler and Bodenhausen, 2002).

When ingroup success reflects negatively on self-esteem:
the contrast process

Although some studies may suggest the presence of an assimilation effect by highlighting the positive impact of upward comparisons with members of the ingroup (Blanton *et al.*, 2000; Mackie, 1984;

Mussweiller and Bodenhausen, 2002), other research points to a radically different result. Major, Sciacchitano, and Crocker (1993) have shown that participants in situations of upward comparisons with members of their ingroup had lower self-esteem than in situations of downward comparison. Such a result seems to illustrate a contrast effect rather than an assimilation effect. However, Brewer and Weber (1994) have shown that a contrast effect on self-evaluations in situations of comparison with members of the ingroup is only observed among members of a dominant group (numerical majority), consistent with the prediction of Tesser's (1988) self-evaluation maintenance model (SEM). The fact that Tesser's model can be applied when members of dominant groups are placed in situations of ingroup comparisons suggests that this comparison information is processed at an interpersonal level. In the experiment conducted by Major and colleagues (1993), participants seemed to have been affected by upward comparisons with members of their ingroup (i.e., people perceived as similar) because these comparisons were assessed at an interpersonal rather than at an intra-group level. The level at which the comparison information is processed may serve to explain the differences in the results between Blanton *et al.*'s (2000) experiment and that of Major *et al.* (1993). The female participants in Blanton *et al.*'s experiment processed the comparisons with members of the ingroup at an intra-group level and assimilated their self-evaluations with the performance of these ingroup members. This explains why their self-esteem was lower in situations of ingroup downward comparisons than in ingroup upward comparisons. As the participants in Major and colleagues' (1993) experiment seemed to have processed the comparison information with members of the ingroup at an interpersonal level, the opposite result was observed: self-esteem was lower in situations of ingroup upward comparisons than in ingroup downward comparisons. We therefore need to know why, in a context of comparison, some individuals process ingroup comparisons at an intra-group level, while others process them at an inter-personal level. We hypothesize that this difference can be explained by the status of the ingroup compared to that of the outgroup in an intergroup context of comparison.

Assimilation as a process reserved for members of subordinate groups: the importance of group identification

In the argument put forth by Mackie (1984) and by Blanton and colleagues (2000), the disparaged image of the ingroup is the key-idea explaining the assimilation process. Thus, the fact of assimilating one's self-evaluations to the performance of members of the ingroup is observed only in members of subordinate groups. This hypothesis is in line with the results obtained by Brewer and Weber (1994) with groups set up experimentally. Indeed, these authors have shown the existence of an assimilation effect of the performance of the ingroup in members of subordinate groups (numerical minority) which was not present in members of the dominant group (numerical majority). This hypothesis also explains the absence of an assimilation process in the participants in Major et al. (1993) who were white males, and therefore members of a dominant group. Moreover, in this experiment, group membership, which was induced experimentally, did not involve any status asymmetry (members of Type X or Type Z groups).

According to Brewer's (1991) optimal distinctiveness model, the fact of being a member of a majority group appears to activate an individual need for differentiation with respect to other members of the group thus making the processes of interpersonal comparisons more salient. Moreover, other findings have shown that group membership is likely to be less salient for majority members than for minority members, and as a result, members of majority groups may make relatively few group-based comparisons (Doise, 1988; McGuire and McGuire, 1988; Smith and Leach, 2004; see also Lorenzi-Cioldi and Chatard, this volume). Thus, even in a context of intergroup comparisons, members of dominant groups seek to differentiate themselves from members of their group therefore processing comparison information issued from members of the ingroup as interpersonal comparison information. On the other hand, members of subordinate groups seem to focus on group membership (Lorenzi-Cioldi, 1988, 1993), processing information stemming from a context of intergroup comparison at an intra or intergroup level (Brewer, 1991). When group members perform in such a way as to invalidate the poor image of the group, there is much to gain in assimilating one's self-evaluations to the success of peers.

Some studies have used indicators to measure the process of assimilation, such as the number of people deemed the same (Simon, Greenberg, Arndt, Pyszczynski, Clement, and Solomon, 1997; Pickett, Silver, and Brewer, 2002), intragroup similarity and coherence (Pickett and Brewer, 2001), or estimated ingroup size (Pickett and Brewer, 2001). However, no indicator supports the explanation in terms of the assimilation process envisaged to account for the effects of intragroup social comparisons in members of subordinate groups (e.g., Blanton et al., 2000; Brewer and Weber, 1994; Collins, 1996, 2000; Stapel and Koomen, 2001). Our suggestion is that the assimilation of self-evaluations to the performance of the ingroup will be rendered possible via group identification.

Group identification may be defined as "*the degree to which the ingroup is included in the self*" (Tropp and Wright, 2001, p. 586). The perceived similarity with members of one's own group and the use of group standards in self-evaluation are strongly related to ingroup identification (e.g., Branscombe, Schmitt, and Harvey, 1999). Moreover, several studies covering a wide range of social groups have shown a positive relationship between the identification to a low-status group and self-esteem (e.g., Bat-Chava, 1994; Branscombe *et al.*, 1999; Jetten, Branscombe, Schmitt, and Spears, 2001). It appears therefore that the costs generated by a low-status social identity may be compensated by the benefits derived from the identification to the group conveying this low-status (e.g., Redersdorff, Martinot, and Branscombe, 2004). Consequently, we hypothesized that the members of a subordinate group in a situation of upward comparison with their peers would tend to emphasize their identification to the ingroup in order to benefit, through a process of assimilation, from the good performance of the latter, thus protecting their self-esteem from unfavorable comparisons.

In recent research (Redersdorff and Martinot, 2003), we tested this hypothesis with members of subordinate groups by studying the effects on both their self-esteem and their group identification, of upward or downward comparisons with members of their own subordinate group or of a dominant outgroup. To create the context of intergroup comparison, the female participants, only women were selected, were told that the research focused on differences in performances between men and women on the dimension of intelligence. As shown in Schmitt, Sylvia, and Branscombe's (2000) experiment which has inspired our own procedure, this inter-gender context of comparison on the dimension of intelligence placed women in a subordinate group position. Participants were randomly assigned to one of the four experimental conditions in the following design: 2 (direction of comparison: downward *vs.* upward) X 2 (group membership of the target of comparison: ingroup (a woman) *vs.* outgroup (a man)). Participants carried out a bogus test deemed to be highly predictive of general intelligence. They were given their personal score and were then informed of someone else's score who could be either a woman (ingroup condition of comparison) or a man (outgroup condition of comparison). This person had performed either better (upward condition of comparison) or not as well (downward condition of comparison) as the participants. Finally, participants filled in a questionnaire which included our different dependent variables and especially a measure of state self-esteem and a measure of gender-group identification. Participants had also filled the measure of identification with women prior to the research, i.e. before any experimental manipulation. This enabled us to calculate difference scores and to see whether the participants' identification with women increased or decreased following the experimental manipulation.

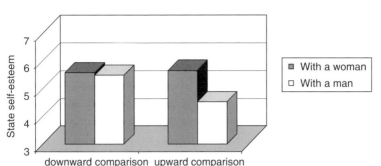

Figure 6.1. State self-esteem in women by social comparison direction, and group membership of comparison target

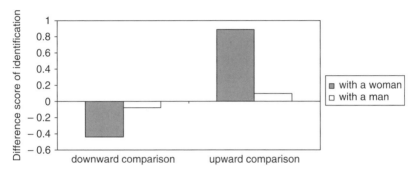

Figure 6.2. Identification with women by social comparison direction, and comparison group

As shown in Figure 6.1, and consistent with our expectations, upward comparisons with another woman did not negatively impact the participants' self-esteem.

The measures of identification with women and more specifically the difference score in identification, enable us to grasp the effects of ingroup social comparisons on self-esteem. Indeed, following an upward comparison, participants who compared themselves with another woman identified more with women, whereas those who compared themselves with a man identified less with women. Moreover, the only score significantly different from zero was observed for women in upward comparison with another woman (see Figure 6.2). We have also shown that in upward comparisons, identification with women serves to mediate the effect of the target's group membership on self-esteem. In line with our expectations, when women are placed in situations of upward comparison with another woman, they tend to protect their self-esteem from these unfavorable comparisons by increasing identification to the ingroup, evidence of a process of assimilation (see cell 5 in Table 6.1). Group identification is therefore perceived as a key factor in explaining the effects of social comparisons with members of one's ingroup on the self-esteem of members of subordinate groups.

Assimilating one's own self-evaluations with the performance of members of the ingroup may be harmful in cases of ingroup downward comparisons. However, no lowering of self-esteem was observed in this particular condition. At first glance, such a result may appear consistent with the idea that ingroup downward comparisons should have no negative effect on self-esteem because they are perceived as potential opportunities for individual social mobility (e.g., Seta and Seta, 1996). Our participants may very well have interpreted their positive performance as a possibility of making it on their own, setting aside their group, which in turn should translate in a decrease of group identification. Although a marginally significant decrease of the identification with women is indeed observed in the ingroup downward comparison condition, it does not appear significantly more important than that observed in the outgroup downward comparison condition. Moreover, given the lack of a significant correlation between identification with women and self-esteem in participants who performed better than another woman, this trend towards a decrease of identification does not appear to be linked to a mechanism of protection of self-esteem. Another explanation for this result may be that individuals placed in situations of downward comparison focus on their personal identity rather than on their social identity (see cell 7 in Table 6.1). In other words, even in comparisons made in an intergroup context, emphasis seems to be put on personal rather than social identity in order to benefit from the effects of downward comparisons. Indeed, research shows that members of disadvantaged groups can highlight the perceived heterogeneity of their group or focus on an individual level of self-categorization rather than on their threatened social identity (e.g., Lee and Ottati, 1995). The trend towards a decrease of the identification with women observed in our participants following downward comparisons with another woman could therefore convey a quest for self-definition as a unique individual rather than a group member.

This research also indicates (Redersdorff and Martinot, 2003) that the only instance of a decrease in self-esteem is observed in a situation of upward comparison with a member of a dominant outgroup (namely a man) (see Figure 6.1). Such a comparison can only confirm the legitimacy of the subordinate status of women. Therefore, the fact of identifying oneself to that group cannot protect self-esteem. A decrease in self-esteem is in line with the result obtained by Blanton *et al.* (2000) with black participants. These participants referred to the performance of white women (members of the dominant outgroup) as standards for self-evaluation, which led to a process of contrast. Therefore, their self-esteem was lower in situations of outgroup upward comparisons than in situations of outgroup downward comparisons. But here again, the results of Major *et al.*'s (1993) research are different from ours and from those observed by Blanton and colleagues. Indeed, in the experiment conducted by Major and colleagues, participants' self-esteem was as positive in situations of outgroup upward comparisons as in outgroup downward comparisons. From this result, Major *et al.* (1993) came to the influential conclusion that: "If the better performance of others could be attributed to differences in group membership between the self and comparison others, the negative implications of unfavourable comparisons for self-esteem would be avoided" (p. 718). In other words, if upward comparisons with outgroup members cannot be avoided, they will be perceived as irrelevant and will not affect self-esteem. But in fact such an argument is contradicted by the decrease in self-esteem of the women in our own experiment in situations of upward comparisons with a man, or of that of black women placed in upward comparisons with a white woman in Blanton *et al.*'s (2000) experiment.

As our own suggestion was that the assimilation of the good performance of members of the ingroup was only observed in members of subordinate groups and therefore was dependent on group status, we hypothesize that the dismissal of a comparison information as irrelevant is also dependent on group status and that only members of dominant groups are in a position to do so. Indeed, the fact of dismissing certain comparison targets as irrelevant points to an asymmetrical relation between the target and the person deeming it irrelevant.

The moderating role of group status

Fiske (1993) argues that if indeed powerful people ignore the powerless, the opposite is much less probable. Fiske and Stevens (1993) show that gender relations are a perfect illustration of this asymmetrical relationship of power. Participants in Major *et al.*'s (1993) experiment were white men, and therefore members of the dominant group. However, given that group membership inducement in this experiment did not concern gender but rather experimentally set up groups devoid of power asymmetry, it may be assumed that participants reacted in their usual way, i.e., as members of a dominant group. This would explain why they did not show any sign of a decrease in self-esteem in situations of outgroup upward comparisons. As members of a dominant group, they are chronically used to dismiss as irrelevant comparison information issued by an outgroup. Their dominant group status could also explain why they are affected by upward comparisons with members of their own group. As mentioned earlier, dominant group membership appears to activate an individual need to differentiate oneself from other group members (Lorenzi-Cioldi, 1988) therefore rendering interpersonal comparison processes more salient (Brewer, 1991). In order to test the moderating role of group status in explaining the effects of social comparisons with the ingroup or the outgroup on self-esteem, we conducted a series of six studies (Martinot, Redersdorff, Guimond, and Dif, 2002; Martinot and Redersdorff, 2002, 2003; Redersdorff and Martinot, 2004).

A first research replicated quite literally Major *et al.*'s (1993) experiment with men, as well as with women (Martinot *et al.*, 2002, exp.1). We were expecting the same results as Major and colleagues (1993) only in the case of men. More specifically, we were predicting lower self-esteem when male participants were placed in situations of upward comparisons with members of their own group. We did not expect upward comparisons with members of the outgroup to affect self-esteem as their dominant group status would enable them to dismiss such comparisons as irrelevant to them. On the other hand, as far as female participants were concerned, we were expecting opposite results, namely that their self-esteem should be lower only in situations of upward comparisons with members of the outgroup. Their subordinate group status would not enable them to dismiss such comparisons as non-informative. On the other hand, and in line with our previous results showing that women protect their self-esteem by increasing identification to their own group in situations of upward comparisons with other women (Redersdorff and Martinot, 2003, exp.1), we were not expecting a decrease in self-esteem in situations of ingroup upward comparisons. These hypotheses were totally validated. As far as the effects of upward comparisons on self-esteem are concerned, we replicated with our male participants the results observed by Major *et al.* (1993), while results obtained with women were diametrically opposite. In this particular replication, only the women reported lower self-esteem in situations of upward comparisons with the outgroup. They seemed unable to dismiss as irrelevant comparison information stemming from the outgroup. In line with our hypothesis, only the men were able to do so as they were not affected by outgroup upward comparisons. On the other hand, in cases where the upward comparison took place with members of the ingroup, women's self-esteem was not negatively impacted while that of men lowered. Men did not seem to rely on an assimilation process to protect their self-esteem in this particular configuration. As far as the effects of downward comparisons are concerned, they were identical in both populations and in line with those observed by Major *et al.* (1993). In order to benefit from the positive effects of the downward comparison information (Major *et al.*, 1993; Brickman and Bulman, 1977), both men and women seemed to minimize or ignore the difference in group membership between their self and the others to whom they were being compared. As suggested before, personal identity appears to take precedence over social identity in situations of downward comparisons.

Although this research indicates differing consequences on the self-esteem of men and women in situations of social comparisons taking place in an intergroup context, one may be tempted to put forward biological reasons to explain the effects observed (e.g., Baron-Cohen, 2003). To ensure that the gender group *status* does indeed account for these effects, and not biologically-based sex differences, two other experiments manipulating group status experimentally were conducted. Our hypothesis was that women contextually placed in a situation of dominant group would react as men did in our replication of Major *et al.* (1993), and that men contextually placed in a situation of subordinate group would react in the same way as the women did in our replication. Indeed, considering the asymmetrical relationship between groups leads us to take into account the circumstances under which a given attribute endows a subordinate or dominant group position in a context of intergroup comparison. For example, from the moment that a domain of comparison is perceived as stereotypically feminine, the referent group changes, and women become the dominant group (e.g., Dovidio, Ellyson, Keating, Heltman, and Brow, 1988). The importance of the sexual connotation linked to the context is therefore essential in the understanding of the asymmetrical relations between men and women and, for this reason, we manipulated the stereotypical connotation of the task, in order to induce either a dominant or a subordinate group status within both, a female population (Martinot *et al.*, 2002, exp.2) and a male population (Redersdorff, 2002, exp.4). These two experiments were carried out following the same procedure, the only difference being the gender of the participants. Participants were told that the objective of the research was to study gender differences thus placing them in a context of intergroup comparison. The task was then presented as either typically female or typically male in order to induce a dominant or subordinate status in our participants. Participants were placed in a comparison situation with members of either the ingroup or the outgroup and their task performance was worse (upward comparison) or better (downward comparison) than the latter. Our main measures were state self-esteem and gender group identification.

Effect of group status on self-esteem of women

In line with our expectations, women placed in a dominant group position (due to the female task label) reacted in the same way as the men did in our replication of Major *et al.*'s (1993) experiment. Indeed women, when exposed to an upward comparison with other women, present a lower self-esteem than in other conditions of comparison (see Figure 6.3). On the other hand, when women compare unfavorably to men (members of the outgroup), they do not seem to be affected by such comparisons. The dominant status of their group appears to enable them to dismiss as irrelevant this comparison information.

As expected, when women as a group hold a subordinate status (due to the male task label), the same results as those obtained with women in our replication of Major *et al.*'s (1993) experiment are observed, i.e., lower self-esteem reported only in situations of upward comparisons with the outgroup. Indeed, women exposed to an upward comparison with men report lower self-esteem than in the other conditions of comparison (see Figure 6.3). The subordinate status of their group does not enable them to dismiss the comparison information stemming from the dominant outgroup as irrelevant (see cell 6 in Table 6.1). On the other hand, as noted previously (Martinot *et al.*, 2002, exp.1; Redersdorff and Martinot, 2003), upward comparisons with other women (the ingroup) do not seem to affect their self-esteem. In this condition, participants' identification with women increased, thus facilitating the assimilation of their self-esteem with the good performance of other women.

Effect of group status on self-esteem of men

In line with our expectations, when men are placed in a dominant group status (due to the male task label), lower self-esteem is reported only in situations of upward comparisons with other men (members of the ingroup), as observed in our replication of Major *et al.* (1993). Therefore, men are unaffected by upward comparisons with women (members of the outgroup), their position as a dominant group enabling them to dismiss this comparison information as irrelevant. Also, as expected, when men hold a subordinate group status (due to the female task label), they report lower self-esteem when placed in a situation of upward comparison with women (members of the outgroup), since their subordinate status does not enable them to dismiss this comparison information as irrelevant. However, they are unaffected by upward comparisons with other men (see Figure 6.3).

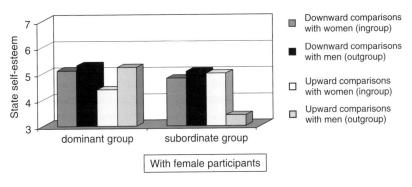

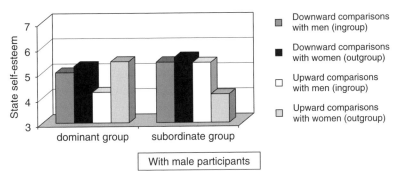

Figure 6.3. State self-esteem in both men and women by group status, social comparison direction, and comparison group

These two studies, one carried out with women (Martinot *et al.*, 2002, exp.2), and the other with men (Redersdorff, 2002, exp.4), point to the necessity of taking into account the status of the ingroup when examining the effects of intergroup comparisons on self-esteem. In line with previous research, (Martinot *et al.*, 2002, exp.1; Redersdorff and Martinot, 2003), they also highlight the fact that information pertaining to group membership of the comparison targets appear to be overlooked in downward comparisons (see cells 3, 4, 7 and 8 in Table 6.1). Individuals (men and women) seem to focus on their personal identity and on the related benefits, rather than on their social identity (cf. Figure 6.3). All these results were replicated making salient other group membership besides gender. By leading participants to self-categorize as members of the group of students in psychology (Martinot *et al.*, 2002, exp.3) or by inducing group membership experimentally (inductive or deductive thinkers) (Martinot and Redersdorff, 2002), the same effects on self-esteem were observed. As they have been demonstrated on varying group memberships, and each time using new experimental procedures, the effects observed can be considered as robust and can be generalized to all context of intergroup comparison involving status asymmetries.

This series of experiments shows that members of subordinate groups protect their self-esteem from upward comparisons with members of their own group by increasing their identification with the ingroup (see cell 5 in Table 6.1). We have not found this particular psychological process in members of dominant groups (Martinot *et al.*, 2002; Redersdorff and Martinot, 2003). On the other hand, the self-esteem of members of a dominant group, who are more focussed on their uniqueness (Lorenzi-Cioldi, 1988, see also Chapter 12, this volume) and are motivated by a desire for interpersonal differentiation (Brewer, 1991), is negatively impacted in situations of upward comparisons with members of their own group (Martinot *et al.*, 2002; see cell 1 in Table 6.1).

Dismissal of comparison information: a mechanism
of self-protection reserved to members of dominant groups

We have also shown that the self-esteem of members of dominant groups remains unaffected by upward comparisons with members of subordinate outgroups, while members of subordinate groups report a decrease in self-esteem in situations of upward comparison with members of a dominant outgroup. This result observed consistently in six different experiments (Martinot *et al.*, 2002; Martinot and Redersdorff, 2002, 2003; Redersdorff, 2002) has enabled us to argue that only the members of dominant groups appear to be in a position to dismiss the relevance of unfavorable comparison information stemming from a subordinate outgroup, thus protecting their self-esteem. However, in these studies, we had no evidence pointing towards a genuine dismissal of the relevance of the outgroup comparison information by members of dominant groups. This is the reason why we included measures of perceived informativeness of the comparison target (Redersdorff and Martinot, 2004) in a seventh study.

In this research, female psychology students were randomly assigned to one of the eight experimental conditions of the design classically used in our research: 2 (group status: dominant *vs.* subordinate) × 2 (comparison direction: downward *vs.* upward) × 2 (comparison group: ingroup *vs.* outgroup). Group status was manipulated via membership to the group of students in psychology. Participants carried out a test said to be linked to intellectual ability. They were told that the French Ministry of Education had published a report showing that the average level of intellectual ability of students varied according to their field of study. Next, they were given the ranking of eight fields of study on the intelligence tests: the group of medical students took first position, the group of philosophy students came last, and the group of psychology students was placed right in the middle. To induce group status, the participants were told that the purpose of the study was to compare two fields of study. In the "subordinate group status" condition, participants thought that the comparison would be made between psychology students and medical students while in the "dominant group status" condition, the comparison was said to be made between psychology students and philosophy students. The participants were then informed of both their personal score at the test and the average score obtained by the comparison group (medicine or philosophy for the "outgroup" condition or psychology for the "ingroup" condition). In situations of downward comparison, the participants saw that their score was better than the comparison group's average score. In situations of upward comparison, they noted that their score was lower than the comparison group's average score. Next the participants were asked to fill in a questionnaire which included our main measures: identification with psychology students, state self-esteem and perceived informativeness of the comparison target.

The results obtained on self-esteem are in line with those observed in previous studies and are once again proof of the robustness of the effects. In a context of comparison where psychology students are placed in a subordinate group position, a lowering of self-esteem is reported only in situations of upward comparison with the dominant outgroup (medical students). In situations of upward comparisons with other students in psychology, participants do not report a lower self-esteem. This is explained by the fact that this type of comparison increases the participants' identification with the group of students in psychology. Once again, this experiment shows that for members of subordinate groups, identification with the ingroup serves as mediator for the effect of the target's group membership on state self-esteem in situations of upward comparisons (see cell 5 in Table 6.1).

In a context of comparison where psychology students are placed in a dominant group position, a lowering of self-esteem is reported only in situations of upward comparison with psychology students, i.e., the ingroup. As expected, psychology students placed in a context where their group is dominant do not report lower self-esteem following upward comparisons with a subordinate group (philosophy students), which points to the fact that they do not perceive this particular comparison information as relevant. The results observed with our measure of perceived informativeness of the comparison target concur with this idea. We ran a 2 (group status: dominant or subordinate) × 2 (comparison

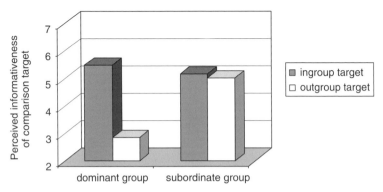

Figure 6.4. Perceived informativeness of the comparison target, by group status and group membership of target

direction: upward or downward) × 2 (group in comparison: ingroup or outgroup) × 2 (rated group target: ingroup or outgroup) mixed ANOVA, with the last factor as a repeated measure. As expected, participants assigned to a dominant group rated their group (psychology students) more self-informative than the subordinate outgroup (philosophy students). Participants assigned to a subordinate group perceived their group as self-informative as the dominant outgroup (medicine students, see Figure 6.4). Moreover, one-sample t tests of the distribution around the theoretical mean confirmed that participants in the dominant status group condition rated the comparison with the subordinate outgroup as not self-informative. Whereas participants in the subordinate status group condition rated the comparison with the dominant outgroup significantly self-informative. This means that when group status is dominant, the participants deem their own group (psychology students) more informative with respect to their personal value that the subordinate outgroup (philosophy students) (see cells 1 and 2 in Table 6.1). This also entails that when the group has a subordinate status, the participants deem the dominant outgroup (medical students) as informative as their own group (psychology students) in gaining knowledge about their personal value. This set of results represents strong support in favor of the hypothesis according to which only the members of dominant groups are in a position to dismiss the relevance of comparison information stemming from the outgroup.

Conclusion

The studies presented in this chapter show that an intergroup level of analysis of the effects of social comparisons on self-esteem is indeed fruitful and necessary as is the analysis of the underlying self-protection mechanisms occurring when social comparisons take place with members of the ingroup or of an outgroup. The asymmetrical relationship that often sets in between groups in a context of comparison plays a decisive role in the way in which individuals will process the comparison information they receive, and consequently in the effects of social comparisons on self-esteem.

First, the comparison information can be processed at an interpersonal level and classic effects of interpersonal comparisons on self-esteem are observed. The series of studies presented here show that when individuals belong to a group placed in a dominant position in the context of intergroup comparison, these individuals appear to process the comparison information at an interpersonal level. They report lower self-esteem in situations of ingroup upward comparisons than in situations of downward ingroup comparisons. In accordance with Brewer's (1991) optimal distinctiveness model, their self-concept drew from personal attributes stressing the uniqueness of the self compared to other people, especially to ingroup members (Brewer, 1991; Brewer and Weber, 1994; Lorenzi-Cioldi, 1988, 1993). Such arguments could explain why individuals who belong to a group with a dominant status do not seem to make use of the possibility of assimilating themselves with the positive performance of ingroup members when the latter perform better than they do (see cell 1 in Table 6.1).

Second, the comparison information can be processed at group level, which contributes towards intragroup assimilation or intergroup contrast effects on self-esteem. This series of studies thus shows that, in a context of intergroup comparison in which their own group holds a subordinate position, and in keeping with Brewer's (1991) optimal distinctiveness model, individuals process comparison information at group level (intragroup and/or intergroup). By increasing group identification, they are therefore able to assimilate their own self-esteem to the success of their peers in situations of upward comparison with members of their own group (see cell 5 in Table 6.1). On the other hand, in a situation of upward comparison with members of the dominant outgroup, members of the subordinate group are not in a position allowing them to dismiss these comparison targets as irrelevant as they deem the dominant group just as informative as their ingroup. They are in that case subjected to a contrast effect and to the negative impact on their self-esteem of an upward comparison (see cell 6 in Table 6.1).

Third, the comparison target may be deemed irrelevant. Only the members of a group holding a dominant status in an intergroup context seem to be able to assess the subordinate outgroup as an irrelevant comparison target and hence remain unaffected by upward comparisons with this outgroup (see cell 2 in Table 6.1).

In short, in intergroup context, and with the necessity of taking into account the relative status of the groups involved, we can predict that individuals will be able to protect themselves from upward comparisons with the ingroup but will be affected by upward comparisons with the outgroup when their own group holds a subordinate status (the converse being the case when their group holds a dominant status). However, group status does not appear to play a role in situations of downward comparisons taking place in an intergroup context. The individuals seem to process these comparisons at an interpersonal level and overlook the information regarding the group membership of their comparison (see cells 3, 4, 7 and 8 in Table 6.1). Although the intergroup context makes the social identity salient, individuals seem able to focus on their personal identity in situations where the self can benefit (Redersdorff and Martinot, 2003, exp.2). Predictions concerning the effects of downward comparisons on self-esteem in an intergroup context do not entail prior knowledge of either the status of the groups involved or of the group membership of the comparison targets. On the other hand, it is essential to place oneself at an intergroup level of analysis to be able to predict and understand the effects on self-esteem of upward social comparisons taking place in an intergroup context.

References

Baron-Cohen, S. (2003). *The essential difference: The truth about the male and female brain*. New York, NY: Basic Books, Inc.

Bat-Chava, Y. (1994). Group identification and self-esteem of deaf adults. *Personality and Social Psychology Bulletin*, *20*, 494–502.

Blanton, H. (2001). Evaluating the self in the context of another: The three-selves model of social comparison assimilation and contrast. In G. B. Moskowitz (ed.), *Cognitive social psychology: The Princeton Symposium on the legacy and future of social cognition* (pp. 75–87). Mahway, NJ: Lawrence Erlbaum Associates.

Blanton, H., Crocker, J., and Miller, D. T. (2000). The effects of in-group versus out-group social comparison on self-esteem in the context of a negative stereotype. *Journal of Experimental Social Psychology*, *36*, 519–530.

Branscombe, N., Schmitt, M. T., and Harvey, R. D. (1999). Perceived discrimination among African-Americans: Attributions, group identification, and consequences for well-being. *Journal of Personality and Social Psychology*, *77*, 135–149.

Brewer, M. B. (1991). The social self: On being the same and different at the same time. *Personality and Social Psychology Bulletin*, *17*, 475–482.

Brewer, M. B. and Weber, J. G. (1994). Self-evaluation effects of interpersonal versus intergroup social comparison. *Journal of Personality and Social Psychology*, *6*, 268–275.

Brickman, P. and Bulman, R. J. (1977). Pleasure and pain in social comparison. In J. M. Suls and R. L. Miller (eds.), *Social comparison processes: Theoretical and empirical perspectives on the self* (pp. 149–186). Washington, DC: Haslted / Wiley.

Collins, R. L. (1996). For better or worse: The impact of upward social comparison on self-evaluations. *Psychological Bulletin, 119,* 51–69.

——— (2000). Among the better ones: Upward assimilation in social comparison. In J. Suls and L. Wheeler (eds.), *Handbook of social comparison* (pp. 159–172). New York: Kluwer Academic/Plenum Publishers.

Crocker, J. and Major, B. (1989). Social stigma and self-esteem: The self-protective properties of stigma. *Psychological Review, 96,* 608–630.

Crocker, J., Major, B., and Steele, C. (1998). Social stigma. In D. Gilbert, S. T. Fiske, and G. Lindzey (eds.), *The handbook of social psychology* (4th edn.) (pp. 504–553), Boston: McGraw Hill.

Doise, W. (1988). Individual and social identities in intergroup relations. *European Journal of Social Psychology, 18,* 99–112.

Dovidio, J. F., Ellyson, S. L., Keating, C. F., Heltman, K., and Brown C. E. (1988). The relationship of social power to visual displays of dominance between men and women. *Journal of Personality and Social Psychology, 54,* 233–242.

Festinger, L. (1954). A theory of social comparison processes. *Human Relations, 7,* 117–140.

Fiske, S. and Stevens L. (1993). What's so special about sex? Gender stereotyping and discrimination. In S. Oskamp and M. Costanzo (eds.), *Gender issues in social psychology* (pp. 173–196). Newburry Park, CA: Sage.

Fiske, S. T. (1993). Controlling other people: The impact of power on stereotyping. *American Psychologist, 48,* 621–628.

Gardner, W. L., Gabriel, S., and Hochschild, L. (2002). When you and I are "we," you are no longer threatening: The role of self-expansion in social comparison processes. *Journal of Personality and Social Psychology, 82,* 239–251.

Greenberg, J., Solomon, S., Pyszcynski, T., Rosenblatt, A., Burling, J., Lyon, D., Simon, L., and Pinel, E. (1992). Why do people need self-esteem? Converging evidence that self-esteem serves an anxiety-buffering function, *Journal of Personality and Social Psychology, 63,* 913–922.

Jetten, J., Branscombe, N. R., Schmitt, M. T., and Spears, R. (2001). Rebels with a cause: Group identification as a response to perceived discrimination from the mainstream. *Personality and Social Psychology Bulletin, 27.*

Jost, J. T. and Banaji, M. R. (1994). The role of stereotyping in system justification and the production of false consciousness. *British Journal of Social Psychology, 33,* 1–27.

Lee, Y.-T. and Ottati, V. (1995). Perceived in-group homogeneity as a function of group membership salience and stereotype threat. *Personality and Social Psychology Bulletin, 21,* 610–619.

Lockwood, P. and Kunda, Z. (1997). Superstars and me: Predicting the impact of role models on the self. *Journal of Personality and Social Psychology, 73,* 91–103.

Long, K. and Spears, R. (1997). The self-esteem hypothesis revisited: Differentiation and the disaffected. In R. Spears, P. J. Oakes, N. Ellemers, and S. A. Haslam (eds.), *The social psychology of stereotyping and group life* (pp. 296–317). Oxford: Blackwell.

Lorenzi-Cioldi, F. (1988). *Individus dominants et groupes dominés. Images masculines et féminines*. Grenoble: Presses Universitaires de Grenoble.

(1993). They all look alike, but so do we … sometimes: Perceptions of ingroup and outgroup homogeneity as a function of sex and context. *British Journal of Social Psychology, 32,* 111–124.

Mackie, D. (1984). Social comparison in high- and low-status groups. *Journal of Cross Cultural Psychology, 15,* 379–398.

Major, B. (1994). From social inequality to personal entitlement: The role of social comparisons, legitimacy appraisals, and group membership. In M. P. Zanna (ed.), *Advances in Experimental Social Experimental* (Vol. xxvi, pp. 293–348). San Diego: Academic Press.

Major, B. and Forcey, B. (1985). Social comparisons and pay evaluations: Preferences for same-sex and same-job wage comparisons. *Journal of Experimental Social Psychology, 21,* 393–405.

Major, B., Sciacchitano, A., and Crocker, J. (1993). Ingroup vs. outgroup comparisons and self-esteem. *Personality and Social Psychology Bulletin, 09,* 711–721.

Manis, M., Biernat, M., and Nelson, T. F. (1991). Comparison and expectancy processes in human judgment. *Journal of Personality and Social Psychology, 61,* 203–211.

Markman, K. D. and McMullen, M. N. (2003). A reflection and evaluation model of comparative thinking. *Personality and Social Psychologicy Review, 7,* 244–267.

Martinot, D. and Redersdorff, S. (2002). Impact of upward comparisons with outgroup members on self-esteem in an asymmetrical intergroup comparison context. *Psychologica Belgica, 42,* 131–149.

(2003). Impact of comparisons with outgroup members on women's self-esteem: role of the stereotypical connotation of the performance context. *International Journal of Psychology, 38,* 348–358.

Martinot, D., Redersdorff, S., Guimond S., and Dif, S. (2002). Ingroup vs. outgroup comparisons and self-esteem: the role of group status and ingroup identification. *Personality and Social Psychology Bulletin, 28,* 1586–1600.

McGuire, W. J. and McGuire, C. V. (1988). Content and process in the experience of self. In L. Berkowitz (ed.), *Advances in experimental social psychology* (Vol. xx, pp. 97–144). New York: Academic Press.

Merton, R. K. and Kitt, A. (1950). Contributions to the theory of reference group behavior. In R. K. Merton and P. F. Lazarsfeld (eds.), *Continuities in social research: Studies in the scope and method of "The American soldier"* (pp. 40–105). New York: Free Press.

Miller, D. T. and Prentice, D. A. (1996). The construction of social norms and standards. In E. T. Higgins and A. W. Kruglanski, *Social psychology: Handbook of basic principles* (pp. 799–829). New York: Guilford Press.

Miller, D. T., Turnbull, W., and McFarland, C. (1988). Particularistic and universalistic evaluation in the social comparison process. *Journal of Personality and Social Psychology, 55,* 908–917.

Morse, S. and Gergen, K. (1970). Social comparison, self-consistency, and the concept of self. *Journal of Personality and Social Psychology, 16,* 148–156.

Mussweiler, T. (2003). 'Everything is relative': Comparison processes in social judgment. The 2002 Jaspars Lecture. *European Journal of Social Psychology*, *33*, 719–734.

Mussweiler, T. and Bodenhausen, G. V. (2002). I know you are, but what am I? Self-evaluative consequences of judging in-group and out-group members. *Journal of Personality and Social Psychology*, *82*, 19–32.

Pickett, C. L. and Brewer, M. B. (2001). Assimilation and differentiation needs as motivational determinants of perceived in-group and out-group homogeneity. *Journal of Experimental Social Psychology*, *37*, 341–348.

Pickett, C. L., Silver, M. D., and Brewer, M. B. (2002). The impact of assimilation and differentiation needs on perceived group importance and judgments of ingroup size. *Personality and Social Psychology Bulletin*, *28*, 546–558.

Redersdorff, S. (2002). Stratégies de protection de l'estime de soi dans un contexte de comparaison intergroupe: une approche expérimentale du rôle du statut du groupe. *Unpublished Doctoral dissertation, Laboratoire de Psychologie Sociale et Cognitive, Université Blaise Pascal, Clermont-Ferrand*.

Redersdorff, S. and Martinot, D. (2003). Impact des comparaisons ascendantes et descendantes sur l'estime de soi: importance de l'identité mise en jeu. *L'Année Psychologique*, *104*, 411–444.

(2004). Identification and perception of target group informativeness as a way to protect self-esteem in an intergroup comparative context. *6th European Social Cognition Network Meeting*, Lisboa, 8–11th September.

Redersdorff, S., Martinot, D., and Branscombe, N. (2004). The impact of thinking about group-based disadvantages or advantages on women's well-being: An experimental test of the rejection-identification model. *Cahiers de Psychologie Cognitive/Current Psychology of Cognition*, *22*, 203–222.

Schmitt, M. T., Silvia, P. J., and Branscombe, N. R. (2000). The intersection of self-evaluation maintenance and social identity theories: Intragroup judgment in interpersonal and intergroup contexts. *Personality and Social Psychology Bulletin*, *26*, 1598–1606.

Seta, J. J. and Seta, C. E. (1996). Big fish in small ponds: A social hierarchy analysis of intergroup biais. *Journal of Personality and Social Psychology*, *71*, 1210–1221.

Sidanius, J. and Pratto, F. (1999). *Social dominance: An intergroup theory of social hierarchy and oppression*. New York: Cambridge University Press.

Simon, L., Greenberg, J., Arndt, J., Pyszczynski, T., Clement, R., and Solomon, S. (1997). Perceived consensus, uniqueness, and terror management: Compensatory responses to threats to inclusion and distinctiveness following mortality salience. *Personality and Social Psychology Bulletin*, *23*, 1055–1065.

Smith, H. J. and Leach, C. W. (2004). Group membership and everyday social comparison experiences. *European Journal of Social Psychology*, *34*, 297–309.

Stapel, D. A. and Koomen, W. (2001). I, we, and the effects of others on me: How self-construal level moderates social comparison effects. *Journal of Personality and Social Psychology*, *80*, 766–781.

Steele, C. (1988). The psychology of self-affirmation: Sustaining the integrity of the self. In L. Berkowitz (ed.), *Advances in experimental social psychology* (Vol. XXI, 181–227), New York: Academic Press.

Suls, J., Gaes, G., and Gastorf, J. W. (1979). Evaluating a sex-related ability: Comparison with same-, opposite-, and combined-sex norms. *Journal of Research in Personality*, *13*, 294–304.

Suls, J. M. and Miller, R. L. (eds.) (1977). *Social comparison processes: Theoretical and empirical perspectives*. Washington, DC: Halsted-Wiley.

Tajfel, H. (1972). La catégorisation sociale. In S. Moscovici (ed.), *Introduction à la psychologie sociale* (pp. 272–302). Paris: Larousse.

    (1974). Social identity and intergroup behavior. *Social Science Information*, *13*, 65–93.

Tajfel, H. and Turner, J. C. (1979). An integrative theory of intergroup conflict. In S. Worchel and W. Austin (eds.), *The social psychology of intergroup relations* (pp. 33–48). Pacific Grove, CA: Brooks/Cole.

    (1986). The social identity theory of intergroup behavior. In S. Worchel and W. Austin (eds.), *Psychology of intergroup relations* (pp. 33–48). Chicago: Nelson-Hall.

Taylor, S. E. and Brown, J. D. (1988). Illusion and well-being: A social psychological perspective on mental health, *Psychological Bulletin*, *103*, 193–210.

Tesser, A. (1986). Some effects of self-evaluation maintenance on cognition and action. In R. M. Sorrentino and E. T. Higgins (eds.), *Handbook of motivation and cognition: Foundations of social behavior* (pp. 435–464). New York: Guilford Press.

    (1988). Toward a self-evaluation maintenance model of social behavior. In L. Berkowitz (ed.), *Advances in experimental social psychology*, (Vol. II, pp. 1–31). Hillsdale, NJ: Erlbaum.

Tesser, A. and Campbell, J. (1983). Self-definition and self-evaluation maintenance. In J. Suls et A. Greenwald (eds.), *Social psychological perspectives on the self* (Vol. II, 1–31), Hillsdale, NJ: Erlbaum.

Tropp, L. R. and Wright, S. (2001). Ingroup identification as the inclusion of ingroup in the self. *Personality and Social Psychology Bulletin*, *27*, 585–600.

Turner, J. C. (1975). Social comparison and social identity: Some prospects for intergroup behaviour. *European Journal of Social Psychology*, *5*, 5–34.

Wood, J. V. (1989). Theory and research concerning social comparison of personal attributes. *Psychological Bulletin*, *106*, 231–248.

7   Attitudes toward redistributive social policies: the effects of social comparisons and policy experience

Donna M. Garcia, Nyla R. Branscombe,
Serge Desmarais, and Stephanie S. Gee

An extensive body of research has examined the factors that shape attitudes toward employment-based redistributive policies such as affirmative action and comparable worth. Empirical work has focused particularly on individualistic predictors of opposition toward these policies, including prejudice or justice beliefs (Bobocel, Son Hing, Davies, Stanley, and Zanna, 1998; Sears, Henry, and Kosterman, 2000). Although some research has considered whether policy support varies as a function of the type of affirmative action program – preferential treatment versus equal opportunity (Bobocel *et al.*, 1998) – little research has assessed how features of employment settings themselves might affect attitudes toward redistributive policies and ideological beliefs. Aspects of the work setting are likely to shape people's beliefs about inequality and group-based policies by cueing different self-categorizations and comparison standards that people draw on when they evaluate their employment outcomes (Tajfel and Turner, 1986; Turner, Hogg, Oakes, Reicher, and Wetherell, 1987). In this chapter, we argue that the presence or absence of gender-based redistributive policies in employment settings convey different identity and comparison information, which then affects people's responses to gender differences in employment outcomes and whether they support or oppose policies that alter these outcomes. We expect that women and men who have conscious experience with redistributive policies will respond differently to these policies and related ideological beliefs than will those who do not have this experience.

Gender discrimination in the workforce

In Western countries, women have made progress in the workplace: their wages have increased, as has their representation in the paid labor force (AFL-CIO, 2004). Despite these advances, working women continue to be clustered in low-paid jobs in Western countries such as Canada and the

USA (AFL-CIO, 2004; Social Development Canada, 2002). Women are still dramatically underrepresented in upper management and they occupy less than 10 percent of senior executive positions (Social Development Canada, 2002). Even those women who do manage to obtain high-status positions experience gender discrimination: they receive fewer and smaller raises, fewer opportunities for advancement and lower wages than do men who are comparable in occupation, education, relocation flexibility, and experience (AFL-CIO, 2004; Stroh, Brett, and Reilly, 1992). Regardless of the type or status of the positions, such gender discrepancies in earnings are common and become increasingly pronounced across the life-span.

In response to gender-based discrimination in the workplace, many organizations have introduced affirmative action and comparable worth policies that are designed to ameliorate gender-based inequities. These policies have, however, created considerable controversy and resentment, and some forms of these policies have been legally challenged as "reverse" discrimination against white men (see Crosby, 2004). Many social scientists have attempted to understand why societies that endorse egalitarian values resist policies that actually promote these ideals (see Crosby, 2004; Sears *et al.*, 2000; Tougas, Brown, Beaton, and Joly, 1995). Although researchers have generated a number of explanations, most theorists have primarily relied on three models to explain resistance to redistributive policies. These three models explain opposition to affirmative action either in terms of negative evaluations of the disadvantaged group (Tougas *et al.*, 1995), a desire to protect highly-valued principles of individualism (Bobocel *et al.*, 1998), or the collective interest of the advantaged group (Bobo, 1998; Tougas *et al.*, 1995). Despite their different foci, all three models assume, to some extent, that opposition to redistributive policies arises from the stable attitudes of perceivers, and overlook the *contextual nature* of beliefs about social inequality (Schmitt, Branscombe, and Kappen, 2003; Schmitt, Ellemers, and Branscombe, 2003). These three models also have in common a tendency to focus on high-status groups and their opposition to redistributive policies but overlook the predictors of low-status group members' support for these policies. Examination of the same factors among both high- and low-status groups could be a very informative means of illuminating the psychological processes underlying policy attitudes.

In this chapter, we take a social identity perspective and consider the role that different types of employment environments might have in shaping *both* men's and women's attitudes toward redistributive policies, *as well as* ideological beliefs. We discuss how aspects of employment settings, specifically their treatment of gender inequality, might influence which social identity, comparison choice, and identity motives are most salient and meaningful when men and women evaluate the favorability of redistributive policies and express related ideological beliefs. We suggest that the presence of affirmative action and comparable worth policies in an employment setting promotes different self-categorizations and comparison types than do employment settings that do not adhere to these policies. Because different self-categorizations and comparison types can lead to different beliefs regarding the magnitude, legitimacy, and stability of discrepancies in employment outcomes, the presence or absence of redistributive policies in a workplace will inevitably affect beliefs regarding the necessity of the policies. Organizations that fail to formally address gender discrimination reinforce people's tendencies to self-categorize at the individual level, make interpersonal comparisons, and focus on personal rather than their group's interests. In contrast, organizations with gender-based redistributive policies are likely to stimulate people to self-categorize in terms of their gender, make intergroup comparisons, and focus on their group's interests rather than self interests. Although the process of evaluating redistributive policies may make group membership salient and lead people to respond on the basis of their group interests (see Crosby, 2004), we suggest this tendency will be especially likely for those who have direct experience with redistributive policies because such experience highlights the implications the policies have for their gender group's interests. In addition, our goal in this chapter is to elucidate how this contextual factor can contribute to variations in policy beliefs within groups as well as between groups.

We begin by considering how the presence or absence of affirmative action and comparable worth policies in employment settings prompts specific self-categorizations. We then discuss how self-categorizations affect comparison processes and how these comparisons in turn shape policy attitudes and related ideological beliefs. Next, we consider how cultural beliefs become reproduced within organizational settings and influence categorization and comparison processes within these organizations. Finally, we present data in which we test the effects of policy experience on men's and women's policy support and beliefs about inequality. We conclude with a discussion of how our findings relate to self-categorization and social comparison theories.

Social identity, self-categorization, and group interests

Self-categorization theory holds that people's responses to justice are contingent on the specific categorization that is salient and relevant within a given context (Turner *et al.*, 1987). How people perceive themselves will have considerable impact on how they understand and respond to social issues such as inequality (Schmitt, Branscombe *et al.*, 2003). In some instances, people will focus on the individual or personal aspects of their identity when determining the fairness of their outcomes; however, many situations highlight the social dimensions of identity, or those aspects of the self that are associated with membership in important and self-relevant groups (Tajfel and Turner, 1986). It is in these instances that social identity, rather than personal identity, will guide people's perceptions of justice. Whether people's appraisals of justice reflect personal interest or group interest will, accordingly, depend upon which level of categorization – personal or social – is most accessible or relevant to them when making their judgments (Schmitt, Branscombe *et al.*, 2003). How justice relates to one's group interests will also depend upon the specific group membership that is salient (e.g., gender or race) and whether existing circumstances benefit or harm the group's identity (Tajfel and Turner, 1986; Turner *et al.*, 1987; Oakes, Haslam, and Turner, 1994). This argument suggests, for example, that a white Canadian woman's attitudes toward redistributive policies will vary depending upon whether her employment context encourages her to think of herself as an individual, a woman, or a white Canadian. In all these cases, the woman's sense of self should lead to a different understanding of how the policies relate to her. She should then respond to the policies accordingly. Indeed, past research (Dubé and Guimond, 1986; Guimond and Dubé-Simard, 1983; Postmes, Branscombe, Spears, and Young, 1999) indicates that when personal identity is salient, people respond in more self-serving than group-serving ways. In contrast, when group identities are salient, people respond to these policies in line with their social identity motives – or group interests (i.e., they work to enhance or protect their ingroup's current position), but not their personal identity concerns – or self interests (see also Branscombe, Spears, Ellemers, and Doosje, 2002). Because low- and high-status groups differ in their socio-structural position, they form oppositional interests. Consequently, members of high- and low-status groups will show the greatest discrepancy in beliefs about inequality and support for corrective measures when the context leads them to define themselves in terms of their social identity and focus on their group rather than their personal self interests (Postmes *et al.*, 1999). We suggest that the contextual cues that prompt people to think in terms of their gender group membership and focus on their group interests are especially likely to be present in organizations that implement affirmative action and comparable worth policies.

Self-categorization theory holds that people will categorize in terms of a social identity when the particular categorization "fits," or is meaningful within the current social context (Oakes, 1987). Fit is determined by the extent to which variations across group membership relate to variations on the focal dimension. If differences on the dimension are perceived to be greater between-groups than within-groups, and the group-based differences are in the expected direction, then the social categorization fits – or is meaningful within – the current context. The relationship between social contextual fit and social categorization is illustrated in a study by Hogg and Turner (1987) who found that participants in a discussion group were more likely to identify in terms of their gender when disagreement on an issue occurred between mixed-sex versus same-sex dyads. Because the correlation between a focal dimension and gender may not always be as clear in daily experiences as it was in that study, other contextual cues may be necessary before a categorization fits the context. For example, as indicated by the stereotype threat literature, beliefs about men's and women's relative math ability might not be meaningful in a math context unless both genders are present (see Inzlicht and Ben-Zeev, 2000) or the relationship between math and gender has been accentuated in some other way (for a review see Steele, Spencer, and Aronson, 2002).

Organizations that implement gender-based redistributive policies make the relationship between gender and reward outcomes clearly salient. Because one key purpose of the policies is to correct for discriminatory practices that disadvantage women and advantage men, organizations that implement the policies in effect acknowledge that employment outcomes are not independent of gender. Moreover, by implementing affirmative action policies, organizations attempt to balance the effects of gender by formally including gender in resource allocations to improve women's opportunities relative to men. Comparable worth differs from affirmative action in that its purpose is to remove the effects of gender from pay structures and ensure that wages are determined on the basis of skill, job responsibility, and qualifications rather than gender. Companies that implement comparable worth policies are required to revaluate women's jobs relative to men's jobs; consequently, these policies make gender a relevant and predominant aspect of men's and women's employment outcomes. Because both affirmative action and comparable worth policies emphasize gender in employment allocations and differentially affect women's and men's interests, their presence in an organization might lead people to develop greater awareness of their gender group's interests, discuss their opinions of the policies more openly and frequently, and become more aware of the gendered nature of policy support. Therefore, we suggest that for men and women who have experience with the policies, gender is more easily accessible and meaningful (i.e., has greater fit) when they express their opinions about redistributive policies than it is for those who have not had experience with the policies. Consequently men and women with policy experience should respond more in line with their group interests compared to men and women without such experience.

Although a salient social identity can heighten people's awareness and concern about their group interests, there are other factors that contribute to whether or not people choose to favor their group's interests. For example, Tajfel and Turner (1979) proposed that people will engage in strategies to promote a positive social identity when the ingroup is central to their self-definition, an intergroup comparison with the salient outgroup is relevant and meaningful, and existing status differences are contestable. The latter two factors emphasize the interactive roles of social identity and social comparison processes: when comparative differences between groups are unstable and illegitimate, a salient social identity can foster intergroup comparisons, which leads to intergroup competition (Tajfel, 1975). However, if comparative differences between the groups are seen as stable and legitimate, people will then focus on interpersonal rather than intergroup competition.

Social identity and comparison processes

Festinger (1954) argued that social experience is fundamentally comparative: because absolute standards are seldom available, people learn to rely on relative standards (i.e., how well they do in comparison to others) in order to assess their attitudes and achievements. Festinger's proposition has been well supported by research demonstrating that people are less concerned with their absolute level of outcomes than they are with their life outcomes relative to the comparison standards that are encouraged by the social environment (for reviews see Diener, 1984; Major, 1994). In this chapter, we use social comparison theory to understand the basis of judgments about redistributive policies and related ideological beliefs. We propose that contextual shifts in comparison standards that influence perceptions of employment outcomes will also influence people's responses to the social policies and ideologies that change or sustain these outcomes (see also Tougas and Beaton, 2002).

Research concerning relative deprivation, (Dubé and Guimond, 1986; Guimond and Dubé-Simard, 1983), wage satisfaction (Crosby, 1982), perceived discrimination (Postmes *et al.*, 1999), pay entitlement (Desmarais and Curtis; 1997a; Major, 1994), and mobility concerns (see Ellemers, 1993) all verify that responses to inequality depend on the nature of the self-comparisons that flow from various self-definitions. For example, women report less entitlement, perceive less discrimination, favor individual over collective mobility strategies, and express less wage dissatisfaction when they make personal-level comparisons rather than intergroup comparisons. For this reason, we expect that men and women who work in employment contexts that foster personal- rather than group-level comparisons will not differ in their endorsement of redistributive policies and ideologies that justify inequality. Differences between women and men in policy support and ideological beliefs will *only* be evident when they work in employment environments that promote group-level categorizations and comparisons. These intergroup processes are possibly limited to organizational settings in which gender is clearly associated with reward allocations (e.g., those where gender-based policies are known to be present).

When group-based comparisons are *not* made meaningful within an environment, the default tendency appears to be for people to think in individualistic terms and rely on personal-level comparisons. Indeed, research demonstrates that when the context prompts social comparisons with others, women and men choose to make interpersonal (or intragroup) comparisons and assess their employment outcomes relative to same-gender others even if opposite-sex and combined-sex wage comparison options are available (Major and Forcey, 1985; Major and Testa, 1989). When social comparison alternative others are absent from the social context, people tend to rely on *intra*personal comparisons and compare their present outcomes with their own past or expected future outcomes (Desmarais and Curtis, 1997a; 2001). Although there is some disagreement about which standard people will tend to draw on – intragroup or intrapersonal – entitlement theorists generally agree that because gender inequality advantages men and disadvantages women, biases in comparison choices contribute to women's lower sense of entitlement relative to men (e.g., Desmarais and Curtis, 1997a; Major, 1994).

There are a number of reasons why people will rely on intragroup or intrapersonal comparisons in many employment settings. First, people tend to choose the comparison option that is most physically salient and perceived as most similar to self (Festinger, 1954; see Major, 1994). Interpersonal comparisons are often preferred because the most similar and proximal comparison choice is oneself (Desmarais and Curtis, 1997a; 1997b). However, when social comparisons are available within the social environment, similarity and proximity may lead people to make intragroup comparisons (see Major, 1994). Ingroup members are more likely than outgroup members to be perceived as similar to oneself on group-defining dimensions; such self-categorization results in the perception of within group similarity relative to between groups (Oakes *et al.*, 1994). Social structural factors also play a role in perceived similarity and the accessibility of comparison options. Societal stereotypes that ascribe different employment-related abilities and expectations to women compared to men encourage individuals to look to their own gender group when trying to assess how well they are doing in the workplace (Major, 1994). Because of occupational gender segregation and wage discrimination, people are more likely to be employed in similar positions and earn similar wages as other members of their gender group, which makes intragroup comparisons more self-relevant and salient (Major, 1994; Redersdorff, Martinot, and Branscombe, 2004).

We propose that personal-level biases are especially pronounced in employment environments that sustain the status quo by failing to implement policies that reduce gender differences in employment outcomes. In these settings, men and women are likely to be more discrepant in terms of wages and occupations than they are in settings that implement formal measures to reduce differences between men and women. If occupational and wage similarity encourage personal-level comparisons, then the greater the magnitude of gender employment discrepancies the more likely intragroup or intrapersonal comparisons will be perceived as relevant and preferred, and intergroup comparisons will be avoided (see also Festinger, 1954; Chapter 15, this volume). Conversely, when the discrepancy is small or reduced, intergroup comparisons should be more likely. Research by Crosby (1982) provides some support for this proposition: although women in low prestige jobs avoided comparing their employment outcomes with men and almost exclusively named female comparison referents, this tendency was reduced among women in high prestige "male-typed" occupations (e.g., dentist and lawyer) who named male comparison referents 40 percent of the time. These findings suggest that as opportunity differences between men and women decrease, women will perceive intergroup comparisons as more self-relevant.

Crosby's (1982) and others' observation that women draw heavily on intragroup (Major and Forcey, 1985; Major and Testa, 1989) or intrapersonal (Desmarais and Curtis, 1997a; 2001) comparisons is disturbing. As noted by these theorists, in systems of inequality, personal-level comparison biases lead women and men to use very different referent standards when assessing their satisfaction with their outcomes. Consequently, personal-level comparisons suppress women's sense of entitlement (see Desmarais and Curtis, 1997a, 2001; Major, 1994), awareness of gender discrimination (Postmes *et al.*, 1999), and interest in collective change (Dubé and Guimond, 1986). If women who work in organizations without redistributive policies rely more on personal-level comparisons and use lower standards than do women who work in settings that promote gender equality, then those women who experience the greatest gender discrepancies in outcomes may actually be the ones who are most satisfied, despite their objective disadvantage. Indeed, Crosby (1982) found that the lower-paid women in her sample who made intragroup comparisons reported greater satisfaction with their employment outcomes than did the higher-paid women who compared themselves to men.

Thus far, we have suggested that an organization's decision to implement or not implement corrective policies will have profound psychological consequences for women and men through their effects on self-categorization and comparison processes. Drawing on self-categorization and social comparison theories, we argued that intragroup biases and their consequences are likely to be pronounced in settings that lack affirmative action and comparable worth policies, but that they will be attenuated in settings that include redistributive policies. In the next section we further explore the effects that the presence or absence of redistributive policies has on policy and ideological beliefs by focussing on the different cultural norms that are reflected in organizations, depending upon their response to gender inequality. We suggest that through the practices they embrace, organizations communicate values concerning resource allocations that influence how people self-define when they consider employment outcomes and the policies that affect the employment status quo. Because organizations are influenced by the greater socio-cultural environment in which they operate, we suggest that standard employment practices will reflect the dominant ideology about resource allocations, which advances individualistic representation of self.

The contextual nature of organizational cultures

Individualistic ideology is ubiquitous in Western societies, despite the prevailing contradictions presented by the continuation of group-based wage and wealth disparity. Although there are many variations of how individualism is conceived and measured (e.g., in terms of the Protestant work ethic, meritocratic beliefs, or conservatism), all conceptualizations of individualism emphasize the individual as the unit of analysis in reward allocations: individuals are responsible for their material and social outcomes because access to societal rewards is a function of self-reliance and individual merit (effort and ability). This focus on individual responsibility in employment outcomes has been adopted in many organizational settings. Organizations have a long history of treating employees as individuals and placing primacy on the individual person in terms of employment possibilities, earning potential, and mobility opportunities (see Haslam, 2001). Because these individualistic representations of reward allocations associate employment outcomes with unique properties of individuals, they encourage men and women in employment settings to self-categorize as individuals and focus on their self interests (Tajfel and Turner, 1986). This tendency is likely to be accentuated in organizations that accept individualistic notions of resource allocations. Ironically, when organizations integrate individualistic, "group-neutral" principles (e.g., color-blind or gender-blind ideologies) into their salary and hiring practices without correcting for existing structural inequalities, they reproduce (or stabilize) and legitimize group-based inequalities. To the extent that these organizations emphasize individual responsibility for employment outcomes, they also promote conceptions of status boundaries between groups as permeable to individual mobility. In contrast, organizations that formally integrate corrective measures into their employment practices with the aim of reducing gender-based discrepancies are likely to encourage self-definition in terms of gender group membership. Moreover, the very presence of redistributive policies in an organization implies that status boundaries between women and men are illegitimate and may be impermeable to individual effort. Because the policies seek to reduce intergroup disparities, people exposed to these policies feasibly also perceive status difference as unstable, or open to change. The differing effects that the presence or absence of redistributive policies has on beliefs about status differences is important because these beliefs have significant implications for how people respond to inequality.

Social identity theory (Tajfel, 1978; Tajfel and Turner, 1979, 1986) argues that people's responses to social inequality depend on whether they conceive of movement across status boundaries as individually or collectively determined. When individuals subscribe to social mobility beliefs and regard status boundaries as permeable to individual effort, they will dissociate from the group and engage in individual mobility strategies. Conversely, when individuals adopt social change beliefs and perceive status boundaries as impermeable to individual effort, they will engage in collective strategies to overcome status differences. According to Tajfel (1978), low-status groups develop social change beliefs when they encounter objectively rigid systems of inequality that they perceive as illegitimate and unstable. Under these conditions, low-status groups will support collective efforts to reduce intergroup boundaries. We expect then, that when status differences between the gender groups are perceived as illegitimate and unstable, women will support gender-based redistributive policies and reject ideologies that justify inequality. The opposite may be true of high-status groups such as men. When gender-based status differences are perceived as insecure and the employment environment constructs them as illegitimate, men should collectively engage in strategies to protect *against* social change. In this case, men should be strongly opposed to redistributive policies relative to women and endorse individualistic ideologies that justify the gender status quo. In contrast, men may show similar support for redistributive policies as women do when the status differences between groups are secure because under these conditions men can afford to show magnanimity and support women's cause (see Platow *et al.*, 1999). Women and men may similarly endorse individualistic ideologies and support redistributive policies when they subscribe to social mobility beliefs and regard intergroup boundaries as permeable because these beliefs will lead to a mutual "motivation to climb the organizational hierarchy" (Schmitt, Ellemers *et al.*, 2003, p. 282). Predictions derived from social identity theory concerning the roles of social mobility beliefs versus social change beliefs have been well-supported empirically, especially among low-status groups (see Branscombe and Ellemers, 1998; Ellemers, 1993; Simon, Hastedt, and Aufderheide, 1997).

Summary of theoretical argument

Social identity theory and self-categorization theory hold that the social context can influence how people perceive and respond to social inequality. We have argued that employment contexts without gender-based redistributive policies differ from employment contexts with those policies in ways that have profound psychological implications. As summarized in Table 7.1, the absence of redistributive policies in an organizational setting promotes individualistic norms, makes personal identity and self-interests salient and meaningful, emphasizes intragroup similarity, and minimizes the relevance of outgroup comparisons. Consequently, men and women will think in terms of their individual identity and make personal level comparisons, which will lower women's sense of wage entitlement and awareness of discrimination. Moreover, both men and women will be likely to perceive status differences as permeable, legitimate, and stable, which leads to a focus on individual mobility strategies. The overall result will be a tendency for women and men to similarly endorse both ideologies that justify the status quo and redistributive social policies. In contrast, settings with redistributive policies in place promote egalitarian norms, make group identity and group

Table 7.1. *The effects of the presence or absence of redistributive policies in organizational settings on self perception, perceptions of structural inequality, and policy support*

	Employment setting	
	Without redistributive policies	With redistributive policies
Salient norms/ideology	Individualistic norms	Egalitarian norms
Identity salience	Personal identity salient	Group identity salient
Identity concerns	Concern with group-interests	Concern with self-interests
Perceptual consequences	Intragroup similarity	Outgroup seen as comparable
Relevance comparison	Outgroup seen as irrelevant	Outgroup seen as relevant
Self-categorization	Individual identity	Social identity
Comparison preferences	Personal-level comparisons	Intergroup comparisons
Perceived wage entitlement	Women lower than men	Women equal to men
Awareness of discrimination	Less awareness	Greater awareness
Perceptions of status-boundaries	Permeable/legitimate/stable	Impermeable/illegitimate/unstable
Belief structure	Social mobility beliefs	Social change beliefs
Behavioural consequences	Individual mobility strategies	Collective mobility strategies
Policy support	No gender differences	Men less supportive than women
Ideological beliefs	Minimal gender differences	Men express greater neosexism and meritocratic beliefs

interests salient, and highlight the relevance of outgroup comparisons. Employees, therefore, will tend to think in terms of their gender and make intergroup comparisons. Consequently, women will feel entitled to equal employment outcomes as men, be more aware of discrimination, and perceive status relations as impermeable, illegitimate, and unstable. The overall result will be that in settings without policies, women will support, and men will oppose, redistributive policies that benefit women. Men will also be motivated to endorse ideologies that help protect their advantaged position. In sum, we expected that the presence or absence of redistributive policies would influence ideological beliefs and policy support within groups as well as between groups. In the next section, we outline how this proposition was tested in a community sample of women and men.

Consequences of experience with redistributive policies

To test our hypotheses concerning the impact of different organizational settings on ideological and policy attitudes, we asked patrons of two public institutions in Ontario, Canada to complete a survey about "perceptions of fairness in regards to monetary and social rewards" (Garcia, Desmarais, Branscombe, and Gee, in press). The first section of the survey asked participants whether they had worked for a company that implemented (a) affirmative action and (b) comparable worth policies. We analyzed the data from the 175 men and women who either answered "yes" or "no/don't know" to both questions. Because the Canadian Employment Equity Act (Department of Justice Canada, 2003) requires employers to inform employees about the presence, purpose, and outcomes of the policies, individuals who have worked for companies with the policies have some knowledge of the policies' implications for their gender group. Thus, we regarded participants who reported that they had worked for companies with affirmative action and comparable worth as an indicator that they had experience with the policies and their effects. In contrast, we considered those who responded "no" or "don't know" as not having experience with the policies or their implications. Therefore, we had four groups of participants in a 2 (participant gender: men or women) $\times$ 2 (policy experience: experience or no experience) between-subjects factorial design.

After indicating their policy experience, participants completed the Perceptions of Meritocracy Inventory (PMI: Garcia, Pancer, Desmarais, and Jackson, 2005) and Neosexism Scale (Tougas et al., 1995). The 17-item PMI (alpha = .85) assesses beliefs that societal rewards are allocated on the basis of individual merit with items such as: "People's wages depend on how well they do their jobs," "Success is possible for anyone who is willing to work hard enough," and "All people have equal opportunity to succeed." The 11-item Neosexism Scale (alpha = .81) assesses contemporary sexism, or the tendency to deny the existence of gender discrimination and includes the items: "Discrimination in the labour force is no longer a problem in Canada," "Women's requests in terms of equality between the sexes are simply exaggerated," and "In past years women have gotten more from government than they deserve."

Following completion of the ideology measures, participants responded to five statements regarding their attitudes toward two types of gender-based redistributive policies – affirmative action (alpha = .78) and comparable worth (alpha = .78). These statements were adapted from Tougas and her colleagues (1995) and assessed participants' beliefs that the policies were favorable, prevented future discrimination, gave unfair advantage to women, corrected for past discrimination, or prevented companies from rewarding individual merit. High scores reflected positive attitudes toward the policies. To emphasize the distinction between affirmative action and comparable worth, we provided participants with a brief description of each policy. Participants read that affirmative action was a hiring policy designed to ensure that women "who are often underrepresented in specific jobs are hired at various levels in a company based on their actual availability in the candidacy pool." That is, we described affirmative action as a quota-based policy that gives preferential treatment to women in hiring procedures and clearly adds group membership into employment decisions. In contrast, participants read that comparable worth was "designed to ensure that pay structures are based on skill and ability rather than gender." Therefore we described comparable worth as a remuneration policy that removed the influence of gender from employment outcomes.

We analyzed responses on the Neosexism and PMI measures as a function of participants' gender and experience with the policies. The analyses for Neosexism produced a main effect of gender and both measures produced a significant Participant Gender x Policy Experience interaction. As illustrated in Figures 7.1 and 7.2, this interaction was driven by the tendency for men with policy experience to express stronger neosexist and meritocratic beliefs in comparison to experienced women and inexperienced men. Although men's responses on these measures differed as a function of their policy experience, women's did not: women expressed similar meritocratic and neosexist beliefs regardless of whether or not they had experience with affirmative action and comparable worth.

We next analyzed the effects of participant gender and policy experience on attitudes toward both affirmative action and comparable worth, with age, education, political affiliation, and the interaction between the latter two variables as covariates. We included these covariates to remain

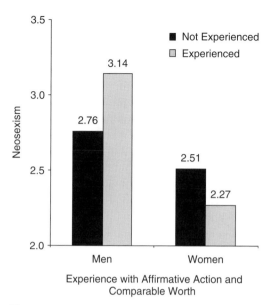

Figure 7.1. Mean responses on the perceptions of meritocracy inventory

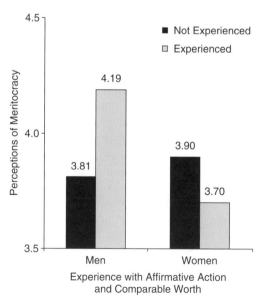

Figure 7.2. Mean responses on the neosexism measures

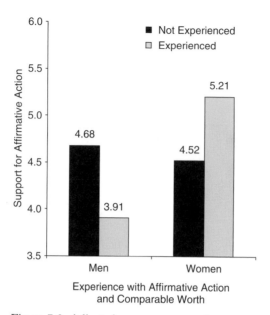

Figure 7.3. Adjusted mean responses for support of affirmative action after controlling for participants' age, education, political orientation, and education × political orientation

consistent with past, related research (e.g., Bobo, 1998). The analyses on the redistributive policy measures produced main effects of gender, which were qualified by significant gender by experience interactions. As shown in Figures 7.3 and 7.4, men and women without policy experience were equally favorable to the policies, whereas women with policy experience were significantly more supportive of the policy than were men with the same experience. We also found effects of policy experience within gender. Women with policy experience were more supportive of the policies than were their inexperienced counterparts. In contrast, men with policy experience were less supportive of both policies than were men who lacked this experience. (For further details of this study, see Garcia *et al.*, in press.)

Overall our findings indicate that policy awareness moderates men's and women's ideological beliefs and attitudes toward both affirmative action and comparable worth. However, because our data are correlational, we must consider whether pre-existing differences between those with and without policy experience account for our findings. For this to be the case, one would expect a main effect of policy experience, which we did not find. We also controlled for the most obvious pre-existing differences by including age, education, political orientation, and the interaction between

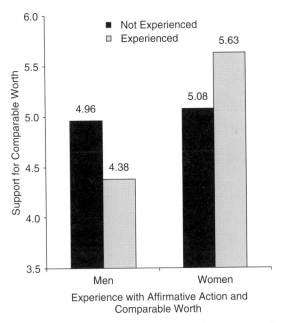

Figure 7.4. Adjusted mean responses for support of comparable worth after controlling for participants' age, education, political orientation, and education × political orientation

education and political orientation as covariates in the policy analyses. A second concern raised by our correlational data is the possibility of reverse causality: that *opposition* led men and *support* led women to be more sensitive to the presence of redistributive policies in their workplace setting. Although it is conceivable that strong attitudes could increase awareness of the presence of the policies, we argue that both strong opposition and strong support should similarly increase sensitivity to the presence of redistributive policies, regardless of gender. We did not find this to be true: scores on the policy measures did not predict whether people reported experience with the redistributive policies, independent of gender.

Implications for organizational psychology

Consistent with recent experimental research (Branscombe *et al.*, 2002; Schmitt, Branscombe, Silvia, Garcia, and Spears, in press), our findings suggest that social comparison at different levels of analysis may generate distinctly different outcomes. We found no gender differences in policy attitudes among those men and women without policy experience, a context in which personal identity and intragroup or interpersonal comparisons are likely. Conversely, among those with policy experience, social identity and intergroup social comparisons are likely to be activated. In this context, we found, as expected, strong gender differences in policy attitudes with men being sharply against redistributive social policies compared to women.

There is some irony in our findings. They suggest that women may be less satisfied with their collective situation in employment environments that attempt to improve women's circumstances compared to settings that disregard and even perpetuate women's disadvantage. However, dissatisfaction and feeling relatively deprived is necessary for women or other low-status group members to develop collective concern on behalf of their group and challenge unfairness (Crosby, 1982). Increased intergroup competition from women and the presence of redistributive policies that reduce men's advantages will also increase men's dissatisfaction and experience of collective threat (Tougas *et al.*, 1995). Therefore, intergroup conflict and the tensions between men and women will be more evident in organizations with system-changing policies than in settings that perpetuate the employment status quo. However, this intergroup tension may dissipate as gender relations become more balanced, with women feeling fairly treated and men no longer feeling they have an advantaged position to protect. In other words, intergroup relations may need to get worse, before they get better.

If both genders are dissatisfied and intergroup competition is enhanced as a result of redistributive policies in an employment environment, then one could argue that such policies promote conflict and are damaging to the productivity and collective well-being of the organization. This argument, however, overlooks two important factors. First, conflict – whether it is interpersonal or intergroup – need not be seen in solely negative terms. Research suggests that some intra-organizational competition will have positive psychological effects on creativity and reasoning and lead to social innovation (Haslam, 2001; Turner, 2005). Second, conflict is not limited to organizational contexts that stimulate intergroup competition. Rather, interpersonal conflict is often intense in individualistic employment environments that emphasize individual achievement, because these environments motivate people to further their self-interests over the interests of their fellow workers (Morris, Avilia, and Allen, 1993). As demonstrated by Morris and colleagues, excessive interpersonal conflict can be damaging to organizational productivity because such conflict plausibly detracts from the collective achievement of the team. In organizations that foster individualistic achievement orientation, workers tend to pursue their personal goals over the collective interests of the organization and are reluctant to contribute to teamwork unless their individual efforts are recognized. Without individual recognition, these employees will engage in "social loafing" and attempt to realize their personal goals by relying on the efforts of others. Thus, organizations have a dilemma: if conflict can be both positive and negative, how can organizations optimize productivity?

The solution may be quite simple. Research indicates that employment environments that encourage *both* competition and cooperation are the most productive (see Haslam, 2001). Cooperation is enhanced when organizations encourage employees to categorize at the collective level and focus on their common organizational identity. Both interpersonal and intergroup tensions can be lessened when people recategorize in terms of a common identity (Gaertner, Rust, Dovidio, Bachman, and Anastasio, 1994), which can induce employees to work for the collective well-being of the organization and appreciate the positively distinct aspects of their organizational identity. Organizations can develop positive identities relative to other organizations by implementing redistributive policies and emphasizing the distinctive ways in which they ensure equal opportunity, a principle highly valued in Western cultures (Sears *et al.*, 2000). Egalitarianism in organizational settings may also improve relations to the extent that diverse individuals working together are "equal team members" with equal standing in the work-team. Equal status relations in diverse settings can reduce intergroup conflict and promote cooperation on collaborative efforts (Gaertner *et al.*, 1994; see Haslam, 2001). Moreover, organizations benefit from diversity if they capitalize on the diverse talents and perspectives available in their workforce (Schneider and Northcraft, 1999). Because these benefits appear to be limited to organizational settings that advocate both cooperation and competition, productivity is likely to be enhanced in organizations that permit the expression of both organizational and group-based identities (Gaertner *et al.*, 1994; see Haslam, 2001). Hence, the most productive organizations are feasibly those that implement redistributive policies and encourage group-level categorizations, but temper the resulting intergroup conflict by providing opportunities for employees to also categorize at the collective level. Perhaps this view is optimistic, but it may be worthwhile to examine empirically whether organizations that implement such policies can reduce conflict by enhancing collective group identities.

Conclusion

We have outlined a number of reasons why employment settings that include redistributive policies in their hiring and wage practices will stimulate different self-categorizations and self-comparison processes and convey different information about status relations than will employment settings without these policies. Although social identity and self-categorization theories provide a theoretical framework that corroborates these proposed effects, we do not directly test whether organizations' treatment of gender inequality shape self-categorizations, comparison processes, and beliefs about status relations, which in turn influence ideological and policy beliefs. Future research could profitably examine how the presence or absence of redistributive policies in organizational settings influences policy beliefs vis-à-vis self-categorization, comparison processes, and beliefs about status relations (i.e., permeability, stability, and legitimacy).

References

AFL-CIO American Federation of Labor and Congress of Industrial Organizations (2004). It's time for working women to earn equal pay. Retrieved December 12, 2004, from http://www.aflcio.org/issuespolitics/women/equalpay/

Bobo, L. (1998). Race, interests, and beliefs about affirmative action: Unanswered questions and new directions. *American Behavioral Scientist*, *41*, 985–1003.

Bobocel, D. R., Son Hing, L. S., Davey, L. M., Stanley, D. J., and Zanna, M. P. (1998). Justice-based opposition to social policies: Is it genuine? *Journal of Personality and Social Psychology*, *75*, 653–669.

Branscombe, N. R. and Ellemers, N. (1998). Coping with group-based discrimination: Individualistic versus group-level strategies. In J. K. Swim and C. Stangor (eds.), *Prejudice: The target's perspective* (pp. 244–267). New York, NY: Academic Press.

Branscombe, N. R., Spears, R., Ellemers, N., and Doosje, B. (2002). Intragroup and intergroup evaluation effects on group behavior. *Personality and Social Psychology Bulletin*, *28*, 744–753.

Crosby, F. J. (1982). *Relative deprivation and working women*. New York: Oxford University Press.

(2004). *Affirmative action is dead: Long live affirmative action*. New Haven, CT: Yale University Press.

Department of Justice Canada (2003). Available from Part I Employment Equity: Employer Obligations Website, http://laws.justice.gc.ca/en/E-5.401/49886.html#rid-49922.

Desmarais, S. and Curtis, J. (1997a). Gender and perceived pay entitlement: Testing for effects of experience with income. *Journal of Personality and Social Psychology*, *72*, 141–150.

(1997b). Gender differences in pay histories and views on payment entitlement among university students. *Sex Roles*, *37*, 623–642.

(2001). Gender and perceived income entitlement among full-time workers: Analyses for Canadian National Samples, 1984 and 1994. *Basic and Applied Social Psychology*, *23*, 169–181.

Diener, E. (1984). Assessing subjective well-being: Progress and opportunities. *Social Indicators Research*, *31*, 103–157.

Dubé, L. and Guimond, S. (1986). Relative deprivation and social protest: The personal-group issue. In J. M. Olson, C. P. Herman, and M. P. Zanna (eds.), *Relative Deprivation and Social Comparison: The Ontario Symposium* (Vol. 4., pp. 201–216). Hillsdale, NJ: Erlbaum.

Ellemers, N. (1993). The influence of socio-structural variables on identity management strategies. In W. Stroebe and M. Hewstone (eds.), *European Review of Social Psychology* (Vol. 4, pp. 27–58). New York: Wiley.

Festinger, L. (1954). A theory of social comparison processes. *Human Relations*, *7*, 117–140.

Gaertner, S. L., Rust, M. C., Dovidio, J. F., Bachman, B. A., and Anastasio, P. A. (1994). The role of a common ingroup identity on reducing intergroup bias. *Small Group Research*, *25*, 224–249.

Garcia, D. M., Desmarais, S., Branscombe, N. R., and Gee, S. S. (in press). Opposition to redistributive employment policies for women: The role of policy experience and group interest. *British Journal of Social Psychology*.

Garcia, D. M., Pancer, S. M., Desmarais, S., and Jackson, L. M. (2005). *The perceptions of meritocracy inventory: Assessing beliefs that societal rewards are allocated on the basis of merit.* Manuscript in preparation.

Guimond, S. and Dubé-Simard, L. (1983). Relative deprivation theory and the Quebec nationalist movement: The cognition-emotion distinction and the personal-group deprivation issue. *Journal of Personality and Social Psychology*, *44*, 526–535.

Haslam, S. A. (2001). *Psychology in organizations: The social identity approach.* London: Sage.

Hogg, M. A. and Turner, J. C. (1987). Intergroup behaviour, self-stereotyping and the salience of social categories. *British Journal of Social Psychology*, *26*, 325–340.

Inzlicht, M. and Ben-Zeev, T. (2000). A threatening intellectual environment: Why females are susceptible to experiencing problem-solving deficits in the presence of males. *Psychological Science*, *11*, 365–371.

Major, B., (1994). From social inequality to personal entitlement: The role of social comparisons, legitimacy appraisals, and group membership. In M. P. Zanna (ed.), *Advances in Experimental Social Psychology* (Vol. 26, pp. 293–355). New York: Academic Press.

Major, B. and Forcey, B. (1985). Social comparisons and pay evaluations: Preferences for same-sex and same-job comparisons. *Journal of Experimental Social Psychology*, *21*, 393–405.

Major, B. and Testa, M. (1989). Social comparison processes and judgments of entitlement and satisfaction. *Journal of Experimental Social Psychology*, *25*, 101–120.

Morris, M. H., Avila, R. A., and Allen, J. (1993). Individualism and the modern corporation: Implications for innovation and entrepreneurship. *Journal of Management*, *19*, 595–612.

Oakes, P. J. (1987). The salience of social categories. In J. C. Turner, M. A. Hogg, P. J. Oakes, S. D. Reicher, and M. S. Wetherell (eds.), *Rediscovering the social group: A self-categorization theory* (pp. 117–141). Oxford: Blackwell.

Oakes, P. J., Haslam, S. A., and Turner, J. C. (1994). *Stereotyping and social reality*. Oxford: Blackwell.

Platow, M. J., Durante, M., Williams, N., Garrett, M., Walshe, L., Cincotta, S., Lianos, G., and Barutchu, A. (1999). The contribution of sport fan social identity to the production of prosocial behavior. *Group Dynamics, 3*, 161–169.

Postmes, T., Branscombe, N. R., Spears, R., and Young, H. (1999). Comparative processes in personal and group judgments: Resolving the discrepancy. *Journal of Personality and Social Psychology, 76*, 320–338.

Redersdorff, S., Martinot, D., and Branscombe, N. R. (2004). The impact of thinking about group-based disadvantages or advantages on women's well-being: An experimental test of the rejection-identification model. *Current Psychology of Cognition, 22*, 203–222.

Schmitt, M. T., Branscombe, N. R., and Kappen, D. (2003). Attitudes toward group-based inequality: Social dominance or social identity? *British Journal of Social Psychology, 42*, 161–186.

Schmitt, M. T., Branscombe, N. R., Silvia, P. J., Garcia, D. M., and Spears, R. (in press). Categorizing at the group-level in response to intragroup social comparisons: A self-categorization theory integration of self-evaluation and social identity motives. *European Journal of Social Psychology*.

Schmitt, M. T., Ellemers, N., and Branscombe, N. R. (2003). Perceiving and responding to gender discrimination at work. In S. A. Haslam, D. van Knippenberg, M. Platow, and N. Ellemers (eds.), *Social identity at work: Developing theory for organizational practice* (pp. 277–292). Philadelphia, PA: Psychology Press.

Schneider, S. K. and Northcraft, G. B. (1999). Three social dilemmas of workforce diversity in organizations: A social identity perspective. *Human Relations, 52*, 1445–1467.

Sears, D. O., Henry, P. J., and Kosterman, R. (2000). Egalitarian values and contemporary racial politics. In D. O. Sears, J. Sidanius, and L. Bobo (eds.), *Racialized politics: The debate about racism in America* (pp. 75–117). Chicago: University of Chicago Press.

Simon, B., Hastedt, C., and Aufderheide, B. (1997). When self-categorization makes sense: The role of meaningful social categorization in minority and majority members' self-perception. *Journal of Personality and Social Psychology, 73*, 310–320.

Social Development Canada, Government of Canada. (2004). Available from Workplace Equity Programs Website, http://www.sdc.gc.ca/en/gateways/topics/wzp-gxr.shtml.

Steele, C. M., Spencer, S. J., and Aronson, J. (2002). Contending with group image: The psychology of stereotype and social identity threat. In L. Berkowitz (ed.), *Advances in experimental social psychology, 34*, 379–439. New York: Academic Press.

Stroh, L. K., Brett, J. M., and Reilly, A. H. (1992). All the right stuff: A comparison of female and male managers' career progression. *Journal of Applied Psychology, 77*, 251–260.

Tajfel, H. (1975). The exit of social mobility and the voice of social change. *Social Science Information*, *14*, 101–118.

(1978). *Differentiation between social groups: Studies in the social psychology of intergroup relations*. London: Academic Press.

Tajfel, H. and Turner, J. C. (1979). An integrative theory of intergroup conflict. In W. G. Austin and S. Worchel (eds.), *The social psychology of intergroup relations* (pp. 33–47). Monterey, CA: Brooks-Cole.

(1986). The social identity theory of intergroup behavior. In S. Worchel and W. G. Austin (eds.), *The psychology of intergroup relations* (pp. 7–24). Chicago: Nelson-Hall.

Tougas, F. and Beaton, A. M. (2002). Personal and relative group deprivation: Connecting the 'I' to the 'we'. In I. Walker and H. J. Smith (eds.), *Relative deprivation: Specification, development, and integration* (pp. 119–135). Cambridge: Cambridge University Press.

Tougas, F., Brown, R., Beaton, A. M., and Joly, S. (1995). Neosexism: Plus ça change, plus c'est pareil. *Personality and Social Psychology Bulletin*, *21*, 842–849.

Turner, J. C. (2005). Explaining the nature of power: A three-process theory. *European Journal of Social Psychology*, *35*, 1–22.

Turner, J. C., Hogg, M. A., Oakes, P. J., Reicher, S. D., and Wetherell, M S. (1987). *Rediscovering the social group: A self-categorization theory*. Oxford: Blackwell.

8   Social comparison and group-based emotions

Vincent Yzerbyt, Muriel Dumont, Bernard Mathieu,
Ernestine Gordijn, and Daniel Wigboldus

Social comparison is a core element of human life (Festinger, 1954; Mussweiler, 2003; Tajfel, 1981; for a collection, see Suls and Wheeler, 2000). This is because comparing oneself to others is the most favored way people use to evaluate themselves. People choose to compare themselves to others with a variety of goals in mind. Obviously, a major concern would be informational: people like to know where they stand in terms of what they think, feel, or do. Are they simply normal or do they happen to be outrageously below or above widely popular standards? Often, people also rely on social comparison to motivate themselves. If getting a kick out of the comparison is the main goal of the comparison then the comparison target is likely to be some person or some group that fares slightly better. Finally, there could also be an explicit attempt at self-enhancement. By finding comparison others who are sufficiently similar yet also somewhat less knowledgeable, strong or likeable than themselves, people make sure that they will come out of the comparison with a feeling of psychological comfort. In short, people's self-knowledge, motivation, and self-esteem crucially hang on the outcome of dozens of daily comparison operations.

Although initially used in interpersonal theory contexts, the social comparison process also comes across as a major player in an impressive series of social psychology theories that focus on intergroup relations. Prominent contributions are for instance relative deprivation theory (Crosby, 1976, 1982; Guimond and Dubé-Simard, 1983; Gurr, 1970; Runciman, 1966; Vanneman and Pettigrew, 1972; Walker and Pettigrew, 1984; for a collection, see Walker and Smith, 2002), social identity theory (Tajfel, 1981; Tajfel and Turner, 1979; Turner, 1975), and self-categorization theory (Hogg and Abrams, 1988; Oakes, Haslam and Turner, 1994; Turner et al., 1987). In all these theoretical perspectives, the selection of a particular social comparison target has been shown to exert a major influence on people's beliefs, feelings, and, indeed, behaviors.

This analysis holds particularly in the case of self-categorization theory (SCT). SCT is often presented as the direct offspring of social identity theory in that social identification holds a prime position in the theoretical apparatus. SCT is mainly concerned with the combined impact of perceivers' a priori expectations regarding their social environment (the normative fit) and the characteristics of the social stimuli in the context (the comparative fit) on the way they draw distinctions between themselves and others (Hogg and Abrams, 1988; Turner *et al.*, 1987). Depending on circumstances, the context will encourage people to appraise the social environment either in interpersonal terms, leading them to contrast themselves with other individuals, or, on the contrary, in intergroup terms, thereby triggering a so-called depersonalization process (see also Chapter 7, this volume). When people depersonalize, their self is construed in such a way that it matches the features of the other members of their group and distinguishes it from those aspects that best represent the members of the outgroup. In other words, when all is said and done, the chief idea in SCT is that people are constantly relying on comparisons to define what they are, be it as individuals or, and perhaps most importantly, as group members (Hogg, 2000).

In the present contribution, we also emphasize the role of social comparison in the development of people's cognitions and actions, much like SCT theorists have done, but we also add the emotional dimension to the picture. We do so in the context of a research program that is concerned with the possibility that people experience emotions not as individuals but indeed as group members. As we show, our empirical work provides strong evidence for the idea that people are capable of feeling emotions not on a strictly individual basis but in terms of their group membership. Importantly, because we believe that social comparison is a central aspect of people's endeavor to build an understanding of their surrounding world, our investigations led us to use social comparison as a most efficient tool in order to shape people's emotional reactions in predictable ways.

In the first section of this chapter, we provide a quick overview of the theoretical and empirical case that can be made for group-based emotions. In the second section, we offer some illustrative examples of our recent empirical work on this front. Before we conclude, our third section is devoted to a discussion of the similarities as well as some differences we see between our model of group-based emotions and research conducted under the banner of relative deprivation theory.

The case for group-based emotions

A little more than a decade ago, Smith (1993, 1999) questioned the then dominant perspective on prejudice and intergroup relations. Rather than adopting a view in which prejudice, stereotypes, and discrimination are distinguished, much in the same way as classical attitude research uses the terms emotion, cognition, and action, Smith (1993) proposed that one would do well to refer instead to the appraisal theories of emotion (Frijda, 1986; Frijda, Kuipers, and ter Schure, 1989; Roseman, 1984; Scherer, 1984, 1988). These theories provide a rich set of propositions linking cognitive appraisals, emotional reactions, and behavioral tendencies. Building upon these efforts in the domain of emotions, Smith (1993) argued that it is possible to go beyond the simplistic expectation that people's responses are feeling negatively or positively, thinking in negative or positive terms, and acting in favor of or against a target group, and account for the variety of reactions that people manifest towards social groups.

To take a simple example, the view that the members of a specific group are wealthy, intelligent, and driven, something most observers would be tempted to call a positive stereotype, is often accompanied by feelings of resentment and envy (Fiske, Cuddy, Glick, and Xu, 2002). Such a pattern is particularly tricky to explain in the unidimensional conception of traditional approaches. In contrast, the same combination poses no difficulty for appraisal theories of emotion because such descriptions of outgroup members may be accompanied by appraisals of deprivation and unjustified disparity in power and status regarding the ingroup. In sum, appraisal theories of emotion, thanks to their complex and probably more realistic description of people's reactions to events in general and social groups in particular, offer a straightforward account for patterns that are far more difficult to explain in terms of a strict continuum ranging from negative to positive.

Smith (1993) did not simply encourage scholars working on prejudice to adopt appraisal theories of emotions. He also addressed the limitation stemming from the fact that appraisal theories of emotion are cast in purely individualistic terms. Strictly speaking, appraisal theories are confined to people's experiences as individuals and have little to say regarding how they may react as members of social groups. Building upon SCT (Turner *et al.*, 1987) as well as on a series of empirical studies showing that people may indeed mentally represent closely-related others in general and the ingroup members in particular as overlapping with the self (Smith, Coats, and Walling, 1999; Smith and Henry, 1996; see also Cadinu and Rothbart, 1996; Otten and Wentura, 2001), Smith (1999) argued that observers could well experience emotions on the basis of appraisals that rest upon concerns and goals defined in social, i.e. intergroup, terms. In other words, individuals carry out a cognitive evaluation of the situation they face bearing in mind that they are group members and not just unique individuals. According to Smith, the resources and obstacles with which the group to which people belong is confronted feed the emotional experience of group members as surely as the resources and obstacles with which the individuals are confronted shape their personal emotional response.

Preliminary evidence for Smith's intergroup emotions theory comes from a series of studies by Mackie, Devos, and Smith (2000) in which the authors tested their idea that the strength of the ingroup position should influence group members' emotions and action tendencies. According to most appraisal theories of emotion, anger (fear) is likely to emerge when people face a negative event, such as a conflict, and see that they do (do not) have the necessary means to stand a fight and, eventually, prevail. Anger (fear) will then translate into action tendencies aimed at confronting (avoiding) the source of conflict. The general scenario used by Mackie *et al.* (2000) is quite straightforward. Participants are asked to specify whether they are members of a group that supports or opposes some controversial issue. They are then asked to examine information suggesting that their opinion group enjoys substantial (versus little) collective support, whereas the other group can count on little (versus substantial) support. The key dependent measures concern group identification, emotional reactions, and action tendencies.

The first study was correlational (Mackie *et al.*, 2000, Exp. 1). Once participants had self-categorized into opponents or supporters of severe punishment for drug use, they were asked to indicate the level of collective support associated with the two opinion groups in presence. They then reported their level of identification with each group. Next, they stated the extent to which the group they had designated as an outgroup made them feel angry and afraid. Finally, they specified the extent to which they wanted to act against the outgroup or move away from it. The predictions are directly concerned with the impact of group resources on individual group members' reactions. To the extent that participants see their group as enjoying many (few) resources, they should experience more anger (fear) and manifest the associated action tendencies.

As predicted, the more participants believed their group enjoyed collective support, the more they felt angry and the more they wanted to challenge the other group. Moreover, anger was found to mediate the impact of perceived collective support on the tendency to confront the other group. It is noteworthy that identification with the ingroup also predicted anger and action tendencies. Furthermore, anger partially mediated the impact of identification on offensive action tendencies. In contrast to this encouraging news regarding anger, no significant results were found for fear and its associated action tendencies.

In a second study, Mackie *et al.* (2000, Exp. 2) manipulated collective support. To do so, they had participants read and evaluate a list of nineteen headlines supposedly taken from newspapers and related to the issue at stake, i.e., whether homosexual couples in long-term relationships should benefit from the same legal rights as married heterosexuals. Whereas the vast majority of headlines (sixteen out of nineteen) supported the ingroup in the "strong-ingroup" condition, only a minority of headlines (three out of nineteen) supported the ingroup in the "weak-ingroup" condition. There was also a control condition in which participants were not presented with any headlines. As would be predicted on the basis of intergroup emotions theory, participants who were made to believe that the ingroup was in a strong (weak) position felt more (less) angry and wanted to oppose the outgroup more (less). Again, anger proved to be a mediator of the impact of collective support on the tendency to confront the outgroup. Replicating earlier findings, feelings of fear and defensive action tendencies remained impervious to the manipulation.

A third study generalized these findings to yet another issue and further showed that members on both sides in relation to an issue reacted similarly to the manipulation of collective support. Rather than fear, the authors now also looked at contempt. In line with intergroup emotions theory, Mackie and colleagues found that appraisals of ingroup strength produced offensive tendencies directed against an opponent group and that anger was a mediator. However, no evidence was found for appraisal generating emotions of contempt, precluding any mediating role to emerge for this emotion in the relation between appraisal and action tendencies.

Several comments can be made about Mackie and colleagues' empirical efforts. First, at a methodological level, we think that it would be highly desirable to include a condition in which people are not members of any of the opinion groups. In other words, it is not entirely clear to what extent the observed reactions truly qualify as group-based emotions, i.e., emotions that are caused and shaped by virtue of one's group membership, as we have no real point of comparison. One piece of correlational evidence indirectly supports this point, however. Identification with the ingroup has indeed been found to amplify the emotion of anger and, in turn, the resulting offensive action tendency (Mackie *et al.*, Exp. 1). This suggests that participants' social identity is indeed at stake. However, the fact that identification was measured only after support was considered poses a problem, and more definitive evidence on this front would be welcome.

Perhaps more strikingly, the authors selected a very specific kind of group, namely opinion groups. Members of such groups are almost by definition hostile to each other. Belonging to one group not only means that one is not a member of the other, but it is also obvious that you are opposed to the other group. The social landscape is defined in terms of two contrasting sides and good news for one group always comes as bitter information for the other group. One is thus facing a clear conflict of interests, a situation in which the level of interdependence stands extremely high. The extent to which the results can be generalized to situations in which interdependence is less negative remains unknown.

Another notable characteristic is that the emotions and action tendencies that are investigated by Mackie and colleagues all point to the outgroup as the prime target. This characteristic makes for a most interesting link with recent work in the content of stereotypes (Fiske, Cuddy, and Glick, 2002; Fiske et al., 2002; Fiske, Xu, Cuddy, and Glick, 1999). Yet it is possible that emotions may be guided by one's group membership without the need for a specific outgroup to be the focal object of the emotional experience. Any event that takes place in which people are engaged on behalf of their group membership may be triggering emotional reactions. At the extreme, events occurring within the ingroup may also be firing group-based emotions.

More crucially, we think that there are essentially two main strategies that one can embrace to provide evidence for the existence of emotions that rest on group membership. One was adopted by Smith, Mackie and colleagues and consists in changing the objective conditions faced by the group to which people belong in the hope that this will change their subjective appraisal of the situation and directly influence their feelings and action tendencies as group members. It should be noted here that one should make sure that the checks used to ascertain the success of the manipulation are clearly distinguished from the cognitive appraisal itself. Also, the cognitive appraisals discussed in most theories of emotion concern a wide variety of dimensions, and it should be useful to examine the impact of a given situation on an extensive range of cognitive appraisals in order to substantiate the model. An exclusive focus on the issue of perceived support and coping resources may constitute too limited a set of antecedents to fully predict people's emotional reactions.

The other strategy, which we implemented in our own research, addresses the self-categorization side of the phenomenon. The idea here is that when people are confronted with specific events, the way perceivers appraise the situation will be crucially influenced by group membership, which provides the lenses through which the situation is being seen. It is at this level that social comparison may exert a critical impact on the unfolding of people's emotional reactions. As it happens, it is also the sort of findings that would provide the most convincing demonstration that emotional reactions and their associated behaviors are grounded in the social identity of perceivers rather than in their personal identity. As a matter of fact, by promoting a particular approach to the social landscape, one may see observers manifest very different reactions.

Our model of group-based emotions explicitly builds on the assumption made by SCT that one of several interpretations of the social world can be promoted depending on a number of contextual and individual factors (Ellemers, Spears, and Doosje, 1999; Oakes, Haslam, and Turner, 1994; Turner *et al.*, 1987). The prediction is that observers will probably appraise an event very differently as a function of the social identity "hat" they are wearing. As a result of this differential appraisal, they will experience different feelings and emotions. This emotional experience, in turn, will translate into specific action tendencies and, eventually, in particular behaviors. Over recent years, we have conducted a number of studies aimed at testing our model of group-based emotions and have accumulated impressive evidence with respect to its unique predictions. As we will see in the next section, the issue of the social comparison is truly a cornerstone of our empirical work on this issue.

Evidence for our model of group-based emotions

When people are confronted with an event that concerns them directly, it is difficult to argue that they are experiencing an emotion rooted in their social identity. This is not to say that people are not reacting in terms of their group membership and that they are not showing intergroup emotions. However, it seems like a tedious enterprise to try and disentangle the personal level of reaction from the social one. A less ambiguous demonstration of the role of group membership in the emergence of emotional experience would come from a setting in which people would be presented with events that do not affect them directly. Negative events are ideal for this purpose. Indeed, people have often been shown to distance themselves from negative events confronted by others (Lerner, 1980). Unless people are really taking seriously their common membership with the victims of hardship (Batson, 1994) and can easily restore a sense of justice, it would seem that their preferred reaction is to blame the victims.

Even more striking is the fact that people tend to use the hardship encountered by fellow ingroup members to reassure themselves that their own lot is not as bad. This phenomenon is well-known in the discrimination literature as the person-group discrimination discrepancy (PGDD) (Crosby, 1976; Taylor, Wright, Moghaddam, and Lalonde, 1990, Taylor, Wright, and Porter, 1994): When asked about their experience of discrimination, members of a disadvantaged social group spontaneously compare themselves with other members of their ingroup so as to conclude that their own outcomes are not as bad as those of other ingroup members (Postmes, Branscombe, Spears, and Young, 1999; see also Chapter 10, this volume). Clearly, thus, discrimination research confirms that, unless they are strongly attached to their group, people are not quick to take the perspective of unfortunate others. Only when a clear intergroup comparison context imposes itself do people manifest group-based rather than person-based reactions.

The above rationale guided our empirical efforts. To ensure that we triggered group-based emotions and not simply personal emotions, we informed participants about harmful events involving protagonists, some of whom could be seen as ingroup or as outgroup members depending on the way participants thought of themselves. That is, in order to influence the bonding with the people affected by the events, we constrained the way participants approached the social landscape by having them endorse one or another of their social identities. In concrete terms, we did so by telling participants that we would *compare* their reactions as a member of a specific ingroup to the reactions of the members of other specific groups. The careful selection of the comparison context induced participants to include the victims of the harmful events in the same group as the one they themselves belonged to or, instead, encouraged them to see the victims as members of an outgroup.

It should be noted that the instructions we used never required our participants to provide us with comparative judgments. In other words, we never asked them to *compare* how they reacted and how they thought the target of the social comparison reacted. We never enquired about whether they thought they were better or worse off than some comparison group. We also avoided asking them to indicate how satisfied or happy they were with what was happening relative to some other group. Simply, by mentioning that we, as experimenters, were envisioning a study that would collect their responses as well as those of the members of a comparison group, we hoped to confine our participants into a particular social identity.

If participants' reactions prove impervious to our manipulation, then it is likely that we are facing person-based reactions. Alternatively, it could also be that a single social identity takes over in all conditions. In both cases, the outcome would be that no difference emerges as a function of the particular social comparison set forth in the instructions. If, on the contrary, the emotional reactions of our participants vary in a lawful manner as a function of the group membership we promoted by way of our social comparison manipulation, then we are in a good position to argue for the presence of group-based emotions. Specifically, we hoped the same emotional reactions would develop among our participants as the ones one would expect to see among the victims of the harmful events only to the extent that the social comparison manipulation induced participants to perceive the victims as fellow ingroup members. Quite a different picture should emerge when the social comparison setting encourages participants to see themselves and the victims as belonging to different groups. This simple yet powerful idea formed the basis of our initial series of studies (Gordijn, Wigboldus, and Yzerbyt, 2001; Gordijn, Wigboldus, Yzerbyt, and Hermsen, 1999; for a review, see Yzerbyt, Dumont, Gordijn, and Wigboldus, 2002).

Initial test of the model

In one illustrative study (Gordijn, Wigboldus, and Yzerbyt, 2001), we confronted participants, students from the University of Amsterdam, with a newspaper article. The story depicted a conflict involving students from Leiden University and the professors and Board at that same university. The latter wanted to implement a series of new policies that would greatly restrict access to the university. Students had not been consulted and strongly opposed the decisions. Mobilization was on its way. Because participants were enrolled at the University of Amsterdam, they could receive the story in a number of ways, namely as students, as people enrolled in Amsterdam, or even as individual observers. We thus decided to channel the way participants approached this conflict by warning them that we were interested in comparing the reactions either of people belonging to different universities or the reactions of students and professors. It is important to note that our social comparison manipulation took place *before* participants' confrontation with the specific story.

The predictions were straightforward. To the extent that participants see themselves as belonging to the same group as the students of Leiden, a reaction that we hoped would be triggered in the condition comparing "students versus professors", they should adopt a perspective similar to the one found among the Leiden students and feel the emotions presumably experienced by these students. In contrast, we expected participants in the condition comparing "different universities" to see themselves and the Leiden students as belonging to different groups. As a consequence, the emotions felt by our participants would be less akin to those presumably experienced by the victims. We also included a control condition in which we did not mention any other rationale for the study than our interest in participants' reactions to the story.

Turning to the dependent variables, participants were asked the extent to which they felt angry (i.e., angry, outraged, and aggressive), happy (i.e., happy, elated, and cheerful), and anxious (i.e., anxious, powerless, and helpless). As a means to check for the manipulation, participants also indicated to what extent they felt similar to students of Leiden University, and to what extent students of Leiden University and students of the University of Amsterdam are similar (averaged to create a similarity index). The predicted interaction between emotion and condition which came out was significant. Participants reported feeling more angry and less happy when they understood that the study aimed at comparing reactions of students to those of professors compared to what was observed in the two other conditions. Interestingly, and showing the discriminant validity of the emotion indices, we found no impact of our manipulation on anxiety, another negative emotion.

It is also interesting to examine the data from the control condition somewhat more closely. As it turns out, participants confronted with a negative event harming a group of people spontaneously tended to distance themselves. Of course, we have no data allowing us to know precisely how these control participants defined the social landscape but it is possible to venture at least one interpretation based on the similarity index. Even though control participants had quite a few reasons to embrace the student identity, they seem to have preferred making a distinction between themselves and the victims. Indeed, the similarity index reveals that control participants did not differ from the participants who were told that the study compared different universities. Both conditions led to lower anger and lower similarity ratings between the Leiden students and the Amsterdam students than the condition in which participants thought the study compared the reactions of students and professors. If anything, control participants felt more different from the victims than participants in any other condition. This pattern is highly reminiscent of the PGDD in that people confronted with victims potentially associated to themselves contrasted away from them.

The above study illustrates the potential impact of selecting one social comparison target rather than another. By encouraging observers to draw particular contours in their social landscape, our manipulation generated divergent patterns of emotional reactions. After this initial success, we went on to conduct several studies in order to address a number of important additional issues. Our *first question* was whether we could extend our argument about the impact of the comparison context to include the issue of action tendencies. Indeed, group-based emotion theory holds that people's emotional reactions should mediate the impact of our social comparison manipulation on action tendencies. A *second important issue* concerns the role of identification. Although we observed that the temporary salience of one identity over another affects the chain of reactions, we wanted evidence that the impact of the contextually salient category would be moderated by the degree of identification with the salient category. Such a pattern would further establish the impact of group membership on emotional reactions and, therefore, the social nature of emotions. *A third question* is whether we could find cases in which an emotion other than anger, such as fear, would show the predicted pattern. *Fourth*, a convincing demonstration of the influence of social as opposed to personal identity on cognitive appraisals, emotions, and action tendencies would be provided if one could encourage observers to embrace the perspective of the victims as well as the perspective of the perpetrators depending on the specific comparison context. *Finally*, although our social comparison manipulation influences the general profile of people's emotional reactions, it would be most compelling to show that people's consensus in emotional reactions is indeed higher when participants are thrown in the same group as the victims than when they approach the situation as individual observers or as members of some less relevant group.

Action tendencies and identification

In order to simultaneously address the mediating role of emotions on action tendencies and the moderating role of identification, we (Yzerbyt, Dumont, Wigboldus, and Gordijn, 2003) conducted a study in which French-speaking students at the University of Louvain in Louvain-la-Neuve, Belgium, learned about a conflict opposing Dutch-speaking students of the University of Ghent to their university authorities. The alleged clash revolved around the unexpected decision to impose English as the language for all Masters-level classes. As before, we relied on social comparison as a means to infuse a different social categorization in our participants *before* they were confronted with the critical event. Also before we presented them with the newspaper article, we measured participants' level of chronic identification with the group they were associated with in their specific condition, namely students in general (as compared to professors) or students from Louvain-la-Neuve (as compared to students from other universities).

Once they had read about the event, participants completed a series of scales pertaining to their emotional reactions (anger, sadness, fear, and happiness). As a specific goal of this study, we also measured their action tendencies. Three of the action tendencies were meant to concern offensive tendencies ("to intervene," "to get angry," "to set oneself against"), three were related to an absence of any reaction and crying ("to do nothing," "to lock oneself at home," "to cry"), three had to do with avoidance tendencies ("to hear no more about it," "to stop thinking about it," "to be reassured"), and three were associated with making fun about the event ("to make fun of it," "to mock it," "to be exuberant about it"). These four sets of action tendencies were selected so as to be closely related to anger, sadness, fear, and happiness, respectively.

As expected, people's emotional reactions were not only higher on anger than on any other emotion, but anger was also the only emotion that proved sensitive to our independent variables. Moreover, and in line with predictions, the pattern of reactions showed that the simultaneous presence of high identification and a group membership stressing the similarity with the victims was conducive to higher levels of anger than any of the three other combinations. In other words, when participants either were led to think of themselves as members of a different category from the victims or felt weakly identified with the category that comprised them and the victims, they reported significantly lower levels of anger.

Turning to action tendencies, initial analyses revealed the presence of three conative syndromes, namely attack, avoidance, and mockery. Clearly, offensive tendencies dominated participants' reactions, followed by avoidance and mockery. The specific categorization imposed on participants through the comparison context combined with their chronic identification lead to the production of a pattern of action tendencies that was entirely consistent with expectations. That is, participants manifested the strongest offensive action tendencies when they had been thrown in the same category as the victims and had initially expressed strong levels of identification with this category. The three other combinations did not differ from each other.

The most important objective of this study was to verify the viability of our mediational hypothesis. The idea here is that contextual categorization and chronic identification join forces in shaping participants' action tendencies via their impact on emotional reactions. In line with the recommendations spelled out by Judd and Kenny (1981) and Baron and Kenny (1986), we implemented a model in which participants, cornered into thinking of themselves as belonging to the same category as the victims (i.e., students in general) and who had expressed a high level of identification with this category, were contrasted with all other participants. This variable was not only shown to predict offensive action tendencies but its impact was significantly reduced and turned out to be non-significant when participants' emotional reactions of anger were taken into account in the model. It is important to note that we found no support for an alternative model, in which offensive action tendencies were used as a mediator for the impact of our independent variables on anger.

In sum, this study provides very strong evidence in favor of our group-based model. We were able to replicate our finding that contextual forces may indeed press people to endorse a particular identity in such a way that their emotional reactions to events are strongly influenced. In line with SCT's proposal that identification would combine with contextual forces to shape people's affective and behavioral reactions, we also extended previous work by showing the role of participants' chronic identification with the category in the emergence of emotional reactions. Finally, we collected firm evidence for the mediational role of emotions. As we expected, adopting a particular social identity does impact on action tendencies through an impact on the emotional experience.

It is also noteworthy that the specific comparison manipulation used here relied on sub-categorization rather than cross-categorization. We either put participants in the shoes of students in general or in the shoes of a subset of students, namely students from their university. In line with other work showing the impact of group boundaries on social behavior and intergroup relations (Gaertner and Dovidio, 2000), our findings show the importance of making salient a common ingroup in that people reacted much like the victims when it was made clear to them that they shared the same group membership as these victims.

Fear and behaviors

One feature of the above empirical demonstrations is that they all focussed on anger as the key emotional reaction. Moreover, we concentrated on emotions and action tendencies but did not provide any evidence for the impact of our manipulation of comparison context on actual behaviors. We addressed these two issues in a series of studies that took advantage of the infamous terrorist attacks against the World Trade Center on September 11, 2001 (Dumont, Yzerbyt, Wigboldus, and Gordijn, 2003).

One of these studies (Dumont *et al.*, Expt. 2) was conducted one week after the events and presented participants with a full-page picture of the Twin Towers burning down in order to remind participants about the event. At this stage, participants were confronted with one of two rationales for the study. Whereas in one condition they were informed that the study concerned a comparison between European and Arab respondents, those in the other condition learned that their responses as Europeans would be compared with those of American respondents. The specific social comparison was thus quite subtle in that the first implicitly defined Europeans and Americans as belonging to the same group of non-Arabs. In contrast, the second comparison made explicit the distinction between Europeans and Americans. One should add that identification with

Europeans that was measured before the presentation of the picture recalling the event was not affected by the manipulation. In addition to a set of questions aimed at tapping participants' emotional reactions and action tendencies, we also measured a series of behaviors that all involved communicating personal information in order to be contacted later on by other people than the experimenters themselves.

Our predictions were that all negative emotions would be very strong, reflecting the immensely tragic nature of the attacks. However, because of the specific appraisals associated with each of the emotions (Frijda, Kuipers, and ter Schure, 1989), we hypothesized that our participants would show some sensitivity to our manipulation, particularly with respect to fear. Specifically, we expected appraisals of sadness and anger to be impervious to the identity manipulation. In the context of September 11th, the fact that neither Europeans nor Americans could have foreseen such a tragic succession of events, along with the certainty that many people had died and suffered because of the attacks and the common belief that little if anything could be done to ever repair the damage, all are elements that should have given rise to sadness amongst both Europeans and Americans. Also, both Europeans and Americans certainly thought that military action against the various countries hosting the terrorists was a possible line of action and that the United States would be reacting to such an attack. These appraisals should have elicited anger among both Europeans and Americans. At the same time, the critical appraisals associated with fear, that is, the uncertainty attached to one's personal future and to the availability of the required coping resources to face other events of a similar nature, should be more likely to vary as a function of whether the ingroup or an outgroup is considered to be the target of the terrorist attacks.

Results confirmed that sadness and anger indeed qualified as relevant emotions as they were strongly reported by participants. These emotions, however, proved to be unaffected by the comparison context. In contrast, and in line with predictions, making salient a comparison context linking participants with victims of the harmful behavior in a common ingroup led them to report more fear than when the comparison context had them categorize the victims as outgroup members. Moreover, we found strong evidence that the comparison context influenced behavioral tendencies. Informing participants that their answers would be compared to those of Arab respondents elicited stronger tendencies to seek information about the events and how they developed, stronger tendencies to provide support and help to the victims, and stronger tendencies to talk about the events with other persons than when it was thought their answers would be compared to those of American respondents.

Finally, whether the behaviors concerned communicating personal data so as to later receive information about terrorist networks, about how to support and help the victims, or about demonstrating for NATO intervention, all proved sensitive to our manipulation. These behaviors would indeed be most relevant if one wished to reduce one's level of uncertainty, regain some subjective control over the situation, and improve self-protection. In fact, as many as 18 percent of participants led to categorize the victims in their ingroup, compared to a mere 3 percent in the other condition, communicated their e-mail address or telephone number in order to receive additional information about a demonstration for NATO intervention.

To sum up, we were able to find evidence for the fact that other emotions than anger prove sensitive to the categorization and identity changes triggered by the manipulation of the comparison context. An important point is that we also demonstrated that the impact of the comparison context extends to behavioral intentions and actual meaningful behaviors.

Victims or perpetrators To further stress the role of social categorization in the emergence of emotions, we wanted to show that the same observers could feel angry or content about a particular event as a function of the particular "social" shoes they were led to walk in. Of course, we also intended to show that our social comparison manipulation would trigger lawful differences in people's appraisal of the very same situation as well as in their behavioral intentions.

Addressing this question allows us to establish a direct link with fascinating research conducted over recent years on the topic of collective guilt. Indeed, a number of authors have started to examine more closely those conditions under which groups and group members may experience guilt and shame with respect to harmful behavior perpetrated by ingroup members on members of other groups. Perhaps the most telling studies in this respect were conducted by Doosje and his colleagues (Doosje, Branscombe, Spears, and Manstead, 1998). In one of these (Doosje *et al.*, 1998, Expt. 2), Dutch participants first completed an identification questionnaire pertaining to their identity as Dutch people. They were then confronted with one of three sets of information about the conduct of Dutch people in one of their former colonies. Depending on conditions, the information was either consistently negative, both negative and positive, or consistently positive. The dependent measures enquired about the extent to which participants felt guilty about the behavior of their fellow citizens and thought that compensation was in order. For obvious reasons, none of the participants could have any direct implication in the historical events that were presented.

Results indicated that participants in the negative conduct condition indeed felt guilty and very much wanted to compensate for their ancestors' misbehavior. The reverse pattern emerged in the positive conduct condition. The most interesting data concern the ambiguous condition. When behaviors posed by the Dutch colonial forces proved to be both positive and negative, only those participants who were not strongly identified expressed guilt and agreed to compensate. In contrast, high identifiers expressed significantly less guilt and were not ready to offer compensation for how their ancestors acted. These findings suggest that identification very much orients people's interpretation of events, even distant ones, thereby shaping their emotional reactions and willingness to engage in specific actions.

In one of our recent studies (Gordijn, Yzerbyt, Wigboldus, and Dumont, in press), our ambition was to show that the very same people could be manipulated into reacting either like victims or perpetrators. This should be possible simply by taking advantage of the existence of social identities linking people to either one of these two kinds of protagonists. Again, we counted on our social comparison manipulation to bring people to think differently about themselves and took advantage of the particular situation with which US universities are confronted, whereby out-of-state students pay more than their in-state colleagues to attend classes. Because it was notorious at the time of the study that most US states faced huge deficits, we informed in-state students from the University of Colorado at Boulder that their State House Representatives had decided to raise the tuition by 35 percent for out-of-state students. This information was conveyed *right after* we had indicated to our participants that we wanted their opinion and reactions on a series of newspaper articles either *as students* (in order to compare them with non-students) or *as Colorado residents* (in order to compare them with people from other states) and had asked them to complete a scale tapping their identification with the relevant category. We then measured participants' appraisals of the policy adopted by Colorado State House Representatives as well as their emotional reactions and action tendencies. Note here that we had never directly examined appraisals in our prior work. We were therefore very curious regarding the perception of legitimacy and justice associated with the policy as a function of the particular social identity we imposed on participants.

To make a long story short, we obtained the predicted significant interaction between identification and the contextually salient identity for all our key dependent variables. So, replicating previous findings, participants thinking of themselves as connected to the victims through the salient identity (students) tended to report more anger when they had initially indicated that they were strongly rather than weakly identified with the category of students. A mirror pattern emerged for participants in the condition where their identity associated them to the perpetrators (Colorado residents). The more these participants identified with their state, the less angry they tended to feel about the policy adopted by their State House Representatives.

In addition to the ubiquitous presence of our omnibus interaction, some nuances are worth mentioning as far as appraisals and action tendencies are concerned. Indeed, our data revealed the presence of two main kinds of legitimacy appraisals, namely how *acceptable* and how *wrong* the situation was perceived to be. Decomposing the interaction pattern into simple effects of identification for each condition revealed slightly different patterns for these two appraisals. First, participants induced to think of themselves as linked to the victims saw the decision as less acceptable as a function of their identification with the group of victims whereas identification to the group of perpetrators failed to show a significant impact. Second, participants led to see themselves as linked to the perpetrators saw the situation as less wrong as a function of their identification with the perpetrators but identification with victims had no impact on this appraisal.

A parallel comment holds for action tendencies. Here, it was possible to distinguish two action tendencies, namely *take action against proposal* and *express support for proposal*. When similarities to the victims were made salient, higher levels of identification were related to stronger willingness to take action against the proposal but the reverse was not true when similarities to the perpetrators were made salient. Rather, in that condition, higher identification was associated with expressing more support for the proposal but identification to the victims failed to induce less support for the proposal.

Globally, one can thus say that when observers were thrown in the group of the victims, identification went hand in hand with finding the situation less acceptable, feeling angry, and intending to take action against the proposal. When participants were cornered into the category of the perpetrators, higher identification made them see the situation as less wrong, feel less angry, and intend to express support for the proposal. Finally, a most compelling piece of evidence regarding the viability of our model of group-based emotions comes from our mediational analyses. As a matter of fact, we found strong evidence that the interactive impact of categorization and identification on participants' action tendencies was mediated by how illegitimate they perceived the situation, which was itself mediated by how angry they felt.

Our present efforts provide very substantial support for the validity of our model of group-based emotions. They nicely complement the findings reported by Doosje and colleagues (1998) in showing that people can be manipulated into approaching a situation from very different perspectives. Depending on the specific social landscape that was activated in their particular case, observers understood the same events, reacted emotionally to them, and intended to do something about them in ways that varied dramatically. Moreover, building upon our argument regarding the impact of categorization on intergroup emotions (Yzerbyt *et al.*, 2002), Wohl and Branscombe (2004) recently conducted an internet study in which Jewish participants assigned more versus less collective guilt for the Holocaust to Germans, expressed more versus less willingness to forgive Germans, and judged genocide as being more versus less pervasive as a function of the specific identities that were activated at the outset of the questionnaire, either Jews (compared to Germans) versus human beings. Again, the message here is that there is definitely more than one identity that observers can embrace when they approach a situation. Our efforts and now other people's work show that, rather than leaving it all up to the observers, one can channel the social identity they adopt so as to orient their subsequent appraisals, emotions, action tendencies, and indeed behaviors.

Emotions and consensus

Our next question concerns another criterion that is generally associated with social reactions namely consensus (Haslam, Oakes, Reynolds, and Turner, 1999; Haslam, Oakes, Turner, McGarty, and Reynolds, 1998; Haslam, Turner, Oakes, Reynolds, Eggins, Nolan, and Tweedie, 1998; Leyens, Yzerbyt, and Schadron, 1994). Indeed, our model of group-based emotions would predict that observers of an event react more like one of the protagonists to the extent that they endorse the same social identity. This prediction can be tested at the level of the emotional profile, i.e., the intensity with which people report the various emotions. A fascinating issue, however, is whether the similarity with the protagonists is also conducive to a more homogeneous reaction among observers. For instance, is it the case that people thrown in the same social category as victims of harmful events experience more consensually the same emotional syndrome, and possibly the one that the victims themselves would experience, than if they are left to approach the event as individuals or as members of an irrelevant category?

To investigate this issue, we adapted an earlier paradigm that involved the presentation of a newspaper article concerning a conflict about the adoption of English as the standard language in the students' curriculum. For the present purpose, we will focus on the most relevant issues of this research (Mathieu, Yzerbyt, and Dumont, 2005, Expt. 1). Our participants, all French-speaking students from the University of Louvain at Louvain-la-Neuve, Belgium, learned that students in Flanders, the Dutch-speaking part of the country, were opposing a decision by their regional government that English would be the sole language used at Masters level. The text expressed in striking terms the shock experienced by the Dutch-speaking students and the level of opposition that grew among them. Before being exposed to the text, however, participants were informed that we were interested in comparing the reactions either of students versus professors (making salient a relevant identity with respect to the victims) or of French-speaking versus Dutch-speaking people (highlighting an irrelevant identity with respect to the victims) regarding various events that had come out in recent news. We also added a control condition in which participants were told that our interest simply focused on people in general (personal identity). As for the dependent variables, participants in the two experimental conditions were asked to complete an identification scale with respect to the social identity that was salient in the condition, i.e. either as a student or as a French-speaking person. We then asked all participants the extent to which they felt a series of emotions reflecting anger, happiness, and sadness.

We first examined the mean responses to these three emotions in the different conditions. We controlled for participants' proficiency in English in order to reduce the impact of individual appraisal on our results. On average, participants experienced more anger than sadness and more sadness than happiness. More interestingly, and in line with earlier findings, both anger and sadness were significantly higher in the relevant identity condition than in the irrelevant identity condition, the personal identity condition falling in between. Neither of these differences between experimental conditions were moderated by identification. Turning to happiness, no significant difference emerged between conditions. However, whereas identification had no influence on happiness in the irrelevant identity condition, a different story emerged in the relevant identity condition: the more participants identified with the relevant identity (students) the less they reported feeling happy. This is exactly what one would expect on the basis of our model of group-based emotions. People are not very happy in general about hearing this story, but they are even less happy when they had indicated that the student identity meant a lot to them.

Our key goal in this study concerned consensus. Our prediction was that higher levels of consensus would be observed in participants' emotional reactions when they were led to see themselves as members of a category that is relevant for the situation, namely the student category. In order to test this hypothesis, we centered our participants' scores for anger, sadness, and happiness in each condition separately and took the absolute difference from the mean so as to obtain distance scores. We then submitted these distance scores to an analysis of covariance using distance of the uncentered score from the midpoint of the scale as the covariate. As expected, the data for anger revealed that the absolute distances were smaller for participants in the relevant identity condition than those in the two other conditions, which did not differ from each other. No significant effect emerged for sadness. With respect to happiness, the consensus tended to be less marked in the relevant identity condition than in the two other conditions. Although this may seem somewhat unexpected, happiness was also the only emotion for which identification turned out to be a moderator. As one would hope, whereas no impact of identification was found in the irrelevant identity condition, the consensus of participants' answers in the relevant identity condition was stronger as a function of identification.

Taken together, these data are extremely compelling indeed. First of all, they are consistent with our earlier findings pertaining to people's average profile of reactions to events. Furthermore, they also confirm the suspicion we had regarding the social consensus that should be observed when people react with some relevant social category in mind. These data are very much in line with other efforts aimed at showing that intergroup contexts and, especially, identities that prove relevant for the topic at hand, increase the consensus in people's reactions (Haslam *et al.*, 1999). The originality of the present demonstration resides in the fact that consensus is shown at the level of emotional reactions rather than in terms of cognitive productions.

Summary

The ambition of the present section was to provide an overview of our research program on group-based emotions. As the description of the studies reveals, social comparison is a crucial ingredient of our experimental strategy aimed at demonstrating the impact of social identity on people's emotions. Clearly, there is a wealth of evidence showing that social comparison is indeed a key element in the emergence of emotions that are based on group membership. In light of the role our research program gives to social comparison, our efforts complement many pieces of research conducted in the framework of the relative deprivation theory. In the next section, we examine the many similarities as well as some differences between our model of group-based emotions and relative deprivation theory.

Group-based emotions and relative deprivation

A central notion underlying relative deprivation theory (Pettigrew, 1967; Runciman, 1966) is that people's actions towards social change originate in their evaluation that the situation that they are facing is not what it should be, compared to some referent. More precisely, *egoistical* or *personal relative deprivation* derives from discontent about one's personal situation compared to other individuals'. In contrast, *fraternal* or *group relative deprivation* arises when people consider that the relative standing of their group, compared to other groups, is undeserved (Ellemers, 2002; Guimond and Tougas, 1999; Kawakami and Dion, 1993, 1995; Walker and Pettigrew, 1984). By comparing their group with one or several other groups, people, especially those who belong to disadvantaged groups, are likely to assess the relative standing of their group as being unfair and illegitimate. As a result, they may experience a sense of deprivation and feelings of displeasure likely to elicit a desire for social change. Importantly, relative deprivation theory suggests that people's involvement in social change does not have to be related to their objective standing but, rather, to their subjective sense of deprivation compared to others.

Clearly, the mechanisms postulated by relative deprivation theory entail striking similarities with our group-based emotion model (Bernstein and Crosby, 1980; Cook, Crosby, and Hennigan, 1977; De La Rey and Raju, 1996; Grant and Brown, 1995; Guimond and Dubé-Simard, 1983; Olson and Hafer, 1996; Tougas, Dube, and Veilleux, 1987). Indeed, both lines of work would argue that a number of factors lead social observers to stick to an individual perspective on events or, instead, to embrace a social identity. Both hold that observers' appraisal of the situation need not be constrained by objective reality. Both suggest that this subjective appraisal is a crucial determinant of observers' feelings. Finally, both approaches put forth the idea that these feelings feed into action tendencies and behaviors. In sum, the evidence accumulated in our research program usefully adds to the impressive amount of data collected by relative deprivation theorists. Together, these contributions provide solid evidence for the idea that group-based emotions are an important facet of social life and, as such, account for intergroup attitudes and behavior (see for example Dambrun and Guimond, 2001; Dion, 1986; Dubé and Guimond, 1986; Grant and Brown, 1995; Guimond, 2003; Guimond and Dambrun, 2002; Guimond and Tougas, 1999; Kawakami and Dion, 1995; Mummendey, Kessler, Klink, and Mielke, 1999; Olson and Hafer, 1996; Pettigrew and Meertens, 1995; Tougas and Beaton, 2002; Vanneman and Pettigrew, 1972; Wright and Tropp, 2002).

Having stressed the similarities between these two lines of work, it is also interesting to examine for a moment a series of useful nuances and distinctions. One issue concerns the status afforded to social comparison.

In one study that nicely illustrates relative deprivation research, Tropp and Wright (1999) looked at deprivation feelings among Latinos and African Americans. Participants were not only led to think of themselves as *individuals* in relation to other members of *their minority* group or in relation to members of *other disadvantaged* groups, or to think of their *minority group* in relation to *other minorities*, but they were also asked to compare *themselves* to members of the *dominant group*, i.e., whites, and to compare *their minority group* to the *dominant group* of whites. The rationale for the comparisons involving whites, and especially the group-level comparison, rests on a simple idea. In order for collective action to be undertaken, Tropp and Wright (1999) argue, people may not only need to perceive their group as being relatively disadvantaged but the target of comparison must also be understood to have had some agency in creating and maintaining the group status hierarchy. In line with the authors' predictions, a comparison with the dominant group led to the accentuation of deprivation reports.

In addition to looking at participants' identification with their minority group and their experience of personal and group relative deprivation in comparison to other minorities and to the dominant group of whites, the authors also distinguished the cognitive and the affective level of reaction (Guimond and Dubé-Simard, 1983; Kawakami and Dion, 1995). These responses were then used to predict participants' support for collective action. Only the identification measure and the affective measure of group relative deprivation in comparison to whites emerged as significant predictors of support for collective action. Interestingly, dropping these two predictors revealed the significant impact of the cognitive measure of group relative deprivation in comparison to whites.

A key message of the above research is that only the group comparison in which the dominant group, i.e., whites, was directly mentioned seemed to hold the active component. As it happens, these findings corroborate the results of a meta-analysis on relative deprivation studies conducted by Smith and Ortiz (2002). They found impressive evidence that collective behavior and attitudes were most strongly related to participants' responses when the question involved an explicit ingroup-outgroup comparison. One should expect people to make different appraisals of deprivation and, as a result, to experience different emotions and adopt different lines of action when they approach an issue from the perspective of one social identity rather than another. The fact that Tropp and Wright (1999) obtained different responses for appraisals and feelings of relative deprivation as a result of varying the definition of the comparison outgroup, either other minorities or whites, is of course reminiscent of our own results (Dumont *et al.*, 2003) which showed that the way respondents defined their ingroup changed subtly, albeit significantly, as a result of the referent group used in the comparison.

Although a change in the comparison group along with the associated modification of the definition of people's ingroup is by no means trivial in its consequences, most of the work we presented in this chapter adopts an even more radical perspective. Indeed, our model is unique in that it combines, on the one hand, the lessons learned from the research on the role of identification, where the spontaneous interpretation of the setting in individual and social terms can be seen to vary as a function of people's level of identification, and on the other hand, the work on the contextual salience of categorization, in which the comparison context is used to make a particular group identity salient. We would therefore argue that relative deprivation research, in spite of its merits, fails to fully take into consideration the flexibility people can manifest in the endorsement of social identities (Oakes, Haslam, and Turner, 1994; Turner *et al.*, 1987). Instead of confronting people with several comparisons simultaneously, as was done by Tropp and Wright (1999) and, for that matter, in most studies on person-group discrimination discrepancy (see Dumont *et al.*, this volume), we corner participants into only one of their many social identities at a time. Because people are capable of witnessing social events and social situations while wearing a variety of different hats, they may end up appraising their environment in radically different ways. As a result, they may or may not experience feelings of deprivation. In short, we argue that it is possible to change people's assessment of relative deprivation and the associated emotional experience by channeling the social identity used to approach the event.

In our opinion, these specific implications of our work on group-based emotions for relative deprivation theory are in fact quite new. The only study that explicitly links intergroup emotions to relative deprivation was reported in a chapter by Smith and Ho (2002). Caucasian Americans were asked to indicate their attitudes and feelings with respect to Asian Americans. Smith and Ho (2002) rightly point out that Asian Americans come across as an intriguing and indeed unexpected prejudiced group. By usual standards, most stereotypes about Asian Americans would be considered as being quite positive. Nevertheless, respondents' emotional reactions seemed to boil down to resentment, envy, and anger rather than respect, admiration, and friendliness. One indication from the study by Smith and Ho (2002) is that their respondents were all the less likely to report anger or resentment if they also seemed to consider Asian Americans as belonging to the same group of Americans as Caucasian Americans. In other words, seeing the two groups as belonging to a common ingroup would seem to be the best antidote against prejudice.

We would argue that our approach, in which social comparison is explicitly relied upon to shape the social landscape, is definitely the way to go in order to draw causal conclusions regarding this conjecture. Clearly, the set of studies we presented in the previous section all testify to the power of social comparison to alter people's appraisals, emotions, and behaviors.

In our model, we insist on the role of chronic identification. This factor has also been singled out by relative deprivation theorists (Guimond and Dubé-Simard, 1983; Smith and Leach, 2004; Tropp and Wright, 1999) as a key triggering factor for people to engage in collective action (Branscombe and Ellemers, 1998; Ellemers, Spears, and Doosje, 1997; Simon, 1998; Simon and Klandermans, 2001; Wright and Tropp, 2002). We would argue that this is the case because high identifiers more than low identifiers read the situation in group terms and, as a result, are more inclined to experience group-based emotions. Indeed, some evidence suggests that, compared to low identifiers, high identifiers are more likely to be angry that their group is being treated poorly and will consider collective action to reduce group-based discrimination (Branscombe and Ellemers, 1998). Interestingly, the role of identification on emotion has seldom been explicitly addressed in terms of moderation as we did in our own work (Tropp and Wright, 1999). Much should be gained by doing so in future research.

From the point of view of our model, the focus of relative deprivation theory is rather narrow. That is, relative deprivation theory would seem to be relevant in a somewhat more limited number of settings than our more general model of group-based emotions. To take but one example, the fact that the achievements of the ingroup dictate people's positive emotional reactions (Boen, Vanbeselaere, and Feys, 2002; Cialdini, Borden, Thorne, Walker, Freeman, and Sloan, 1976) would not fall under the umbrella of relative deprivation (in fact, most scholars would spontaneously categorize this work under the "BIRG" label) but they do illustrate our model of group-based emotions as surely as cases where feelings of anger or resentment presumably dominate. In other words, many group-based emotions other than anger or resentment, on which relative deprivation research has mainly focussed, are also important. We think that our work provides evidence for this and can therefore be used to provide a more differentiated explanation of intergroup behavior.

Finally, our model of group-based emotion differs somewhat from closely-related perspectives on social emotions (Smith, 1993) and from earlier contributions inspired by relative deprivation theory in its conception of the target of the emotional experience. For the vast majority of relative deprivation theorists, the focus is on the appraisal of the group's position in society. For Smith (1993, 1999), the outgroup is the prime emotional target (Mackie, Devos, and Smith, 2000). Our model, and indeed our empirical studies, suggest that group-based emotions can be experienced on a more general basis. As far as we are concerned, any group-relevant event may trigger emotional experiences. This allows for the intuitively appealing possibility that emotions emerge on a social basis even for ingroup-related events. We thus strongly recommend that not only emotions towards the outgroup be considered as a valid group-based emotion.

Conclusion

We started this chapter by presenting Smith's (1993) theory of intergroup emotions. Criticizing traditional perspectives on prejudice in the intergroup relations literature, Smith (1993) argued that emotional reactions in the social sphere go beyond a simple opposition between positive and negative affect and insisted that they are in fact multifaceted and cover a rich range of reactions. Borrowing from cognitive appraisal theories, Smith proposed that a series of dimensions organize people's subjective assessments of their social environment, which then feed into emotional experiences and guide behaviors. He also relied on the self-categorization theory and recent empirical evidence to propose that the way people see themselves may depend in very significant ways on the groups that they are associated with. In a similar vein, he then suggested that emotions, rather than being strictly individual experiences, can very much be shaped by people's group membership. Smith (1999) noted that in this regard, his theory had much in common with earlier efforts conducted under the banner of relative deprivation theory (Smith and Ho, 2002). Along with his colleagues, Smith also collected encouraging evidence showing the impact of appraisals on the emergence of intergroup emotions (Mackie, Devos, and Smith, 2000).

Our own contribution in this domain has been to suggest that appraisals as a determinant of emotional reaction and behavioral tendencies is only one side of the intergroup emotions coin. Another crucial aspect of group-based emotions is the particular social identity that is at work in the context. Indeed, we argued that the specific categorization that is operating in people's minds does more than organize their social landscape. It also commands their interpretation of the events they are confronted with, thereby triggering specific emotions along with the associated behavioral tendencies. In fact, because social comparison is such a central aspect of people's endeavor to understand their surrounding world, our investigations led us to use social comparison as a most efficient tool in order to shape people's emotional reactions in predictable ways.

Over an impressive number of studies, based on very different events, using participants from different countries, investigating different emotions, manipulating either explicitly, or more subtly, the way people categorize themselves, we were able to provide evidence for the validity of our model of group-based emotions. It is obvious that our specific take on the issue of group-based emotions has a lot in common with the research on relative deprivation. In fact, relative deprivation work is uniquely important to our own research in that it clearly demonstrates the implications of social comparison. The originality of our work is that we have taken the theoretical propositions of self-categorization theory regarding the flexibility of social identity and people's sensitivity to contextual forces perhaps more seriously than ever before and shown how the same people may approach things in dramatically different ways as a function of how they categorize themselves.

Clearly, the data we have accumulated in our research program confirm that the way people define the social landscape exerts a most dramatic impact on their appraisals, emotions, action tendencies, and indeed behaviors. The fact that our social comparison manipulation was successful in so many different settings, and the finding that not only the emotional profile but also its degree of consensus were affected, lend impressive support to the idea that the emotional reactions reported by our participants were group-based and not responses deriving from strictly personal considerations. In view of this, we think that our research on group-based emotions provides persuasive evidence that people can indeed experience emotions on behalf of their social identity (see also, Yzerbyt, in press). The special status afforded to social comparison in our empirical efforts made us keenly aware of the numerous connections between the work on social emotions and the work on relative deprivation. We hope that the present chapter, by promoting the idea of further comparing and contrasting these two lines of research, will foster cross-fertilization.

References

Baron, R. M. and Kenny, D. A. (1986). The moderator-mediator variable distinction in social psychological research: Conceptual, strategic, and statistical considerations. *Journal of Personality and Social Psychology, 51*, 1173–1182.

Bernstein, M. and Crosby, F. J. (1980). An empirical examination of relative deprivation theory. *Journal of Experimental Social Psychology 16*, 442–456.

Batson, C. D. (1994). Prosocial motivation: Why do we help others? In A. Tesser (ed.), *Advanced social psychology* (pp. 333–381). Boston: Mcgraw-Hill.

Boen, F., Vanbeselaere, N., and Feys, J. (2002). Behavioral consequences of fluctuating group success: An internet study of soccer-team fans. *Journal of Social Psychology, 142*, 769–781.

Branscombe, N. R. and Ellemers, N. (1998). Coping with group-based discrimination: individualistic versus group-level strategies. In J. Swim and C. Stangor (eds.), *Prejudice: The target's perspective* (pp. 83–103). New York: Academic Press.

Cadinu, M. R. and Rothbart, M. (1996). Self-anchoring and differentiation processes in the minimal group setting. *Journal of Personality and Social Psychology*, *70*, 661–677.

Cialdini, R. B., Borden, R. J., Thorne, A., Walker, M. R., Freeman, S., and Sloan, R. L. (1976). 'Basking in reflected glory: Three (football) field studies', *Journal of Personality and Social Psychology*, *34*, 366–375.

Cook, T. D., Crosby, F., and Hennigan, K. M. (1977). The construct validity of relative deprivation. In J. M. Suls and R. L. Miller (eds.), *Social comparison processes*. Washington, DC: Hemisphere.

Crosby, F. (1976). A model of egoistic relative deprivation. *Psychological Review*, *83*, 85–113.

(1982). *Relative deprivation and working women*. New York: Oxford University Press.

Dambrun, M. and Guimond, S. (2001). La théorie de la privation relative et l'hostilité envers les Nord-Africains. *International Review of Social Psychology*, *14*, 57–89.

De La Rey, C. and Raju, P. (1996). Group relative deprivation: Cognitive versus affective components and protest orientation among Indian South Africans. *Journal of social psychology*, *136*, 579–588.

Dion, K. L. (1986). Responses to perceived discrimination and relative deprivation. In J. M. Olson, C. P. Herman, and M. P. Zanna (eds.), *Relative deprivation and social comparison: The Ontario Symposium* (Vol. IV, pp. 159–179). Hillsdale, NJ: Erlbaum.

Doosje, B., Branscombe, N. R., Spears, R., and Manstead, A. S. R. (1998). Guilty by association: When one's group has a negative history. *Journal of Personality and Social Psychology*, *75*, 872–886.

Dumont, M., Yzerbyt, V. Y., Wigboldus, D., and Gordijn, E. H. (2003). Social categorization and fear reactions to the September 11th terrorist attacks. *Personality and Social Psychology Bulletin*, *29*, 1509–1520.

Dubé, L. and Guimond, S. (1986). Relative deprivation and social protest: The personal group issue. In J. M. Olson, C. P. Herman, and M. P. Zanna (eds.), *Relative deprivation and social comparison* (pp. 201–216). Hillsdale, NJ: Erlbaum.

Ellemers, N. (2002). Social identity and relative deprivation. In I. Walker, and H. J. Smith, (eds.). *Relative deprivation: Specification, development and integration*. Cambridge: Cambridge University Press.

Ellemers, N., Spears, R., and Doosje, B. (1997). Sticking together or falling apart: Ingroup identification as a psychological determinant of group commitment versus individual mobility. *Journal of Personality and Social Psychology*, *72*, 617–626.

(1999). *Social identity: Context, commitment, content*. Oxford: Blackwell.

Festinger, L. (1954). A theory of social comparison processes. *Human Relations*, *7*, 117–140.

Fiske, S. T., Cuddy, A. J., and Glick, P. (2002). Emotions up and down: Intergroup emotions result from perceived status and competition. In D. M. Mackie and E. R. Smith (eds.). *From prejudice to intergroup emotions: Differentiated reactions to social groups* (pp. 247–264). Philadelphia, PA: Psychology Press.

Fiske, S. T., Cuddy, A. J. C., Glick, P., and Xu, J. (2002). A model of (often mixed) stereotype content: Competence and warmth respectively follow from perceived status and competition. *Journal of Personality and Social Psychology, 82,* 878–902.

Fiske, S. T., Xu, J., Cuddy, A. C., and Glick, P. (1999). (Dis)respecting versus (dis)liking: Status and interdependence predict ambivalent stereotypes of competence and warmth. *Journal of Social Issues, 55,* 473–489.

Frijda, N. H. (1986). *The emotions.* Cambridge: Cambridge University Press.

Frijda, N. H., Kuipers, P., and ter Schure, E. (1989). Relations among emotion, appraisal, and emotional action readiness. *Journal of Personality and Social Psychology, 57,* 212–228.

Gaertner, S. L. and Dovidio, J. F. (2000). *Reducing intergroup bias: The common ingroup identity model.* Philadelphia, PA: Psychology Press.

Gordijn, E. H., Wigboldus, D., Hermsen, S., and Yzerbyt, V. (1999). Categorisatie en boosheid: De invloed van negatief outgroup gedrag (Categorization and anger: The influence of negative outgroup behavior). In D. Van Knippenberg, C. K. W. De Dreu, C. Martijn, and C. Rutte (eds.). *Fundamentele Sociale Psychologie, 13.* Tilburg: Tilburg University Press.

Gordijn, E. H., Wigboldus, D., and Yzerbyt, V. (2001). Emotional consequences of categorizing victims of negative outgroup behavior as ingroup or outgroup. *Group Processes and Intergroup Relations, 4,* 317–326.

Gordijn, E., Yzerbyt, V. Y., Wigboldus, D., and Dumont, M. (in press). Emotional reactions to harmful intergroup behavior: The impact of being associated with the victims or the perpetrators. *European Journal of Social Psychology.*

Grant, P. R. and Brown, R. (1995) From ethnocentrism to collective protest: responses to relative deprivation and threats to social identity. *Social Psychology Quarterly, 58,* 195–211.

Guimond, S. (2003). Stigmatisation et mouvements sociaux. In J.-C. Croizet and J.-P. Leyens (eds.), *Mauvaises réputations* (pp. 257–281). Paris: Armand Colin.

Guimond, S. and Dambrun, M. (2002). When prosperity breeds intergroup hostility: The effects of relative deprivation and relative gratification on prejudice. *Personality and Social Psychology Bulletin, 28,* 900–912.

Guimond, S. and Dubé-Simard, L. (1983). Relative deprivation theory and the Quebec movement: The cognition-emotion distinction and the person-group deprivation issue. *Journal of Personality and Social Psychology, 44,* 526–535.

Guimond, S. and Tougas, F. (1999). Sentiments d'injustice et actions collectives: la privation relative. Dans R. Y. Bourhis and J.-P. Leyens (eds.), *Stéréotypes, discrimination et relations intergroupes* (pp. 201–231). Sprimont, Belgium: Mardaga.

Gurr, T. R. (1970). *Why men rebel.* Princeton: Princeton University Press.

Haslam, S. A., Oakes, P. J., Reynolds, K. J., and Turner, J. C. (1999). Social identity salience and the emergence of stereotype consensus. *Personality and Social Psychology Bulletin, 25,* 809–818.

Haslam, S. A., Oakes, P. J., Turner, J. C., McGarty, C., and Reynolds, K. J. (1998). The group as a basis for emergent stereotype consensus. In W. Stroebe and M. Hewstone (eds.). *European review of social psychology* (Vol. VIII, pp. 203–239). Chichester, UK: Wiley.

Haslam, S. A., Turner, J. C., Oakes, P. J., Reynolds, K. J., Eggins, R. A., Nolan, M., and Tweedie, J. (1998). When do stereotypes become really consensual? Investigating the group-based dynamics of the consensualization process. *European Journal of Social Psychology, 28,* 755–776.

Hogg, M. A. (2000). Social identity and social comparison. In J. Suls and L. Wheeler (eds.), *Handbook of social comparison: Theory and research* (pp. 401–421). New York: Kluwer/Plenum.

Hogg, M. A. and Abrams, D. (1988). *Social identification: A social psychology of intergroup relations and group processes.* London: Routledge.

Judd, C. M. and Kenny, D. A. (1981). Process analysis. Estimating mediation in treatment evaluations. *Evaluation Review, 5,* 602–619.

Kawakami, K. and Dion, K. L. (1993). The impact of salient self-identities on relative deprivation and action intentions. *European Journal of Social Psychology, 23,* 525–540.

(1995). Social identity and affect as determinants of collective action. *Theory and Psychology, 5,* 551–577.

Lerner, M. J. (1980). *The belief in a just world: A fundamental delusion.* New York: Plenum.

Leyens, J.-Ph., Yzerbyt, V., and Schadron, G. (1994). *Stereotypes and social cognition.* London: Sage.

Mackie, D. M., Devos, T., and Smith, E. R. (2000). Intergroup emotions: Explaining offensive action tendencies in an intergroup context. *Journal of Personality and Social Psychology, 79,* 602–616.

Mathieu, B., Yzerbyt, V. Y., and Dumont, M. (2005). Group-based emotions: *Consensus as further evidence of their social nature.* Manuscript submitted for publication. Catholic University of Louvain at Louvain-la-Neuve.

Mummendey, A., Kessler, T., Klink, A., and Mielke, R. (1999). Strategies to cope with negative social identity: Predictions by social identity and relative deprivation theory. *Journal of Personality and Social Psychology, 76,* 229–245.

Mussweiler, T. (2003). Comparison processes in social judgment: Mechanisms and consequences. *Psychological Review, 110,* 472–489.

Oakes, P. J., Haslam, S. A., and Turner, J. C. (1994). *Stereotyping and social reality.* Oxford: Basil Blackwell.

Olson, J. M. and Hafer, C. L. (1996). Affect, motivation, and cognition in relative deprivation research. In R. M. Sorrentino and E. T. Higgins (eds.), *Handbook of motivation and cognition: The interpersonal context* (Vol. III, pp. 85–117). New York: Guilford.

Otten, S. and Wentura, D. (2001). Self-anchoring and in-group favoritism: An individual profile analysis. *Journal of Experimental Social Psychology*, *37*, 525–532.

Pettigrew, T. F. (1967). *Social evaluation theory: Convergencies and applications*. Nebraska Symposion on Motivation, 241–315.

Pettigrew, T. F. and Meertens, R. W. (1995). Subtle and blatant prejudice in western Europe. *European Journal of Social Psychology*, *25*, 57–75.

Postmes, T., Branscombe, N. R., Spears, R., and Young, H. (1999). Personal and group judgments of discrimination and privilege: Resolving the discrepancy. *Journal of Personality and Social Psychology*, *76*, 320–338.

Roseman, I. J. (1984). Cognitive determinants of emotion: A structural theory. In P. Shaver (ed.), *Review of personality and social psychology: emotions, relationships, and health* (pp. 11–36). Beverly Hills, CA: Sage.

Runciman, W. G. (1966). *Relative deprivation and social justice*. Berkeley, CA: University of California Press.

Scherer, K. R. (1984). On the nature and function of emotion: A component process approach. In K. R. Scherer and P. Ekman (eds.), *Approaches to emotion* (pp. 293–317). Hillsdale, NJ: Erlbaum.

(1988). Criteria for emotion-antecedent appraisal: A review. In V. Hamilton, G. H. Bower, and N. H. Frijda (eds.), *Cognitive perspectives on emotion and motivation* (pp. 89–126). Norwell, MA: Kluwer Academic.

Simon, B. (1998). Individuals, groups, and social change: On the relationship between individual and collective self-interpretations and collective action. In C. Sedikides, J. Schopler and C. A. Insko (eds.), *Intergroup cognition and intergroup behavior* (pp. 257–282). Mahwah, NJ: Erlbaum.

Simon, B. and Klandermans, B. (2001). Politicized collective identity: A social psychological analysis. *American Psychologist*, *56*, 319–331.

Smith, E. R. (1993). Social identity and social emotions: toward new conceptualizations of prejudice. In D. M. Mackie and D. L. Hamilton (eds.). *Affect, cognition, and stereotyping: Interactive processes in group perception.* (pp. 297–315). San Diego, CA: Academic Press.

(1999). Affective and cognitive implications of a group becoming part of the self: New models of prejudice and of the self-concept. In D. Abrams and M. A. Hogg (eds.), *Social identity and social cognition* (pp. 183–196). Oxford: Basil Blackwell.

Smith, E. R., Coats, S., and Walling, D. (1999). Overlapping mental representations of self, in-group, and partner: Further response time evidence and a connectionist model. *Personality and Social Psychology Bulletin*, *25*, 873–882.

Smith, E. R. and Henry, S. (1996). An in-group becomes part of the self: response time evidence. *Personality and Social Psychology Bulletin*, *22*, 635–642.

Smith, E. R. and Ho, C. (2002). Prejudice as intergroup emotion: Integrating relative deprivation and social comparison explanations of prejudice. In I. Walker and H. Smith (eds.), *Relative deprivation: Specification, development, and integration* (pp. 332–348). Cambridge: Cambridge University Press.

Smith, H. J. and Leach, C. (2004). Group membership and everyday social comparison experiences. *European Journal of Social Psychology*, *34*, 297–308.

Smith, H. J. and Ortiz, D. J. (2002). Is it just me? The different consequences of personal and group relative deprivation. In I. Walker and H. Smith (eds.), *Relative deprivation: Specification, development, and integration* (pp. 91–115). Cambridge: Cambridge University Press.

Suls, J. and Wheeler, L. (2000), *Handbook of social comparison: Theory and research.* New York: Kluwer Academic/Plenum Publishers.

Tajfel, H. (1981). *Human groups and social categories: Studies in social psychology.* Cambridge: Cambridge University Press.

Tajfel, H. and Turner, J. C. (1979). An integrative theory of intergroup conflict. In W. G. Austin and S. Worchel (eds.), *The social psychology of intergroup relations* (pp. 33–48). Monterey, CA: Brooks/Cole.

Taylor, D. M., Wright, S. C., Moghaddam, F. M., and Lalonde, R. N. (1990). The personal/group discrimination discrepancy: Perceiving my group, but not myself, to be a target for discrimination. *Personality and Social Psychology Bulletin, 16*, 254–262.

Taylor, D. M., Wright, S. C., and Porter, L. E. (1994). Dimensions of perceived discrimination: The personal/group discrimination discrepancy. In M. P. Zanna and J. M. Olson (eds.), *The psychology of prejudice: The Ontario symposium* (Vol. VII, pp. 233–255). Hillsdale, NJ: Erlbaum.

Tougas, F. and Beaton, A. M. (2002). Personal and group relative deprivation: Connecting the "I" to the "we". In I. Walker and H. Smith, *Relative deprivation: Specification, development, and integration* (pp. 119–136). Cambridge: Cambridge University Press.

Tougas, F., Dubé, L., and Veilleux, F. (1987). Privation relative et programmes d'action positive. *Revue canadienne des sciences du comportements, 19*, 167–177.

Tropp, L. R. and Wright, S. C. (1999). Ingroup identification and relative deprivation: An examination across multiple social comparisons. *European Journal of Social Psychology, 29*, 707–724.

Turner, J. C. (1975). Social comparison and social identity: Some prospects for intergroup behaviour. *European Journal of Social Psychology, 5*, 5–34.

Turner, J. C., Hogg, M. A., Oakes, P. J., Reicher, S. D., and Wetherell, M. S. (1987). *Rediscovering the social group: A self-categorization theory.* New York: Basil Blackwell.

Vanneman, R. D. and Pettigrew, T. F. (1972). Race and relative deprivation in the urban United States. *Race, 13*, 461–485.

Walker, I. and Pettigrew, T. F. (1984). Relative deprivation theory: an overview and conceptual critique. *British Journal of Social Psychology, 23*, 310–310.

Walker, I. and Smith, H. J. (2002). *Relative deprivation: Specification, development, and integration.* Cambridge: Cambridge University Press.

Wohl, M. J. A. and Branscombe, N. R. (2004). Importance of social categorization for forgiveness and collective guilt assignment for the Holocaust. In N. R. Branscombe and B. Doosje (eds.), *Collective guilt: international perspectives* (pp. 284–305). Cambridge: Cambridge University Press.

Wright, S. C. and Tropp, L. (2002). Collective action in response to disadvantage: Intergroup perceptions, social identification and social change. In I. Walker and H. Smith (eds.), *Relative deprivation: Specification, development, and integration* (pp. 200–236). Cambridge: Cambridge University Press.

Yzerbyt, V. Y. (in press). The politics of social contexts: Shaping the social landscape as a means to regulate beliefs, emotions, and behaviors. In P. A. M. van
Lange (ed.), *Bridging social psychology: The benefits of transdisciplinary
approaches*. Hillsdale, NJ: Erlbaum.

Yzerbyt, V. Y., Dumont, M., Gordijn, E., and Wigboldus, D. (2002). Intergroup
emotions and self-categorization: The impact of perspective-taking on reactions to victims of harmful behavior. In D. Mackie and E. Smith (eds.), *From
prejudice to intergroup emotions* (pp. 67–88), Philadelphia, PA: Psychology
Press.

Yzerbyt, V. Y., Dumont, M., Wigboldus, D., and Gordijn, E. (2003). I feel for us:
The impact of categorization and identification on emotions and action
tendencies. *British Journal of Social Psychology*, *42*, 533–549.

9 The counter-intuitive effect of relative gratification on intergroup attitudes: ecological validity, moderators and mediators

Michaël Dambrun, Serge Guimond, and Donald M. Taylor

After five decades of research revealing that relative deprivation (RD) is a central variable in the explanation of intergroup prejudice, recent research suggests that the opposite of RD, the relatively ignored relative gratification (RG), is also an important determinant of prejudice. This chapter summarizes both recent studies and current development in this line of research. After presenting several experiments that test the respective effects of both RD and RG on intergroup attitudes, we address the question of the ecological validity of the RG effect. By looking at South African data, we show that the effect of RG on prejudice is not merely a laboratory artefact, nor is it limited to the French intergroup context. Finally, in the last part, we focus more directly on the "understanding" dimension by testing both moderators and mediators of the RG effect.

Understanding intergroup conflict and the factors that contribute to stereotyping and prejudice is a fundamental problem that has attracted the attention of social psychologists for many years. This chapter examines a new theoretical perspective in the explanation of prejudice. This perspective suggests that Relative Gratification (RG), the complete opposite of Relative Deprivation (RD), is a powerful determinant of various forms of negative or hostile intergroup attitudes. In common with relative deprivation theory (Walker and Smith, 2002), social identity theory (Tajfel and Turner, 1986), Equity Theory (Walster, Walster, and Berscheid 1978), and the five-stage model of intergroup relations (Taylor and McKirnan, 1984), this new perspective based on RG shares the assumption that social comparison processes are fundamental to an understanding of intergroup conflict (see Taylor and Moghaddam, 1994 for an overview of these theories). However, unlike the almost exclusive attention given in these approaches to various forms of *negative* or *unfavorable* social comparisons, focussing on RG leads to a radically different perspective because it suggests that *favorable* social comparisons can also generate outgroup hostility (Guimond and Dambrun, 2002).

To understand the concept of RG, it is necessary to consider first the concept of RD from which it originates. Thus, we begin by a very brief review of the evidence on the relations between RD and intergroup attitudes.

Being *unsatisfied* and prejudice: the basic effect of RD

Relative deprivation theory is often considered as one of the main theoretical perspectives in the explanation of prejudice (Jones, 2002; Nelson, 2002). Central to the theory are a number of important distinctions between various types of RD. First, the cognitive component of RD, the perception of deprivation, can be distinguished from its affective component, the sense of injustice, dissatisfaction, anger or resentment that one can experience as a result of this perceived deprivation (Cook, Crosby, and Hennigan, 1977). Second, RD can occur at different levels of analysis, depending on the type of comparison involved (Guimond and Tougas, 1994; see also Redersdorff and Guimond, this volume). Thus, Runciman (1966) distinguished egoistical or personal RD from fraternal or group RD. In the case of personal RD, the individual is dissatisfied about his or her own personal situation as a result of a comparison revealing that he or she is worse off than other individuals. In the latter case, the individual is dissatisfied with the position of the ingroup as a whole compared to that of an outgroup. Research has shown in a consistent and reliable manner that the affective component of group RD is the most important predictor of intergroup attitudes and behaviors (Dambrun and Guimond, 2001; Dubé and Guimond, 1986; Guimond and Dubé-Simard, 1983; Moghaddam and Perrault, 1992; Taylor, Moghaddam, and Bellerose, 1989; Tougas and Beaton, 2002; Wright and Tropp, 2002). For example, a comprehensive study of prejudice towards immigrants in Europe found strong evidence for the role of group RD, but not for personal RD (see Pettigrew, Jackson, Ben Brika, Lemaine, Meertens, Wagner, and Zick, 1998). Specifically, in France, The Netherlands, UK, and West Germany, people who feel that their ingroup has been, over the last five years, economically worse off than the outgroup display more ethnic prejudice than others, especially more blatant forms of prejudice. No such relation was observed when the focus was personal RD. This is consistent with earlier evidence obtained in the United States (see Vanneman and Pettigrew, 1972). More recently, Duckitt and Mphuthing (2002) using a four-month longitudinal design also found, consistent with past research, that measures of affective group RD can reliably predict outgroup prejudice in South Africa. Thus, the hypothesis that people who feel that their ingroup as a whole is deprived compared to an outgroup will be more likely than others to express prejudice has been strongly supported. Yet, virtually all research in this area is correlational in nature, leaving open the question of causality. Group RD may very well be a source of greater prejudice but prejudice could very well lead to greater feelings of group RD. The longitudinal design used by Duckitt and Mphuthing (2002) is a definite improvement over past research but still does not allow for strong causal inferences. To address this problem, Guimond and Dambrun (2002) designed a series of experiments to test the effect of RD on prejudice. Included in their design were a condition of RD in which feelings of deprivation were experimentally manipulated, a control group, and a condition of RG, the opposite of RD, in which feelings of gratification were experimentally manipulated. This three-group design raised a new question: what effect might RG have on prejudice?

Being *satisfied* and prejudice: the basic effect of RG

The first hypothesis in the experiment that systematically manipulated RD and RG was straightforward: compared to the control condition, the RD condition was expected to yield higher levels of ethnic prejudice. Using a 15-item scale of prejudice developed on the basis of previous research, Guimond and Dambrun (2002) indeed found clear evidence in support of this hypothesis. French university students who were led to experience greater feelings of dissatisfaction about the relative economic position of their ingroup displayed reliably higher scores on the measure of ethnic prejudice, compared to the control group. The second hypothesis about the effect of RG was less straightforward. Relative deprivation theorists have long argued that when people perceive that they are better off than others, that is when the outcome of a social comparison is favorable, the result is a state of "relative gratification," the opposite of RD (e.g. Martin, 1981; Smith, Spears, and Oyen, 1994). However, virtually all research related to RD theory has focussed on RD, not on RG, so that little is known about the role of RG in intergroup relations. One assumption was that since RD is expected to increase prejudice, RG, the opposite of RD, should be associated with a decrease in prejudice. But apart from its logical basis, there was little in terms of psychological processes that supported this prediction. Counter-intuitively, in exploring the possible role of RG, arguments can be presented to suggest that it too might be associated with higher levels of prejudice (see Guimond and Dambrun, 2002).

The most basic argument arises from the social function of prejudice. Why do people have prejudiced attitudes? What social function do these attitudes serve? The clear answer for many scholars is that prejudice has the function of providing a justification for economic and social privileges. This position is well articulated within Social Dominance Theory (Sidanius and Pratto, 1999). Sidanius and Pratto take the position that all major forms of prejudice are instances of what they call "legitimizing myths." This concept is defined as "attitudes, values, beliefs, stereotypes, and ideologies that provide moral and intellectual justification for the social practices that distribute social value within the social system." (Sidanius and Pratto, 1999, p. 45) Primary examples of legitimizing myths are racism, which attempts to justify racial inequality, and sexism, which seeks to justify gender inequality. Thus, from the perspective of social dominance theory, racial or ethnic prejudice are essentially beliefs and attitudes that seek to justify racial or ethnic inequality. It follows that if people perceive that their ingroup is economically privileged, they will be motivated to endorse attitudes and beliefs that justify this privilege. In other words, when people are in a privileged position, they should display higher levels of prejudice in order to justify their advantages. Because RG, by definition, involves a situation where people judge that they are better off than others (Kawakami and Dion, 1995), Guimond and Dambrun (2002) hypothesized that, compared to the control condition, the RG condition in their experiments would also lead to higher levels of ethnic prejudice. In two experiments involving different operationalizations of RG, Guimond and Dambrun (2002) found striking evidence in support of this hypothesis. In fact, the evidence for the effect of RG was even more pronounced than that for RD. For example, in the second experiment, the effect of RD was evident on the 15-item scale of prejudice but not on any additional measures. In contrast, the effect for RG was observed not only on the prejudice scale, but equally on additional measures such as ingroup bias, immigration policy preference, and even discriminatory behavioral intention. Consistently, the effect of RG on the 15-item scale of prejudice accounts for a greater percentage of explained variance (14.4 percent) than the effect of RD (9.1 percent). Finally, additional analyses of the data from this experiment reveal that participants in the RG condition display significantly more stereotypic judgments of "Arabs" ($M = .82$) than the participants in the control condition ($M = .43$; $F (1, 79) = 4.93$, $p < .029$). By contrast, the effect of RD on stereotyping was not significant.

These results strongly support the hypothesis that RG leads to negative evaluations and stereotypical judgments of outgroups. However, the robust finding is exclusively based on traditional or explicit attitude scales, which does not exclude an alternative interpretation of the effect of RG. It is possible that the manipulation of RG, by virtue of its very positive and unexpected nature, might mobilize a substantial portion of an individual's cognitive resources. Several studies have shown that, in certain circumstances, individuals will control and minimize their negative social attitudes when filling in a questionnaire (Fazio, Jackson, Dunton, and Williams, 1995; Sigall and Page, 1971). If indeed in the RG condition, the cognitive resources of the participants are taxed, they might exert less control over their responses (Gilbert and Hixon, 1991). This, in turn, would lead to an increase of the level of prejudice expressed. In order to examine (among other things) this alternative interpretation of the effect of RG, Dambrun and Guimond (2004) tested the impact of economic RG on prejudice using two different measuring techniques: a traditional, explicit measure allowing participants to control their responses, and an implicit measure (i.e. a lexical decision task), by definition much less controllable (Fazio and al., 1995; Wilson, Lindsey, and Schooler, 2000; Wittenbrink, Judd, and Park, 1997). If indeed the effect of RG is only observed using the explicit measure, this would support the hypothesis that a decrease in cognitive resources may explain RG. On the other hand, if the effect of RG arises for both the explicit and the implicit measure, this would tend to invalidate the hypothesis of a decrease in cognitive resources. Consistent with our expectations, the results of the study showed that the effect of RG on prejudice toward Arabs is observed both on the explicit and the implicit measure. Thus, in RG condition, the participants were significantly quicker than in the control condition to associate the subliminal prime "Arab" with negative adjectives and the prime "French" with positive adjectives. It therefore seems that RG triggers a strikingly negative pattern of intergroup attitudes.

In these studies, relative gratification was manipulated in terms of economic expectations. A second series of studies was carried out in order to examine whether the effect of RG was limited to this manipulation, or if it reflected a more general process that would be observable in different domains of comparison.

Inducing "superior intelligence": the effect of RG in a new context

In this study (Dambrun and Guimond, 2000), we examined whether gratifying individuals on a non-economic and non temporal dimension would generate effects similar to those observed for economic gratification. We chose to gratify – or not – psychology students ($N = 60$) on the level of intelligence of their ingroup. Specifically, in the RG condition, participants were to read a purported report from "Student Services." This report stated that several studies had compared the intellectual abilities of psychology students and law students. In France, the status of law students is higher than that of psychology students, the latter holding a rather low status within the student community. The results of this fictitious report were straightforward; psychology students were more intelligent than law students. Indeed, on several intelligence tests (i.e. IQ, etc.), graphs showed mean scores substantially higher for psychology students compared to law students. In the control condition, the participants were not given feedback on intelligence. Consistent with our expectations, analyses of the items serving as manipulation checks revealed that the participants in the RG condition were more likely to agree that the abilities of psychology students were higher than those of law students ($M = 3.26$) relative to the participants in the control condition ($M = 2.56$; $F (1, 59) = 4$, $p < .05$). The second step involved examining whether the experimental manipulation had an effect on the level of prejudice participants showed toward an ethnic target stigmatized in France (e.g. Arabs). Prejudice towards Arabs was measured using a seven-point scale comprising sixteen items (e.g. "The rate of criminality would be lower if Arabs were sent back to their countries of origin") that had been validated in other studies (see Dambrun, 2001; Dambrun, 2004). For the present experiment, the reliability of the scale was satisfactory (Cronbach alpha $= .88$). Our hypothesis regarding RG was confirmed in that participants in the RG group ($M = 2.99$) expressed significantly more prejudice toward Arabs than participants in the control group ($M = 2.46$; $F (1, 59) = 6.68$, $p < .012$). Perceiving one's ingroup in a gratifying manner on the dimension of intelligence significantly increased the level of prejudice of the participants towards a stigmatized outgroup (i.e. Arabs).

Next, we examined whether this effect could be generalized to any ethnic group, whatever its status. The participants were asked to express their attitude toward several ethnic groups who varied according to their status; low status outgroups (Arabs, Turks), high status outgroups (Swiss, English) and ingroup (French). The results are presented in Figure 9.1. As far as the ingroup and the high status outgroups are concerned, no differences appear between the two experimental conditions. On the other hand, participants in the RG condition are significantly less favorable toward low status outgroups (Arab and Turk) than participants in the control condition (respectively, $F (1, 58) = 5.16$, $p < .027$; $F (1, 58) 4.07$, $p < .049$). Thus, the effect of RG does not generalize to any ethnic group, but does seem to generalize to low status ethnic groups.

It is interesting to notice the gap between the experimental manipulation where the groups manipulated are students and the effects observed on ethnic rather than student targets. If indeed psychology students in RG condition feel the need to justify their situation by calling upon prejudice, we should logically observe an effect at the level of student

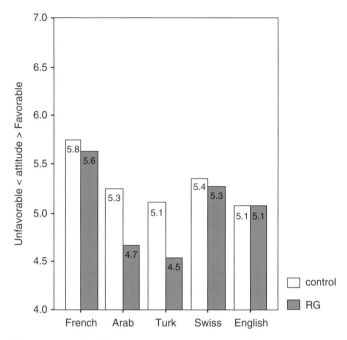

Figure 9.1. The effect of intelligence RG on different ethnic targets

targets; participants (all of whom are psychology students) should express less favorable attitudes towards law students in RG condition rather than in control condition. In order to explore this possibility, we examined the attitudes of participants towards different groups of students; the ingroup (psychology students), the target outgroup (law students), two other high status outgroups (economy students and maths students) and a low status outgroup (philosophy students). The results are presented in Figure 9.2. Contrary to our hypothesis, the experimental manipulation had no effect on the attitudes of participants towards law students. Attitudes towards the two other high status groups (i.e. maths and economy) were not affected either by RG. Only the attitudes towards philosophy students (low status) are significantly different in the two experimental conditions ($F(1, 58) = 4.26, p < .044$). Participants in the RG group are significantly less favorable towards philosophy students ($M = 4.9$) than those in the control group ($M = 5.6$). In short, it appears that RG generates prejudice only towards low status groups.

Further support for the idea that the RG effect is closely related to the existence of a status hierarchy was found in a study conducted by

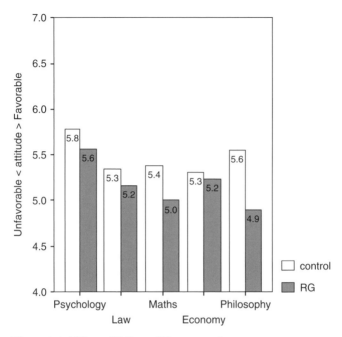

Figure 9.2. Effect of RG on different student targets

Guimond, Dif and Aupy (2002). High school students, ten to eighteen years old, from Clermont-Ferrand, France participated in this study. They were told that an important scientific research was being conducted and that to take part in it, they would have to do three tasks. The first two tasks, it was explained, would assess their level of creativity, a special dimension ostensibly found in previous research to be highly predictive of obtaining a very good position in society in the future. The third task would involve answering a questionnaire to find out their opinions about school life.

This high school was selected for the study because it comprises two groups of students: those in the regular program who enjoy a high status within the school system relative to others who belong to special classes in a program called "Segpas," designed for students presenting extreme learning difficulties. In short, students in the "Segpas" represent a some-what stigmatized, low status group, within this system. One of the main hypothesis of the study was that regular students receiving positive feed-back, suggesting that their class did better on the creativity test than the class of Segpas (relative gratification condition), would display more negative evaluations of the Segpas than regular students not receiving any positive feedback (control condition). Strong support for this hypothesis was obtained (see Guimond *et al.*, 2002). The regular students were asked to indicate their impressions of the Segpas, and of their own group, on several different attributes, some positive and some negative. There was evidence of ingroup bias in all conditions, that is, even regular students in the control condition, as members of a high status group, displayed a more favorable evaluation of their own group than the outgroup. However, this ingroup bias was significantly stronger among students in the relative gratification condition. In fact, the only condition where outgroup derogation was observed, that is a tendency to actually attribute more negative traits to the outgroup than to the ingroup, was in the relative gratification condition.

If, indeed, RG leads to higher levels of prejudice and outgroup derogation, would RG also promote the approval of ultra-conservative political ideologies of extreme right-wing political groups such as the "Front National" in France? This possibility was examined using a correlational design. We (Dambrun, Maisonneuve, Duarte, and Guimond, 2002; $N = 290$) measured RG with two items (i.e. "I consider that the French have high intellectual abilities," "When I think about the intellectual abilities of the French, I feel satisfied"; $r = .49$, $p < .001$). Prejudice towards Arabs was measured using a scale comprising 23 items (alpha = .92). Extreme right-wing attitudes were measured using a scale developed for the purpose of this study (6 items; alpha = .72). The results revealed, as expected, that prejudice towards Arabs is significantly and positively predicted by RG in terms of intelligence ($r = .25$, $p < .001$). The more participants perceive the "French" as gratified with respect to intelligence, the more they express negative attitudes towards Arabs. Moreover, the attitude of individuals towards the *Front National*, although highly predicted by prejudice towards Arabs ($r = .59$, $p < .001$), is also significantly related to the RG measure ($r = .15$, $p < .01$). The more RG participants perceive, the more favorable they are towards the extreme right-wing political group.

The ecological validity of the effect of relative gratification

While the effect of relative deprivation on prejudice has been documented in several countries, such as the United States (Vanneman and Pettigrew, 1971), India (Tripathi and Strivastava, 1981), South Africa (Appelgryn and Nieuwoudt, 1988), and Western Europe (Dambrun and Guimond, 2001; Pettigrew and Meertens, 1995), the effect of gratification has been limited to psychology students in France. It is essential that the validity of RG be tested in new cultural contexts. Moreover, it is essential to test the validity of the RG effect on representative samples, beyond the usual psychology students. With this in mind, Dambrun, Taylor, McDonald, and Crush (2005) carried out a study on a representative sample of South Africans.

The effect of relative gratification on attitudes towards immigrants in South Africa

Recent data from the Southern African Migration Project (SAMP), based on representative samples, show that immigrants are currently a prime target of prejudice in South Africa (Dambrun and Taylor, 2003; Mattes, Taylor, Poore, and Richmond, 1999). Not only are African immigrants openly disparaged, but European and North American immigrants are too. In this context, Dambrun, Taylor, McDonald, and Crush (2005) tested the potential impact of relative gratification on attitudes towards immigrants in South Africa. Specifically, the predictions derived from two models were tested. The first model is based on relative deprivation theory and predicts a linear relationship between perceived relative deprivation and hostility towards immigrants (e.g. Pettigrew and Meertens, 1995). The second model is based on both relative deprivation theory and relative gratification theory, and predicts a quadratic relationship between the relative gratification-deprivation continuum and hostility towards immigrants. According to the traditional approach, the relative gratification-deprivation continuum should be positively and linearly linked to hostility towards immigrants. The more individuals perceive themselves as deprived relative to immigrants, the more likely they are to express negative attitudes towards them. On the other hand, taking into account the effect of relative gratification leads to a different prediction. Not only should perceived relative deprivation be linked to intergroup hostility, but so should perceived relative gratification. Taking into account the effect of relative gratification leads to the prediction of a quadratic relationship between the relative gratification-deprivation continuum and intergroup hostility. This quadratic relationship can be labelled a V-Curve (Dambrun *et al.*, 2005; Grofman and Muller, 1973; Guimond and Dambrun, 2002).

Dambrun *et al.* (2005) jointly tested the validity of the linear model and of the quadratic model on a sample of 1,600 South Africans representative of the South African population. The sample comprised 800 women and 800 men between the age of 16 and 99 years old (average age = 38.3). Several ethnic groups were represented: 869 blacks, 372 whites, 208 coloured and 151 Indians/Asians. Perceived relative gratification-deprivation was measured with a reliable and valid scale comprising eight items similar in content and design to those traditionally used. In terms of intergroup attitudes, participants were asked to evaluate their own ethnic

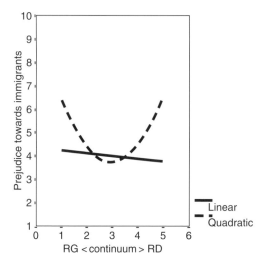

Figure 9.3. Linear and quadratic relationships between the RG-RD continuum and prejudice towards immigrants

group and several groups of immigrants on a 10-point scale ranging from strongly unfavorable (1) to strongly favorable (10). A measure of prejudice towards immigrants was obtained by subtracting the average of the evaluations of groups of immigrants from the evaluation of the ingroup. The results are presented in Figure 9.3. While the linear model is not significantly predictive of the measure of prejudice towards immigrants, the quadratic model is significantly linked to this measure ($p < .0001$). As shown quite clearly in Figure 9.3, perceived RG and perceived RD are both associated with a high level of prejudice towards immigrants.

These results seem to confirm those underscored in the French context using experimental methods. It seems that the effect of RG is neither a laboratory artefact nor a phenomenon limited to the French context. It would seem possible to conclude that the effect of RG is a relatively robust phenomenon that can be found in other intergroup contexts.

Understanding the effect of RG

One important avenue for understanding the phenomenon of RG involves identifying the moderators, i.e. the variables that either limit or exacerbate the effect of RG on intergroup attitudes. This also entails identifying the mechanisms underlying the effect of RG, i.e. identifying the mediating variables.

The moderators of the effect of RG

In the course of this research program, we have mainly tested the moderating power of the socio-economic status.

The socio-economic status. The moderating effect of socio-economic status in the relation between RG and intergroup attitudes was successfully tested in the study conducted by Dambrun, Taylor, McDonald, and Crush (2005) on the data from South Africa. In that study, our prediction was that the target group of the effect of RG would be dependent on the socio-economic status of individuals. Specifically, when people perceive economic RG, they are motivated to maintain their advantaged position by derogating groups that are perceived as potential competitors. It has long been demonstrated that the perception of economic competition is associated with intergroup hostility (Campbell, 1965; LeVine and Campbell, 1972; Sherif, 1966) and derogation of immigrants (Esses, Jackson, and Armstrong, 1998; Jackson and Esses, 2000). In the context of RG, we argued that low and high SES people do not perceive the same competitors. According to the instrumental model of group conflict, "for dimensions relevant to obtaining resources, groups that are similar to the ingroup are more likely to be seen as competitors." (Esses, Jackson, and Armstrong, 1998, p. 704) Thus, low SES South Africans who perceive RG should perceive low status immigrants as potential competitors (e.g. African immigrants in South Africa), but would tend to disregard high status immigrants as potential competitors (e.g. western immigrants in South Africa). Because, in this specific case, low status immigrants should be perceived as more threatening than high status immigrants, we hypothesized that, among *low SES South Africans*, RG would be more strongly associated with prejudice towards African immigrants than with prejudice towards western immigrants.

Among high SES South Africans experiencing RG, we hypothesized the opposite pattern of results. We argued that high status immigrants would be perceived as more threatening than low status immigrants, by high SES people perceiving economic RG. Consequently, we hypothesized that, among *high SES South Africans*, economic RG would be more strongly associated with greater levels of prejudice towards high status immigrants (western immigrants) than with low status immigrants (African immigrants).

The results clearly validated our hypotheses. Indeed, while the effect of economic RG on prejudice towards African immigrants was observed only in the case of South Africans of low socio-economic status, the effect of RG on prejudice towards western immigrants was observed only in individuals of high socio-economic status. The socio-economic status clearly appears to be a moderating factor of the effect of economic RG on intergroup attitudes. It seems that the socio-economic status allows for a prediction as to which group will become the target of prejudice among people in a state of economic gratification.

The mediators of the effect of RG

With the identification of the mechanisms underlying the effect of RG as our main objective, we tested the mediating power of several variables through a series of studies. Satisfaction or positive emotion, perceived improvement, social dominance orientation (SDO), fulfilment of expectations, and social identification were tested in turn as possible mediators.

Satisfaction and perceived improvement: the affective and cognitive components of RG. A number of studies have shown that the affective component of RD mediates the effect of group RD on social attitudes and behaviors. Guimond and Dubé-Simard (1983), for instance, have shown that the effect of the perceived inequality between two groups (cognitive component) on support for a social movement is mediated by feelings of dissatisfaction (cognitive component) stemming from an unfavorable comparison between the situation of the ingroup and that of the outgroup (for similar findings, see De La Rey and Raju, 1996; Grant and Brown, 1995; Tougas, Dubé and Veilleux, 1987). With this in mind, Guimond and Dambrun (2002) examined whether the affective (positive emotion) and/or cognitive (perceived improvement) components played a mediating role in the effect of intergroup RG on intergroup attitudes.

Based on the studies conducted by Bodenhausen, Kramer, and Süsser (1994), we could predict that a favorable comparison induced by RG would lead to a positive emotion, and that this positive emotion, surprisingly can generate negative stereotyping. Bodenhausen, Kramer, and Süsser (1994) have argued that when people are in a happy mood, they are more likely to use heuristic processing strategies. Since group stereotypes represent a cognitive heuristic, it follows that people will be more likely to rely on stereotypes when processing information in a happy mood. Because group stereotypes can be negative in valence, a happy mood may lead to more negative intergroup attitudes. Research has provided experimental evidence consistent with such an analysis (Bodenhausen *et al.*, 1994; Forgas and Fiedler, 1996).

Contrary to our hypothesis derived from Bodenhausen *et al.*'s (1994) model, Guimond and Dambrun (2002; experiment 2) showed that only perceived improvement mediates the effect of intergroup RG on prejudice (see Figure 9.4). The affective component was indeed linked to the effect of intergroup RG in such a way that participants in the RG

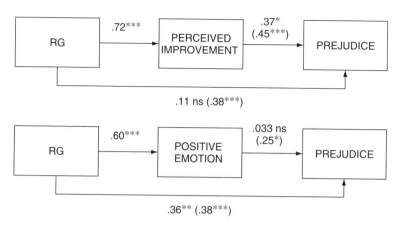

Figure 9.4. Affective and cognitive components of RG as potentials mediators

condition expressed a higher level of general satisfaction than participants in the control condition, but this effect did not mediate the impact of RG on prejudice (see Figure 9.4). Results stemming from the manipulation of RG on the dimension of intelligence proved even more convincing. In that study, emotions such as happiness, and joy were measured. Contrary to an emotional interpretation, participants in the RG condition did not show an emotional level ($M = 5.3$) different from that of participants in the control condition ($M = 5.4$; $F < 1$). Thus, contrary to the effect of relative deprivation which is mediated by a negative emotion (affective component), the effect of RG appears more mediated by its cognitive component. When participants are placed in a situation of intergroup relative gratification, they perceive an improvement in the situation of their ingroup, which in turn triggers negative intergroup attitudes. Why? Insofar as prejudice may be conceptualized as a cognitive tool used to justify or legitimize social inequalities favorable to the ingroup (Crocker, Major, and Steele, 1998), it may well be that participants in a situation of intergroup RG need to justify this fact, and hence call upon prejudice more frequently. This hypothesis should be tested directly in future studies. However, several studies testing the role of social dominance orientation (SDO) and fulfilment of expectations are beginning to shed light on this issue.

Social dominance orientation. Social dominance theorists have argued and shown that dominant social groups, and individuals scoring high on social dominance orientation (SDO), are more likely than others to subscribe to a wide variety of "legitimizing myths" including racism and sexism (see Pratto, Sidanius, Stallworth, and Malle, 1994). Their findings indicate that SDO can affect not just attitudes toward a particular target group but attitudes toward a whole range of groups and social ideologies (see also Pratto, 1999; Sidanius and Pratto, 1999). The reason for this is that all these attitudes and beliefs share the same function: to justify inequality. Similarly, by placing individuals in a privileged position and giving them access to a dominant status, the RG condition may have triggered the need to justify this position which was expressed by denigrating not simply a particular group but various outgroups.

The mediating effect of SDO was tested, with contrasting results. First, the study carried out by Guimond and Dambrun (2002, experiment 2) showed that participants in a condition of intergroup gratification expressed a significantly higher level of SDO than participants in a control condition. In other words, in a situation of RG, participants are more in favor of social inequalities between groups and for the domination of subordinate groups by dominant groups, which seems quite compatible with the hypothesis concerning the need for justification. However, this same study does not allow us to conclude that SDO is a mediator of the effect of RG on prejudice. When SDO was statistically controlled, the effect of RG on prejudice was not significantly reduced. In short, it seems unlikely that SDO can explain the effect of RG on prejudice. At the most, it appears that it can be seen as a partial mediator. This implies that the underlying justification process cannot, on its own, explain the effect of RG and that other mechanisms must come into play.

Fulfilment of expectations. In their paper titled "The strange case of relative gratification and potential for political violence," Grofman and Muller (1973) suggest that perceived improvement could generate positive expectations that individuals may wish to fulfil. Insofar as prejudice may be seen as a tool serving to justify social inequalities, it is quite likely that individuals wishing to fulfil their positive expectations may resort to it. We tested this hypothesis in a recent study (Dambrun and Hecquet, 2004) for which a new experimental manipulation of relative gratification was applied. Specifically, employment forecasts for women and men were manipulated in such a way that female participants, all of whom were psychology students, were led to believe that employment prospects were significantly better for women than for men. In the control condition, information was given to suggest the idea that employment prospects were the same for both gender groups. The attitudes of female participants towards men and women were measured using an attribution task of positive and negative traits. A measure of gender attitude was obtained by subtracting the average of positive evaluations of the outgroup from that of the ingroup. First, the attitude of female participants towards men was significantly more positive in the control condition ($M = -.98$) than in the RG condition ($M = -.67$; F (1, 82) $= 4.43$, $p < .038$), thus confirming the effect of RG in a new context. Second, in line with the fulfilment of expectations hypothesis, compared to participants in the control condition ($M = -.31$), the female participants in the RG condition were significantly more eager to see the induced forecasts materialize ($M = .37$; F (1, 82) $= 6.51$, $p < .013$). Unfortunately, this fulfilment of expectations process does not significantly mediate the effect of RG on the measure of attitudes. As was the case for the effect of SDO, the fulfilment of expectations process appears compatible with the mediating effect of the cognitive component of RG. Indeed, the fact of resorting to prejudice is conceptualized as a cognitive construction of justification enabling to maintain and/or achieve improvement. It seems, however, that a totally different mechanism may be more important.

Social identification. According to social identity theory (SIT; Tajfel and Turner, 1979), people are motivated to maintain or achieve a positive social identity. Because the self-concept is partially derived from group membership that positively influences self-esteem through favorable intergroup comparisons, people tend to identify more strongly with the group to which they belong than with outgroups. In the context of RG, people may identify even more strongly with their social group. A favorable intergroup comparison, such as a perceived economic improvement in the country or a perceived improvement in group status would underlie a state of relative gratification. In this context, it can be argued that people will feel more pride in their own group and will be more attracted to it (see Doosje, Spears, and Ellemers, 2002). This should result in stronger ingroup identification among people perceiving RG. It has been relatively well established that stronger ingroup identification is associated with increases in ingroup bias and outgroup derogation (e.g. Perreault and Bourhis, 1999). Consequently, on the basis of SIT, we predict a mediational model in which group identification mediates the effect of RG on intergroup attitudes. Dambrun *et al.* (2005) tested this hypothesis in the context of South Africa. Results clearly showed that identification with the participants' own ethnic group totally mediated the effect of RG on prejudice towards African immigrants and partially mediates the effect of RG on prejudice towards immigrants from western countries. Thus, this study points to the mediating role of social identification in explaining the effect of RG. In the RG condition, participants are led to identify more with their own ethnic group, and this triggers more prejudice towards ethnic outgroups.

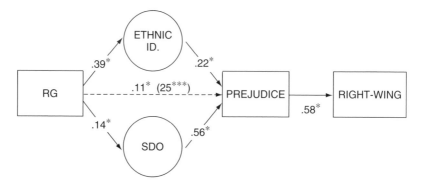

Figure 9.5. Ethnic identification and SDO as two independent mediators of the effect of RG on prejudice and right-wing political attitudes
Note: Ethnic id. Ethnic identification; SDO = social dominance orientation; Right-wing extreme right-wing political attitudes; $N = 290$.

Testing both social identification and SDO as independent mediators. With the sample used by Dambrun, Maisonneuve, Duarte, and Guimond (2002; $N = 290$), we proposed that both the mediating role of ethnic identification and SDO should be tested. Specifically, we tested a model according to which the effect of "intelligence" RG on ethnic prejudice would be mediated through two variables: the strength of identification with the ingroup and SDO. Furthermore, the model proposed that the effects of ingroup identification and SDO on support for an extreme right-wing political party would be mediated by ethnic prejudice (see Figure 9.5). Ethnic identification was measured using ten items stemming from various measures of social identification (alpha = .87). The sixteen items suggested by Pratto *et al.* (1994) were used to measure SDO (alpha = .88). This model (Figure 9.5) was tested with a structural equation modelling program (E.Q.S. 5.7; Bentler and Wu, 1995). The standardized coefficients were obtained using the "Maximum Likelihood Method of Estimation" ("M.L."). A non-significant Chi-square (X^2) and indices above or equal to .90 (*CFI; GFI;* et *NFI*) indicate that the model is valid and appropriate. First, we tested the model shown in Figure 9.5, without the dotted line between RG and prejudice. Statistics yielded a significant Chi-square, albeit quite low (X^2 (5) = 25.06, $p < .001$) and a model highly in line with the data. Indeed, the different indices are all high (*CFI* = .94; *GFI* = .97; *NFI* = .93). The same model with the dotted line included did not yield a significant statistical improvement (X^2 (4) = 20.09, $p < .001$; *CFI* = .95; *GFI* = .97; *NFI* = .94). However, when ethnic identification and SDO were statistically controlled, even though the link between RG and pre-judice was substantially reduced, it remained significant ($\beta_1 = .256$, $t = 4.50$, $p < .001$; $\beta_2 = .11$, $t = 2.23$, $p < .027$). Ethnic identification and SDO are indeed the two mediators of the effect of RG. However, it is likely that other variables mediate the effect of RG on ethnic prejudice. As far as the attitude towards the extreme right-wing is concerned, it is fully mediated by the measure of ethnic prejudice. In the model presented in Figure 9.5, the relationship between RG and attitudes towards the extreme right is non-existent ($\beta = .00$). It should be noted that this model explains 38 percent of the variance with respect to prejudice, and 33 percent of the variance in attitudes towards the extreme right-wing, which is substantial.

Conclusion

Over the past several decades, RD theorists have documented the role of RD in the explanation of intergroup attitudes and behaviors, suggesting that the more people feel deprived, the more likely they are to display outgroup prejudice. The theoretical implication of this legacy of research is that the less people feel deprived, the less likely they are to display negative intergroup attitudes and behaviors. In the present chapter, we have argued and demonstrated clearly that relative gratification may play an important role and substantially improve our understanding of prejudice.

Since the first studies highlighting the effect of RG (Guimond and Dambrun, 2002), significant headway has been made. First, it appears that the effect of RG is not circumscribed to the socio-economic context. Indeed, a manipulation involving a totally different dimension (i.e. intelligence) shows similar effects to those initially observed. It is therefore likely that the effect of RG reflects a general process. Second, the study carried out with a representative sample of the population of South Africa (Dambrun et al., 2005) seems to support the ecological validity of the effect of RG. Clearly, the effect of RG is not merely a laboratory artefact. The studies highlighting the moderators and mediators of RG confirm this fact, since clearly identified psychosocial processes seem to underlie it. However, as suggested by the last results presented in this chapter, it seems that other mediators besides those examined up until now underlie the effect of RG. More generally speaking, it is important that, in future studies, we manage to understand why the effect of RG mainly triggers prejudice towards at times indirect and essentially low status targets. Indeed, in the studies presented here, especially in the first part of the chapter, a gap is frequently observed between the targets manipulated (law students) and the targets of prejudice (e.g. ethnic minorities). Understanding this shift most certainly represents one of the main challenges of future studies.

References

Appelgryn, A. E. and Nieuwoudt, J. M. (1988). Relative deprivation and the ethnic attitudes of Blacks and Afrikaans speaking Whites in South Africa. *Journal of Social Psychology*, *128*, 311–323.

Bentler, P. M. and Wu, E. J. C. (1995). *EQS for windows user's guide*. Encino, CA: Multivariate Software, Inc.

Bodenhausen, G. V., Kramer, G. P., and Süsser, K. (1994). Happiness and stereotypic thinking in social judgment. *Journal of Personality and Social Psychology*, *66*, 621–632.

Campbell, D. T. (1965). Ethnocentric and other altruistic motives. In D. Leaven (ed.), *Nebraska symposium on motivation* (Vol. XIII, pp. 183–311). Lincoln, NE: University of Nebraska Press.

Cook, T. D., Crosby, F., and Hennigan, K. M. (1977). The construct validity of relative deprivation. In J. M. Suls and R. L. Miller (eds.), *Social comparison processes*. Washington, DC: Hemisphere.

Crocker, J., Major, B., and Steele, C. (1998). Social stigma. In D. Gilbert, S. Fiske, and G. Lindzey (eds.), *Handbook of social psychology* (4th edn.). Boston: McGraw-Hill.

Dambrun, M. (2001). *Dominance sociale et préjugés: la régulation sociale des cognitions intergroupes*. Doctoral dissertation, Laboratoire de Psychologie Sociale et Cognitive, Université Blaise Pascal, Clermont-Ferrand published in *Thèses à la carte*. Reference: 01CLF20009 – 288 pages – ISBN: 2–284–03961-8

(2004). Belief in paranormal determinism as a source of prejudice towards disadvantaged groups: "The dark side of stars." *Social Behavior and Personality: An International Journal*, *32*, 627–636.

Dambrun, M. and Guimond, S. (2000). *Inducing "superior intelligence": The effect of relative gratification on intergroup attitudes in a new context*. Unpublished data. Université Blaise Pascal, France.

(2001). La théorie de la privation relative et l'hostilité envers les Nord-Africains. [Relative deprivation theory and hostility towards North Africans]. *Revue Internationale de Psychologie Sociale/International Review of Social Psychology*, *14*, 57–89.

(2004). Implicit and explicit measures of prejudice and stereotyping: do they assess the same underlying knowledge structure? *European Journal of Social Psychology*, *34*, 663–676.

Dambrun, M. and Hecquet, C. (2004). *Relative gratification and fulfilment of expectations*. Unpublished data. Université Blaise Pascal, France.

Dambrun, M., Maisonneuve, C., Duarte, S., and Guimond, S. (2002). Modélisation de quelques déterminants psychosociaux de l'attitude envers l'extrême droite. [Modelling the social-psychological determinants of support for extreme right-wing movements] *Les Cahiers Internationaux de Psychologie Sociale*, *55*, 49–63.

Dambrun, M. and Taylor, D. M. (2003). *Intergroup attitudes in post-apartheid South-Africa: Foreigners as a prime target of prejudice*. Report #1 for the Southern African Migration Project (SAMP), January 2003. Unpublished Report, McGill University, Canada.

Dambrun, M., Taylor, D. M., McDonald, D., and Crush, J. (2005). The relative deprivation-gratification continuum and attitudes towards immigrants in South Africa: a test of the v-curve hypothesis. Manuscript under review.

De La Rey, C. and Raju, P. (1996). Group relative deprivation: Cognitive and affective components and protest orientation among Indian South Africans. *The Journal of Social Psychology*, *136*, 579–588.

Doosje, B., Spears, R., and Ellemers, N. (2002). Social identity as both cause and effect: The development of group identification in response to anticipated and actual changes in the intergroup status hierarchy. *British Journal of Social Psychology*, *41*, 57–76.

Dubé, L. and Guimond, S. (1986). Relative deprivation and social protest. In J. M. Olson, C. P. Herman, and M. P. Zanna (eds.). *Relative deprivation and social comparison: the Ontario symposium*. Hillsdale, NJ: Lawrence Erlbaum.

Duckitt, J. and Mphuthing, T. (2002). Relative deprivation and intergroup attitudes – South Africa before and after the transition. In I. Walker and H. J. Smith (eds.), *Relative deprivation: specification, development and integration* (pp. 69–90). Cambridge: Cambridge University Press.

Esses, V. M., Jackson, L. M., and Armstrong, T. L. (1998). Intergroup competition and attitudes toward immigrants and immigration: An instrumental model of group conflict. *Journal of Social Issues*, *54*, 699–724.

Fazio, R. H., Jackson, J. R., Dunton, B. C., and Williams, C. J. (1995). Variability in automatic activation as an unobtrusive measure of racial attitudes: A bona fide pipeline? *Journal of Personality and Social Psychology*, *69*, 1013–1027.

Forgas, J. P. and Fielder, K. (1996). Us and them: mood effects on intergroup discrimination. *Journal of Personality and Social Psychology*, *70*, 28–40.

Gilbert, D. T. and Hixon, J. G. (1991). The trouble of thinking: activation and application of stereotypic beliefs. *Journal of Personality and Social Psychology*, *60*, 509–517.

Grant, P. R. and Brown, R. (1995) From ethnocentrism to collective protest: responses to relative deprivation and threats to social identity. *Social Psychology Quarterly*, *58*, 195–211.

Grofman, B. N. and Muller, E. N. (1973). The strange case of relative gratification and potential for political violence: the V-curve hypothesis. *American Political Science Review*, *57*, 514–539.

Guimond, S. and Dambrun, M. (2002). When prosperity breeds intergroup hostility: the effects of relative deprivation and relative gratification on prejudice. *Personality and Social Psychology Bulletin*, *28*, 900–912.

Guimond, S. and Dubé-Simard, L. (1983). Relative deprivation theory and the Quebec nationalist movement: the cognition-emotion distinction and the personal-group deprivation issue. *Journal of Personality and Social Psychology*, *44*, 526–535.

Guimond, S., Dif, S., and Aupy, A. (2002). Social identity, relative group status, and intergroup attitudes: when favourable outcomes change intergroup relations ... for the worse. *European Journal of Social Psychology*, *32*, 739–760.

Guimond, S. and Tougas, F. (1994). Sentiments d'injustice et actions collectives: la privation relative. In R. Y. Bourhis and J.-P. Leyens (ed.). *Stéréotypes, discrimination et relations intergroupes*. Liège: Mardaga.

Jackson, L. M. and Esses, V. M. (2000) Effects of perceived economic competition on people's willingness to help empower immigrants. *Group Processes and Intergroup Relations*, *3*, 419–435.

Jones, M. (2002). *Social psychology of prejudice*. Upper Saddle River, NJ: Prentice Hall.

Kawakami, K. and Dion, K. L. (1995). Social identity and affect as determinants of collective action: Toward an integration of relative deprivation and social identity theories. *Theory and Psychology*, *5*, 551–577.

LeVine, R. A. and Campbell, D. T. (1972). *Ethnocentrism: Theories of conflict, ethnic attitudes, and group behavior*. New York: Wiley.

Martin, J. (1981). Relative deprivation: a theory of distributive injustice for an era of shrinking resources. *Research in Organizational Behavior*, *3*, 53–107.

Mattes, R., Taylor, D. M., Poore, A., and Richmond, W. (1999). Still waiting for the barbarians: South African attitudes to immigrants and immigration. *Southern African Migration Project*. Migration policy Series No. 14. Cape Town: Idasa.

Moghaddam, F. M. and Perreault, S. (1992). Individual and collective mobility strategies among minority group members. *Journal of Social Psychology*, *132*, 343–357.

Nelson, T. D. (2002). *The psychology of prejudice*. Boston: Allyn and Bacon.

Perrault, S. and Bourhis, R. Y. (1999). Ethnocentrism, social identification and discrimination. *Personality and Social Psychology Bulletin*, *25*, 92–103.

Pettigrew, T. F. and Meertens, R. W. (1995). Subtle and blatant prejudice in western Europe. *European Journal of Social Psychology*, *25*, 57–75.

Pettigrew, T. F., Jackson, J. S., Ben Bricka, J., Lemaine, G., Meertens, R. W., Wagner, U., and Zick, A. (1998). Outgroup prejudice in Western Europe. *European Review of Social Psychology*, *8*, 241–273.

Pratto, F. (1999). The puzzle of continuing group inequality: piecing together psychological, social, and cultural forces in social dominance theory. In M. P. Zanna (eds.). *Advances in experimental social psychology*, (Vol. XXXI, pp. 191–263). New York: Academic Press.

Pratto, F., Sidanius, J., Stallworth, L. M., and Malle, B. F. (1994). Social dominance orientation: A personality variable predicting social and political attitudes. *Journal of Personality and Social Psychology*, *67*, 741–763.

Runciman, W. G. (1966) *Relative deprivation and social justice*. London: Routledge and Kegan Paul.

Sherif, M. (1966). *Group conflict and co-operation: Their social psychology*. London: Routledge and Kegan Paul.

Sidanius, J. and Pratto, F. (1999). *Social dominance: An intergroup theory of social hierarchy and oppression*. New York: Cambridge University Press.

Sigall, H. and Page, R. (1971). Current stereotypes: A little fading, a little faking. *Journal of Personality and Social Psychology*, *18*, 247–255.

Smith, H. J., Spears, R., and Oyen, M. (1994). The influence of personal deprivation and salience of group membership on justice evaluations. *Journal of
Experimental Social Psychology*, *30*, 277–299.

Tajfel, H. and Turner, J. C. (1986). The social identity theory of intergroup
behaviour. In S. Worchel and W. G. Austin (eds.), *Psychology of Intergroup
Relations*. Chicago: Nelson-Hall.

Taylor, D. M. and McKirnan, D. J. (1984). A five stage model of intergroup
relations. *British Journal of Social Psychology*, *23*, 291–300.

Taylor, D. M. and Moghaddam, F. M. (1994). *Theories of intergroup relations:
International social psychological perspectives*. Westport, CT: Praeger.

Taylor, D. M., Moghaddam, F. M., and Bellerose, J. (1989). Social comparison
in an intergroup context. *Journal of Social Psychology*, *129*, 499–515.

Tougas, F. and Beaton, A. M. (2002). Personal and group relative deprivation:
Connecting the "I" to the "we." In I. Walker and H. Smith, *Relative depriva-
tion: Specification, development, and integration* (pp. 119–136). Cambridge:
Cambridge University Press.

Tougas, F., Dubé, L., and Veilleux, F. (1987). Privation relative et programmes
d'action positive. *Revue Canadienne des Sciences du Comportements*, *19*,
167–177.

Tripathi, R. C. and Strivastava, R. (1981). Relative deprivation and intergroup
attitudes. *European Journal of Social Psychology*, *11*, 313–318.

Vanneman, R. D. and Pettigrew, T. F. (1972) Race and relative deprivation in the
urban United States. *Race*, *13*, 461–486.

Walker, I. and Smith H. J. (eds.) (2002). *Relative deprivation: Specification, development, and integration*. Cambridge: Cambridge University Press.

Walster, E., Walster, G., and Berscheid, E. (1978). *Equity: theory and research*.
Boston: Allyn and Bacon.

Wilson, T. D., Lindsey, S., and Schooler, T. Y. (2000). A model of dual attitudes.
Psychological Review, *107*, 101–126.

Wittenbrink, B., Judd, C. M., and Park, B. (1997). Evidence for racial prejudice
at the implicit level and its relationship with questionnaire measures. *Journal
of Personality and Social Psychology*, *72*, 262–274.

Wright, S. C. and Tropp, L. (2002). Collective action in response to disadvantage: Intergroup perceptions, social identification and social change. In
I. Walker and H. Smith (eds.), *Relative deprivation: Specification, development,
and integration* (pp. 200–236). Cambridge: Cambridge University Press.

10 Social comparison and the personal-group discrimination discrepancy

Muriel Dumont, Eléonore Seron, Vincent Yzerbyt, and Tom Postmes

This chapter is about the correspondence between the psychology and social reality of devalued group membership. Well-being and the subjective satisfaction with life are, at best, modestly related to the objective conditions in which that life takes place. Often, members of minorities or otherwise devalued groups experience similar levels of self-esteem as members of objectively more privileged groups (for a review, see Crocker and Major, 1989). More surprisingly, they report very low levels of personal discrimination even if they are fully aware of the extent to which their group is discriminated against (Crosby, 1982). Thus, it would *appear* that they perceive themselves as less vulnerable to discrimination than the average member of their group. This discontinuity between judgments of discrimination for self and group has been called the *personal-group discrimination discrepancy* or PGDD (Crosby, 1982; Taylor, Wright, and Porter, 1994). It is a very robust effect that is found in a wide variety of devalued groups (Taylor, Wright, Moghaddam, and Lalonde, 1990).

The purpose of this chapter is to elaborate on prior work examining the role of social comparison processes in personal and group judgments of discrimination. Specifically, we consider the different goals and motivations involved in these perceptions and elaborate on the hypothesis that is being tested when personal versus group judgments of discrimination are made. One of the most significant consequences of social comparison activities is that they can alter feelings of entitlement, perceptions of being discriminated against, and the perceived relevance of various social categories. This chapter highlights some cognitive and motivational factors that lead to the selection of certain social comparison targets over others, the conditions leading to testing either similarity or dissimilarity hypotheses when comparing the self or the ingroup to these targets, and the consequences that this has for self- and group-evaluations in the context of discrimination. The first part of this chapter focusses on personal discrimination and examines why and how social comparison processes contribute to people's low sense of personal vulnerability to discrimination. The second part concentrates on group discrimination and considers why and how social comparison processes contribute to people's perception of group discrimination and to a sense of relative group deprivation.

The argument developed below is threefold. First, we draw on prior research to specify cognitive and motivational factors that lead to the selection of different comparison standards in judgments of personal and group discrimination. Second, we propose that in each judgment pertaining to discrimination, the hypothesis being tested with respect to the comparison target is likely to be a dissimilarity hypothesis. This is expected to create a contrast effect leading devalued group members to perceive themselves as less vulnerable to discrimination than their ingroup, and their ingroup as more discriminated against than the outgroup. Third, we propose that the goals and motivations guiding these social comparison preferences are of a different nature when personal or group evaluations of discrimination are made.

Personal and group discrimination: social comparisons of a different nature

The earliest attempts to explain the discrepancy between perceived personal and group discrimination focussed on motivational aspects and centered on the hypothesis that perceived low personal discrimination results from denial, or minimization, of discrimination experiences (Crosby et al., 1989), although exaggeration of group discrimination may also result in the observed discrepancy (Taylor et al., 1994). In recent years, however, evidence has accumulated to suggest that personal and group judgments could be viewed as two cognitive processes of a different nature. Indeed, the existence of different underlying comparative judgments (Major, 1994; Postmes, Branscombe, Spears, and Young, 1999), or different informational bases (Kessler, Mummendey, and Leisse, 2000) have been considered as possible reasons for the emergence of the discrepancy (see also Quinn, Roese, Pennington, and Olson, 1999).

It is widely assumed that individuals tend to make interpersonal or intragroup comparisons between themselves and others when evaluating personal discrimination. When evaluating group discrimination, however, intergroup comparisons between a salient outgroup and one's ingroup are more likely. To illustrate the point, Postmes et al. (1999) reported empirical evidence that personal and group ratings are of a qualitatively different nature. Instead of comparing two different measures for the personal and group judgments, these authors asked women to make explicit comparisons between themselves and other ingroup members (personal intragroup comparisons), between themselves and outgroup members (personal intergroup comparisons), and between their ingroup as a whole and the outgroup. By using these explicit comparative measures as predictors for the more general personal and group ratings (i.e. ratings for which the comparison target was not explicit) Postmes *et al.* (1999) provided evidence that, when reporting personal discrimination, members of devalued groups spontaneously compared themselves with other ingroup members, whereas group discrimination was based on spontaneous comparisons with the outgroup. Postmes *et al.* (1999) also showed that group, but not personal discrimination reports, were specifically sensitive to social motivations such as ingroup identification or audience concerns. The implication is that the very act of making a particular comparison activates different motives which are likely to draw upon relevant aspects of identity (personal or social) implicated in these comparisons.

Personal discrimination and intragroup comparisons

1.   Selection of the comparison target

The very act of social comparison depends upon comparability, which implies similarity at some superordinate level (Asch, 1952; Festinger, 1954; Merton, 1957). Thus, personal judgments of disadvantage are likely to be based, at least partly, on comparisons with ingroup others (e.g., Major, 1994). Similarly, Mussweiler (2003) argues that the choice of the comparison standard depends on a holistic assessment of the target-standard similarity. Consistent with this reasoning, shared group membership has been shown to assume a prominent role in the comparison process (Mussweiler and Bodenhausen, 2002).

However, it is not always the case that fellow ingroup members are chosen as standards of comparison. Blanton, George, and Crocker (2001) showed that women made intragroup comparisons with other women to gauge their satisfaction with a pay rate when it was framed as compensation for past work. In contrast, when it was framed as part of an offer for future employment, women made intergroup comparisons with men to gauge their satisfaction with the pay rate, and they were much less content. Thus, depending on the nature of the question (and the temporal perspective bound up in it), intragroup or intergroup comparisons were preferred. This change in the focus of comparison lead to radically different outcomes in terms of people's satisfaction about their situation. Thus, intragroup comparisons seem to be preferred on a default basis because of the greater comparability with other ingroup members. However, contextual cues are likely to affect the relevance of the comparison standard and may suggest that intergroup comparisons are more appropriate.

In addition to their availability and assumed diagnosticity, intragroup comparisons may also echo some personal needs. Indeed, a large body of work has examined the relationship between social comparisons and self-esteem. Typically, social comparisons with others who are doing poorly (downward comparisons) are thought to generate positive feelings and to contribute to well-being (Taylor, Buunk, and Aspinwall, 1990; Wills, 1981; Wood, Taylor, and Lichtman, 1985), whereas comparisons with others who are doing well (upward comparisons) are thought to have negative affective consequences (Morse and Gergen, 1970). Despite the fact that members of a devalued group are potentially confronted with repeated instances of upward comparisons as a consequence of the objective social position of their group, Crocker and Major's (1989) review revealed that members of a devalued group manifested surprisingly undamaged self-esteem and suggested that members of a devalued group use comparison processes in order to protect their self and cope with their unfavorable status. Specifically, these authors argued that preference for intragroup social comparison and avoidance of intergroup upward comparison protect self-esteem.

Martinot, Redersdorff, Guimond, and Dif (2002) provided evidence that comparisons with members of a valued outgroup harmed devalued group members' self-esteem, and further asserted the importance of group status in determining self-esteem and self-protection strategies in social comparison situations. In a series of studies, they compared members of dominant and subordinate groups as they were exposed to upward or downward social comparisons with either ingroup or outgroup members. The results showed that members of subordinate groups suffered most from upward comparisons with members of dominant outgroup, resulting in lower self-esteem. In contrast, the self-esteem of members of dominant groups was lowest when they were confronted with upward comparisons with members of the dominant ingroup (see also Schmitt and Branscombe, 2002). In other words, both members of subordinate and of dominant groups suffer from upward comparisons with members of the dominant group. Furthermore, additional data from Martinot *et al.* (2002) suggested that members of subordinate groups benefit from upward comparisons with an ingroup member by associating themselves with the success of the ingroup and increasing their group identification (see Martinot and Redersdorff, this volume, for additional evidence).

Martinot *et al.* (2002)'s conclusions seem much more consistent with Schmitt and Branscombe (2002) than with Crocker and Major (1989). Specifically, Martinot *et al.* (2002) suggest that "*it may be difficult for women to avoid unfavourable social comparisons with men and dismiss them as non-self-relevant.*" (p. 1598) Consistent with Blanton *et al.*'s (2001) findings, when women do make intergroup comparisons, they are unhappy about them. Although these comparisons are likely to be aversive and unpleasant, underprivileged groups still do seem to make them occasionally. Martinot *et al.*'s (2002) findings are not necessarily incompatible with the idea of deliberately avoiding intergroup comparisons when possible. Indeed, their results show the consequences of a given (forced) comparison on self-esteem but remain uninformative about which comparison would *spontaneously* be made. On the other hand, these results support the hypothesis that devalued group members will avoid these comparisons if possible because they are harmful to self-esteem.

2.   Hypothesis being tested and resulting assimilation or contrast

Detailing the cognitive mechanisms involved in processes of comparative evaluation, Mussweiler (2003) considers that selecting a comparison target is only one of the steps in the process. He argues that, after the comparison standard has been selected, comparison and evaluation still have to take place. In his selective accessibility model, Mussweiler (2003) proposed that, once the standard of comparison has been selected, social comparison involves a selective search for evidence indicating similarity to the comparison other. This is the comparison in itself. This selective test of a similarity hypothesis typically increases the accessibility of consistent self-knowledge and leads to the assimilation of one's self-evaluation towards the comparison standard. However, in situations in which people focus on differences between themselves and the comparison standard, contrasted self-evaluations are more likely to occur (Mussweiler, 2001).

According to Mussweiler (2003), whether similarity or dissimilarity is tested depends on whether one is generally similar or dissimilar to the comparison standard. An initial focus on similarities and the subsequent test of a similarity hypothesis can be expected to be the default option in most situations. It is only when people are forced to use a dissimilar standard of comparison, i.e. because such a standard is highly accessible, particularly salient for the critical domain, or because it is the only available standard, that dissimilarity is being tested instead of the default similarity hypothesis. The evaluation stage then integrates the collected information into one's self-evaluation and results in either assimilation or contrast to the standard of comparison (for more details, see Mussweiler, Rüter, and Epstude, this volume).

The role of group membership and social identity has also been examined in the context of social comparisons (Brewer and Weber, 1994;

Hogg, 2000; Mussweiler and Bodenhausen, 2002; Mussweiler, Gabriel, and Bodenhausen, 2000). Consistent with the idea developed above, Mussweiler and Bodenhausen (2002) provided evidence that spontaneous intragroup comparisons primarily involved the activation of individuated self-knowledge indicating similarity with the ingroup. As a consequence, subsequent self-evaluations were assimilated toward the ingroup. Spontaneous comparisons with outgroup members, however, primarily involved the activation of more categorical self-knowledge stressing difference from the outgroup. As a consequence, self-evaluations were contrasted away from the outgroup comparison targets (Mussweiler and Bodenhausen, 2002). Is it, however, always the case that intragroup comparisons lead to similarity testing and assimilation effects?

In the context of the research on perceived discrimination, the PGDD seems quite inconsistent with assimilation effects toward the ingroup. Rather, it is often argued that members of the devalued group are motivated to search for dissimilarity and contrast when they evaluate personal discrimination (Crosby et al., 1989). Because personal and group ratings have been found to involve different social comparison activities (Postmes et al., 1999), examining the difference score of personal and group ratings may be an inappropriate basis to draw such conclusions. However, there may well be some validity to the argument that devalued group members seek to positively differentiate from the ingroup discrimination that threatens their group. Indeed, in line with Self-Categorization Theory, one can hypothesize that there are conditions under which people would be motivated to focus on differences with ingroup members, despite their overarching similarity deriving from the superordinate category (e.g., when personal identity is salient; Turner and Onorato, 1999).

Several pieces of evidence suggest that contrast from the ingroup may occur when people contemplate the level of personal discrimination that they experience. For instance, Quinn and Olson (2003) used specific measures that make the comparison standard explicit. This allowed a precise evaluation of "where" the discrimination experienced by the participants stood in comparison to the proposed standard. Specifically, items were anchored from "*I feel less discriminated against than other women*" to "*I feel more discriminated against than other women.*" Through the use of such a comparative measure, members of the devalued group were invited to indicate very clearly whether they contrasted themselves from the ingroup, or not. As it turns out, Quinn and Olson's (2003) data mirrored the PGDD and confirmed that women reported being personally less discriminated against than other women. Contrast rather than assimilation thus seems to result from an explicit intragroup comparison.

In fact, these authors conducted two experiments in which the manipulations were expected to lead people to assimilate to the ingroup versus contrast themselves from the ingroup as a function of whether similarity or dissimilarity was suggested. In the first experiment, the framing of the questions was varied such that either the self was compared to the ingroup or the ingroup was compared to the self. The literature has shown that people more readily see the group as being similar to the self than the other way around (Codol, 1975). Results showed that when the self was compared to the ingroup, a comparison that invites contrast, women reported less personal vulnerability in comparison to the ingroup than when the ingroup was compared to the self, a comparison that invites assimilation. In a second experiment, Quinn and Olson (2003) provided external information indicating self-ingroup (dis)similarity. Results showed that when the available information suggested dissimilarities rather than similarities, women reported less personal vulnerability in comparison to the ingroup. Again, women contrasted themselves more from the ingroup when dissimilarity rather than similarity was suggested. Importantly, the contrast between perceived discrimination of the self and perceived discrimination of the ingroup appeared robust and persisted both when the group was compared to the self and when the self was compared to the group. In fact, the divergence in perceived discrimination for the self and the group only disappeared when externally generated information made the similarity between self and ingroup unquestionable. As noted by Quinn and Olson (2003), it seems that *"the threatening nature of discrimination overrides the default tendency to test for self-ingroup similarity and instead motivates individuals to seek evidence that they will not share the plight of their group."* (p. 235)

Evidence collected in our laboratory with similar measures making the standard of comparison explicit lends further support to our reasoning. Specifically, Dumont, Postmes, Seron, and Yzerbyt, (2004) tested the hypothesis that self-protective motivations lead devalued group members to contrast from the ingroup and perceive themselves as being less vulnerable to discrimination than their ingroup. We reasoned that threatening situations should foster people's self-protective motivations. Self-ingroup comparisons on discrimination issues are likely to be painful and threatening to devalued group members. This sense of threat, we propose, induces them to search for self-ingroup dissimilarity as a way to satisfy their self-protective needs. Of course, the more devalued their group, the greater the urgency for group members to dissociate themselves from the adverse effects of their group's disadvantage. In other words, members of the devalued group should be particularly tempted to deny, or at least minimize, their personal experience of discrimination under threatening

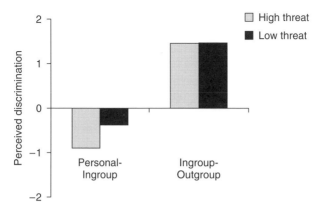

Figure 10.1. Perceived personal and group discrimination as a function of threat

circumstances. Such denial of discrimination would manifest itself through lower levels of reported personal discrimination. Because the measures are explicitly comparative, we would expect greater contrast between the level of discrimination people perceive for their ingroup and what they admit is applicable to themselves.

In a first study, we (Dumont *et al.*, 2004) used a stereotype threat manipulation to enhance women's motivations to self-protect. Stereotype threat partly consists of threats to the individuals because of their social group membership (Steele and Aronson, 1995). Specifically, participants were first confronted with either a threatening or non-threatening math test. Then, unrelated to the math task, the general level of perceived discrimination was assessed. Participants made direct comparisons between themselves and their ingroup, between themselves and the outgroup, and between ingroup and outgroup. Consistent with past theorizing that considers denial to be a tendency to distance the self from the ingroup (Crosby *et al.*, 1989), denial was evident in intragroup comparisons. As can be seen in Figure 10.1, the default tendency of these female participants is to consider themselves less discriminated against than their ingroup. This tendency was significantly stronger in a condition which placed participants under stereotype threat.

A second study built on Higgins' work on self-regulation to directly manipulate motives of self-protection (e.g., Higgins, 1998). We directly induced either a prevention or a promotion focus among women. Using this conceptually related but practically quite different manipulation, we perfectly replicated this pattern of data. Women with a prevention focus contrasted more strongly from their gender ingroup than women with a promotion focus. Interestingly, manipulation of personal motives has a specific impact on the self-ingroup comparisons. That is, inter-group comparisons remained totally unaffected by our manipulation of self-protection motives.

Clearly, the above empirical evidence is consistent with the idea that personal motivations affect the degree to which members of devalued group seek to differentiate themselves from those aspects of their ingroup which present personal risks to themselves. When self-protective motives have been aroused, people are more inclined to make contrastive ingroup comparisons, testing for dissimilarity between themselves and ingroup others. As a result, a very low level of personal discrimination is perceived. Interestingly, these self-protective motives do not in the least affect the level of discrimination that the ingroup as a whole is seen to endure. Group discrimination seems to be high, irrespective of the manipulations. In sum, these studies confirm that intragroup comparisons do not necessarily lead to assimilation, or to tests of similarity with the comparison standard. In fact, quite the opposite was observed in the context of discrimination, especially when self-protective motives were made salient.

To sum up, when people are led to assess their personal levels of discrimination, they are likely to make intragroup comparisons. Such comparisons are likely to be most diagnostic and relevant for both cognitive and motivational reasons. Unlike other social comparison processes, however, these judgments with essentially similar others do not elicit assimilative comparisons, but rather contrast from the ingroup. The degree to which this contrast emerges covaries with the degree of threat experienced, and the degree to which self-protection is sought. It can be inferred that the more the group in question is discriminated against, the bigger the search for a self-serving contrast between ingroup and self should be.

Group discrimination and intergroup comparisons

1.   Selection of the comparison target

In the case of group judgments of discrimination, the referent is much less ambiguous than for personal judgments. Technically speaking, group judgments may elicit comparisons with either the self, more valued outgroups – dominant groups – or devalued outgroups. Still, asking for a judgment about the group should more readily lead people to compare at the group level since this dimension is made salient by the question.

It is notable that in the contemporary literature on social comparison, intergroup comparisons are generally ignored. In fact, the literature is almost exclusively concerned with self-evaluations and target-other comparisons (e.g., Major, 1994; Mussweiler, 2003). Still, devalued groups are part of a large social structure which likely includes at least one dominant group and several other devalued groups (Rothberger and Worchel, 1997; Tropp and Wright, 1999). That is, intergroup comparisons with each one of these groups are possible. In contrast to comparison processes underlying self-evaluations, we think that selection of the comparison group for group evaluations does not necessarily result from the standard's similarity to the ingroup. Rather, it is most likely that availability or salience of potential comparison referents determines which group is compared to the ingroup. For a devalued group such as women, the dominant group of men immediately comes to mind (see Postmes *et al.*, 1999; Quinn *et al.*, 1999) although other more similar devalued groups, i.e. similar in that they are discriminated against and have comparable status, could equally serve as the comparison standard.

We see two main reasons for the dominant group of men to be more salient and preferred over any other group as the comparative standard. First, the gender dimension is bipolar and, as a result, one group calls for the other. Second, the issue of discrimination itself suggests that one group is being discriminated against by a specific other group. Logically thus, the dominant group is made salient because of the very aspect under judgment. The same reasoning holds for any devalued group that is specifically related to a single dominant group, i.e. blacks, immigrants, linguistic minorities. Another reason for preferring the dissimilar dominant group as the comparison standard resides in the fact that groups are partly defined through their distinctiveness from other groups (Oakes, Haslam, and Turner, 1994). Therefore, comparisons with dissimilar groups provide more diagnostic and relevant information for ingroup evaluations. Even if, or because, it is largely dissimilar to the devalued ingroup, the salient dominant outgroup becomes the favorite comparison standard for group judgments.

As shown by Tropp and Wright (1999), the relative status of the comparison standard may be particularly relevant for the level of deprivation that is being experienced. Specifically, these authors asked devalued group members to rate their feelings of deprivation compared to the dominant group and compared to other minorities. Results showed that people felt more deprived compared to the dominant group than compared to other minorities. This is of particular interest since group relative deprivation (rather than personal or egoistic relative deprivation) has been shown to serve as initial impetus for actions directed at changing the status and outcomes of the ingroup (Dion, 1986; Guimond, 2003; Hafer and Olson, 1993; Kessler and Mummendey, 2002). Thus, the initiation of collective action depends on the low status group's willingness to engage in a comparison with the group that is seen to be responsible for the subordinate status of the ingroup. In other words, intergroup comparison with the dominant group may be of particular importance to elicit relative deprivation feelings, need for social changes and desire to act against the group that is to blame for the disadvantaged position of the ingroup.

Acknowledgment of group discrimination is not without consequences for people's social identity. Indeed, when asked about their ingroup standing, people's social identity becomes salient and is appraised in comparison with the outgroup on relevant dimensions (Tajfel, 1981). If the comparison is in favor of the ingroup, then the resulting identity is seen as positive. On the contrary, if the comparison is in favor of the outgroup, as is likely to be the case for members of a devalued group, the outcome of comparison reflects negatively on people's social identity and they may try to improve the situation. For instance, when the ingroup is seen to occupy a relatively disadvantaged position, people may evaluate how easy it is to move from one group to another. That is, they assess whether intergroup boundaries are permeable, taking into account whether the intergroup status hierarchy is legitimate and stable, in order to infer whether individual upward mobility is possible (Tajfel and Turner, 1979; Taylor and McKirnan, 1984). Research reveals that when intergroup boundaries seem permeable, people's attention is focussed on personal identities, personal outcomes, and interests. In short, people adopt an "individual mobility orientation." (Tajfel, 1981) This orientation is marked by decreased ingroup identification, that is, dissociation from the disadvantaged ingroup, and a preference for individual actions aimed at improving the individual's own position.

In a series of studies, Wright and colleagues (Wright, 1997; Wright and Taylor, 1998; Wright *et al.*, 1990a) investigated the effects of tokenism on collective actions. Tokenism is defined as an intergroup context in which very few members of a disadvantaged group are accepted into positions usually reserved for members of the advantaged group, whereas access is systematically denied for the vast majority of disqualified disadvantaged group members. They showed that when as few as 2 percent of ingroup members are allowed access to advantaged positions, individual actions become the favorite response. Wright (1997) suggested that tokenism or highly restricted boundary permeability leads to preferring individual over collective action through focussing devalued group members' attention on their personal identity and encouraging interpersonal social comparisons with the few successful tokens who now hold high status positions. As a result, egoistic relative deprivation may occur and translate into individual mobility actions.

In a similar vein, Taylor and McKirnan (1984) propose that individual mobility motivations encourage interpersonal upward comparisons with others – ingroup or outgroup members – who are similar on dimensions relevant to the requirements for entry into the advantaged group. Consistent with this view, a series of studies have provided evidence that upward comparisons may indeed be beneficial at an individual level in that they provide positive role models, for instance in helping victimized populations to cope with their situation (Collins, 1996). The key aspect here is that such upward comparisons with outgroup members serve a self-enhancement rather than self-evaluation purpose. To be sure, by encouraging interpersonal upward social comparisons, for individual mobility and self-enhancement motivations, tokenism refocusses attention away from the intergroup comparisons and reduces the chances of perceiving group discrimination, feeling group deprivation, and undertaking collective actions.

In contrast, when intergroup boundaries are perceived to be closed, and the status hierarchy as illegitimate and unstable, attention is focussed on social identities, group outcomes and interests, and people adopt a "social change orientation." (Tajfel, 1981) This orientation is marked by increased identification with the ingroup an increase in intergroup social comparisons and a consequent enhanced motivation to improve the ingroup's position through social creativity and/or collective action (see Ellemers, 1993; Tajfel and Turner, 1979). It is thus when social change is perceived as a possible solution to an undesirable situation that intergroup comparisons, at least on the part of devalued group members, are most likely.

Both external and internal barriers can affect the perception of boundary permeability (Wright and Tropp, 2002). On the one hand, physical and structural factors can serve as external barriers that reduce the chances to move from the disadvantaged group to a more advantaged social group. For instance, ascribed characteristics (e.g. gender, race), norms and practices (e.g. direct or institutional prejudice or discrimination), or geographical distances between groups, can all prevent members of the disadvantaged group from leaving their group and joining the outgroup. However, self-categorization theory posits that people can simultaneously hold multiple identities and that, in each context, different categorizations can be salient depending on accessibility and fit (Turner et al., 1987). Even if women would hardly become men, or blacks become whites, they can hope to join the group of people that will allow them to benefit from the higher status social positions, jobs, and salaries. Even if both categorizations covary strongly, the relevant dimension or the intergroup boundary to cross then is not that of gender or race, but that of job status instead. This means that women, for example, are confronted with a much less firm boundary. The level of self-representation, as a qualified job applicant, or as a woman, or a black, thus affects which boundary is seen to be relevant to cross and the perception of its permeability may elicit either interpersonal or intergroup comparisons respectively.

In the discussion above, we deliberately talk of "perceived" permeability, for one should not risk ignoring the personal and social-psychological factors which can throw up internal barriers to social mobility and which also affect preferences for making interpersonal or intergroup comparisons and behavioral strategies. For example, strong ingroup identification increases solidarity, and thereby reduces the perceived permeability of group boundaries. Thus, ingroup identification makes intergroup comparisons with the dominant group more relevant and fraternal relative deprivation and collective actions more likely (e.g. Branscombe and Ellemers, 1998; Ellemers *et al.*, 1997; Tropp and Wright, 1999; Wann and Branscombe, 1995; Wright *et al.*, 1990b). Similarly, Postmes *et al.* (1999) showed that the level of identification significantly predicts perceived group discrimination, whereas reported personal discrimination was not affected (see also Ellemers *et al.*, 1999; Guimond, 2003; Operario and Fiske, 2001; Petta and Walker, 1992).

However, identification should not be seen as an individual difference variable, predestining one's relation to the group (Turner, 1999). Identification is not rooted firmly in individuality, yet at the same time it is not exclusively determined by contextual factors at the inter-group level either – there are intra-group factors such as respect and acceptance which feed it (cf. Branscombe *et al.*, 2002; Postmes and Branscombe, 2002). There is also an important ideological dimension to identification and ideology is (once again) not dictated by intergroup forces alone. Finally, identification is inevitably also influenced by intergroup factors: it is increased by situational factors influencing social identity salience (Turner *et al.*, 1987) as well as long-term factors such as minority status (e.g., Lorenzi-Cioldi, in press). Our view on the matter is that identification's influence in intergroup matters is so pervasive precisely because, through taking account of the social-psychological as well as the social-structural, it reflects what level of social comparison is most meaningful to the individual within the group.

Corroborating this argument, Doosje, Ellemers, and Spears (1995) provided evidence that, when compared negatively to a relevant outgroup, high identifiers perceive both ingroup and outgroup as more homogeneous than low identifiers. Furthermore, Spears, Doosje, and Ellemers (1997) showed that people who identify strongly with the devalued ingroup tend to self-stereotype more. This is in contrast to low identifiers, who depend more on contextual cues in determining appropriate comparison and behaviors, and who are more strategic in adapting their behavior to take the best out of each situation (Ellemers *et al.*, 1999, for extensive evidence and discussion; Kelly and Breinlinger, 1996). Postmes and colleagues (1999) showed that this extends to low identifiers' perception of group discrimination: the nature of the audience to which reports were directed made no difference for highly identified women, but low identified women reported more group discrimination in front of a female than a male audience. These studies suggest that highly identified group members live their life in intergroup or group-based terms, whereas low identifiers may use these terms to suit their needs in life.

It would thus appear that for highly identified group members, the intergroup context is more of a given than it is for low identifiers. Possibly, highly identified group members would also hold rather more firm and extensive representations of their ingroup. In contrast, low identifiers may be more inclined to construe images of the ingroup depending on the context and audience. Low identified group members should therefore use only a limited representation of the ingroup as a basis for their group judgment, and be more dependent on contextually-induced motives. Returning to Postmes and colleagues' (1999) study, facing a female audience should heighten low identified women's awareness that groups of women are discriminated against. Faced with a male audience, on the contrary, low identified women may become less aware of discrimination, and they certainly seem less motivated to express this. As a result, low identifiers' perceptions of group discrimination are likely to be more unstable.

To be sure, this reasoning is speculative and it is not clear yet whether audience effects such as the ones reported by Postmes *et al.* (1999) are due to compliance with the audience's expected assessment of discrimination, or with activation of different informational sets (cf. Kessler *et al.*, 2000), or both. Nevertheless, it is clear that both internal characteristics and external cues combine to affect the selection of the comparison standard. The resulting perception of disadvantage will depend on the relative weight and direction of these two forces.

2.   *Hypothesis being tested and resulting assimilation or contrast*

Although current empirical efforts guided by Mussweiler's selective accessibility model (2003) only speak to social comparisons devoted to self-assessment, this model should be applicable to group assessment as well. In the context of group discrimination, a comparison between the devalued ingroup and the dominant outgroup should be associated with an initial holistic assessment of dissimilarity. Actually, people might be drawn to making these comparisons as a means of indicting the outgroup. A selective search of evidence indicating that the ingroup is dissimilar to the outgroup should then be initiated, resulting in increased accessibility of knowledge that is inconsistent across both groups, i.e. instances of discrimination. The evaluation stage then consists of integrating the collected information into the ingroup's evaluation. Then, the devalued ingroup should be contrasted to the dominant outgroup, resulting in perceiving high levels of group discrimination. Although this model has not been tested at the group level yet, its assumptions are perfectly consistent with the literature on perception of discrimination or relative deprivation studies.

This chapter extends prior work examining the role of social comparison processes in personal and group judgments of discrimination. Specifically, we elaborate what goals and motivations are involved in the social comparison, we examine which hypothesis is tested during the comparison process, and what consequences may result at both levels of judgment. Empirical research on social comparison in the PGDD literature indeed suggests that different goals and motivations guide the social comparison process at personal and group levels, resulting in a different choice for a referent. Both contextual cues such as similarity salience and motivational factors such as self-esteem maintenance, may explain devalued group members' tendency to prefer intragroup comparisons when evaluating personal discrimination. In the case of group evaluations, cognitive salience of the dominant group due to its chronic accessibility (as is the case for people highly identified with their devalued ingroup) or due to its frequent association with the devalued ingroup, especially in the context of discrimination, would lead this group to be the favorite comparison standard when judging group discrimination. Moreover, motivational factors related to social identification such as the desire for group improvement call for intergroup social comparisons, or any other distinctive referent.

We further propose that, when asked about discrimination, members of the devalued group will always contrast both themselves and the ingroup to the referent. That is, contrary to what happens in many contexts in which similarity testing and assimilation are assumed to be the default options (Mussweiler, 2003), we propose that discrimination issues lead people to seek differentiation, resulting in contrasted self and ingroup evaluation. Indeed, the perception of dissimilarity would undoubtedly contribute to preserving self-esteem (contrast at the personal level) and boost social identification and improve the ingroup's status (contrast at the group level).

By gathering evidence coming from both social comparison and PGDD literatures, we hope to have extended our knowledge and understanding of the PGDD phenomenon. Indeed, we think that shedding more light on yet unexplored facets of the role of social comparison processes in the personal-group discrimination discrepancy would contribute to a better understanding of this intriguing and fascinating phenomenon.

References

Asch, S. E. (1952). *Social psychology*. Englewood Cliffs, NJ: Prentice-Hall.

Blanton, H., George, G., and Crocker, J. (2001). Contexts of system justification and system evaluation: Exploring the social comparison strategies of the (not yet) contented female worker. *Group Processes and Intergroup Relations, 4,* 126–137.

Branscombe, N. R. and Ellemers, N. (1998). Coping with group-based discrimination: Individualistic strategies versus group-level strategies. In J. K. Swim and C. Stangor (eds.), *Prejudice: The target's perspective*. San Diego: Academic Press.

Brewer, M. B. and Weber, J. G. (1994). Self-evaluation effects of interpersonal versus intergroup social comparison. *Journal of Personality and Social Psychology, 66,* 268–275.

Codol, J.-P. (1975). "Effet PIP" et conflit de normes. *L'Année Psychologique, 75,* 127–145.

Collins, R. L. (1996). For better or worse: The impact of upward social comparison on self-evaluations. *Psychological Bulletin, 119,* 51–69.

Crocker, J. and Major, B. (1989). Social stigma and self-esteem: The self-protective properties of stigma. *Psychological Review, 96,* 608–630.

Crosby, F. J. (1982). *Relative deprivation and working women*. New York: Oxford University Press.

Crosby, F. J., Pufall, A., Snyder, R. C., O'Connell, M., and Whalen, P. (1989). The denial of personal disadvantage among you, me, and all the other ostriches. In M. Crawford and M. Gentry (eds.), *Gender and thought: psychological perspectives* (pp. 79–99). New York: Springer-Verlag.

Dion, K. L. (1986) Responses to perceived discrimination and relative deprivation. In J. M. Olson, C. P. Herman, and M. P. Zanna (eds.), *Relative deprivation and social comparison: The Ontario Symposium* (Vol. IV, pp. 159–179). Hillsdale, NJ: Lawrence Erlbaum.

Doosje, B., Ellemers, N., and Spears, R. (1995). Perceived intragroup variability as a function of group status and identification. *Journal of Experimental and Social Psychology, 31,* 410–436.

Dumont, M., Postmes, T., Seron, E., and Yzerbyt, V. (2004). The motives to deny personal discrimination: The impact of stereotype threat and regulatory focus. *Paper submitted for publication.*

Ellemers, N. (1993). The influence of socio-cultural variables on identity management strategies. In W. Stroebe and M. Hewstone (eds.), *European Review of Social Psychology* (Vol. IV, pp. 27–57). Chichester: John Wiley.

Ellemers, N., Spears, R., and Doosje, B. (1997). Sticking together or falling apart: Ingroup identification as a psychological determinant of group commitment versus individual mobility. *Journal of Personality and Social Psychology*, *72*, 617–626.

(eds.) (1999). *Social identity: Context, commitment, content*. Oxford: Blackwell.

Festinger, L. (1954). A theory of social comparison processes. *Human Relations*, *7*, 117–140.

Guimond, S. (2003). Stigmatisation et mouvements sociaux. In J.-C. Croizet and J.-P. Leyens (eds.), *Mauvaises réputations* (pp. 257–281). Paris: Armand Colin.

Hafer, C. L. and Olson, J. M. (1993). Beliefs in a just world, discontent, and assertive actions by working women. *Personality and Social Psychology Bulletin*, *19*, 30–38.

Higgins, E. T. (1998). Promotion and prevention: regulatory focus as a motivational principle. In M. P. Zanna (ed.), *Advances in Experimental Social Psychology*, Vol. xxx, pp. 1–46. San Diego, CA: Academic Press.

Hogg, M. A. (2000). Social identity and social comparison. In J. Suls and L. Wheeler (eds.), *Handbook of social comparison: theory and research* (pp. 401–421). New York: Plenum.

Kelly, C. and Breinlinger, S. (1996). *The social psychology of collective action: Identity, injustice and gender*. London: Taylor and Francis.

Kessler, T. and Mummendey, A. (2002). Sequential or parallell processes? A longitudinal field study concerning determinants of identity-management strategies. *Journal of Personality and Social Psychology*, *82*, 75–88.

Kessler, T., Mummendey, A., and Leisse, U.-K. (2000). The Personal-Group Discrepancy: Is there a common information basis of personal and group judgment? *Journal of Personality and Social Psychology*, *79*, 95–109.

Lorenzi-Cioldi, F. (in press). Group status and individual differentiation. In T. Postmes and J. Jetten (eds.), *Individuality and the group: Advances in social identity*. London: Sage.

Major, B. (1994). From social inequality to personal entitlement: The role of social comparisons, legitimacy appraisals, and group membership. In M. Zanna (ed.), *Advances in experimental social psychology* (Vol. xxvi, pp. 293–355). New York: Academic Press.

Martinot, D., Redersdorff, S., Guimond, S., and Dif, S. (2002). Ingroup versus outgroup comparisons and self-esteem: The role of group status and ingroup identification. *Personality and Social Psychology Bulletin*, *28*, 1586–1600.

Merton, R. K. (1957). *Social theory and social structure*. New York: The Free Press.

Morse, S. and Gergen, K. J. (1970). Social comparison, self-consistency, and the concept of self. *Journal of Personality and Social Psychology*, *16*, 148–156.

Mussweiler, T. (2001). 'Seek and ye shall find': Antecedents of assimilation and contrast in social comparison. *European Journal of Social Psychology*, *31*, 499–509.

(2003). Comparison processes in social judgment: mechanisms and consequences. *Psychological Review*, *110*, 472–489.

Mussweiler, T. and Bodenhausen, G. V. (2002). I know you are but what am I? Self-evaluative consequences of judging ingroup and outgroup members. *Journal of Personality and Social Psychology*, *82*, 19–32.

Mussweiler, T., Gabriel, S., and Bodenhausen, G. V. (2000). Shifting social identities as a strategy for deflecting threatening social comparisons. *Journal of Personality and Social Psychology*, 79, 398–409.

Oakes, P. J., Haslam, S. A., and Turner, J. (1994). *Stereotyping and social reality*. Oxford: Blackwell.

Operario, D. and Fiske, S. T. (2001). Ethnic identity moderates perceptions of prejudice: Judgments of personal versus group discrimination and subtle versus blatant bias. *Personality and Social Psychology Bulletin*, 27, 550–561.

Petta, G. and Walker, I. (1992). Relative deprivation and ethnic identity. *British Journal of Social Psychology*, 31, 285–293.

Postmes, T. and Branscombe, N. R. (2002). Influence of long-term racial environmental composition on subjective well-being in African Americans. *Journal of Personality and Social Psychology*, 83, 735–751.

Postmes, T., Branscombe, N. R., Spears, R., and Young, H. (1999). Personal and group judgments of discrimination and privilege: Resolving the discrepancy. *Journal of Personality and Social Psychology*, 76, 320–338.

Quinn, K. A. and Olson, J. M. (2003). Framing social judgment: Self-ingroup comparison and perceived discrimination. *Personality and Social Psychology Bulletin*, 29, 228–236.

Quinn, K. A., Roese, N. J., Pennington, G. L., and Olson, J. M. (1999). The personal/group discrimination discrepancy: The role of informational complexity. *Personality and Social Psychology Bulletin*, 25, 1430–1440.

Rothberger, H. and Worchel, S. (1997). The view from below: Intergroup relations from the perspective of the disadvantaged group. *Journal of Personality and Social Psychology*, 73, 1191–1205.

Schmitt, M. T. and Branscombe, N. R. (2002). The meaning and consequences of perceived discrimination in disadvantaged and privileged social groups. *European Review of Social Psychology*, 12, 167–200.

Spears, R., Doosje, B., and Ellemers, N. (1997). Self-stereotyping in the face of threats to group status and distinctiveness: The role of group identification. *Personality and Social Psychology Bulletin*, 23, 538–553.

Steele, C. M. and Aronson, J. (1995). Stereotype threat and the intellectual test performance of African-Americans. *Journal of Personality and Social Psychology*, 69, 797–811.

Tajfel, H. (1981). *Human groups and social categories: studies in social psychology*, Cambridge: Cambridge University Press.

Tajfel, H. and Turner, J. C. (1979). An integrative theory of intergroup relations, in W. G. Austin and S. Worchel (eds.), *Psychology of intergroup relations*. Monterey: Brooks-Cole.

Taylor, D. M. and McKirnan, D. J. (1984). A five-stage model of intergroup relations. *British Journal of Social Psychology*, 23, 291–300.

Taylor, D. M., Wright, S. C., and Porter, L. E. (1994). Dimensions of perceived discrimination: the personal/group discrimination discrepancy. In M. P. Zanna and J. M. Olson (eds.), *The psychology of prejudice: The Ontario Symposium*, (Vol. VII, pp. 233–255). Hillsdale: Erlbaum.

Taylor, D. M., Wright, S. C., Moghaddam, F. M., and Lalonde, R. N. (1990). The personal/group discrimination discrepancy: Perceiving my group, but not myself, to be a target for discrimination. *Personality and Social Psychology Bulletin, 16,* 254–262.

Taylor, S. E., Buunk, B. P., and Aspinwall, L. G. (1990). Social comparison, stress and coping. *Personality and Social Psychology Bulletin, 16,* 74–89.

Tropp, L. R. and Wright, S. C. (1999). Ingroup identification and relative deprivation: An examination across multiple social comparisons. *European Journal of Social Psychology, 29,* 707–724.

Turner, J. C. (1999). Some current issues in research on social identity and self-categorisation theories. In N. Ellemers, R. Spears and B. Doosje (eds.), *Social identity: Context, commitment, content* (pp. 68–89). Oxford: Basil Blackwell.

Turner, J. C., Hogg, M. A., Oakes, P. J., Reicher, S. D., and Wetherell, M. S. (1987). *Rediscovering the social group: A self-categorization theory.* New York: Blackwell.

Turner, J. C. and Onorato, R. S. (1999). Social identity, personality, and the self-concept: A self-categorizing perspective. In T. R. Tyler and R. M. Kramer (eds.), *The psychology of the social self. Applied social research* (pp. 11–46). Mahwah, NJ: Lawrence Erlbaum Associates.

Wann, D. L. and Branscombe, N. R. (1995). Influence of level of identification with a group and physiological arousal on perceived intergroup complexity. *British Journal of Social Psychology, 34,* 223–235.

Wills, T. A. (1981). Downward comparison principles in social psychology. *Psychological Bulletin, 90,* 245–271.

Wood, J. V., Taylor, S. E., and Lichtman, R. R. (1985). Social comparison in adjustment to breast cancer. *Journal of Personality and Social Psychology, 49,* 1169–1183.

Wright, S. C. (1997). Ambiguity, shared consensus and collective action: Generating collective protest in response to tokenism. *Personality and Social Psychology Bulletin, 23,* 1277–1290.

Wright, S. C. and Taylor, D. M. (1998). Responding to tokenism: Individual action in the face of collective injustice. *European Journal of Social Psychology, 28,* 647–667.

Wright, S. C., Taylor, D. M., and Moghaddam, F. M. (1990a). Responding to membership in a disadvantaged group: From acceptance to collective action. *Journal of Personality and Social Psychology, 58,* 994–1003.

(1990b). The relationship of perceptions and emotions to behavior in the face of collective inequality. *Social Justice Research, 4,* 229–250.

Wright, S. C. and Tropp, L. R. (2002). Collective action in response to disadvantage: Intergroup perceptions, social identification, and social change. In I. Walker and H. J. Smith (eds.), *Relative deprivation. Specification, development and integration* (pp. 200–236). Cambridge: Cambridge University Press.

Part Three

Culture: comparison processes within
and across cultures

11   Stereotype content across cultures as a function of group status

Susan T. Fiske and Amy J. C. Cuddy

People want to know where they stand. Groups care deeply about where other groups stand. When a new group immigrates in significant numbers, people first ask whether they come with friendly or hostile intent. Do they come to cooperate, participate, and assimilate, or do they come to exploit, compete, and steal? Naturally, people want to know who may help or harm them. However, immediately after determining who is friend and who is foe, people want to know whether the other is capable of enacting those intentions. A fundamental question is the group's perceived status and from it follows their perceived capability to enact their intent, for good or ill.

To an extraordinary degree, people assume that groups of high status deserve it. As we will see, people all over the world agree that rich people, professionals, employers, and entrepreneurial immigrants achieve their high status with traits reflecting intelligence, competence, capability, and skill. Conversely, people all agree that others who are poor, homeless, drug addicted, or unemployed likewise deserve it because they are stupid, incompetent, incapable, and unskilled.

As our data will indicate, the strength of this effect is huge. In the senior author's career spanning decades, she has never observed correlations of these magnitudes. Why should people be so convinced that those with high status are endowed with superior competence and those of lower status are denied the same traits? This chapter explores the evidence and the reasons for this status endowment effect.

Social status and competence

Recently, we have developed the Stereotype Content Model (SCM), a theory of group stereotypes suggesting that groups array in a space defined by perceived competition and perceived group status (Fiske, Cuddy, Glick, and Xu, 2002). From perceived competition, observers infer lack of warmth, friendliness, and trustworthiness, and from perceived status, people infer competence; our theory emphasizes the two-dimensional space. Here, because the current volume focusses on comparison, we just focus on perceived group status, which is a relative judgment.

According to the SCM, people infer that other people's traits reflect their social status. Several factors incline people to this inference. All complex societies are hierarchically organized (Sidanius and Pratto, 1999). Stereotypes come from perceived economic, geographic, normative, and power relationships among groups (Eagly and Kite, 1987; LeVine and Campbell, 1972; Linssen and Hagendoorn, 1994; Poppe, 2001; Poppe and Linssen, 1999).

The perceived link between a group's societal outcomes and its competence serves several functions. This link may represent a group-level correspondence bias, namely, that people's behavior (in this case, their position) reflects their traits (Gilbert and Malone, 1995). Or it might reflect just-world thinking, namely, that people get what they deserve (Lerner and Miller, 1978). At the level of groups, it justifies the system (Jost and Banaji, 1994) and legitimates power–prestige rankings (Berger, Rosenholtz, and Zelditch, 1980; Ridgeway and Berger, 1986).

The link is not a foregone conclusion and the opposite viewpoint is conceivable: cultural stereotypes could instead reflect group-level sour grapes. A bigot might reason that the high-status outgroup inherited, lucked out, or cheated, so they do not deserve their position and they actually are stupid. Consider comments about royal families being stupid or a rich heir who was "born on third base and thinks he hit a triple."

Many intergroup stereotypes turn in part on consciousness of power relations; stereotypes justify the status quo (Berger *et al.*, 1980; Fiske, 1993; Glick and Fiske, 2001; Jost and Banaji, 1994; Jost and Burgess, 2000; Ridgeway and Berger, 1986). Envious stereotypes devolve on that high-competence but low-warmth lot who seem to be doing better than others. Prideful stereotypes belong to those ingroups or emblems of society that serve as reference groups, possessing both high status and the competence to achieve it. United States datasets have found the predicted correlations between perceptions of status and competence (Fiske *et al.*, 2002). Central and Eastern European stereotypes also support this competence-status prediction (Phalet and Poppe, 1997; Poppe and Linssen, 1999). Similarly, in ratings of European nations, perceived economic power predicts perceived competence (Poppe, 2001; Poppe and Linssen, 1999). Also, person perception (Wojciszke, Baryla, and Mikiewicz, 2003) demonstrates respect based on perceived status, as mediated by perceived competence. Stereotypes based on social structure legitimate an unfair, uncontrollable status quo (Glick and Fiske, 2001). Status correlates with competence stereotypes, justifying the apparent meritocracy. System-justification legitimates such political and economic group inequalities (Jost and Banaji, 1994). Superordinate groups justify their advantage by viewing the status quo as fair, and even subordinate groups endorse this view because it explains their own outcomes. For example, belief in a just world (Lerner and Miller, 1978) and the western cultural ideology of the Protestant Work Ethic (Katz and Haas, 1988; Kay and Jost, 2003) provide moral justification for the unequal distribution of resources: groups with high-status, well-paying jobs must have earned them through talent and hard work; groups on the bottom deserve it because they are incompetent and lazy.

Additionally, people may simply infer a group's traits from their social position. In interpreting behavior, westerners over-use internal dispositions, ignoring the influence of the situation (Gilbert and Malone, 1995; Jones, 1979; Ross, 1977). Thus, when a group is supposedly over-represented in high-status positions, people may attribute this outcome to the group's perceived competence.

Status and competence in Asian settings

These explanations – system justification, just-world beliefs, the Protestant Work Ethic and dispositional bias – while plausible in the western context, plant the seeds of doubt for an eastern context. First, culture shapes the ideologies that legitimate prejudice (Cohen and Nisbett, 1994; Crandall, D'Anello, Sakalli, Lazarus, Wieczorkowska, and Feather, 2001; Glick *et al.*, 2000, 2004). Collectively-held ideologies shape what people see as good and bad, thereby stipulating which groups will become the targets of which prejudice. For example, individualistic North Americans score particularly high in just-world beliefs (Loo, 2002), which morally justify good and bad outcomes, perhaps reinforcing the perceived status-competence relationship. Similarly, the Protestant Work Ethic lauds economically successful individuals and groups. Collectivistic cultures, without the Protestant Work Ethic and typically lower in just-world beliefs, might not generate the same link.

Second, North Americans are more likely than members of some other cultures to attribute people's behaviors and outcomes (competition, status) to dispositions (warmth, competence) as opposed to situational factors (Choi, Nisbett, and Norenzayan, 1999; Miller, 1984). Cultures without such a strong dispositional bias might not infer traits from structural outcomes. If not universal, the status-competence link might be emphasized more in individualistic, dispositional, meritocratic ideologies.

Thus, our inquiries required not only going outside the US, to Europe, but beyond, to the Asian and Middle Eastern settings. If the status-endowment effect extends that far, it approaches a potential human universal.

Overview of the international studies

Any discussion of pancultural phenomena requires testing across multiple cultures. So we tested the status-competence hypothesis by varying across cultures the two central factors that might have been driving the effects in the United States: perceivers and target groups. American perceivers might be influenced by unique norms, ideologies, and attribution biases that exclusively support our proposed principles. Likewise, the status-competence relationship might be embedded in American society's unusually heterogeneous mélange of groups or in its unique immigration history. For these reasons, we tested our proposed principles across multiple non-American perceivers and target groups.

We collected data from seventeen non-US samples representing fourteen nations. We gathered data from eleven samples in nine European nations (seven EU members – Belgium, France, Germany, Netherlands, Portugal, Spain, and U.K – and two non-EU members – Bulgaria and Norway), three East Asian nations (Hong Kong, Japan, and S. Korea), Costa Rica, and Israel (two samples – Jewish and Muslim).

In a first study, we used the same target groups as in our US studies, but surveyed a non-US sample of perceivers (Belgium). If the perceived status-competence relationship stems from characteristics specific to the perceivers' culture, it should fail to generalize to non-US respondents. Next, varying target groups, nine European nations rated the then current fifteen EU member nations, which constituted an alternative, pre-determined set of relevant groups, thereby eliminating concerns about biased selection of target groups and the potentially restricted applicability of the model to US target groups. In the third set of studies, seven samples from six nations (five samples from collectivistic cultures – Costa Rica, Hong Kong, Israeli-Muslim, Japan, and S. Korea; two from individualistic cultures – Belgium and Israeli – Jewish) rated lists of relevant groups in their respective societies; the groups were generated in preliminary studies in the same populations. This combined emic-etic (insider-outsider) approach unites culturally indigenous approaches to data collection (i.e., indigenous lists of groups) with imported approaches (i.e., our scales; Hui and Triandis, 1985). The goal is to make cross-cultural comparisons using equivalent stimuli, while simultaneously using ecologically-valid qualities of the construct of interest. This approach can provide a relatively unbiased test of our hypothesis – that in each sample perceived status would correlate positively with competence ratings.

Method and results

Samples and participants One thousand five hundred and thirty-five respondents from fourteen nations completed the questionnaire (Cuddy *et al.*, 2004). University students largely comprised all samples, which were 60 percent female with an average age of twenty-one. The samples included: 124 students (40 in Sample 1, 41 in Sample 2, 43 in Sample 3) at the Catholic University of Louvain at Louvain-la-Neuve, Belgium; 100 students at the Institute of Sociology, Sofia, Bulgaria; 150 students at the Université Blaise Pascal, Clermont-Ferrand, France; 98 students at the Eberhard-Karls-Universitaet Tuebingen, Germany; 122 students at Leiden University, Netherlands; 40 students at the University of Tromso, Norway; 102 students at the University of Lisbon, Portugal; 199 students at the University of Granada, Spain; 41 students at Cardiff University, Wales; 122 students at the University of Costa Rica; 60 students at the Chinese University of Hong Kong; 82 students at the University of Tsukuba in Japan; 91 students at the Ewha Women's University in South Korea; and 100 Muslim students and 104 Jewish students at Tel-Aviv University in Israeli.

Questionnaire and procedure As noted, different samples rated different groups. A Belgian sample rated groups from American studies (Fiske *et al.*, 2002, Study 2), but translated into French. Samples from the nine European countries rated the fifteen then-current member nations of the EU (Austria, Belgium, Denmark, Finland, France, Germany, Greece, Ireland, Italy, Luxembourg, Netherlands, Portugal, Spain, Sweden, and United Kingdom). Seven samples from six nations (five from collectivistic cultures – Costa Rica, Hong Kong, Israeli-Muslim, Japan, and S. Korea; two from individualistic cultures – Belgium and Israeli-Jewish) rated their own lists of relevant groups, generated in preliminary studies (described below). Like the groups used in American studies, these groups varied on race, gender, socio-economic status, occupation, religion, immigration history, etc.

Preliminary Groups-Listing Study. In seven samples, in their respective native languages, participants read and answered the following three questions (from Fiske *et al.*, 2002, Study 2):
1. Off the top of your head, what various types of people do you think today's society categorizes into groups (i.e., based on ability, age, ethnicity, gender, occupation, race, religion, etc.)?
2. What groups are considered to be of very low status by [Belgian/Costa Rican/Hong Kong/Israeli/Japanese/South Korean] society?

Table 11.1. *Scales*

Competence
As viewed by society, how ... are members of this group?
Competent, confident, capable, and skillful
Status
How prestigious are the jobs typically achieved by members of this group?
How economically successful have members of this group been?
How well-educated are members of this group?

---

3. What groups, based on the same criteria used in the first question, do you consider yourself to be a member of?

Question 1 aimed at getting participants to list relevant social groups in the least constrained way. In US studies, this question typically yielded lists that included neither very low status outgroups that might fit the pure antipathy model of prejudice, nor did it typically generate ingroups. Questions 2 and 3 were intended to insure that all types of groups would be listed. Groups listed by at least 15 percent of participants were included on the final questionnaire. In all samples, the number of groups was between twenty and twenty-seven.

Questionnaire. Participants rated the social groups on items measuring competence (competent, confident, skillful, able) and status (prestigious jobs, economic success, high education level), in addition to warmth (warm, nice, friendly, and sincere) and competitiveness (resources, more power, and special breaks). (See Table 11.1 for complete wording. For a complete discussion of warmth and competitiveness, see Fiske *et al.*, 2002.) The scales were developed and refined over the course of several studies (Fiske *et al.*, 2002; Fiske, Xu, Cuddy, and Glick, 1999). The original list of traits included both positive and negative items and many items unrelated to warmth and competence. Principal components factor analyses consistently pointed to two trait factors – one reflecting warmth and the other reflecting competence. Negative traits did not consistently load onto one factor, so they were dropped from the lists. For each nation, translators converted the questionnaire to the relevant language and all independent back-translations were satisfactory. Scale reliabilities were sufficiently high for all scales in all samples, competence (alpha = .67 to .85); and status (alpha = .69 to .84).

Using five-point scales (1 = *Not at all*; 5 = *Extremely*), participants read, "We ... are interested in how different groups are considered by [Belgian/German/Hong Kong etc] society. We are not interested in your personal opinions, but in how you believe others view these groups." The instructions aimed to reduce social desirability concerns and to draw on perceived societal stereotypes as culturally-shared knowledge, as in our earlier work.

Results

In all seventeen samples, exactly as hypothesized, perceived status highly correlated with competence ratings, average $r = .77$, range $= .55$ (Israel-Muslim) to .87 (Hong Kong and Spain), all $ps < .01$. This held both for samples from relatively individualistic societies (average $r = .78$) and from relatively collectivistic societies (average $r = .71$). Table 11.2 presents the status-competence correlations for all samples. Figure 11.1 depicts the strong relationship between status and competence averaged across EU samples, showing the fifteen EU nations scattered on competence and status ratings. Figure 11.2 depicts the status-competence relationship in a collectivistic sample, Hong Kong, showing the groups scattered on competence and status ratings. These correlations land in the ballpark of good reliabilities, but the status and competence items clearly are not measuring the same construct twice. Note that the status questions ask demographic questions (jobs, education, wealth), whereas the competence items ask about individual personality traits (see Table 11.1).[1]

All of the samples were demographically homogeneous, having come from college student populations, limiting our ability to compare responses of higher- and lower-status demographic groups. However, sex-based status differences favoring men are pervasive across cultures (Harris, 1991), and most of these samples included both female and male respondents. In all samples, analyses revealed no significant differences or trends between responses based on participants' sex; for female and male participants the status-competence correlation was equally high.

What does it mean?

The current findings converge with growing evidence from studies of specific groups: some overarching principles of prejudice and stereotyping may be pancultural, while some of their manifestations are culturally idiosyncratic. The overarching principles that have been tested thus far include high-level constructs, such as social structure (Glick *et al.*, 2000, 2004), cultural ideologies (Crandall *et al.*, 2001), and threats to resources and values (Stephan *et al.*, 2000, 1998), all of which hold up across varied perceivers. To this we can now add that perceived high-status endows its occupants with perceived competence, confidence, and capability.

---

[1] One status item – "well-educated" – could be viewed as having substantial overlap with one competence item – "skillful." In all samples but one (Germany), re-analyses of the data without "skillful" revealed no significant decreases in the strength of the status-competence correlation.

Table 11.2. *Status-competence correlations, all studies*

Study	Status-Competence r
US, students	.88*
Fiske et al., 2002b, Study 2 ($n = 147$)	
US, national sample	.83*
Cuddy, Fiske, and Glick, 2004, ($n = 571$)	
Belgium, students, US groups ($n = 40$)	.75*
EU nations	
Belgium ($n = 43$)	.72*
France ($n = 150$)	.63*
Germany ($n = 98$)	.68*
Netherlands ($n = 122$)	.84*
Portugal ($n = 102$)	.85*
Spain ($n = 199$)	.87*
UK ($n = 41$)	.85*
EU combined ($n = 755$)	.89*
Non-EU members	
Bulgaria ($n = 100$)	.72*
Norway ($n = 40$)	.84*
Collectivistic samples	
Costa Rica ($n = 121$)	.73*
Hong Kong ($n = 60$)	.87*
Japan ($n = 83$)	.75*
South Korea ($n = 91$)	.64*
Israeli samples	
Israel – Jewish ($n = 104$)	.83*
'Israel – Muslim ($n = 100$)	.55*

Note: $^*p < .01$

At the same time, some specific manifestations of these principles vary depending on culture and other contextual factors. For example, the groups considered relevant in each society do vary somewhat (Cuddy et al., 2004), the contents of particular groups' stereotypes often vary between cultures (Dion, Pak, and Dion, 1990; Shaffer, Crepaz, and Sun, 2000; Wheeler and Kim, 1997), as do the endorsement of prejudice-legitimizing ideologies (Crandall et al., 2001) and the relative weights of different intergroup threats in predicting prejudice (Stephan et al., 2000, 1998). Our research suggests that in any culture, a group's competence stereotype can be predicted from their status relative to other groups. However, culture influences the status a given group will have in a given society. As a result, specific group stereotypes vary across cultures.

Prior investigations all have focussed on prejudice toward specific groups; none has proposed general stereotyping principles that will hold

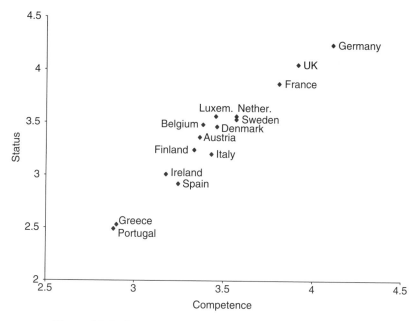

Figure 11.1. Status-competence correlation in EU nations' average ratings of each other

across varied perceivers *and* groups. The SCM provides a set of rules that emphasizes similarities in the basic structure of intergroup relations. The research summarized here suggests that this basic framework remains intact across cultures, allowing us to predict how groups are likely to be stereotyped on competence, based on their perceived status relative to other groups in their respective society.

Other research reflects the psychological bases of status inequality. In this volume, Glick reports data from twenty-five nations for Ambivalent Sexism toward women (Ambivalent Sexism Inventory; ASI) and seventeen nations for Ambivalence toward Men (Ambivalence toward Men Inventory; AMI). The ASI and AMI national averages relate strongly to the Power Distance Index (PDI), even when the Gender Empowerment Measure (GEM) is partialed out. The ASI and AMI scales not only reflect inequality, but also tap underlying values that support it (since the PDI measures support for social hierarchy).

In all this correlational data, causal direction is an issue. Correlations linking status to competence are encouraging for our model. However, correlations are only correlations. One could reasonably argue that social status precedes the perceived traits of groups and so logically should be

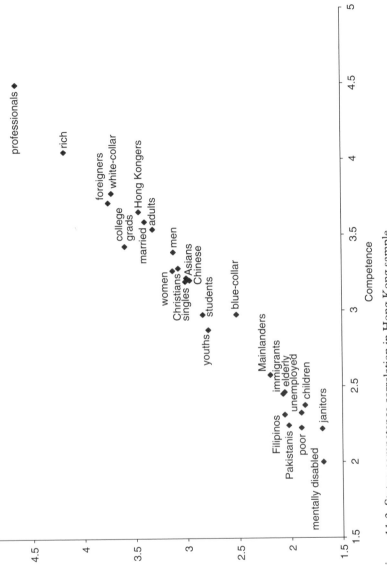

Figure 11.2. Status-competence correlation in Hong Kong sample

prior and therefore potentially causal. Indeed, experimental interpersonal research supports this causal direction. For example, conspicuous random assignments to low-status (e.g., clerks) or high-status (e.g., managers) roles cause people to perceive themselves (Langer and Benevento, 1978) and others (Humphrey, 1985) as less or more competent, respectively. But one could argue the opposite, that the groups' actual or perceived competence gives them their place in society. We do not deny this possibility, but we focus on perceptions.

Our methods aimed to capture stereotypes as culturally-shared, as opposed to personal, beliefs. Thus, we invoked a common frame of reference by asking people to report *society's* views of groups. One might argue that this approach obscures individuals' true beliefs, failing to reflect an accurate representation of the social world. However, people reliably project their own beliefs and feelings onto the beliefs and feelings of others (e.g., Marks and Miller, 1987). This "false consensus effect" generalizes to the domain of stereotyping; personal stereotypes highly correlate with reported cultural stereotypes (Gordijin, Koomen, and Stapel, 2001; Krueger, 1996). Moreover, mere exposure to (even without endorsement of) cultural stereotypes strongly influences perceptions and behavior toward outgroups (e.g., Gaertner and Dovidio, 1986). The importance of these findings is reflected in the field's increasing focus on cultural stereotypes (e.g., Jost, Pelham, Sheldon, and Sullivan, 2003; Glick and Fiske, 2001; Rudman and Fairchild, 2004).

Still, it is possible that personal stereotypes might not always correspond with cultural stereotypes. For the data presented here, participants not only rated outgroups – they also rated some of their own demographic ingroups and reference groups. Thus, comparisons of personal and cultural stereotypes might be particularly relevant here. In western samples, there is some evidence of ingroup and reference group favoritism on warmth and competence (Cuddy *et al.*, 2004). Yet across samples and cultures, female (lower status) and male respondents (higher status) reported equally high status-competence correlations. In SCM data collected from a representative United States sample (Cuddy, Fiske, and Glick, 2005), we found very few differences when comparing demographic groups by age, sex, religion, socio-economic status, race/ethnicity, and region of the country (e.g., Northeastern US, Southern US). These findings again underscore the power of dominant cultural stereotypes as shared meaning systems. When using this common frame of reference (i.e., society's views), even members of low status, disadvantaged groups rate higher status groups as more competent. Our ongoing research explores this issue more deeply by asking people to report either cultural or personal stereotypes (Leslie, Constantine, Fiske, Dunham, and Banaji, 2005); early data indicate that people report similar status hierarchies on more personal measures. However, compared to societal measures, they even more acutely believe that high-status people have some faults (lack of warmth) and low-status people have some virtues (warmth).

For us, the main lesson of this persistent, high, and troubling correlation is that people want to believe in the meaning of social hierarchies. This propensity has many names, most recently system justification (Jost and Banaji, 1994; Jost *et al.*, 2003). But individuals differ in their defense of the status quo hierarchies, according to their social dominance orientation (Overbeck, Jost, Mosso, and Flizik, 2004), their conservative ideology (Jost, Kruglanski, Glasner, and Sullaway, 2003), and belief in a just world (Jost and Burgess, 2000). Cultures vary, too, as our data indicate. Nevertheless, the correlations are always high and always positive, showing that, according to world-wide human belief, who you are depends on where you stand.

Author note

For help with data collection we thank Peter Glick (Lawrence University, WI, USA), Stephanie Demoulin and Jacques-Philippe Leyens (Catholic University of Louvain, Belgium), Michael Bond (Chinese University of Hong Kong), Jean-Claude Croizet (Université Blaise Pascal, Clermont-Ferrand, France), Ed Sleebos and Naomi Ellemers (Leiden University, Netherlands), Tin Tin Htun (Japan Women's University) and Mariko Yamamoto (University of Tsukuba, Japan), Hyun-Jeong Kim (Ewha Women's University, South Korea), Greg Maio (Cardiff University, Wales), Judith Perry (University of Tromso, Norway), Kristina Petkova and Valery Todorov (Institute of Sociology, Sofia, Bulgaria), Rosa Rodriguez-Bailon, Elena Morales, and Miguel Moya (University of Granada, Spain), Nadim Rouhana (Tel-Aviv University, Israel), Vanessa Smith and Rolando Perez (University of Costa Rica), Jorge Vala (University of Lisbon, Portugal), and Rene Ziegler (Eberhard-Karls-Universitaet Tuebingen, Germany).

References

Berger, J., Rosenholtz, S. J., and Zelditch, M. (1980). Status organizing processes. *Annual Review of Sociology*, 6, 479–508.
Choi, I., Nisbett, R. E., and Norenzayan, A. (1999). Causal attribution across cultures: Variation and universality. *Psychological Bulletin*, *125*, 47–63.
Cohen, D. and Nisbett, R. E. (1994). Self-protection and the culture of honor: Explaining Southern violence. *Personality and Social Psychology Bulletin*, *20*, 551–567.

Crandall, C. S., D'Anello, S., Sakalli, N., Lazarus, E., Wieczorkowska, G., and Feather, N. T. (2001). An attribution-value model of prejudice: Anti-fat attitudes in six nations. *Personality and Social Psychology Bulletin*, *27*, 30–37.

Cuddy, A. J. C., Fiske, S. T., and Glick, P. (2005). *The BIAS map: behaviors from intergroup affect and stereotypes*. Manuscript under review.

Cuddy, A. J. C., Fiske, S. T., Kwan, V., Glick, P., Demoulin, S., Leyens, J.-Ph., Bond, M. H., *et al.* (2004). *Is stereotyping culture-bound? A cross-cultural comparison of stereotyping principles reveals systematic similarities and differences*. Manuscript under review.

Dion, K. K., Pak, A. W., and Dion, K. L. (1990). Stereotyping physical attractiveness: A sociocultural perspective. *Journal of Cross Cultural Psychology*, *21*, 158–179.

Eagly, A. H. and Kite, M. E. (1987). Are stereotypes of nationalities applied to both women and men? *Journal of Personality and Social Psychology*, *53*, 451–462.

Fiske, S. T. (1993). Controlling other people: The impact of power on stereotyping. *American Psychologist*, *48*, 621–628.

Fiske, S. T., Cuddy, A. J. C., Glick, P. S., and Xu, J. (2002). A model of (often mixed) stereotype content: Competence and warmth respectively follow from perceived status and competition. *Journal of Personality and Social Psychology*, *82*, 878–902.

Fiske, S. T., Xu, J., Cuddy, A. J. C., and Glick, P. S. (1999). (Dis)respecting versus (dis)liking: Status and interdependence predict ambivalent stereotypes of competence and warmth. *Journal of Social Issues*, *55*, 473–489.

Gaertner, S. L. and Dovidio, J. F. (1986). The aversive form of racism. In J. F. Dovidio and S. L. Gaertner (eds.), *Prejudice, discrimination, and racism*. Orlando, FL: Academic Press.

Gilbert, D. T. and Malone, P. S. (1995). The correspondence bias. *Psychological Bulletin*, *117*, 21–38.

Glick, P. and Fiske, S. T. (2001). Ambivalent stereotypes as legitimizing ideologies: Differentiating paternalistic and envious prejudice. In J. T. Jost (ed.), *The psychology of legitimacy: Emerging perspectives on ideology, justice, and intergroup relations* (pp. 278–306). New York: Cambridge University Press.

Glick, P., Fiske, S. T., Mladinic, A., Saiz, J. L., Abrams, D., Masser, B., *et al.* (2000). Beyond prejudice as simple antipathy: Hostile and benevolent sexism across cultures. *Journal of Personality and Social Psychology*, *79*, 763–775.

Glick, P., Lameiras, M., Fiske, S. T., Eckes, T., Masser, B., Volpato, C., and Manganelli, A. M. *et al.*, (2004). Men are bad but bold (and women are wonderful but weak): hostile as well as benevolent attitudes toward men predict gender inequality in 16 nations. *Journal of Personality and Social Psychology*, *86*, 713–728.

Gordijn, E. H., Koomen, W. and Stapel, D. A. (2001). Level of prejudice in relation to knowledge of cultural stereotypes. *Journal of Experimental Social Psychology*, *37*, 150–157.

Harris, M. (1991). *Cultural anthropology* (3rd edn.). New York: Harper Collins.

Hui, C. H. and Triandis, H. C. (1985). Measurement in cross-cultural psychology: A review and comparison of strategies. *Journal of Cross Cultural Psychology*, *16*, 131–152.

Humphrey, R. (1985). How work roles influence perception: Structural-cognitive processes and organizational behavior. *American Sociological Review, 50,* 242–252.

Jones, E. E. (1979). The rocky road from acts to dispositions. *American Psychologist, 34,* 107–117.

Jost, J. T. and Banaji, M. R. (1994). The role of stereotyping in system-justification and the production of false consciousness. *British Journal of Social Psychology, 33,* 1–27.

Jost, J. T. and Burgess, D. (2000). Attitudinal ambivalence and the conflict between group and system justification motives in low status groups. *Personality and Social Psychology Bulletin,* 293–305.

Jost, J. T., Pelham, B. W., Sheldon, O., and Sullivan, B. N. (2003). Social inequality and the reduction of ideological dissonance on behalf of the system: Evidence of enhanced system justification among the disadvantaged. *European Journal of Social Psychology, 33,* 13–36.

Jost, J. T., Glasner, J., Kruglanski, A., and Sulloway, F. (2003). Political conservatism as motivated cognition. *Psychological Bulletin, 129,* 339–375.

Katz, I. and Haas, R. G. (1988). Racial ambivalence and American value conflict: Correlational and priming studies of dual cognitive structures, *Journal of Personality and Social Psychology, 55,* 893–905.

Kay, A. C. and Jost, J. T. (2003). Complementary justice: Effects of "poor but happy" and "poor but honest" stereotype exemplars on system justification and implicit activation of the justice motive. *Journal of Personality and Social Psychology, 85,* 823–837.

Krueger, J. (1996). Personal beliefs and cultural stereotypes about racial characteristics. *Journal of Personality and Social Psychology, 71,* 536–548.

Langer, E. J. and Benevento, A. (1978). Self-induced dependence. *Journal of Personality and Social Psychology, 36,* 886–893.

Lerner, M. J. and Miller, D. T. (1978). Just world research and the attribution process: Looking back and ahead. *Psychological Bulletin, 85,* 1030–1051.

Leslie, L., Constantine, V., Fiske, S., Dunham, Y., and Banaji, M. (2005). *The Princeton quartet: Changing public and private stereotype content.* Manuscript under review.

LeVine, R. A. and Campbell, D. T. (1972). *Ethnocentrism: Theories of conflict, ethnic attitudes, and group behavior.* Oxford: Wiley.

Linssen, H. and Hagendoorn, L. (1994). Social and geographical factors in the explanation of the content of European nationality stereotypes. *British Journal of Social Psychology, 33,* 165–182.

Loo, R. (2002). A psychometric and cross-national examination of a belief in a just-world scale. *Journal of Applied Social Psychology, 32,* 1396–1406.

Marks, G. and Miller, N. (1987). Ten years of research on the false consensus effect: An empirical and theoretical review. *Psychological Bulletin, 102,* 72–90.

Miller, J. G. (1984). Culture and the development of everyday social explanation. *Journal of Personality and Social Psychology, 46,* 961–978.

Overbeck, J. R., Jost, J. T., Mosso, C. O., and Flizik, A. (2004). Resistant versus acquiescent responses to ingroup inferiority as a function of social dominance orientation in the USA and Italy. *Group Processes and Intergroup Relations*, 7, 35–54.

Phalet, K. and Poppe, E. (1997). Competence and morality dimensions of national and ethnic stereotypes: A study in six eastern-European countries. *European Journal of Social Psychology*, 27, 703–723.

Poppe, E. (2001). Effects of changes in GNP and perceived group characteristics on national and ethnic stereotypes in central and eastern Europe. *Journal of Applied Social Psychology*, 31, 1689–1708.

Poppe, E. and Linssen, H. (1999). In-group favouritism and the reflection of realistic dimensions of difference between national states in Central and Eastern European nationality stereotypes. *British Journal of Social Psychology*, 38, 85–102.

Ridgeway, C. L. and Berger, J. (1986). Expectations, legitimating, and dominance behavior in task groups. *American Sociological Review*, 51, 603–617.

Ross, L. (1977). The intuitive psychologist and his shortcomings: Distortions in the attribution process. In L. Berkowitz (ed.), *Advances in Experimental Social Psychology* (Vol. x, pp. 174–221). New York: Academic Press.

Rudman, L. A. and Fairchild, K. (2004). Reactions to counterstereotypic behavior: The role of backlash in cultural stereotype maintenance. *Journal of Personality and Social Psychology*, 87, 157–176.

Shaffer, D. R., Crepaz, N., and Sun, C. R. (2000). Physical attractiveness stereotyping in cross-cultural perspective: Similarities and differences between Americans and Taiwanese. *Journal of Cross Cultural Psychology*, 31, 557–582.

Sidanius, J. and Pratto, F. (1999). *Social dominance: An intergroup theory of social hierarchy and oppression.* Cambridge: Cambridge University Press.

Stephan, W. G., Diaz Loving, R., and Duran, A. (2000). Integrated threat theory and intercultural attitudes: Mexico and the United States. *Journal of Cross Cultural Psychology*, 31, 240–249.

Stephan, W. G., Ybarra, O., Martinez, C. M., Schwarzwald, J., and Tur Kaspa, M. (1998). Prejudice toward immigrants to Spain and Israel: An integrated threat theory analysis. *Journal of Cross Cultural Psychology*, 29, 559–576.

Wheeler, L. and Kim, Y. (1997). What is beautiful is culturally good: The physical attractiveness stereotype has different content in collectivistic cultures. *Personality and Social Psychology Bulletin*, 23, 795–800.

Wojciszke, B., Baryla, W., and Mikiewicz, A. (2003). Two dimensions of interpersonal attitudes: Liking is based on self-interest, respect is based on status. Unpublished manuscript, Polish Academy of Science.

12 The cultural norm of individualism and group status: implications for social comparisons

Fabio Lorenzi-Cioldi and Armand Chatard

Western societies value personal autonomy and interpersonal distinctiveness. These values have substantial implications for people's comparison strategies. In western societies, the default comparison other is the individual rather than the group. People thus tend to engage in interpersonal rather than intergroup comparisons (Festinger, 1954). However, in this chapter, we argue for a two-stage model in which group status moderates this general, shared tendency. Members of high-status groups embody the values of society to a greater extent than do members of low-status groups. Hence, they emphasize individual comparisons more often than do subordinates. This status moderation is illustrated by research examples carried out in a variety of domains.

Cultural values and social comparison processes among the dominants and the subordinates

Western societies value beliefs in the uniqueness and separateness of individuals. These beliefs emphasize individualist or egocentric characteristics of the person such as independence, autonomy, achievement, and competitiveness. The prototypical western person is deemed an "independent, self-contained, autonomous entity who comprises a unique configuration of internal attributes such as traits, abilities, motives, and values, and behaves primarily as a consequence of these internal attributes." (Markus and Kitayama, 1991, p. 224) People in western societies strive for idiosyncrasies, inner potentials, excellence, and praise interpersonal diversity. Accordingly, they tend to make comparison at the personal level rather than the group level (Snyder and Fromkin, 1980), and to confer more value on individual than collective behavior (Lalonde and Silverman, 1994). As Jetten, Postmes, and McAuliffe (2002) cogently asserted, people in western societies display collectivism through strong individualism.

Such normative dynamics is usually examined on an *intercultural* basis. Large-scale comparative research shows that western cultures value individuals' distinctiveness and uniqueness, whereas non-western cultures (referring in most empirical investigations to Far East cultures) value ingroup harmony and individual responsibility to groups (e.g., Fiske, Kitayama, Markus, and Nisbett, 1998; Iyengar, Lepper, and Ross, 1999; Markus and Kitayama, 1991; Triandis, 1994). In the present chapter, we maintain that normative dynamics can be advantageously studied on an *intracultural* basis (Lorenzi-Cioldi, 2002a). The starting premise of this analysis is that social structure impacts people's tendency to adhere to superordinate or macro-cultural values. More specifically, a group position in the social structure determines the group members' degree of proximity to the shared prototype of the self-contained person. Thus, although in western societies individualism is an ideal defining a common system of reference in relation to which all people define themselves, those who belong to groups endowed with status and power fit this cultural imperative more closely, and can better enact it.

It follows from the above that the existence of shared values does not preclude heterogeneity between social groups. According to Deschamps (1982): "[Groups] are not pre-existing closed spheres each of which would be able to engender its own specific system of meanings. It cannot therefore be said that each group has its own interpretations and values; groups exist as something which is concrete and 'objective' only in the context of some values which are common to the society as a whole." (pp. 87–88) The logic of this argument entails that it is not the system of values which determines the diversity of groups, but, quite on the contrary, a common, homogeneous system of values. Tajfel's contention – that intergroup discrimination is stronger when group comparisons take place within a common system of reference – exemplifies this point (e.g., Turner, Brown, and Tajfel, 1979; see also Kessler and Mummendey, 2002). The existence of shared values is associated with the fact that members of the high-status group set the standard of the culturally valued behavior against which members of the low-status group define themselves (Smith and Zàrate, 1992). Thus, the latter do not single themselves apart in terms of criteria which are internal to their group; they do this starting from points of reference which are offered to them by a relevant higher status group (see Apfelbaum, 1979). Elsewhere, we have discussed the impact of this intracultural status dynamics on social identity phenomena (Lorenzi-Cioldi, 2002b, 2004a, 2004b). We showed that shared norms are conducive to diverging paths of social identification in terms of individuated high-status groups and depersonalized low-status groups. The focus of the present chapter is on the impact of this status dynamics on social comparison processes.

To set the stage of this analysis, it is important to note that people compare themselves to others not only in terms of their abilities and opinions, but also in terms of a vast array of social identity elements (groups, status symbols, material goods, etc.). By definition, a group status is a comparative notion that is based on conceptions of inequality: one's group membership status is not superior or inferior in any absolute sense; it is so within a status hierarchy, that is in comparison to other groups. However, people in high-status positions adhere more intensely to the prototype of the self-contained person than those in low-status positions. Thus, they come to define themselves as unique persons rather than undifferentiated, homogeneous group members. The crucial point here is that the dominants' elusive references to collective aspects of their identity, for the benefit of references to the person and his/her freedom from role constraints, are the very consequence of their superior status. Social comparison strategies are thus contingent on the group membership status: for high-status people, horizontal, personal comparisons prevail over intergroup comparisons; for those in low-status positions, vertical, intergroup comparisons take priority over the personal (Hagendoorn, 1995; Lorenzi-Cioldi, 2004b).

A compelling hypothesis that ensues from this reasoning is that the choice of a comparison other tends to differ at unequal status positions. For members of high-status groups, the individual other is the default. However, their comparison strategies testify to some flexibility. Specifically, the group is called on in specific situations, namely when group-level comparisons are contextually salient (see Turner, Hogg, Oakes, Reicher, and Wetherell, 1987). For members of low-status groups, the collective other is the default, engendering a chronic accessibility of group-level comparisons. This higher accessibility boosts the saliency of collective identifications in most situations.

There is suggestive evidence for this role of group status on comparison dynamics. Let us mention just two examples taken from the sociological and the socio-psychological research in the domain of self-perception. Studies on spontaneous descriptions of the self show that people in individualist societies, as well as members of high-status groups in these societies, indulge in ego-autonomy contents such as personality traits, dispositions, and preferences. Conversely, people in collectivist societies, as well as members of low-status groups in individualist societies, put more emphasis on their group memberships and social roles, even in the absence of explicit comparisons with the outgroup (e.g., McGuire, 1984). This status effect has been replicated in western cultures using a variety of status cues, such as gender (Lorenzi-Cioldi, 1994), level of education (Deschamps, Lorenzi-Cioldi, and Meyer, 1982), ethnicity (Lorenzi-Cioldi and Meyer, 1984), and professional role (Guillaumin, 1972; Serino, 1994). Collectively, these studies provide evidence of the low-status group members' tendency to put strong emphasis on their group membership when describing themselves. Furthermore, a number of surveys suggest that collective memberships among the disadvantaged are often of such overwhelming salience that additional prestige accruing from education or occupational status hardly impacts on the group members' identification. To illustrate, whites with higher education or prestigious occupations subjectively identify as high-status persons, whereas blacks who succeed in the same mobility attempts continue to subjectively identify as blacks (Jackman and Jackman, 1983).

Of more relevance for the present purpose are experimental demonstrations of this chronic salience of group membership among the disadvantaged. Pichevin and Hurtig (1996), and Lorenzi-Cioldi (1991), showed that context variables, namely the numerical ratio of the gender groups and the dimensions of intergroup comparisons, altered the perceptual salience of the male but not the female sex-membership. The latter remained highly accessible and readily available for use in all situations. Likewise, studies on the uniqueness and deindividuation phenomena suggest that women, compared to men, show more resistance and tolerance of (or lack of concern about) threats to their personal uniqueness (Festinger, Gerard, Hymovitch, Kelley, and Raven, 1952; Fromkin, 1972), and better fit or adaptation to strongly depersonalized groups (Lorenzi-Cioldi and Doise, 1990).

In what follows, we provide empirical illustrations of this two-stage intracultural analysis. The following section shows that a shared norm of the self-contained person organizes self-representations and representations of other people and social activities in the society at large. To illustrate the second stage, we then introduce the participant group status as a moderator of this general tendency towards personal uniqueness.

The pervasiveness of individual comparisons

Two recent studies related to advertising will illustrate our assumption that in western societies at large there is a shared norm of the self-contained person that is spontaneously used to organize perceptions of objects and people.

Social representations of prestige. Twenty-four male and thirty-six female randomly selected adults rated the prestige conveyed by advertisements of a variety of goods (clothes, shoes, watches, cars, etc.) on a series of content dimension, using a ten-point scale ($10 = very\ important$) (Lorenzi-Cioldi, 2000). A principal component analysis of these responses yielded a two-dimensional solution that explains 52 percent of the total variance. The results are shown in Figure 12.1.

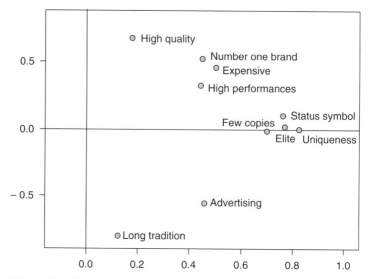

Figure 12.1. Principal components analysis of "What confers prestige to a goods"
Note: Components 1 (horizontal) and 2 (vertical) of the two-dimensional solution.

Component 1 refers to a general conception of social status ("It is a status symbol") in terms of items that convey the idea of *small numbers* and *rarity* (e.g., "It is meant for an elite"; "It is produced in few copies"). It is noteworthy that the item "It arouses feelings of personal uniqueness" loads significantly on this dimension. This item suggests that the capacity of the goods to propel some sense of personal uniqueness and dissimilarity from other people, rather than the goods' intrinsic characteristics, is the key determinant of how prestige comes to goods. The goods' intrinsic characteristics emerge on the second component. This dimension highlights a more standard quality-oriented conception of the prestige of goods. It opposes the goods' quality, price, and the prestige of the brand, to the brand's tradition and its advertising. Thus, the emphasis on individuals' uniqueness, on their membership in a small group, and their mutual comparisons at the individual level emerge as a coherent organizing principle of the acknowledgment of the goods' prestige.

Gendered cars ... but with one hell of a personality. Lorenzi-Cioldi (2001) asked a sample of eighty-seven male and fifty-seven female owners of a new car to rate their car on twenty attributes (seven-point scales). A principal components analysis of these responses yielded a four-dimensional

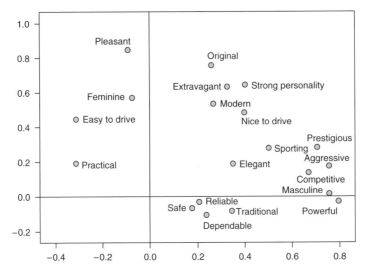

Figure 12.2. Principal components analysis of the descriptions of one's own car
Note: Components 1 (horizontal) and 2 (vertical) of the four-dimensional solution.

solution explaining 60 percent of the total variance. Figure 12.2 shows the results of this analysis.

Component 1 stresses a masculine stereotype (e.g., "Masculine," "Competitive," "Powerful"), and component 2 a feminine stereotype ("Feminine," "Pleasant," "Easy to drive"). The analysis of the participants' factor scores corroborates this interpretation: men, along with people with higher earnings, adhere altogether to the masculine dimension and women adhere to the feminine dimension. More importantly, however, the prominence of a few, distinctive items, namely "Has a strong personality," "Extravagant," and "Original," appears on *both* components. These items clearly suggest the importance of differentiating oneself as a unique person when purchasing a car. Accordingly, one's car may be either "Masculine" or "Feminine," so to speak, but in any event it must have a personality of its own. In short, people engage in purchase behaviors that reflect a preference for gender related possessions, without relinquishing a shared and prized norm of cultural individualism.

Group status and adherence to individualist values

Recall the premises of our intracultural analysis. On the one hand, people in western societies strive to define themselves in terms of autonomy and independence. On the other, only members of high-status groups succeed altogether in this effort. This idea was tested in a series of questionnaire studies using gender as an indicator of group status (Lorenzi-Cioldi and Dafflon, 1998; Lorenzi-Cioldi, 2002a). Gender was used because the content of sex-stereotypes along the constructs of agency and communion bears links with the content of cultural stereotypes along the individualism-collectivism distinction. By and large, the male stereotype has an instrumental or agentic tone, while the female stereotype propounds more expressive, relational, or communal contents (Eagly, 1987; Eagly and Kite, 1987; Gilligan, 1982; Markus and Oyserman, 1989). As a consequence, in western societies, men and women differ as groups according to the degree of proximity of their ingroup norms to the shared cultural norm of the self-contained person: men match it more closely than women (Amâncio, 1997; Rosenkrantz, Vogel, Bee, Broverman, and Broverman, 1968).

In accordance with a common finding in intercultural research, the first hypothesis of these studies was that there would be a general tendency for participants to endorse the belief in the self-contained person. However, based on our intracultural framework, this trend was expected to be qualified by the participant status. Hypothesis 2 stated that members of the high-status group, i.e. men, would perceive themselves, and be perceived by others, as possessing the attributes of the shared cultural norm, whereas members of the low-status group, i.e. women, would perceive themselves, and be perceived by others, as possessing intermediate and average levels of both the shared norm and the ingroup, more relational norm. Thus, the dominant norm of the self-contained person and the respective ingroup norms would coincide, and grow in strength, for judgments of male targets, and would conflict, and cancel each other out, for judgments of female targets.

Male and female Swiss College students ($Ns = 511$ men, 713 women) judged the extent to which various attributes applied to "people in general" (Study 1), to "men" and "women" (Studies 2 and 3), to "Occidentals" and "Orientals," and to their self (Studies 3 and 4). Two attributes representing each culture were selected in a pilot study: the western *individual* norm was represented by "independent" (positive valence) and "individualistic" (negative); the non-western *collective* norm was represented by "collectivistic" (positive) and "follower" (negative). (In addition, alternative designations of the attributes were used, for instance "conformist" for the negative pole of the collective norm; however, the findings were unaffected by these variations; see Lorenzi-Cioldi, 2002a, pp. 63ff, for details).

As expected on the basis of the literature on intercultural self-perception, the results showed that "people in general" were credited higher scores of attributes related to the individual than the collective norm. Likewise, judgments of "Occidentals" displayed a striking individual flavor, whereas those of "Orientals" displayed a corresponding collective flavor. Finally, differences between male and female participants, in general and across targets, were not reliable, except for self-perceptions (see below). These preliminary results attest that the ideal, in a western culture, is the self-contained person, and that western people attribute another, more communal and connected ideal, to non-western cultures.

Consistent with hypothesis 1, all the targets, including the participants' self, were overall ascribed more attributes related to the individual rather than the collective norm. However, in accordance with hypothesis 2, this individual-based perception of the targets was qualified by the targets' social status. On the one hand, consistent with the literature on sex-role stereotypes (Rosenkrantz et al., 1968), judgments of "men" paralleled closely those of "people in general": these two targets were ascribed more of the individual than the collective norm. On the other hand, demonstrating the lack of parallelism between the representations of the male and the female groups, judgments of female targets, as well as women's self, matched neither those of "men" and "people in general," nor those of "Occidentals" and "Orientals." These lower status targets were ascribed similar and intermediate levels of the individual and the collective norms. Finally, the results showed that the participants judged their self similarly to their gender ingroup: men described themselves by means of the behaviors related to the individual norm, whereas women attributed to their self comparable levels of both individual and collective behaviors. Nonetheless, self-descriptions were overall less extreme than the descriptions of groups of people (see also Doise and Lorenzi-Cioldi, 1991).

Study 4 introduced a prime for the judgments of the targets. In one condition, participants were told that the study aimed at investigating how people perceive themselves and others as a function of their gender. In the other condition, the instructions stressed that the interest of the study was on how people perceive themselves and others as a function of their cultural membership (West vs. Far East cultures). The participants then judged their self and the gendered targets (condition 1), or their self and the cultural targets (condition 2), on the normative and counter-normative attributes used in the previous studies. The results regarding self-perception are presented in Figure 12.3.

Besides replicating the above effects, the analysis of self-perception yielded an interaction between the prime condition, the participant gender, and the norm. The prime had no effect on women's self-ratings: women consistently described themselves with similar levels of the individual and the collective norms. Men, on the contrary, showed

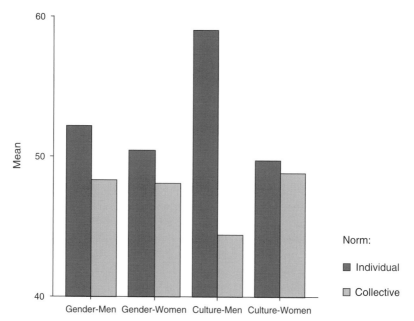

Figure 12.3. Self-perception of male and female college students according to the gender vs. cultural prime: individual and collective norms

Note: 100 mm scale ranging from "does not apply at all" (0) to "applies entirely" (100), for each norm. Attributes related to the individual norm (independent and individualistic) on the one hand, and to the collective norm (collectivist and follower, or conformist) on the other hand, were collapsed.

a robust shift in self-perception according to the prime. It is obvious from Figure 12.3 that men's tendency to describe themselves using more of the individual than the collective norm gained prominence under the cultural prime. That is, when describing themselves as members of the larger western culture, compared to members of the male category, men showed a stronger self-perception in terms of the shared norm of the self-contained person.

A detailed analysis of the means further revealed that this increased adherence to the shared norm under the cultural prime was due to a large increase in the endorsement of the *negative* pole of the norm ("individualistic"), not the positive ("independent"). It is worth noting that this latter phenomenon, though surprising at first glance, is compatible with recent findings in the field of social attribution. Research on the ultimate attribution error – the tendency to underscore dispositional forces as opposed to situational forces in explaining a target's behavior – shows that in western cultures this bias tends to occur irrespective of the desirability of the target's behavior (Beauvois, Gilibert, Pansu, and Abdelaoui, 1998). In particular, members of powerful or dominant groups explain their desirable behavior, as well as their undesirable behavior, by internal causes, even if in this process they downplay their inherent motivation to present themselves in a positive way. They thus take the individual norm to extremes, attributing to themselves negative characteristics such as disproportionate individualism, aggressiveness, self-assurance, or competitiveness. This phenomenon casts doubts upon the allegedly universality, or "panculturality," of the self-enhancement motive (Taylor and Brown, 1988; Sedikides, Gaertner, and Toguchi, 2003). People in high-status positions seem to agree to relinquish this motive in order to adhere as intensely as possible to an individual-based self-conception.

At a more general level, the results presented so far suggest that group status is a key variable in determining the group members' self-conceptions in terms of individualistic, or collectivistic contents. According to social identity theory, individualistic self-conceptions should elicit interpersonal comparisons, whereas collectivistic self-conceptions should elicit intergroup comparisons (Tajfel and Turner, 1986). Therefore, for members of the dominant group, the default comparison other should be another person in most circumstances, unless those people are explicitly instructed to compare with the outgroup. For members of the subordinate group, the default other should be the outgroup, and this chronic accessibility of the collective should arise even in the absence of any explicit instruction to compare oneself at the group level.

There is some evidence for this difference. Hogg and Turner (1987), for instance, used gender as a cue for categorization and created a condition in which sex-category membership was expected to be salient (discussion in an inter-sex group), and another condition in which idiosyncratic and personal features were expected to be salient (discussion in an intra-sex dyad). In line with self-categorization theory (Turner *et al.*, 1987), the authors found that, when asked to rate their degree of sex-typicality, male and female participants perceived themselves as being more typical of their own sex when they interacted in an intergroup rather than an interpersonal setting. Upon closer inspection of these results, however, we can notice that changes in self-perception occurred mainly for male participants (for female participants, the corresponding changes did not reach conventional levels of significance, cf. Hogg and Turner, 1987, p. 331; see also Lorenzi-Cioldi, 1991).

Do males show a general tendency to change their self-perception more than females as a function of the comparative context? This finding, along with other findings reviewed in the first section of this chapter, suggests that changes in self-evaluation as a function of the comparative context are specific to members of the dominant group, not the subordinate group. Of course, social comparisons are important for everyone (Buunk and Mussweiler, 2001; Festinger, 1954; Wood and Wilson, 2003). However, the consequences of comparisons with ingroup and outgroup members may be different, at least in magnitude, for members of the dominant group and for members of the subordinate group. Our analysis so far suggests that status plays a role in shaping the kind of self-representation that one can observe among gender groups, with men having more individual-centered self-definitions, and women more group-centered self-definitions. This difference has implications for people's tendency to spontaneously adopt individual or group comparisons. For women, group comparison may be more common than for men. As a result, we predict that by varying the salience of between-group comparisons we can impact more strongly men's judgments than women's. In the concluding section of this chapter, we examine evidence that provides a direct test of this prediction about the effects of intra- and intergroup social comparisons among gender groups.

The importance of the comparative context

To test the hypothesis that group comparisons have different effects among men and women, a study was carried out in four countries (Belgium, France, Switzerland, and Tunisia) (Chatard, Guimond, Lorenzi-Cioldi, and Désert, 2005). Participants ($Ns = 711$ French speaking students, 249 men and 462 women) were asked to describe themselves in various contexts. These descriptions were made on eight gender stereotypic traits, selected on the basis of previous studies (Guimond, Chatard, Martinot, Crisp and Redersdorff, in press). The feminine stereotype comprised "Feel that human relations are important," "Caring," "Family oriented," and "Affectionate"; the masculine stereotype comprised "Boastful," "Dominant," "Often use coarse language," and "Selfish." In a control condition, the participants provided self-descriptions in the absence of any explicit comparison other ("I am …"). In the other two conditions, the comparison other was either the other ingroup members, or the outgroup ("Compared with *men/women* in general, I am …"). Finally, participants provided descriptions of "men in general" and "women in general" on the same traits.

These latter judgments can be used to test the a priori gender classification of the traits. Consistent with previous findings reported in this chapter, the descriptions of the target groups, either "men in general," or "women in general," were more sex-typed than self-descriptions. The feminine traits were systematically attributed to "women in general" more than "men in general," and the masculine traits were systematically attributed to "men in general" more than "women in general" (see also Désert and Leyens, this volume). In addition, in terms of self-ratings, the feminine and masculine traits were negatively correlated. Hence, a global measure of self-description can be constructed, by averaging the four masculine traits with the four reversed feminine traits (see Bem, 1985; Lorenzi-Cioldi, 1991). Thus, high scores on this measure indicate a stronger use of the male than the female stereotype (that is, more selfish and dominant, and less family oriented and affectionate).

These self-descriptions were analyzed using participant gender, comparison context (intragroup vs. intergroup vs. neutral), and country as between-subject variables. This analysis yielded a reliable interaction involving participant gender and comparative context. This interaction indicated that men's self-descriptions, but not women's, were moderated by the comparison other. Consistent with self-categorization theory (Turner et al., 1987), male students described themselves in the control condition as they did in the intragroup condition, but these descriptions were overall different from those provided in the intergroup condition. In this latter condition, men judged themselves as being more masculine. No reciprocal pattern of ratings was found for female participants. There were no differences in women's self-descriptions as a function of the comparison context. Women testified to a higher accessibility of the female stereotype: they described themselves as being "feminine" in comparison to other ingroup members, to outgroup members, and in the absence of any explicit comparison other (see Figure 12.4). Furthermore, women described themselves similarly to their gender ingroup in all comparison conditions. Men also described themselves similarly to their ingroup, but they did so only in the intergroup context of comparison. In addition, these effects were not qualified by the country variable. It should finally be noted that these findings bear out what Guimond et al. (in press) have already found in other studies carried out in France and England. All in all, these findings indicate that, consistent with our analysis, men are more affected by intergroup comparisons than women, who, whatever the context, take into account group level social comparisons in their self-descriptions. These data testify to the crucial importance of the participant group status in explaining shifts in self-perception according to the comparative context.

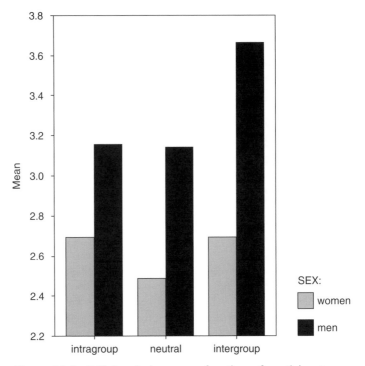

Figure 12.4. Self-descriptions as a function of participant sex and comparative context
Note: General measure of self-description ranging from 1 (feminine) to 7 (masculine).

Conclusions

In this chapter, we presented a two-stage intracultural analysis of norm endorsement in status hierarchies and its implications for social comparison phenomena. The first stage of this analysis asserts that in western cultures a norm of the self-contained, autonomous person is shared by everybody. The second stage qualifies this general tendency by the social status of the individuals' group membership: the shared norm appears to be differently activated among high-status and low-status group members. High-status people embody this norm more strongly than low-status people, and they do so to the point of endorsing negative behaviors, as long as these behaviors are normatively consistent – that is, if they preserve and sustain an autonomous self-image. These processes influence the kind of social comparison strategies people adopt: interpersonal comparisons are the default among the dominants and intergroup comparisons are the default among the subordinates.

To extend Markus and Kitayama's claim that "The notion of the autonomous individual in continuous tension with the external collective is 'natural' only from a particular cultural perspective," (1994, p. 570) our intracultural analysis suggests that the poles of this tension, namely personal distinctiveness and depersonalization, are likely to be represented in western cultures by groups differing in social status. Dominant groups show strong conformity to the norm of the self-contained person. They thus identify with their group but, concomitantly, lay emphasis on each group member's unique qualities and differences from others at the individual level. Conversely, the subordinates' distance from this norm calls attention to their group membership, and leads them to engage in more collective forms of comparison with other people.

Members of dominant groups emphasize the person's independence or uniqueness – the western shared norm – when judging themselves. Individualism, independence, and autonomy are valued traits in western societies (e.g., Fiske et al., 1998) and are systematically attributed more to members of the dominant group than the subordinate group. Members of high-status groups perceive themselves and are perceived in a more heterogeneous, individualistic, and "personalized" manner than do members of lower status groups, who remain more closely connected to their ingroup in their self-construal processes (see Lorenzi-Cioldi, 1998). Accordingly, the dominants are more likely than the subordinates to display diverse facets of their identity, either personal or collective, as a function of the social context. Consistent with Tajfel's assertion (1978) that the tendency of an individual to perceive the self as being relevant in some ways to his/her group membership will increase as a function of "the clarity of his awareness that he is a member of a certain group," (p. 39) subordinate groups would have more group-consciousness and higher accessibility of the group membership, in most situations (see also Josephs, Markus, and Tafarodi, 1992). Besides, a host of studies shows that the subordinates report more group-consciousness on personality scales (e.g., Fiske, 2001; Pinel, 1999), and that they are more group-schematic than the dominants (Hurtig and Pichevin, 1990; Lorenzi-Cioldi, 1991; Simon and Hamilton, 1994). Consistent with these findings, research on psychological androgyny has documented that women have a lower proclivity than men for blending group stereotypes into an androgynous self-conception (Lorenzi-Cioldi, 1994). Much research has indeed documented that status discrepancies can account for many presumed sex differences in social behaviors (Conway, Wood, Dugas, and Pushkar, 2003; Conway, Pizzamiglio, and Mount, 1996; Eagly, 1987; LaFrance, Hecht, and Levy Paluck, 2003; Lorenzi-Cioldi, 1998).

There is considerable evidence that social comparisons with ingroup members are conducive to assimilation effects whereas comparisons with outgroup members lead to contrast effects (Mussweiler and Bodenhausen, 2002). But there is also evidence that social status affects social comparisons in different ways (e.g., Branscombe, Spears, Ellemers, and Doosje, 1999; Brewer and Weber, 1994; Martinot, Redersdorff, Guimond, and Dif, 2002). This has led us to propose that gender, as a status cue, shapes the extent to which people define themselves when they compare with other ingroup members or with the outgroup. Because men define themselves with contents that refer to independence and individuals' uniqueness in front of the collective representation of their ingroup, they change their self-perception and define themselves as they define their group when they shift from an ingroup context to an outgroup one. A similar change would not be discernible in the self-perception of women because they would be dependent, more than men, on the collective representation of their ingroup.

In conclusion, the present chapter has documented that individualistic self-perceptions are inescapable in western societies. However, it has also illustrated that members of high status groups endorse more strongly this cultural norm than members of low status groups, and that this difference has profound implications for social comparison processes.

References

Amâncio, L. (1997). The importance of being male: Ideology and the context in gender identities. *Revue Internationale de Psychologie Sociale*, 2, 79–94.

Apfelbaum, E. (1979). Relations of domination and movements for liberation: An analysis of power between groups. In S. Worchel and W. Austin (eds.), *The social psychology of intergroup relations* (pp. 188–204). Chicago: Nelson-Hall.

Beauvois, J.-L., Gilibert, D., Pansu, P., and Abdelaoui, S. (1998). Internality attribution and intergroup relations. *European Journal of Social Psychology*, 28, 123–140.

Bem, S. L. (1985). Androgyny and gender schema theory: A conceptual and empirical integration. In T. B. Sonderegger (ed.), *Psychology and Gender, Nebraska Symposium on Motivation*, 32, Lincoln: University of Nebraska Press.

Branscombe, N. R., Ellemers, N., Spears, R., and Doosje, B. (1999). The context and content of social identity threat. In N. Ellemers and R. Spears (eds.), *Social identity: Context, commitment, content* (pp. 35–58). Oxford: Blackwell Science.

Brewer, M. B. and Weber, J. G. (1994). Self-evaluation effects of interpersonal versus intergroup social comparison. *Journal of Personality and Social Psychology*, 66, 268–275.

Buunk, B. P. and Mussweiler, T. (2001). New directions in social comparison research. *European Journal of Social Psychology*, 31, 467–475.

Chatard, A., Guimond, S., Lorenzi-Cioldi, F., and Désert, M. (2005). Domination masculine et identité de genre. *Les Cahiers Internationaux de Psychologie Sociale.*

Conway, M., Pizzamiglio, M. T., and Mount, L. (1996). Status, communality, and agency: Implications for stereotypes of gender and other groups. *Journal of Personality and Social Psychology, 71,* 25–38.

Conway, M., Wood, W. J., Dugas, M., and Pushkar, D. (2003). Are women perceived as engaging in more maladaptive worry than men? A status interpretation. *Sex Roles, 49,* 1–10.

Deschamps, J.-C. (1982). Social identity and relations of power between groups. In H. Tajfel (ed.), *Social identity and intergroup relations* (pp. 85–98). Cambridge: Cambridge University Press.

Deschamps, J.-C., Lorenzi-Cioldi, F., and Meyer, G. (1982). *L'échec scolaire.* Lausanne: Favre.

Doise, W. and Lorenzi-Cioldi, F. (1991). L'identité comme représentation sociale. In V. Aebischer, J. P. Deconchy, and E. M. Lipianski (eds.), *Idéologies et représentations sociales* (pp. 273–286). Fribourg: DelVal.

Eagly, A. H. (1987). *Sex differences in social behavior: A social-role interpretation.* Hillsdale: Erlbaum.

Eagly, A. H. and Kite, M. E. (1987). Are stereotypes of nationalities applied to both women and men? *Journal of Personality and Social Psychology, 53,* 451–462.

Festinger, L. (1954). A theory of social comparison processes. *Human Relations, 7,* 117–140.

Festinger, L., Gerard, H. B., Hymovitch, B., Kelley, H. H., and Raven, B. (1952). The influence process in the presence of extreme deviates. *Human Relations, 5,* 327–346.

Fiske, A. P., Kitayama, S., Markus, H. R., and Nisbett, R. A. (1998). The cultural matrix of social psychology. In D. T. Gilbert, S. T. Fiske, and G. Lindzey (eds.), *The handbook of social psychology* (Vol. II, pp. 915–981). New York: Oxford University Press.

Fiske, S. T. (2001). Social and societal pragmatism. In K. Deaux and G. Philogène, *Representations of the social,* (pp. 249–255). Oxford: Blackwell Publishers.

Fromkin, H. L. (1972). Feelings of interpersonal undistinctiveness: An unpleasant state. *Journal of Experimental Research in Personality, 6,* 178–185.

Gilligan, C. (1982). *In a different voice: Psychological theory and women's development.* Cambridge, MA: Harvard University Press.

Guillaumin, C. (1972). *L'idéologie raciste: Genèse et langage actuel.* Paris: Mouton.

Guimond, S., Chatard, A., Martinot, D., Crisp, R., and Redersdorff, S. (in press). Social comparison, self-stereotyping, and gender differences in self-construals. *Journal of Personality and Social Psychology.*

Hagendoorn, L. (1995). Intergroup biases in multiple group systems: The perception of ethnic hierarchies. In W. Stroebe and M. Hewstone. *European Review of Social Psychology, 6,* 199–228.

Hogg, M. A. and Turner, J. C. (1987). Intergroup behaviour, self-stereotyping and the salience of social categories. *British Journal of Social Psychology, 26,* 325–340.

Hurtig, M. C. and Pichevin, M. F. (1990). Salience of the sex category system in person perception: Contextual variations. *Sex Roles, 22,* 369–395.

Iyengar, S. S., Lepper, M. R., and Ross, L. (1999). Independence from whom? Interdependence with whom? Cultural perspectives on ingroups versus outgroups. In D. A. Prentice (ed.), *Cultural divides: Understanding and overcoming group conflict* (pp. 273–301). New York: Russell Sage Foundation.

Jackman, M. R. and Jackman, R. W. (1983). *Class awareness in the United States.* Berkeley and Los Angeles, CA: University of California Press.

Jetten, J., Postmes, T., and McAuliffe, B. J. (2002). "We're all individuals": Group norms of individualism and collectivism, levels of identification and identity threat. *European Journal of Social Psychology, 32,* 189–207.

Josephs, R. A., Markus, H. R., and Tafarodi, R. W. (1992). Gender and self-esteem. *Journal of Personality and Social Psychology, 63,* 391–402.

Kessler, T. and Mummendey, A. (2002). Sequential or parallel processes? A longitudinal field study concerning determinants of identity-management strategies. *Journal of Personality and Social Psychology, 82,* 75–88.

LaFrance, M., Hecht, M. A., and Paluck, E. L. (2003). The contingent smile: A meta-analysis of sex differences in smiling. *Psychological Bulletin, 129,* 305–334.

Lalonde, R. N. and Silverman, R. A. (1994). Behavioral preferences in response to social injustice: The effects of group permeability and social identity salience. *Journal of Personality and Social Psychology, 66,* 78–85.

Lorenzi-Cioldi, F. (1991). Self-stereotyping and self-enhancement in gender groups. *European Journal of Social Psychology, 21,* 403–417.

(1994). *Les Androgynes.* Paris: Presses Universitaires de France.

(1998). Group status and perceptions of homogeneity. *European Review of Social Psychology, 9,* 31–75.

(2000). *Représentations sociales du prestige de produits représentés sur des affiches publicitaires.* Unpublished data, Université de la Suisse Italienne, Lugano.

(2001). *L'achat d'une voiture.* Unpublished data, Université de la Suisse Italienne, Lugano.

(2002a). *Expériences sur les groupes dominants et dominés: Les perceptions de l'homogénéité des groupes.* Bern: P. Lang.

(2002b). *Les représentations des groupes dominants et dominés: Collections et agrégats.* Grenoble: Presses Universitaires.

(2004a). *Lower status group homogeneity as a function of the salience of the relationship between high-status and low-status groups.* Manuscript submitted for publication.

(2004b). *Group status and individual differentiation.* Manuscript submitted for publication.

Lorenzi-Cioldi, F. and Dafflon, A. C. (1998). Norme individuelle et norme collective, I: Representations du genre dans une société individualiste. *Swiss Journal of Psychology, 57,* 124–137.

Lorenzi-Cioldi, F. and Doise, W. (1990). Levels of analysis and social identity. In D. Abrams and M. Hogg (eds.), *Social identity theory* (pp. 71–88). New York: Harvester.

Lorenzi-Cioldi, F. and Meyer, G. (1984). *Semblables ou différents?* Geneva: International Labor Office.

Markus, H. R. and Kitayama, S. (1991). Culture and the self: Implications for cognition, emotion, and motivation. *Psychological Review, 98*, 224–253.

Markus, H. and Kitayama, S. (1994). The cultural construction of self and emotion: Implications for social behavior. In S. Kitayama and H. Markus (eds.), *Culture and emotion* (pp. 89–130). Washington, DC: American Psychological Association.

Markus, H. and Oyserman, D. (1989). Gender and thought: The role of the self-concept. In M. Crawford and M. Gentry (eds.), *Gender and thought* (pp. 100–127). New York: Springer Verlag.

Martinot, D., Redersdorff, S., Guimond, S., and Dif, S. (2002). Ingroup versus outgroup comparisons and self-esteem: The role of group status and ingroup identification. *Personality and Social Psychology Bulletin, 28*, 1586–1600.

Mussweiler, T. and Bodenhausen, G. (2002). I know you are but what am I? Self-evaluative consequences of judging ingroup and outgroup members. *Journal of Personality and Social Psychology, 82*, 19–32.

McGuire, W. J. (1984). Search for the self: Going beyond self-esteem and the reactive self. In R. A. Zucker, J. Aronoff, and A. I. Rabin (eds.), *Personality and the prediction of behavior* (pp. 73–120). New York: Academic.

Moskowitz, D. S., Suh, E. J., and Desaulniers, J. (1994). Situational influences on gender differences in agency and communion. *Journal of Personality and Social Psychology, 66*, 753–761.

Pichevin, M. F. and Hurtig, M. C. (1996). Describing men, describing women: Sex membership salience and numerical distinctiveness. *European Journal of Social Psychology, 26*, 513–522.

Pinel, E. C. (1999). Stigma consciousness: The psychological legacy of social stereotypes. *Journal of Personality and Social Psychology, 76*, 114–128.

Rosenkrantz, P., Vogel, S., Bee, H., Broverman, I., and Broverman, D. M. (1968). Sex-role stereotypes and self-concepts in college students. *Journal of Clinical and Consulting Psychology, 32*, 287–285.

Sedikides, C., Gaertner, L., and Toguchi, Y. (2003). Pancultural self-enhancement. *Journal of Personality and Social Psychology, 84*, 60–79.

Serino, C. (1994). La somiglianza e la differenza fra sé e gli altri: un tema sotteso alla rappresentazione sociale della malattia mentale. In G. Bellelli (ed.), *L'altra malattia* (pp. 309–334). Naples: Liguori.

Simon, B. and Hamilton, D. L. (1994). Self-stereotyping and social context: The effects of relative in-group size and in-group status. *Journal of Personality and Social Psychology, 66*, 699–711.

Smith, E. R. and Zarate, M. A. (1992). Exemplar-based model of social judgment. *Psychological Review, 99*, 3–21.

Snyder, C. R. and Fromkin, H. L. (1980). *Uniqueness: The human pursuit of difference*. New York: Plenum.

Tajfel, H. (1978). (ed.) *Differentiation between social groups*. New York: Academic Press.

Tajfel, H. and Turner, J. C. (1986).The social identity theory of intergroup behaviour. In S. Worchel and W. G. Austin (eds.), *Psychology of intergroup relations* (pp. 7–24). Chicago: Nelson-Hall.

Taylor, S. E. and Brown, J. D. (1988). Illusion and well-being: A social psychological perspective on mental health. *Psychological Bulletin*, *103*, 193–210.

Triandis, H. C. (1994). Major cultural syndromes and emotion. In S. Kitayama and H. R. Markus (eds.), *Emotion and culture: Empirical studies of mutual influence*, (pp. 285–308). Washington, DC: American Psychological Association.

Turner, J. C., Hogg, M. A., Oakes, P. J., Reicher, S. D., and Wetherell, M. S. (1987). *Rediscovering the social group*. Oxford: Blackwell.

Turner, J. C., Brown, R. J., and Tajfel, H. (1979). Social comparison and group interest in ingroup favouritism. *European Journal of Social Psychology*, *9*, 187–204.

Wood, J. V. and Wilson, A. E. (2003). How important is social comparison? In M. R. Leary (ed.), *Handbook of self and identity* (pp. 344–366). New York: Guilford Press.

13 Ambivalent sexism, power distance, and gender inequality across cultures

Peter Glick

Although some anthropologists dispute the universality of patriarchy and argue that the hunter-gatherer groups in which humans evolved were egalitarian (Salzman, 1999), agricultural and industrial societies are typically dominated by men, who monopolize the highest status positions in powerful social institutions, such as business, government, and organized religion (Carli and Eagly, 2001; Harris, 1991; Sidanius and Pratto, 1999). Societies are typically structured by a gendered division of labor that reflects prescriptive gender roles, which both create and reinforce gender hierarchy (Eagly and Wood, 1999). It is not surprising, then, that gender is a primary psychological category in both social and self-perception. When perceiving others, gender categorization occurs automatically and (judging by the frequency with which people within categories are confused with each other) predominates over other forms of categorization such as race (Taylor, Fiske, Etcoff, and Ruderman, 1978). In self-perception, gender categorization is a basic aspect of self-definition (Bem, 1981).

Given the importance of gender in self and social perception, as well as the regularity with which men and women interact in daily life, cross-gender social comparisons have the potential to occur frequently. Such comparisons potentially have important implications for maintaining or challenging gender inequality. For example, if female employees compare their salaries with male coworkers and find that they are paid less, they might challenge the fairness of the organization or initiate a lawsuit. In contrast, if such comparisons are discouraged (e.g., by a norm that salaries ought not to be disclosed) or legitimized (e.g., by different job classifications), the hierarchy is maintained.

This chapter considers the implications of two basic premises: (a) cross-gender comparisons (social comparisons between men and women) have the potential to reinforce or to challenge inequality between the sexes and (b) cultural ideologies can influence the frequency and content (and, therefore, the effects) of such comparisons. These premises will be explored by considering two kinds of hierarchy-legitimizing

(Sidanius and Pratto, 1999) ideologies that have been validated in cross-cultural research – power distance (a general belief in the legitimacy of social hierarchy; Hofstede, 2001) and ambivalent gender ideologies (traditional beliefs that more specifically encompass beliefs about both men and women, which have subjectively hostile and benevolent content; Glick and Fiske, 1996, 1999, 2001). Endorsement of power distance beliefs is known to inhibit cross-gender comparisons (Chapter 15, this volume) and it is suggested here that ambivalent gender ideologies shape the content of those comparisons (when they are made). Data from twenty-five nations are presented to establish the relationships between power distance, ambivalent gender ideologies, and gender inequality. These data support the contention that power distance and ambivalent sexism are complementary ideologies that not only reflect societal gender inequality, but act to legitimize it.

Social comparisons and social hierarchy

Theories of social stability and change recognize social comparison processes as central to system-maintenance. For example, relative deprivation theory (Runciman, 1966) posits that social change occurs when the "have-nots" compare themselves to the "haves" and feel relatively deprived (and angry) as a result. This theory suggests that intergroup comparison poses a danger to the stability of a hierarchy. Thus, one strategy for inhibiting group-based challenges to the status quo would be to inhibit intergroup comparisons altogether (see Chapter 15, this volume). If individuals only compare to members of their own group, fraternal (i.e., group-based) deprivation, which is known to be more important than egoistical or personal relative deprivation as a catalyst for social movements and social change (Dambrun and Guimond, 2001; Dubé and Guimond, 1986; Grant and Brown, 1995; Runciman, 1966; Walker and Smith, 2002), cannot occur.

Because men and women often interact, however, it seems unlikely that cross-gender comparisons would never occur (even if their frequency can be reduced). A second means by which cross-gender social comparisons can be enlisted to justify inequality is to shape their content so that they create a perception of fairness. Equity theory (Adams, 1965) suggests that some people are willing to accept poorer outcomes than others so long as these differences are perceived to be equitable, reflecting the other person's greater talents, investments, or efforts. Thus even if between-group comparisons occur within a hierarchical society, they do not necessarily create a sense of unfairness as long as the content of those comparisons can be shaped to justify the discrepancies in group outcomes. For example, workers may tolerate managers' vastly greater pay so long as they believe that managers have superior education and specialized skills that warrant their higher salaries.

Tajfel (1981) also points out that social change movements do not occur if group differences in outcome are perceived to be legitimate. Additionally, he suggested such movements also require the belief that the hierarchy is unstable (i.e., that it can be changed). Social comparisons that reinforce the perceived stability of the system can therefore also support hierarchy by undermining the motivation to try to change it.

In sum, norms regarding social comparison processes can maintain group-based inequality by (a) *encouraging within-group and inhibiting between-group comparisons* and (b) when between-group comparisons are made, *promoting between-group comparisons that enhance the perceived legitimacy or stability of differences in group outcomes*. These can be viewed as complementary, sequential strategies for maintaining the status quo: the first limits the number of between-group comparisons made by members of subordinated groups and the second renders these comparisons harmless when they do occur. The role of cultural ideologies in this process may lie in their power to create norms that govern the social comparison process; in particular, norms that inhibit or determine the content of between-group comparisons. More specifically, power distance beliefs and ambivalent gender ideologies may support gender inequality by, in the first case, reducing cross-gender comparisons (see Chapter 15) and, in the second case, by molding the content of those comparisons (when they occur).

Power distance

Power distance is a construct developed by Hofstede (1980, 2001) concerning the perceived relationship between dominants and subordinates; it represents "the extent to which the less powerful members of institutions and organizations within a country expect and accept that power is distributed unequally." (Hofstede, 2001, p. 98) Thus, power distance is thought to reflect a general cultural value that legitimizes hierarchy and power differences between individuals (i.e., interpersonal power); it can be viewed as similar in concept to the idea of social dominance orientation (Sidanius and Pratto, 1999), except that the latter addresses acceptance of power differences *between groups*. One advantage of the power distance concept, however, is that extensive cross-cultural research has established Power Distance Index (PDI) values for over fifty nations (Hofstede, 2001), allowing for extensive cross-cultural comparisons.

Although power distance is assessed by polling individuals' perceptions and beliefs, Hofstede (2001) argues that it is a system-level characteristic.

The three original measures that compose the PDI do not achieve internal consistency reliability at the individual level, but do reliably distinguish between work organizations or nations when aggregated. These measures (originally developed within an occupational context) are the degree to which non-managerial employees: (a) believe that their peers are generally afraid to disagree with their superiors, (b) perceive superiors to prefer non-consultative (e.g., autocratic) decision-making styles, and (c) themselves prefer their superiors to use such non-consultative styles. It is the last item that most directly taps a value dimension legitimating hierarchy and power differences, whereas the others assess a climate in which power is exercised without consultation with subordinates. In short, the PDI appears to tap a mixture of how power is actually used as well as how subordinates tolerate its use.

Two potential criticisms of Hoftstede's index concern its generalizability (from work organizations to national cultures) and validity. Although Hofstede's measures were originally geared to assessing work organizations, they have been generalized as reflecting wider cultural values. Hofstede (2001) has amassed a considerable amount of research showing stability in the PDI for various nations and has been careful to use stratified samples of occupations to ensure that the PDI value for each nation is not an artifact of differences in the occupations that are assessed, thereby answering the first criticism. The second criticism concerns the content validity of the items as measures of a general value that legitimizes hierarchy in that only one item directly assesses subordinates' *preference* for non-consultative decision-making. Other researchers (see Chapter 15 in this volume, as well as Brockner *et al.*, 2001; Early and Erez, 1997; Maznevski, DiStefano, Gomez, Nooderhaven, and Wu, 1997) have developed more obviously content valid (and more reliable, at the individual level of analysis) measures of power distance using items such as "There should be established ranks within society with everyone occupying their rightful place regardless of whether that place is high or low in the ranking." (Brockner *et al.*, 2001) So far, these measures have confirmed Hofstede's classification of nations (using the PDI) as being relatively high or low in power distance. Thus, although Hofstede's PDI measure might be improved upon, it appears to assess an important cultural quality, the extent to which social hierarchy is viewed (especially by subordinates) to be a legitimate, even desirable, way to structure the society.

In fact, there is evidence that power distance is related to the inhibition of between-group comparisons. Guimond and his colleagues (2005; see Chapter 15) found that people in high versus low power distance cultures were more likely to make within-gender and less likely to make between-gender comparisons. Thus there is at least preliminary evidence that the cultural value of power distance discourages cross-gender social comparisons, which, in turn, is likely to reinforce gender hierarchy.

While power distance may be related to the frequency of cross-gender comparisons, another set of ideologies that are specific to gender relations may shape their content. Ambivalent gender ideologies are traditional beliefs that imply social comparisons between men and women that bolster the perceived legitimacy and stability of gender hierarchy.

Ambivalent gender ideologies

Ambivalent sexism theory (Glick and Fiske, 1996, 1999, 2001) notes that gender relations are unique in the degree to which they simultaneously exhibit group-based differences in power along with intimate interdependence between the groups. These two structural facts are hypothesized to spawn ambivalent gender ideologies that reconcile and legitimate men's simultaneous dominance over and dependence upon women. These ideologies make implicit and explicit social comparisons between men and women that reinforce gender inequality by suggesting that (a) both sexes benefit from traditional gender roles and the differences in power that accompany them and (b) that male dominance is natural and inevitable.

More specifically, male dominance is hypothesized to foster hostile ideologies that assign each sex negative traits: women (relative to men) are viewed as weak and not deserving to be in charge, but men (relative to women) are viewed as having the bad traits associated with power (e.g., arrogance). At the same time, intimate interdependence is hypothesized to create benevolent ideologies that assign subjectively favorable traits to both sexes: women (relative to men) are viewed as wonderful (even if weak) creatures and men (relative to women) are viewed as heroic protectors and providers.

Ambivalent ideologies about women are tapped by the Ambivalent Sexism Inventory (ASI; Glick and Fiske, 1996), which includes hostile sexism (HS) and benevolent sexism (BS) scales. Ambivalent ideologies about men are tapped by the Ambivalence toward Men Inventory (AMI; Glick and Fiske, 1999), which includes hostility toward men (HM) and benevolence toward men (BM) scales.

Hostile and benevolent attitudes toward women

HS items (e.g., "Women seek to gain power by getting control over men" and "Women are too easily offended") implicitly compare women unfavorably to men, primarily expressing hostility toward women who pursue equal rights, power over men, or traditionally masculine roles. In contrast, BS items (e.g., "A good woman ought to be set on a pedestal by her man" and "Women, compared to men, tend to have a superior moral sensibility") imply male-female comparisons that favor women, but only those women who enact traditionally feminine roles that serve men. Across samples from nineteen nations around the world, a very similar factor structure was found providing support for the pervasiveness of these dimensions of hostile and benevolent sexism (Glick *et al.*, 2000). This research also demonstrated that even though the two scales reflect different attitudinal valences (with HS predicting negative and BS positive spontaneous stereotypes of women), these attitudes are not psychologically dissonant, as evidenced by consistently positive correlation between them. Rather, they represent a coordinated system of rewards (BS) and punishments (HS) aimed at reinforcing male dominance and traditional gender roles (Glick, Diebold, Bailey-Werner, and Zhu, 1997).

The positive correlation between HS and BS is especially strong when national means are the unit of analysis. Glick *et al.* (2000, 2004) found that among individual respondents the HS-BS correlation is moderate (typically around .30 to .50), but in cross-national comparisons of sample means the correlation is around .90 (i.e., if people – both men and women – within a nation score high on HS, they invariably score high on BS). Furthermore, both scales correlate negatively with national measures of gender equality published by the United Nations. These results are consistent with the idea that HS and BS are (a) shared ideologies within cultures that, (b) work hand-in-hand to justify and reinforce gender inequality.

That subjectively benevolent views of women are related to gender inequality fits Jackman's (1994) views about paternalistic prejudices. Given their intimate interdependence with (and therefore reliance on) women, men seek to avoid overtly hostile relations (reserving hostility for those women who get "out of line"). Instead, they prefer to offer incentives (affection, resources, protection) for women to comply with traditional roles. The standard conception of prejudice as an antipathy (Allport, 1954) fails to capture this dynamic. BS, however, may be a particularly potent legitimizing ideology because it can undermine women's resistance to inequality by promising that men will use their greater power to protect and provide for women.

Furthermore, BS gives women a positive dimension of intergroup comparison with men (e.g., BS items include the notions that women are more "pure" and "moral" than men) that reinforces rather than threatens patriarchy. Such comparisons may boost women's collective self-esteem, but the positive traits BS attributes to women (e.g., purity and innocence) suit them to lower status, supporting roles, rather than to a rough and tumble competition for status and power (see also Jackman, 1994). Thus, BS may only serve to placate women to be content with their lot. Indeed, Jost and Kay (2005) found that mere exposure to BS scale items led women to score higher on a measure of system justification (the perception that society is generally fair).

Hostile and benevolent attitudes toward men

Traditional ideologies about men are similarly complex, ambivalent, and also related to gender inequality. BM is the mirror image of BS, extolling women's need for men who will provide for and protect them (e.g., "Every woman needs a man who will cherish her") as well as men's heroic qualities that make them good protectors and providers (e.g., "Men are less likely to fall apart in emergencies than women are"). HM at first blush may appear to delegitimize patriarchy because it expresses resentment of men's power (e.g., "Most men sexually harass women, even if only in subtle ways, once they are in a position of power over them") and disparage men (e.g., "Men would be lost in this world if women weren't there to guide them"). Yet Glick *et al.*'s (2004) cross-cultural research has shown that HM and BM correlate positively with each other and with the ASI scales (HS and BS) both among individuals and in cross-national comparisons. Additionally, both HM and BM correlate negatively with the United Nations' measures of actual gender equality (in cross-national comparisons). As was the case with HS and BS, the correlations of the AMI scales with each other and with the ASI scales were much stronger (typically in the .70 to .90 range) in cross-national comparisons, suggesting that HM and BM (at both the individual, but especially the systemic level) are complementary legitimizing ideologies to HS and BS.

Although it is not surprising that viewing men as protectors and providers (BM) legitimizes their greater power (indeed, these roles require men to have power to enact them), it may seem odd that resentment of men's power and disparagement of men (HM) somehow is related to the justification of patriarchy. The key to this conundrum is that HM, though resentful, involves an implicit social comparison that views men as naturally and inevitably dominant (e.g., "Men will always fight to have greater control in society than women"). Although HM may not legitimize male power, it seems to reinforce its perceived stability, which Tajfel (1981) suggested to be an equally important factor in eliciting subordinates' resignation to social inequality. Furthermore, HM is itself likely to be caused by gender inequality. Certainly, the greater the inequality, the more women are likely to show resentment of men. The point here is that the beliefs embedded in this resentment undermine, rather than promote attempts at social change because the traits HM attributes to men suggest the inevitability of male dominance.

Traditional stereotypes of men have similar hostile content, attributing traits to men that, though negatively evaluated, are nonetheless associated with achieving and maintaining power (e.g., arrogance, callousness, selfishness). Eagly and Mladinic (1994) have shown that stereotypes of men are, overall, less positive than stereotypes of women precisely because of the negatively evaluated traits associated with dominance. Glick *et al.* (2004) showed that HM predicts negatively evaluated stereotypes of men, but that these negative traits are associated with power and status. Men may be willing to accept these stereotypes, embracing (to some degree) a social comparison in which their gender group is less positively evaluated so long as the comparison implies that they "have what it takes" to achieve and maintain power. Glick *et al.* (2004) found that HM, despite its negative valence toward their own group, was endorsed more strongly by men in gender-traditional as compared to egalitarian nations, suggesting a "macho" male self-image in which men's "bad" traits are celebrated (Mosher and Sirkin, 1984). In short, HM and BM reflect the traditional stereotype of men as "bad but bold" (i.e., as having the negative as well as positive traits associated with power), with the former being viewed as a concomitant of the latter.

In summary, ambivalent gender ideologies imply social comparisons between women and men that: (a) legitimize gender inequality as a fair exchange in which men use their greater power to protect and provide for women (so long as women, in return, comply with the traditional roles that serve men) and (b) reinforce the perceived stability of gender inequality by implying that men, as compared to women, have traits that naturally and inevitably suit them for dominance.

Cross-national correlations: ideologies and gender equality

Power distance is a more general set of beliefs that legitimize social hierarchy, whereas ambivalent gender ideologies more specifically address relations between women and men. As cultural values, how are they related? Are they complementary tools of social control, with cultures that endorse power distance also typically endorsing ambivalent gender ideologies? Are each of these ideologies related to actual gender inequality? The remainder of this chapter uses data from twenty-five nations to examine the interrelationships between power distance, ambivalent gender ideologies, and actual gender inequality across nations.

The relationship between power distance and ambivalent gender ideologies

It is not a foregone conclusion that, at a national level of analysis, the PDI ought to correlate with the ASI and AMI scales or with gender inequality. Whereas the ASI and AMI tap belief in a *group-based gender hierarchy*, power distance beliefs were originally conceived as a generalized ideology that legitimizes *interpersonal hierarchy*. As Hofstede (2001) notes, "power in relationships between groups is not just a replication of power between people within groups." (p. 84) In contrast to the power distance construct, ambivalent sexism theory posits a complex set of ambivalent, yet interlocking beliefs that specifically legitimize gender hierarchy (not tolerance of hierarchy more generally).

Yet there is an underlying commonality between the PDI and the ASI/AMI scales that may cause them to correlate in cross-national comparisons: each is hypothesized to legitimize social inequality. Additionally, the finding (see Chapter 15, this volume) that cross-gender social comparisons are inhibited in high power distance cultures specifically implicates power distance in the maintenance of gender hierarchy, which is the domain of ambivalent gender ideologies. Finally, Hofstede's conception of power difference, like ambivalent sexism theory, recognizes that power can be exercised and legitimated in a paternalistic fashion. Two of the three items that compose Hofstede's (2001) PDI deal with the ways in which dominants exercise power, lumping together two types of doing so: autocratic and "persuasive/paternalistic" (p. 86) methods. The former is more representative of hostile and the latter of benevolent sexism. That power distance encompasses hostile and "benevolent" (paternalistic) styles of exercising power increases the likelihood that both benevolent and hostile gender ideologies correlate with the PDI.

It is possible, however, that correlations between the PDI and the ASI/AMI scales might differ for men and women. Power distance specifically focuses on the beliefs of subordinates about dominants' ways of exercising power. In contrast, the ASI and AMI scales tap the attitudes of both dominants (men) and subordinates (women) toward their own and the other group. Hofstede (1980) reasoned that subordinates have the most accurate view of power differences. Further, because people are always likely to accept power differences they profit from, dominants may not be as likely to vary in their acceptance of power differences across cultures as are subordinates. Given that the PDI focusses on subordinates' perceptions, women (the subordinated group), as compared to men, might exhibit a stronger correlation between ambivalent gender ideologies and the PDI. Cross-national correlations between men's and women's scores on the ASI and AMI scales, however, are quite strong (Glick *et al*, 2000, 2004) making differential correlations less likely, and indicating a strong degree of consensus among men (dominants) and women (subordinates) with respect to these legitimizing ideologies.

Moya, Poeschl, Glick, Páez, and Sedano (2005) explored the relationship of the PDI (using data from Hofstede, 2001) with HS and BS (using data from Glick *et al.*, 2000) in cross-national comparisons. This chapter expands upon their analyses by using a larger data-set (sexism scores for twenty-five rather than twenty nations, with larger sample sizes within some of the nations examined by Moya *et al.*, 2005). In addition, I incorporate cross-cultural data on the AMI (HM and BM) scales (using data from Glick *et al.*, 2004; although AMI data were only available for seventeen nations). Sample sizes per nation for the ASI and AMI data range from about 100 to over 2,600, with an average sample size of approximately 400 men and 400 women. It is important to note that, with some exceptions, the samples from which sexism scale scores have been obtained are not random, national samples but instead over-represent university students. Nevertheless, the two cross-national studies from which the scores were obtained (Glick *et al.*, 2000, 2004) consistently showed negative correlations between sample averages on the sexism scales and independent indices of national gender equality, suggesting that the samples are at least to some degree representative of national attitudes and conditions. PDI values were obtained from Hofstede (2001) and from Basabe, Páez, Valencia, Gonzalez, Rime, and Diener (2002).

Additionally, to examine how national averages on the PDI (as well as the ASI and AMI scales) relate to gender hierarchy, the actual degree of gender equality was indexed by the Gender Empowerment Measure (GEM; obtained from the United Nations' Development Programme, 2002) which measures women's (relative to men's) representation in powerful occupational roles, both in business (e.g., percentage of managers, administrators, and professional workers who are women) and government (e.g., percentage of members of parliament who are women).

Table 13.1 lists: (a) men's and women's averages on the ASI and AMI scales, (b) PDI values, and (c) GEM values of 25 nations (seventeen nations only for AMI scales; also GEM was not available for two nations and PDI for one nation). In Table 13.1, nations are listed in descending order according to PDI value.

Is the PDI related to ambivalent gender ideologies? Table 13.2 reveals that the ambivalent gender ideologies tapped by the ASI and AMI are strongly related to the PDI in cross-national comparisons. Furthermore, this relationship with PDI holds true for both men's and women's

Table 13.1. *National means on power distance, gender ideologies, and gender equality*

Nation	Men's scores				Women's scores				PDI	GEM
	HS	BS	HM	BM	HS	BS	HM	BM		
Cuba	3.66	3.43	2.96	3.52	3.07	3.81	3.61	3.11	81	.46
Mexico	2.95	2.50	2.34	2.41	2.01	2.11	2.82	1.83	81	.52
Syria	3.14	3.57	2.76	2.90	2.61	3.98	3.57	3.58	80	.32
Nigeria	3.35	3.36	–	–	2.50	3.64	–	–	77	–
Singapore	2.80	2.75	2.43	2.65	2.26	2.71	2.57	2.52	74	.59
Brazil	2.64	2.55	–	–	1.68	2.33	–	–	69	.37
Colombia	3.10	2.80	2.15	3.02	2.51	2.88	3.02	2.03	67	.47
Turkey	3.11	2.59	2.62	3.01	2.34	2.72	3.50	2.40	66	.28
Belgium	2.51	1.93	–	–	1.80	2.04	–	–	65	.60
Peru	2.75	2.82	2.55	2.66	2.54	2.94	2.81	2.23	64	.52
Zimbabwe	3.20	2.95	–	–	2.07	3.10	–	–	64	–
Chile	3.04	3.04	–	–	2.22	3.02	–	–	63	.42
Portugal	2.86	2.45	2.04	2.33	2.04	2.20	2.67	1.57	63	.55
S. Korea	2.91	2.67	–	–	2.03	2.56	–	–	60	.29
Taiwan	2.86	2.90	2.34	2.41	2.24	2.60	3.13	2.38	58	.49
Spain	2.61	2.60	2.32	2.05	1.83	2.19	2.96	1.82	57	.62
Japan	2.38	2.40	–	–	2.28	2.34	–	–	54	.47
Italy	2.67	2.21	2.18	2.12	1.90	2.25	2.76	1.81	50	.52
S. Africa	3.44	3.20	–	–	2.41	3.45	–	–	49	.53
Argentina	2.50	2.32	2.02	2.18	2.02	2.23	2.82	1.87	49	.42
United States	2.24	2.30	1.85	1.85	1.60	2.02	2.34	1.47	40	.68
Netherlands	1.97	2.19	2.21	1.85	1.72	1.91	2.64	1.69	38	.69
Australia	2.31	2.22	1.98	1.95	1.86	1.97	2.16	1.74	36	.66
England	2.29	2.15	2.23	2.14	1.85	1.93	2.14	1.82	35	.59
Germany	2.60	2.52	2.19	2.45	1.91	2.54	2.71	2.00	35	.69

Table 13.2. *Correlations of ambivalent gender ideologies with power distance and gender equality*

Index	Men's scores				Women's scores			
	HS[a]	BS[a]	HM[b]	BM[b]	HS[a]	BS[a]	HM[b]	BM[b]
Correlations								
PDI	.70**	.60**	.66**	.74**	.60**	.59**	.71**	.66**
GEM	−.51*	−.44*	−.51*	−.64*	−.41*	−.46*	−.73*	−.58*
Partial correlations								
PDI controlling for GEM	.56**	.43*	.51*	.58*	.48*	.40 +	.49*	.47*
GEM controlling for PDI	−.22	−.18	−.18	−.36	−.11	−.22	−.53*	−.30

[a] $n = 25$ for correlations with PDI; $n = 24$ for correlations with GEM
[b] $n = 17$ for all correlations and partial correlations
$+ p < .10,$
$* p < .05,$
$** p < .01$

national averages on the ASI and AMI scales. The correlation of ASI and AMI averages with the PDI is statistically significant in all cases and the magnitudes of the correlations show little variation, ranging from .59 to .74. Thus, it appears that nations that are high (versus low) in power distance are also those in which both men and women endorse ambivalent gender ideologies about both sexes.

The relationship of ideologies to gender equality

Table 13.2 also shows that women's and men's national averages on the ASI and AMI scales are negatively correlated to the GEM. Similarly, national PDI scores are negatively related to national GEM scores ($r = -.55$, $p < .01$). Thus, nations that score highly on ambivalent gender ideologies and/or on power distance exhibit less actual gender equality.

Of course, the fact that the PDI and ambivalent gender ideologies correlate negatively with gender equality does not allow for causal inferences. Nevertheless, these data are at least consistent with the idea that these ideologies both reflect and, more importantly, reinforce gender inequality by legitimizing it. A less interesting possibility is that any causal relationship that exists is unidirectional such that cultural differences in the PDI and in ambivalent gender ideologies are purely the consequence (and not a cause of) existing gender inequality. In other words, this alternative suggests that the ideologies are solely a by-product of inequality, rather than a set of values that seek to promote inequality by casting hierarchy as legitimate.

Fortunately, partial correlations allow a test of this unidirectional alternative. If cultural differences in endorsement of the PDI and of the ASI and AMI scales are unidirectionally caused by actual gender inequality, then partialing out the GEM (that is, controlling for a measure of each nation's actual degree of gender equality) should significantly diminish or erase the relationship between these ideologies. If, in contrast, the PDI and the ambivalent gender ideologies are related because they both represent values that *seek to legitimize hierarchy*, but whose level of endorsement in a culture is not merely a reflection of the existing degree of hierarchy, they should still correlate once actual gender inequality is controlled.

Table 13.2 reports the partial correlations of national averages on the ASI and AMI scales with the PDI once the GEM (an index of actual gender equality) is controlled. The correlations of the PDI with the ASI and AMI scales remain strong and statistically significant (with only one being reduced to marginal significance). These partial correlations cannot confirm that there is a direct relationship between the PDI (a cultural value that tolerates hierarchy) and ambivalently sexist ideologies, but do show that the relationships between these putative legitimizing ideologies hold when a crucial third variable – the actual degree of gender equality – is controlled. The significant partial correlations of ASI and AMI scores to a general measure of preference for hierarchy (PDI) bolster Glick *et al.*'s (2000, 2004) contentions that all of the ambivalent gender ideologies (including BS, which is subjectively benevolent toward the subordinated group, and HM, which expresses some resentment of, as well as resignation to, male dominance) are values that legitimize hierarchy and are not simply passive reflections of an existing hierarchy.

Another way of addressing these issues is to examine the relationship of the ambivalent gender ideologies to actual gender equality while controlling for the PDI. If sexist attitudes are determined by the degree of objective inequality in a culture, then controlling for the PDI ought not to affect the relationship of the ASI and AMI scales to gender equality. If, instead, controlling for the PDI diminishes the relationships between sexist ideologies and actual gender equality this would be consistent with the notion that the sexist ideologies (like the PDI) assess the *perceived legitimacy* of hierarchy.

The bottom panel of Table 13.2 reveals that once the PDI is partialed out, most of the sexism scales no longer predict gender inequality.

Consistent with the prior analysis, this suggests that the sexist ideologies do not simply reflect inequality, but measure its perceived legitimacy. The one exception in which controlling for the PDI did not reduce a correlation to nonsignificance, was women's endorsement of HM. In other words, even when the PDI was controlled, women express more HM when there is less actual gender equality in their nation. This exception is consistent with the contention that HM reflects women's resentment of men's power (even if it may reinforce the perceived stability of that power). In contrast, Glick *et al.* (2004) argued that men's endorsement of HM reflects acceptance of a macho group-image (men as arrogant and callous) that, though unflattering in some ways, reinforces their power. For women, the degree of resentment may (not surprisingly) be directly determined by their relative lack of power compared to men.

Differences within cultures: the gender gap in endorsement of ambivalent gender ideologies

The strong correlations between men's and women's national averages on the ambivalent gender ideologies suggest a considerable degree of cultural consensus on the perceived legitimacy of gender hierarchy. However, differences *within-cultures* between men's and women's average scores on the ASI and AMI scales show that the consensus between the dominant and subordinate gender groups is not complete. Women almost invariably score lower on HS and higher on HM than men do (Glick *et al.*, 2000, 2004), showing a tendency for women to reject an ideology that is hostile toward their own group, but to accept one that vents hostility toward men (even if the latter still reinforces male dominance). For the benevolent ideologies, men are typically more likely than women to accept BM (a positive characterization of men as protectors and providers that also explicitly suggests women ought to serve men at home). Sex differences on BS, in contrast, show much more inconsistency across cultures, with men sometimes scoring higher than women, small or nonsiginificant sex differences in many nations, and women sometimes scoring higher than men.

Cross-national variations in the sex differences in ASI and AMI scores across nations are not random (Glick *et al.*, 2000, 2004). In nations where men's average HS scores were higher, the gender gap between men and women on HS increased. Thus, although women in nations where men expressed a high degree of HS also scored higher on HS compared to women in low HS nations (illustrating social consensus pressures to accept this legitimizing ideology), they simultaneously evinced some resistance (relative to the men in their nation) to embracing a justification of gender inequality that is hostile toward members of their own group. The gender gap in HM showed a similar effect, with the gender gap reversed. Men showed increasing resistance to endorsing HM as strongly as women in those nations where women's HM was highest. Recall that HM (like HS) is highest among both sexes the more that there is gender inequality. But in these nations, women's expressed hostility to men's power increases relative to men's. Men in more traditional (as compared to egalitarian) cultures are more likely to endorse HM (e.g., to agree that men will always seek greater power over women and exhibit the negative traits that accompany their power), but there appears to be a limit to the degree to which men will embrace this less than flattering portrayal of their own group (even if it reinforces the perceived stability of their power).

Across nations, the variations in the HS and HM gender gaps consistently relate to average scores on these scales (e.g., greater endorsement of HS across nations predicts the gender gap in HS). In contrast, the BS gender gap is robustly related to national averages on all of the ASI and AMI scales; the more gender-traditional the nation, the more likely it is that women will score at least as highly as men on BS. In other words, in more gender-traditional nations, women exhibit an increased preference, relative to men, for men to treat them paternalistically. Because it taps a subordinated group's preference for a paternalistic system, this variation in the BS gender gap may be related to power distance. Alternatively, as Glick *et al.* (2000, 2004) suggest, women's greater endorsement of BS relative to men in the most gender-traditional cultures may simply reflect a pragmatic choice for the least risky way to deal with men's entrenched dominance over them (see also Jackman, 1994). With few independent resources and faced with the likelihood of hostility from men should they challenge men's power, women in gender-traditional cultures may find it safest to endorse BS to elicit affection, protection, and provision (rather than hostility) from men.

Does the PDI relate to sex differences in scores on the ASI and AMI scales? As noted above, *within nations* men typically score higher than women on HS and BM, but lower on HM, and the gender gap on BS varies from men scoring higher than women to women scoring higher than men. Are cross-cultural variations in these gender gaps related to power distance? Gender gap scores were created for each nation by computing the difference between men's and women's scores on each ASI and AMI scale (e.g., men's average on HS – women's average on HS). These gender gap scores were then correlated with national PDI values. As Table 13.3 reveals, only one of these correlations attained significance, the gender gap on BS was significantly negatively correlated

Table 13.3. *Correlations of gender gaps in ASI/AMI scores with power distance and gender equality*

	HS gap[a]	BS gap[a]	HM gap[b]	BM gap[b]
PDI	.30	−.42*	−.38	.24
GEM	−.26	.37+	.59*	−.18
PDI controlling for GEM	.15	−.22	−.04	.16
GEM controlling for PDI	−.13	.20	.48+	−.04

[a] $n = 25$ for correlations with PDI; n = 24 for correlations with GEM
[b] $n = 17$ for all correlations
$+p < .10$,
$*p < .05$

with PDI. This correlation indicates that in high (as compared to low) PDI nations, women's BS scores are more likely to equal or exceed men's. In the highest PDI nations (the top quintile in the sample), women's BS significantly exceeded men's scores in three of five nations (Syria, Cuba, Nigeria); in contrast, for nations in the lowest quintile on PDI, men outscored women on BS in three of five nations (Australia, Netherlands, United States). The other nations in the top and bottom quintiles showed no significant gender difference.

Again, it is possible that this variation in the gender gap on BS scores is not directly related to power distance values, but rather is an artifact of the relationship of both the PDI and of variation in the BS gender gap to actual gender inequality. Glick *et al.* (2000, 2004) argued that, within gender-traditional cultures, women's relatively greater acceptance of BS in comparison to men may be a pragmatic choice, reflecting their limited options. If this is the case, the correlation between the PDI and the BS gender gap ought to diminish or disappear when actual gender equality (measured by the GEM) is controlled. As Table 13.3 shows, this was indeed the case as the partial correlation of the BS gender gap with the PDI became non-significant when controlling for the GEM. However, as Table 13.3 also reveals, the correlation between the GEM and the BS gender gap also dropped from marginal significance to nonsignificance when the PDI was controlled. Thus it is possible that cross-cultural variations in the BS gender gap are partly due to differences in the tendency to accept legitimizing ideologies and are partly driven by actual gender inequality.

Examination of the correlations between the GEM and gender gaps on the ASI/AMI scales (see Table 13.3) reveals another interesting effect: the gap in HM (which is always in the direction of women scoring higher than men) diminishes in more gender-equal nations (as compared to nations with less gender equality). This relationship remains once the PDI is controlled. This effect is consistent with the finding (reported above) which suggested that women's HM (in contrast to HS, BS, and BM) scores may directly reflect the degree of gender equality in their society, with inequality increasing women's HM due to resentment of their lower status, lower power position.

Implications and conclusions

Within a hierarchical society, intergroup social comparisons can delegitimize power differences by drawing people's attention to the unfair treatment of different groups. Alternatively, depending on the content of those comparisons, they can increase the perceived legitimacy and/or stability of power differences by suggesting that each group's characteristics suit them for different positions in society. Thus, cultural ideologies can support intergroup hierarchy either by inhibiting cross-group comparisons (to reduce the salience of unequal outcomes) or by influencing the content of those comparisons to reinforce the perceived legitimacy and stability of the hierarchy. With respect to gender inequality, power distance appears to do the former (see Chapter 15) and I have argued that ambivalent gender ideologies do the latter. These strategies can be viewed as complementary, successive lines of defense that maintain social hierarchy: the first line of defense is to avoid intergroup comparisons entirely, but when they do occur, the second line of defense is to shape their content in a manner that reinforces rather than challenges the hierarchy. The cross-national comparisons made here support the notion of complementary ideologies – cultures that endorse high power distance (i.e., exhibit a general preference for hierarchy) also tend to endorse ambivalent gender ideologies (which increase the perceived legitimacy and stability of gender hierarchy).

In cross-national comparisons, power distance and ambivalent gender ideologies are negatively related to actual gender equality (as measured by the GEM). This finding is consistent with the idea that each set of values reflects and promotes social inequality. The relationships between the PDI and national averages on the ASI and AMI scales, however, remain significant when the actual degree of gender equality in each nation is statistically controlled. Given that the PDI taps a generally supportive attitude toward social hierarchy, its continuing correlation with the ASI and AMI scales once a measure of actual gender equality is partialed out supports the notion that ambivalent gender ideologies measure values that promote (and not just reflect) inequality. I have suggested here that one of the mechanisms by which the ambivalent gender ideologies accomplish their support for inequality is through shaping the content of cross-gender comparisons, but a direct test of this social comparison mechanism awaits further research.

The social comparisons that support gender inequality are quite complex. Ambivalent gender ideologies may appear to be contradictory because they express both positive and negative comparative beliefs about each gender group. Yet these apparently ambivalent beliefs are all positively correlated to each other and negatively correlated to actual gender equality. This holds true even for comparisons that assign positively evaluated characteristics to the subordinate gender group (BS) and negative characteristics to the dominant gender group (HM). Traditional gender ideologies foster some social comparisons that favor women, but only on dimensions that suit them to subordinate and supporting roles, as well as some comparisons that disfavor men, but by attributing them with qualities that (though disliked) characterize them as designed to dominate. The relationships of hostile and benevolent ideologies about both sexes to power distance support the contention that these ambivalent intergroup comparisons form an interlocking set of justifications for gender hierarchy. Justifications of other hierarchical group distinctions may likewise demonstrate ambivalence. For instance, Kay and Jost (2003) have shown that "rich but miserable" and "poor but happy" stereotypes are related to individuals' acceptance of a class hierarchy. Thus it is possible that other group-based hierarchies, not just gender hierarchy, may be legitimized and sustained not only by intergroup comparisons that favor dominants, but also by those that, at first glance, appear to favor subordinates.

References

Adams, J. S. (1965). Inequity in social exchange. In L. Brekowitz (ed.). *Advances in experimental social psychology* (Vol. II, pp. 267–299). New York: Academic Press.

Allport, G. (1954). *The nature of prejudice*. Cambridge, MA: Addison-Wesley.

Bem, S. L. (1981). Gender schema theory: A cognitive account of sex-typing. *Psychological Review, 88*, 354–364.

Besabe, N., Páez, D., Valencia, J., Gonzalez, J. L., Rimé, B., and Diener, E. (2002). Culutral dimensions, socioeconomic development, climate, and emotional hedonic level. *Cognition and Emotion, 16*, 103–125.

Brockner, J., Ackerman, G., Greenber, J., Gelfand, M. J., Francesco, A. M., Chen, Z. X., Leung, K., Bierbrauer, G., Gomez, C., Kirkman, B. L., and Shapiro, D. (2001). Culture and procedural justice: The influence of power distance on reactions to voice. *Journal of Experimental Social Psychology*, *37*, 300–315.

Carli, L. L. and Eagly, A. H. (2001). Gender, hierarchy, and leadership. *Journal of Social Issues*, *57*, 629–636.

Dambrun, M. and Guimond, S. (2001). La théorie de la privation relative et l'hostilité envers les Nord-Africains [Relative deprivation theory and hostility towards North Africans]. *International Review of Social Psychology*, *14*, 57–89.

Dubé, L. and Guimond, S. (1986). Relative deprivation and social protest: The personal–group issue. In J. M. Olson, C. P. Herman, and M. P. Zanna (eds.), *Relative deprivation and social comparison: The Ontario symposium* (Vol. IV; pp. 201–216). Hillsdale, NJ: Lawrence Erlbaum.

Eagly, A. H. and Mladinic, A. (1994). Are people prejudiced against women? Some answers from research on attitudes, gender stereotypes and judgments of competence. In W. Stroebe and M. Hewstone (eds.). *European Review of Social Psychology*, (Vol. V, pp. 1–35). New York: Wiley.

Eagly, A. H. and Wood, W. (1999). The origins of sex differences in human behavior: Evolved dispositions versus social roles. *American Psychologist*, *54*, 408–423.

Early, P. C. and Erez, M. (1997). *The transplanted executive*. New York: Oxford University Press.

Glick, P., Diebold, J., Bailey-Werner, B., and Zhu, L. (1997). The two faces of Adam: Ambivalent sexism and polarized attitudes toward women. *Personality and Social Psychology Bulletin*, *23*, 1323–1334.

Glick, P. and Fiske, S. T. (2001). Ambivalent sexism. In M. P. Zanna (ed.), *Advances in experimental social psychology* (Vol. XXXIII, pp. 115–188). Thousand Oaks, CA: Academic Press.

(1999). The ambivalence toward men inventory: differentiating hostile and benevolent beliefs about men. *Psychology of Women Quarterly*, *23*(3), 519–536.

(1996). The ambivalent sexism inventory: differentiating hostile and benevolent sexism. *Journal of Personality and Social Psychology*, *70*, 491–512.

Glick, P., Fiske, S. T., Mladinic, A., Saiz, J, Abrams, D., Masser, B., Adetoun, B., Osagie, J., Akande, A., Alao, A., Brunner, A., Willemsen, T. M., Chipeta, K., Dardenne, B., Dijksterhuis, A., Wigboldus, D., Eckes, T., Six-Materna, I., Expósito, F., Moya, M., Foddy, M., Kim, H-J., Lameiras, M., Sotelo, M. J., Mucchi-Faina, A., Romani, M., Sakalli, N., Udegbe, B., Yamamoto, M., Ui, M., Ferreira, M. C., and López, W. L. (2000). Beyond prejudice as simple antipathy: Hostile and benevolent sexism across cultures. *Journal of Personality and Social Psychology*, *79*, 763–775.

Glick, P., Lameiras, M., Fiske, S. T., Eckes, T., Masser, B., Volpato, C., Manganelli, A. M., Pek, J., Huang, L., Sakalli-Ugurlu, N., Castro, Y. R., D'Avila Pereira, M. L., Willemsen, T. M., Brunner, A., Six-Materna, I., and Wells, R. (2004). Bad but bold: Ambivalent attitudes toward men predict gender inequality in 16 nations. *Journal of Personality and Social Psychology*, *86*, 713–728.

Grant, P. R. and Brown, R. (1995) From ethnocentrism to collective protest: responses to relative deprivation and threats to social identity. *Social Psychology Quarterly*, *58*, 195–211.

Guimond, S., Branscombe, N., Brunot, S., Buunk, B. P., Chatard, A., Désert, M., Garcia, D., Haque, S., Martinot, D., and Yzerbyt, V. (2005). Culture, gender, and the self: variations and impact of social comparison processes. Manuscript submitted for publication.

Harris, M. (1991). *Cultural anthropology* (3rd edn.). New York: HarperCollins.

Hofstede, G. (1980). *Culture's consequences: International differences in work-related values*. Beverly Hills, CA: Sage.

(2001). *Culture's consequences: Comparing values, behaviors, institutions, and organizations across nations* (2nd edn.). Thousand Oaks, CA: Sage.

Jackman, M. R. (1994). *The velvet glove: Paternalism and conflict in gender, class, and race relations*. Berkeley, CA: University of California Press.

Jost, J. T. and Kay, A. C. (2005). Exposure to benevolent sexism and complementary gender stereotypes: Consequences for specific and diffuse forms of system justification. *Journal of Personality and Social Psychology*, 88, 498–509.

Kay, A. C. and Jost, J. T. (2003). Complementary justice: Effects of "poor but happy" and "poor but honest" stereotype exemplars on system justification and implicit activation of the justice motive. *Journal of Personality and Social Psychology*, 85, 823–837.

Maznevski, M. L., DiStefano, J. J., Gomez, C., Nooderhaven, N. G., and Wu, P. (1997). *Variations in cultural orientations within and among five countries*. Paper presented at the Academy of International Business annual meeting, Monterrey, Mexico.

Mosher, D. L. and Sirkin, M. (1984). Measuring a macho personality constellation. *Journal of Research in Personality*, 18, 150–163.

Moya, M., Poeschl, G., Glick, P., Páez, D., and Sedano, I. F. (2005). Sexisme, masculinité-féminité et facteurs culturels [sexism, masculinity-femininity, and cultural factors], *Revue Internationale de Psychologie Sociale*, 18, 141–167.

Runciman, W. G. (1966). *Relative deprivation and social justice*. London: Routledge and Kegan Paul.

Salzman, P. C. (1999). Is inequality universal? *Current Anthropology*, 40, 31–61.

Sidanius, J. and Pratto, F. (1999). *Social dominance: An intergroup theory of social hierarchy and oppression*. Cambridge: Cambridge University Press.

Tajfel, H. (1981). *Human categories and social groups*. Cambridge: Cambridge University Press.

Taylor, S. E., Fiske, S. T., Etcoff, N. L., and Ruderman, A. J. (1978). Categorical and contextual bases of person memory and stereotyping. *Journal of Personality and Social Psychology*, 36, 778–793.

United Nations Development Programme (2002). *Human development report 2002*. New York: Oxford University Press.

Walker, I. and Smith, H. J. (eds.) (2002). *Relative deprivation: Specification, development and integration*. New York: Cambridge University Press.

14 Social comparisons across cultures I: Gender stereotypes in high and low power distance cultures

Michel Désert and Jacques-Philippe Leyens

Very different social roles are generally assigned to women and men (Eagly, 1987). These roles are translated into stereotypical beliefs about typically female attributes and typically male attributes (Williams and Best, 1986, 1990). Women, for instance, are supposed to be sweet and nurturing. These characteristics are even considered desirable for them. By contrast, men are viewed as cold, domineering, and egotistic. These stereotypes overlap with self-perceptions of women and men (Bem, 1974), and they are not restricted to western countries. Similar data about the self-perceptions of female and male dimensions have been obtained from both men and women in Germany, Japan, Italy, France, Spain, etc. (Lenney, 1991; Lorenzi-Cioldi, 1993; Moya, 1993). Despite some disparities, men from all these cultures see themselves as having more male attributes than do women and the reverse is true for women concerning female attributes. Such a consensus led some authors (Bakan, 1966; Gabriel and Gardner, 1999) to think that it reflects sexual differences that are genetically determined.

Costa, Terracciano, and McCrae (2001), however, made an intriguing finding. In their cross-cultural research based on the five-factor model of personality, they found that differences in personality traits between men and women were greater in western countries than in African and Asian ones. First, these data do not conform to the genetic explanation for the differences between genders. If these differences were genetically determined, they should not vary as a function of the society in which they are studied. Second, Costa *et al.*'s (2001) findings are surprising because male and female roles are thought to have become more homogeneous in European and North American countries than in Asian and African ones. Stated otherwise, cultural evolution has led to greater equality between women and men in western countries. If differences in terms of status and social roles between men and women have decreased, why is it that their relative self-construals differ more than those obtained in Asian and African societies, which have not followed the same equalitarian line?

The present chapter aims at verifying whether Costa *et al.*'s (2001) findings generalize from personality traits of individuals to gender stereotypes such as nurturance, agency, and ability in math and sciences applied to women and men in general. It is well known that women are underrepresented in scientific and mathematical fields (Hyde, Fennema, and Lamon, 1990) as well as at the top levels of power hierarchies (Ellemers *et al.*, 2004; see also Chapter 7, this volume). In other words, the most socially valued domains and the most powerful ones are least accessible to women. These facts are related to gender stereotypes. On the one hand, women are supposed to be less talented than men in math and sciences. On the other hand, the personality characteristics that are typically attributed to women, such as sweetness and nurturance, are not ideal to fit high-status professional positions. Such positions are more in line with male personality attributes like coldness and dominance. These gender stereotypes are found in many countries (Williams and Best, 1990). By contrast, one has to note that, during the last thirty years, inequalities between men and women have diminished, notably in the western world. When people became aware of the amount of existing sexual discriminations, means were taken to suppress them. This effort was met with some success. However, if blatant sexism has decreased, Glick and Fiske (1999) note that a more ambiguous and ambivalent one has replaced it. Also, if the number of women has become more numerous in scientific domains and in prestigious positions, women remain a minority. One can summarize the present situation by saying that the equality between women and men has become a goal that is not yet achieved. Our question is whether this situation is reflected at the level of gender stereotypes. Are women from western societies less targeted by negative gender stereotypes than women from other countries where no effort is made to reduce the gap existing in favor of men?

To answer this question, we measured in several countries/cultures the beliefs that men and women hold about gender stereotypes. To compare the different cultures, we used the concept of Power Distance (PD) proposed by Hofstede (1980). This concept refers to the perception that individuals from a given culture have about social inequalities. Are inequalities between persons occupying different hierarchical positions normal and even desirable? Cultures with a high PD (e.g., Malaysia) tend to view status and power differences between individuals as legitimate. To the contrary, cultures with a low PD (e.g., Switzerland) consider such differences undesirable and illegitimate.

The PD concept has been less studied than other ones, such as the difference between collectivist and individualist societies, which was also proposed by Hofstede (1980; Hofstede and McCrae, 2004).

Recently, however, PD has regained interest among several researchers (see Chapters 13 and 15, this volume). Brockner *et al.* (2001), for instance, showed that low PD cultures have difficulties accepting that their hierarchical superior takes decisions without conciliation; people from high PD cultures, on the contrary, have no problem with such authoritarian situations.

We believe that the PD concept can be very helpful for our purpose. Recent research by Moya *et al.* (2005) shows that, in high PD cultures, men have a score of hostile sexism much greater than women. This difference is reduced in low PD countries. Moreover, Glick and Fiske (1999) defend the idea that sexism is essentially the belief that men and women are not, and should not be equal. It follows from this reasoning that, in high PD cultures, people and especially men should have strong gender stereotypes. An alternative hypothesis is also plausible. Results obtained by Moya, Poeschl, Glick, Páez, and Sedano (2005) may be due to the type of measures they used. It could be that sexism is quite close to PD, when it is viewed as a means to deal with the legitimacy of greater equality between genders as proposed by Glick and Fiske (1999). In this context, what will happen to gender stereotypes such as nurturance versus agency and ability in math and sciences? Remember that Costa *et al.* (2001) found fewer differences between genders (in terms of self-construal) in western countries (characterized by a low or medium PD according to Hofstede) than in Asian countries (typified by a high PD).

To verify whether high PD cultures have stronger gender stereotypes than low PD cultures, we conducted a cross-cultural study with four countries. Participants had to evaluate their gender and the other one on a series of stereotypical dimensions. Research dealing with such topics typically focuses on the agentic/communal dimension. We took this dimension into account in our study, but we also asked our participants to rate a more rarely investigated dimension, that is, the relative ability in math and sciences (Guimond and Roussel, 2001).

When discussing the results, we will present System Justification Theory (Jost and Hunyady, 2002) and interpret the findings in a dialectical way. Indeed, the two authors of this chapter think that the data presented here are quite challenging for System Justification Theory.

Method

Participants

Seven hundred and forty two students from France, Belgium, Switzerland, and Malaysia participated in the study. The number of males in our samples was slightly lower (N = 291) than the number of females

(N = 444), but was consistent from one country to another. Since some age differences between the countries was noted, this variable was covaried in the analyses reported here under.

Material

A French version of the questionnaire was given to the participants in France, Belgium, and Switzerland. It was translated in Malay language for the Malaysian participants.

The first part of the questionnaire consisted of a series of items designed to measure power distance beliefs (Brockner *et al.*, 2001). Six items were included in the present study. "People are better off not questioning the decisions of those in authority," "There should be established ranks in society with everyone occupying their rightful place regardless of whether that place is high or low in the ranking," and "An organization is most effective if it is clear who is the leader and who is the follower" are three examples of these items. The six items were averaged to form a power distance beliefs scale (Cronbach's alpha = .54). The participants answered through seven-point scales (1 = strongly disagree; 7 = strongly agree). High scores on the scale meant that the participants believed that the inequities of power are natural and even desirable in society. Based on the ranking of cultures reported by Hofstede (1980), we expected Malaysia to obtain the highest score and Switzerland the lowest score. France and Belgium were expected to be in the middle.

The second part of the questionnaire dealt with the gender stereotypes. Fourteen items, based on previous research (Guimond and Roussel, 2001; Williams and Best, 1986), were presented in random order. For each item, the participants had to decide how much it was descriptive of "men in general" and of "women in general." Principal component factor analyses, with varimax rotation, were computed separately for the evaluations of "men in general" and "women in general." The two analyses revealed a three-factors pattern (eigen values greater than 1) accounting for 50, 19 percent ("women in general") and 50, 23 percent ("men in general") of the total variance. The items loading highest on the first factor were "human relations are important to me," "affectionate," "good at taking care of others," and "family oriented." They constituted the relational/interdependent dimension of the gender stereotype. The items loading on the second factor were those associated with the agentic/independent dimension of gender stereotype: "boastful," "selfish," "dominant," and "often use coarse language." The third factor was constituted of the items "gifted in math" and "gifted in science." Difference scores were computed to obtain a measure of stereotype for each item. A positive score meant that the item was stereotypically associated with women, while a negative score was obtained for items stereotypically associated with males. Amongst each of the three subscales of gender stereotypes, the difference scores were then averaged in a single score.

Results

Power distance beliefs

A 2 (sex: male vs. female) by 4 (country: Belgium, France, Malaysia, Switzerland) ANOVA yielded a significant main effect of country, F (3, 734) $= 39.77$, $p < .0001$. Switzerland has the lowest score ($M = 2.74$). Belgium ($M = 3.01$) and France ($M = 3.18$) score higher than Switzerland and do not differ from each other. Malaysia has clearly the highest score of our sample ($M = 3.81$). A significant effect of sex was also observed, F (1, 734) $= 4.54$, $p < .035$. Males ($M = 3.38$) scored higher on power distance than did females ($M = 3.11$). The country by sex interaction was not significant.

Gender stereotypes

Based on the pattern of results of the power distance beliefs, the "country" variable (four levels) was recoded in a three-levels variable, named "culture's power distance" (low, medium, or high power distance). The gender stereotypes were analyzed with a 2 (gender of the participants: male vs. female) by 3 (culture: low power distance, medium power distance, high power distance) by 2 (target's gender: male vs. female) mixed design ANOVA, with two between-participants factors (participants' gender and culture) and one within-participants factor (target's gender).

Relational/interdependent stereotype

Consistent with former studies on gender stereotypes, women ($M = 5.83$) are seen as possessing more relational/interdependent traits than men ($M = 4.52$), F (1, 728) $= 18.75$, $p < .0001$. An interaction between target's gender and participants gender is also observed, F (1, 728) $= 5.97$, $p < .015$. As can be seen in Table 14.1, female participants in our samples share a stronger gender stereotype along the relational/interdependent dimension than male participants do. Otherwise stated, females report bigger differences between men and women on this dimension (M women $- M$ men $= 1.41$) than males do (M women $- M$ men $= 1.16$).

Table 14.1. *Means for attribution of the relational/interdependent dimension to men and women, as a function of participants' gender*

	Participants' gender	
	Female	Male
Attributions to women	5.89	5.74
Attributions to men	4.48	4.58

Table 14.2. *Means for attribution of the relational/interdependent dimension to men and women, as a function of culture and participants' gender*

		Target's gender	
		Female	Male
Low power	Attribution to men	4.45	4.08
Distance culture	Attribution to women	5.56	5.41
Medium power	Attribution to men	4.44	4.42
Distance culture	Attribution to women	5.88	5.61
High power	Attribution to men	4.67	5.14
Distance culture	Attribution to women	6.28	6.17

The analysis reveals also a participants' gender by power distance by target's gender interaction, $F(2, 728) = 5.45, p < .005$. As can be seen in Table 14.2, males in low power distance cultures are sharing a stronger gender stereotype concerning the relational/interdependent dimension (M women – M men = 1.33) than women do (M women – M men = 1.12). In medium power distance cultures and even more, in high power distance cultures, the contrary is observed: males make less difference between men and women (Mean difference = 1.19 and 1.02 in medium and high power distance cultures respectively) on the relational/interdependent dimension, while women display a stronger stereotype (M difference = 1.44 and 1.61 in medium and high power distance cultures respectively).

Agentic/independent dimension

A main effect of the target's gender is observed, $F(1, 728) = 11.27$, $p < .001$. Overall, the participants of our samples consider that the

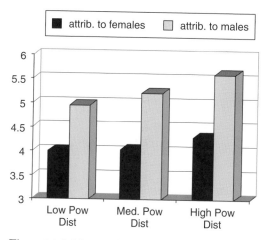

Figure 14.1. Means of attributions of agentic/independent characteristics to men and women, as a function of culture

agentic/independent dimension is a masculine more than a feminine trait ($M = 5.25$ and 4.09 for male and female target respectively). The analysis also reveals an interaction between target's gender and culture, $F (2, 728) = 3.10$, $p < .05$. As Figure 14.1 shows, the higher the power distance of the culture considered, the bigger the difference that was made between attributions to men and attributions to women on the agentic/independent dimension (Mean difference = 0.95, 1.17, 1.29 for low power distance, medium power distance, and high power distance cultures respectively). Stated otherwise, participants from high power distance cultures share a stronger gender stereotype concerning masculine characteristics. No other main effect or interaction was observed.

Ability in math/science dimension

Overall, men are considered as more gifted in science and math ($M = 5.31$) than women ($M = 4.45$) are, but this difference is only marginally significant, $F (1, 722) = 2.96$, $p < .09$. This study does not show thus a strong gender stereotype in the domain of math and sciences. The interaction between culture and target's gender is significant, $F (2, 722) = 3.68$, $p < .03$. As can be seen in Figure 14.2, the higher the power distance of the culture considered, the less difference is made between men and women concerning their abilities in maths and in science. This means that the gender stereotype concerning math and science ability is stronger in low power distance cultures than in high

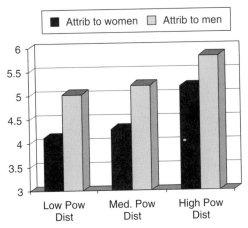

Figure 14.2. Means of attributions of gift in math and science to men and women, as a function of culture

power distance cultures! The analysis also reveals a significant interaction between participants' gender and target's gender, F (1, 722) = 5.81, p <.02. Female participants (M = 5.35, 4.40 for the attribution of gift in math and science to men and women, respectively) hold a stronger gender stereotype against their group in the math/science domain than male participants do (M = 5.25, 4.52 and, for the attribution of gift in math and science to men and women, respectively). The second order interaction between participants' gender, culture and target's gender was not significant.

Discussion Like previous research (Williams and Best, 1990), this cross-cultural study shows that women are seen as more communal, less agentic, and somewhat less gifted in math and sciences than men. Moreover, the gender differences for communality and ability in math and sciences are more strongly recognized by women than by men. The originality of the present research resided in the comparisons of these stereotypes as a function of power distance (Hofstede, 1980). Power Distance had an influence on the stereotypes of communality and ability in math and sciences. As PD increased, women and men accentuated communality, but they did so especially for their own gender. Finally, there was a negative relation between PD and the difference between men and women for their ability in math and sciences.

We think that the results reported here are very challenging for System Justification Theory (SJT, Jost and Banaji, 1994). This theory can be summarized by four general presuppositions and predictions. First, in the step of Social Dominance Theory (Sidanius and Pratto, 1999), SJT supposes that all societies are hierarchical. Without proposing such a general claim, other theories like Social Identity Theory (Tajfel, 1981) work with the idea that structural factors contribute to inequalities between groups such as the African Americans and the European Americans.

Second, SJT predicts that people justify the system in which they live. Jost and colleagues (e.g., Jost and Banaji, 1994; Jost and Hunyady, 2002) recognize that other and older theories predicted the same phenomenon. They claim, however, that their theory is specific and original because it involves the whole system rather than individuals or groups. The "Belief in a Just World" (Lerner, 1980), for instance, is supposed to work at the individual level while Social Identity Theory (Tajfel, 1981) would apply to the group level. This claim is controversial. On the one hand, the level of analysis in SJT is not clear; for instance, when members of groups are considered, differences between groups and correlations at the individual level are often calculated, without a look at societal variables. On the other hand, other theories consider the global system level. The premises of the "Beliefs in a Just World" theory are also "systemic" because they rely on the societal ideology of Protestant Work Ethic. Social Identity Theory (Tajfel, 1981) also takes into account the whole surrounding system by insisting on structural variables such as legitimacy, stability, and permeability that characterize the differences between groups. What makes the difference between SJT and the other theories such as BJW and SIT is that SJT views the system as a "fatum," as a given forever when the other theoretical propositions involve a tension within the system that may lead it to its change.

As a consequence, SJT proposes that dominant groups will behave and view the world so as to maintain their privileges. This point is hardly original. It is accepted by anyone working in the inter-group domain, and has been theorized by SIT and SDT, among others.

The fourth prediction of SJT is the most controversial one. According to system justification theorists, dominated groups will necessarily accept their lower position and will even internalize the view of the dominant groups about them. SDT (Sidanius and Pratto, 1999) first adopted this viewpoint to abandon it later on (e.g., Federico and Levin, 2004) and SIT has always been opposed to this simplistic perspective that does not take into account the constraints of social reality (Spears, Jetten, and Doosje, 2001).

It is this last point that will lead the interpretation of our data. Indeed, if one considers only what is specific to SJT, and not to other theories such as social dominance and social identity theory, one has to look at the responses of the dominated group, that is, women. Do our data show that low-status groups such as women necessarily accept, and even internalize, the values of higher status to justify the surrounding system? The results on PD beliefs clearly constitute a negative answer to the question. First, the level of PD beliefs varied much from countries to countries, showing a great variability of the supposed "system justification" motive. Second, in three of the four countries constituting the whole sample of the study, the difference between groups is seen as illegitimate. Even the mean of the fourth country does not reach the middle of the scale. Stated otherwise, in none of the four countries were the inequalities between groups considered desirable, and they were found particularly undesirable in three of them. The PD data show that dominated groups do not "necessarily" accept the existing system, even though they may differ in the intensity of their conception of the system as legitimate or illegitimate.

Moreover, SJT leads to contradictory hypotheses in terms of stereotyping. Jost and Hunyady (2002, H3, p. 119) postulate that "people will defend and justify the social system in response to threat by using stereotypes to differentiate between high- and low-status groups to a greater degree." One could argue that the evolution of western countries towards greater equality between men and women constitutes a threat against the system. By reaction and in order to maintain the status quo, men and women should utilize stereotypes to further differentiate themselves. In accordance with this reasoning, we indeed found that men and women from low PD societies (i.e., those where hierarchical differences are disputed) expressed greater gender differences in scientific and math abilities than did people from high PD. The latter result seems to support SJT. However, in the same paper, Jost and Hunyady (2002, H 6–8, pp. 121–122) present other hypotheses that go against our findings. Following the authors, subscribing to the legitimacy of the system and its outcomes leads to self-blame and acceptance of responsibility for being in a state of disadvantage. Moreover, the system justification levels are expected to be "higher in societies in which social and economic inequality is more extreme rather than less extreme." (H18, p. 123) We observed the contrary. First, it is in high PD countries, which most accept inequalities, that women perceived themselves as *most* competent! Second, it is in the low PD countries, where gender differences are low, that women perceived themselves as *less* competent!

Turning to the interpretation of the nurturance data, it should be noted that, in SJT research, competence has traditionally been opposed to sociability. Whereas competence was a typical attribute of high-status, dominant groups, sociability was characteristic of low-status, dominated groups (for a review, see Jost and Hunyady, 2002). For instance, students from an elite American university were confronted with those from a regional university. Students from both universities agreed to associate the elite university with intelligence and ambition and to associate the regional university with fun-loving and friendliness (Jost et al., 2002, Study 1). We will come back later on to this example and similar ones. For the moment, we will question the hierarchy between competence and sociability. In her model of Stereotype Content, Fiske and her colleagues (Fiske, Xu, and Cuddy, 1999; Glick and Fiske, 2001) report that people categorize groups along two dimensions: competence and warmth (or sociability). Most of the groups fall into the ambivalent quadrants of the model, that is, the high-competence but low-warmth (e.g., feminists) and the low-competence but high-warmth (e.g., housewives). A few groups, such as people on welfare or who are homeless, fall into the completely negative quadrant, i.e., low-competence and low-warmth. Only the ingroup or a special reference group is seen as high in both competence and warmth.

Contrary to SJT, the Stereotype Content Model (Fiske, Cuddy, and Glick, 2002) does not oppose competence and sociability but treats them as orthogonal, independent. It is true that competence, and not sociability, correlates with status (Fiske, Xu, and Cuddy, 1999). This result does not mean that sociability, such as nurturance, is not something desirable, which may contribute to a dominant status. If it were not so, it would be difficult to understand why people choose to characterize their ingroup as high in competence and in sociability. Our data also show that competence and sociability are not necessarily linked. We calculated the correlations between the ratings that women attributed to themselves for nurturance and ability in math and sciences. In low PD countries, $r = -.65$ and supports SJT. In the high PD country, $r = +.13$ and does not support SJT. The variability of the relation between competence and sociability suggests that such a relation should be considered with great care.

Research on infra-humanization (for reviews, see Demoulin, Leyens, and Paladino, 2004; Leyens, Cortes, and Demoulin 2003) also questions the presupposed lower status of sociability and warmth. According to this research, people vindicate a higher status for their group, relative to outgroups, by claiming a greater possession of uniquely human characteristics. These characteristics are precisely refined emotions such as love, tenderness, compassion, etc., that is, characteristics that are associated with nurturance. Both the SCM and the infra-humanization theory raise doubts as to whether the nurturance stereotype claimed by women should necessarily be considered a sign of acceptance of their low status in society.

The same reasoning may be applied for the lesser ability of women in math and sciences. For obvious reasons, this lesser ability may not be considered an advantage for women. Extensive research has shown women often under-perform men in math and sciences, due to social settings (Spencer, Steele, and Quinn, 1999). It is outside the scope of this chapter to review the literature on the topic (Désert, Croizet, and Leyens, 2002; Steele, Spencer, and Aronson, 2002 for a review). Our point is that it should not be considered sexist to recognize the existence of a gap between men and women in math and sciences performances. Sexism begins when this gap is attributed to different inner characteristics between men and women. Recognition of a fact (Spears, Jetten, and Doosje, 2001) does not necessarily mean acceptance. It is extremely important that dominated groups realize that they are dominated. Otherwise, why should they react? This recognition, and subsequent reaction, is in perfect agreement with the consequences of collective deprivation (see chapter 8 in this volume). This "collective deprivation" may very well explain that women see the gap as greater than do men.

It is noteworthy that most of the SJT research calling for status quo from the part of dominated groups has utilized variables that correspond to reality. In the above example with students from an elite university and a regional one, the low-status students associated the elite university with ambition and their regional university with friendship. These associations are merely constrained by the reality. It is purely speculative to say that they represent acceptance and internalization of the system. In other studies (see Jost and Hunyady, 2002), students are told that alumni from their university do much better or worse than alumni from a competing university. Not surprisingly, participants in these studies report that students of their university are more or less competent and hard working than those of the other university. In other words, people reproduce the reality they have been told about.

Our discussion is not at all in opposition to a view of stereotypes as explanatory devices of reality (Leyens, Yzerbyt, and Schadron, 1994). To the contrary, we strongly believe that human beings need to explain their and others' behaviors. We also agree with the fact that women are discriminated against, relative to men. We believe, however, that stereotypes may not have the same meaning and function for dominant male groups and for dominated female groups. According to the groups, nurturance may mean over-emotional or compassionate; competence may imply intelligence or hard work (Peabody and De Raad, 2002). For dominant groups, stereotypes may be used to explain existing reality or to maintain a status quo. For dominated groups, stereotypes may represent acceptance of a reality to be changed, recognition of their specificity, or a means to attract attention to their unjustly discriminated position. In extreme cases, stereotypes of dominated groups may probably also correspond to submission to the system, but our findings obtained in different countries, with different views about the legitimacy of inequalities, did not support this last possibility.

References

Bakan, D. (1966). *The duality of human existence*. Boston: Beacon Press.
Bem, S. L. (1974). The measurement of psychological androgyny. *Journal of Consulting and Clinical Psychology, 42*, 155–162.
Brockner, J., Ackerman, G., Greenberg, J., Gelfand, M. J., Francesco, A.-M., Chen, Z. X., Leung, K., Birbrauer, G., Gomez, C., Kirkman, B. L., and Shapiro, D. (2001). Culture and procedural justice: The influence of power distance on reactions to voice. *Journal of Experimental Social Psychology, 37*, 300–315.
Costa Jr., P. T., Terracciano, A., and McCrae, R. R. (2001). Gender differences in personality traits across cultures: Robust and surprising findings. *Journal of Personality and Social Psychology, 81*, 322–331.
Demoulin, S., Leyens, J. P., and Paladino, M. P. (2004). Dimensions of "uniquely" and "non-uniquely" human emotions. *Cognition and Emotion, 18*, 71–96.
Désert, M., Croizet, J.-C., and Leyens, J.-Ph (2002). La menace du stéréotype: une interaction entre situation et identité. [Stereotype threat: an interaction between situation and identity]. *L'Année Psychologique, 102*, 555–576.
Eagly, A. H. (1987). *Sex differences in social behavior: A social-role interpretation*. Hillsdale, NJ: Erlbaum.
Ellemers, N., van den Heuvel, H., and de Gilder, D. (2004) The underrepresentation of women in science: Differential commitment or the queen bee syndrome. *British Journal of Social Psychology, 43*, 315–338.
Federico, C. M. and Levin, S. (2004). Intergroup biases as a function of reflected status appraisals and support for legitimizing ideologies: Evidence from the USA and Israel. *Social Justice Research, 17*, 47–73.
Fiske, S. T., Cuddy, A. J. C., and Glick, P. (2002). A model of (often mixed) stereotype content: Competence and warmth respectively follow from perceived status and competition. *Journal of Personality and Social Psychology, 82*, 878–902.
Fiske, S. T., Xu, J., and Cuddy, A. C. (1999). (Dis)respecting versus (dis)liking: Status and interdependence predict ambivalent stereotypes of competence and warmth. *Journal of Social Issues, 55*, 473–489.
Gabriel, S. and Gardner, W. L. (1999) Are there "his" and "hers" types of interdependence? The implications of gender differences in collective versus relational interdependence for affect, behavior, and cognition. *Journal of Personality and Social Psychology, 77*, 642–655.

Glick, P. and Fiske, S. T. (1999). Gender, power dynamics, and social interaction. In M. M. Ferree and J. Lorber, *Revisioning gender* (pp. 365–398). Thousand Oaks, CA: Sage Publications.

(2001). Ambivalent sexism. In M. P. Zanna (ed.), *Advances in experimental social psychology* (Vol. xxxiii, pp. 115–188). Thousand Oaks, CA: Academic Press.

Guimond, S. and Roussel, L. (2001). Bragging about one's school grades: gender stereotyping and students' perception of their abilities in science, mathematics, and language. *Social Psychology of Education, 4,* 275–293.

Hofstede, G. (1980). *Culture's Consequences: International Differences in Work-Related Values.* Beverly Hills: Sage.

Hofstede, G. and McCrae, R. R. (2004). Personality and culture revisited: Linking traits and dimensions of culture. *Cross-cultural Research, 38,* 52–88.

Hyde, J. S., Fennema, E., and Lamon, S. J. (1990). Gender differences in mathematics performance: A meta-analysis. *Psychological Bulletin, 107,* 139–155.

Jost, J. T. and Banaji, M. R. (1994). The role of stereotyping in system-justification and the production of false consciousness. *British Journal of Social Psychology, 33,* 1–27.

Jost, J. T. and Hunyady, O. (2002). The psychology of system justification and the palliative function of ideology. In W. Stroebe and M. Hewstone (eds.), *European Review of Social Psychology, 13,* 111–153. Chichester: John Wiley & Sons.

Jost, J. T., Pelham, B. W., and Carvallo, M. R. (2002). Non-conscious forms of system justification: Implicit and behavioral preferences for higher status groups. *Journal of Experimental Social Psychology, 38,* 586–602.

Lenney, E. (1991). Sex roles: The measurement of masculinity, femininity, and androgyny. In J. P. Robinson and P. R. Shaver (eds.), *Measures of personality and social psychological attitudes* (pp. 573–660). San Diego, CA: Academic Press.

Lerner, M. (1980). *The belief in a just world: A fundamental delusion.* New York: Plenum.

Leyens, J.-Ph., Yzerbyt, V. Y., and Schadron, G. (1994). *Stereotypes and social cognition.* London: Sage.

Leyens, J. P., Cortes, B., and Demoulin, S. (2003). Emotional prejudice, essentialism, and nationalism: The 2002 Tajfel Lecture. *European Journal of Social Psychology, 33,* 703–717.

Lorenzi-Cioldi, F. (1993). They all look alike, but so do we sometimes: Perceptions of in-group and out-group homogeneity as a function of sex and context. *British Journal of Social Psychology, 32,* 111–124.

Moya, M., Poeschl, G., Glick, P., Páez, D., and Sedano, I. F. (2005). Sexisme, masculinité-féminité et facteurs culturels [Sexism, masculinity-femininity, and cultural factors], *Revue Internationale de Psychologie Sociale, 18,* 141–167.

Peabody, D. and De Raad, B. (2002). The substantive nature of psycholexical personality factors: A comparison across languages. *Journal of Personality and Social Psychology, 83,* 983–997.

Sidanius, J. and Pratto, F. (1999). *Social dominance: An intergroup theory of social hierarchy and oppression.* New York: Cambridge University Press.

Spears, R., Jetten, J., and Doosje, B. (2001) The (il)legitimacy of ingroup bias: From social reality to social resistance. In J. T. Jost and B. Major, *Psychology of legitimacy: Emerging perspectives on ideology, justice, and intergroup relations.* (pp. 332–362). New York: Cambridge University Press.

Spencer, S. J., Steele, C. M., and Quinn, D. (1999). Under suspicion of inability: Stereotype threat and women's math performance. *Journal of Experimental Social Psychology, 35,* 4–28.

Steele, C. M., Spencer, S. J., and Aronson, J. (2002) Contending with group image: The psychology of stereotype and social identity threat. In M. P. Zanna (ed.), *Advances in experimental social psychology* (Vol. xxxiv, pp. 379–440). San Diego, CA: Academic Press.

Tajfel, H. (1981). *Human groups and social categories. Studies in social psychology.* Cambridge: Cambridge University Press.

Williams, J. E. and Best, D. L. (1990). *Sex and psyche: Gender and self viewed cross-culturally.* Thousand Oaks, CA: Sage Publications.

(1986). Sex stereotypes and intergroup relations. In S. Worchel and W. G. Austin (eds.), *Psychology of intergroup relations* (pp. 244–259). Chicago: Nelson-Hall.

15   Social comparisons across cultures II: Change and stability in self-views – experimental evidence

S. Guimond, A. Chatard, N. R. Branscombe, S. Brunot,
A. P. Buunk, M. A. Conway, R. J. Crisp, M. Dambrun,
M. Désert, D. M. Garcia, S. Haque, J.-P. Leyens,
F. Lorenzi-Cioldi, D. Martinot, S. Redersdorff, and
V. Yzerbyt

This chapter reports on the results of a cross-cultural study of the effects of social comparison on self-construal among eight nations/cultures. It follows a previous report on five of these cultures (Guimond, Branscombe, Brunot, Buunk, Chatard, Désert, Garcia, Haque, Martinot, and Yzerbyt, 2005) and is linked to the previous chapter outlining some findings of the study in terms of gender stereotyping.

Past research and the specific contributions found in this volume indicate that social comparison processes are involved in many different attitudes and social behaviors. At the most general level, social comparison is a fundamental process by which knowledge is acquired. Indeed, most social psychologists would agree that social comparison is perhaps first and foremost critical for the creation of self-knowledge. To know who we are, we compare ourselves with others, or with ourselves in the past (see Part One, this volume). Some major developments in personality and social psychology have occurred by studying the self across cultures (see Berry, Poortinga, Segall, and Dasen, 1992; Markus and Kitayama, 1991; Shweder and Bourne, 1984; Triandis, 1989; see also Lorenzi-Cioldi and Chatard, this volume). For example, in their influential paper, Markus and Kitayama (1991) reviewed evidence suggesting that the self is defined in fundamentally different ways in western as opposed to eastern cultures. The western conception of self, and for several decades the only conception as far as social and personality psychologists were concerned, is that of an individual who is separate, autonomous, and composed of a set of discrete traits, abilities, and motives. This is referred to as the independent self by Markus and Kitayama (1991) who pointed out that the eastern conception is much more an interdependent self. In this conception, the self is inevitably defined by its relationship with others. The interdependent self is a self that is inherently linked to others, rather than being defined as separate from others.

Such a cultural theory of the self has made it clear that much can be learned by looking at psychology from a cross-cultural perspective. It revealed that some of the most basic constructs of psychology, such as notions of person and selfhood, had to be considered as cultural constructions. This view subsequently influenced research in many different directions (Markus, Kitayama, and Heiman, 1996). Curiously, however, the role of social comparison processes in the genesis of these different self-views across cultures has not been considered, let alone systematically studied (Lehman, Chiu, and Schaller, 2004; Smith and Bond, 1999). The first objective of our research was to begin to fill this gap. Although the study was to some extent exploratory, it was designed in a way that it could test a number of specific hypotheses. Previous theory and research allowed us to formulate specific predictions before the study was carried out. These predictions relate first to cross-cultural variations in the type of comparisons that people may seek, and second, to the effects of these comparisons on self-definition. These two points are developed in turn, setting the stage for a look at empirical results bearing on these predictions. We conclude by considering briefly some of the implications of these results.

Cross-cultural variations in social comparison preference

The universalist perspective in cross-cultural psychology suggests that although certain cognitive processes may be universal, their manifestation can vary considerably across cultures (Berry et al., 1992; Sedikides, Gaertner, and Toguchi, 2003; see also Fiske and Cuddy, this volume). Thus, whereas social comparison may be found in all cultures, the form it takes can differ across cultures. As the previous chapters indicate, people can engage in at least two major forms of social comparison corresponding respectively to an individual level of analysis and to a group level of analysis. If a man compares himself with his wife, and the fact that his wife is a woman is not seen as relevant, then this is a social comparison at the individual level. But if the man compares himself as a man, with his wife specifically because she is a woman, then this is a group level social comparison.

Although it may appear at first sight to be a flimsy distinction, we know that the consequences of making individual level social comparisons versus group level social comparisons can differ sharply (see Part Two, this volume). Research related to relative deprivation theory has repeatedly shown that feelings of personal relative deprivation associated with individual level social comparison lead to different outcomes compared to feelings of group relative deprivation associated with group-based social comparisons (Abeles, 1976; Dambrun and Guimond, 2001; Guimond and Dubé-Simard, 1983; Hafer and Olson, 1993; Walker and Smith, 2002). For example, Pettigrew and Meertens (1995) found that across four European countries, only group relative deprivation predicts prejudice against immigrants and foreigners, not personal relative deprivation. Similarly, in a field experiment, Guimond, Dif, and Aupy (2002) have shown that a positive feedback placing participants in a position where they compare favorably with others has a strikingly different psychological impact if it is defined at the individual level or at the group level. Indeed, to explain collective action and social change, group-based social comparisons are of fundamental importance. As Wright and Tropp (2002) state: "the roots of disruptive collective action, the kind of collective action most likely to change the existing social structure, can be found in (. . .) the propensity to make group-level social comparisons with a dominant outgroup that lead to strong feelings of collective relative deprivation . . . ." (p. 228)

This suggests that identifying the conditions under which people display the propensity to make group-level social comparisons, or individual level ones, can be of considerable social importance. However, a basic theoretical difficulty arises in this respect when one considers current research in social comparison. Some have suggested that there is very little evidence that people do engage in group-based social comparisons. To the contrary, there are clear indications that most people are reluctant to do so. Using a diary-based methodology, Smith and Leach (2004) examined, in a detailed manner, the type of social comparisons that people seem to spontaneously engage in. They report an overwhelming tendency for people to engage in individual level social comparisons and very few cases where group level comparisons are made. This is, of course, one of the major outcomes of the elaborate program of research of Zagelfka and Brown reported in Chapter 5 of this volume. Their general finding is also that people make temporal comparisons and intragroup comparisons, but they very rarely engage in intergroup comparisons.

One possible conclusion that can be drawn from this research is that Festinger (1954) was right all along. He argued that people could perhaps engage in intergroup comparisons at the "phantasy level" but that in reality, most people compare themselves with others who are close to themselves and belong to the same group. This view is still pervasive within social psychology. Researchers working within the tradition of research established by Festinger tend to equate social comparison with interpersonal comparison (see Suls and Wheeler, 2000). Intergroup comparisons are seen as theoretically irrelevant. But even researchers looking at intergroup relations often subscribe to this view. The main study suggesting that intergroup comparisons are not relevant is that of Major, Sciacchitano, and Crocker (1993). They examined the effects of ingroup and outgroup comparisons on self-esteem and found that out-group comparisons had little effect. This study is now widely cited as evidence that inter-group comparisons are not relevant or informative, only intra-group comparisons are (e.g., Tyler and Smith, 1999). Crocker and Blanton (1999) summarize the state of knowledge as follows: "people often prefer comparisons with ingroup members. Festinger (1954) originally suggested this preference for comparison with similar others and his idea has since received wide empirical support (e.g., Gastorf and Suls, 1978; Major, Sciacchitano, and Crocker, 1993; Major, Testa, and Bylsma, 1991; C. T. Miller, 1982, 1984). People may seek comparisons with those similar to them because such comparisons are particularly informative standards ...." (p. 174) In fact, Crocker and Blanton (1999) make it clear that this conclusion applies especially to gender.

In the same vein, Major (1994) argues that: "people tend to make intragroup rather than intergroup comparisons when estimating what they deserve, in part because of the greater availability and diagnosticity of the former." (p. 308) Most of this research and theorizing has been carried out in western societies in which a strong emphasis is placed on personal identity and individual achievements. Consequently, it is perhaps not surprising to find a focus on individual level social comparison. However, assuming that people do not make inter-group comparisons because they are largely irrelevant and uninformative raises a basic pro-blem: how can group relative deprivation emerge? How can people feel that their ingroup is deprived relative to an outgroup if they do not engage in inter-group comparisons? In this context, the analysis of social change and the role of group relative deprivation in such an analysis seems quite problematic. Fortunately, the problem may be more apparent than real. First, there is now solid evidence to suggest that the general conclusion reached by Major, Sciacchitano, and Crocker (1993) needs to be revised and this is explained in detail by Martinot and Redersdorff (see Chapter 6, this volume). Second, a theoretical solution to this problem was proposed several years ago by Tajfel (1974, 1981).

Tajfel's theoretical solution

This solution was proposed in the early days of Social Identity Theory, even before it was called Social Identity Theory, in the unpublished

Katz-Newcomb lectures given by Tajfel (1974), but the ideas may also be found in the book published in 1981: *Human Groups and Social Categories*. In this book, there is a section entitled "social comparison and relative deprivation" in which Tajfel argues that the criteria of similarity that is so fundamental in the case of individual level social comparison is replaced by the criterion of legitimacy in the case of intergroup comparison: "Social comparisons between groups which may be highly dissimilar are based on the perceived legitimacy of the perceived relationship between them." (Tajfel, 1981, p. 265)

Tajfel (1974, 1981) points out the importance of this view for a social psychology of social change and suggests more specifically, that groups perceived as non-comparable can become comparable, under conditions of perceived illegitimacy (see Turner and Brown, 1978; Turner, Brown, and Tajfel, 1979). This view is also found in the five-stage model of intergroup relations (Taylor and McKirnan, 1984). According to this model, group relations go through a series of stages and social comparison processes are one of the critical factors that differentiate between the stages. During Stage 1 (clearly stratified intergroup relations), social comparisons are hypothesized to be restricted to the intra-group level. But social comparisons are expected to become "inter-group" in later stages, as the inter-group structure is perceived as less stable and more open to change. Yet, and this is underlined by Zagefka and Brown in their chapter also, very little research has examined these propositions. Instead, theorists simply argued repeatedly that only inter-individual comparisons are important.

In contrast, our study was set up so that it could provide a cross-cultural test of Tajfel's hypothesis. We selected participants from cultures that are known to vary on the dimension of power distance (PD; Hofstede, 1980). Power distance refers to the extent to which inequality among persons in different positions of power in a given culture is viewed as a natural (and even desirable) aspect of the social order (Hofstede and McCrae, 2004). Cultures receiving a high score on this dimension are those in which norms legitimize differences in power whereas cultures receiving a low score are those in which norms reduce power differences among people (see Brockner, Ackerman, Greenberg, Gelfand, Francesco Chen, Leung, Birbrauer, Gomez, Kirkman, and Shapiro, 2001). Power distance is therefore quite close conceptually to what Tajfel had in mind when he wrote about the perceived legitimacy of the inter-group structure. Cultures high in power distance are systems in which group-based inequality is perceived as legitimate. But cultures low in power distance are, to the contrary, systems in which inequalities of power tend to be perceived as illegitimate. The analyses presented by

Glick, in Chapter 13 of this volume, relating ambivalent gender ideologies to power distance and gender inequality among twenty-five cultures confirm both the importance of power distance as a cultural dimension and its theoretical relevance as a measure of the perceived legitimacy of inequality. Thus, comparing low and high power distance cultures on social comparison processes allows for a direct test of Tajfel's basic hypothesis. The scale of social comparison orientation (SCO) developed by Gibbons and Buunk (1999) was used for that purpose.

Although there was no reliable measure of the tendency to engage in inter-group social comparison when the study was conducted, the SCO scale proved to be a valuable instrument in several studies with widely different populations in terms of the frequency of making interpersonal social comparisons (see Chapter 1 by Buunk and Gibbons, this volume). Using this scale, we predicted a main effect of culture on this measure with people from cultures high in power distance expected to display higher scores indicating a stronger propensity to make individual level social comparisons than those low in power distance. Guimond *et al.* (2005) found support for this hypothesis with people from Malaysia, a high power distance culture, scoring higher than others on SCO. Our purpose here will be to further test this hypothesis by adding three more countries in the analysis: Switzerland, the UK, and Tunisia.

The effects of intragroup and intergroup comparisons across cultures

A second set of predictions dealt with the effects of social comparison on self-construal and the extent to which these effects vary across cultures. A series of investigations by Heine, Lehman, Peng, and Greenhlotz (2002) have revealed the fundamental theoretical and methodological import of social comparison for cross-cultural research. At the methodological level, they point out that people in a culture will evidently use other people in their own culture as comparison standards. Canadians will use other Canadians as reference group, not people from China or Peru. Similarly, the Japanese will use other people in Japan as reference standards, not Canadians. This simple fact has tremendous implications for cross-cultural research. It means that when Canadians are asked to indicate on a standard Likert-type scale how nationalist they are for example, this rating is likely to reflect the fact that they use other Canadians as the referent in their estimations. Likewise the same ratings by Japanese people will reflect the use of other Japanese as their reference group. In other words, when cross-cultural comparisons of these ratings are drawn, there is a confound with the reference groups that people are using.

At the theoretical level, this analysis is also quite challenging. It reveals that social comparison processes need to be taken into account in studies seeking to compare people from different cultures. To be able to understand and make theoretical sense of the cross-cultural similarities or differences that are observed on Likert-type rating scales, one needs to enter into the equation the role of social comparison. Thus, Heine *et al.* (2002) show that manipulating the reference group enhances the expected cultural differences in individualism between East Asians and North Americans. More specifically, among samples of individuals having experienced both cultures, the hypothesis that Canadians are more individualist and less collectivist than the Japanese was strongly supported when participants were instructed to compare themselves with members of the other cultural group. However, it was disconfirmed when they were instructed to compare themselves with members of their own culture. This suggests that cross-cultural differences in individualism, often assumed to reflect long-standing and enduring psychological differences, can in fact vary substantially as a function of the comparative frame of reference.

Allick and McCrae (2004) have recently disputed the claims put forward by Heine *et al.* (2002). Secondary analyses of data from thirty-six cultures using the five-factor model of personality revealed reliable relations between cultures and trait profiles. They concluded that "Although the reference group effect may potentially attenuate cross-cultural comparisons, it cannot explain the systematic variation and pattern of personality differences across the world." (p. 24) Our study allows for an examination of the validity of these two points of view as they apply to the stability of gender differences in self-construal across cultures.

Gender differences in self-construal

In a manner similar to the work pointing to strong cultural differences in self-definition (e.g., Markus and Kitayama, 1991), research has revealed reliable differences in the self-concept of women and men (see Cross and Madson, 1977; Gabriel and Gardner, 1999; Glick and Fiske, 2001; Helgeson, 1994; Josephs, Markus and Tafarodi, 1992; Kemmelmeier and Oyserman, 2001; Moskowitz, Suh, and Desaulniers, 1994; Sidanius, Pratto, and Bobo, 1994; Wood, Christensen, Hebl, and Rothgerber, 1997). More specifically, women's self-construal is believed to be chronically relationally focused, reflecting an interdependent or relational self-concept. In contrast, men's self-construal is said to be much more that of an independent, autonomous, and self-assertive individual who is largely concerned with himself, not with others.

Furthermore, and consistent with the implication of the theoretical perspective of Allick and McCrae (2004), research has revealed that these sex differences in self-construal are invariant across cultures (Kashima, Yamagushi, Kim, Choi, Gelfand, and Yuki, 1995). Among participants from five cultures, selected to represent both individualist and collectivist cultures, self-construal was found to vary across cultures but gender differences in relational self-construal were invariant. This view was re-stated recently by Kashima, Kokubo, Kashima, Boxall, Yamaguchi, and Macrae (2004) in a study comparing Australian and Japanese students (see also Gabriel and Gardner, 1999). These findings are consistent with Allick and McCrae (2004) and the five-factor model of personality which suggests that personality traits represent relatively invariant "biologically-based basic tendencies." (p. 25, see also Hofstede and McCrae, 2004)

However, according to the analysis developed by Heine *et al.* (2002), differences in trait ratings across groups should depend on social comparison. To the extent that social comparison processes vary across cultures, then gender differences in self-construal should be variable rather than fixed across cultures. As noted above, there are reasons to expect some systematic variations in social comparison across cultures. Furthermore, in a program of research on gender differences in self-construal, Guimond, Chatard, Martinot, Crisp, and Redersdorff (in press) independently developed a very similar paradigm to that used by Heine *et al.* (2002). The results revealed, consistent with Heine *et al.* (2002), that gender differences in self-construal are not fixed or enduring. Rather, they vary in systematic manner as a function of social comparison.

On the basis of Self-Categorization Theory (Onorato and Turner, 2004; Ryan, David, and Reynolds, 2003; Turner, 1999; Turner, Hogg, Oakes, Reicher, and Wetherell, 1987; Turner, Oakes, Haslam, and McGarty, 1994; Turner and Onorato, 1999), Guimond *et al.* (in press) argued that gender differences in self-construal reflect a process of self-stereotyping such that, in certain social contexts, women and men define the self by using attributes that are typical of their respective gender groups. The results of four studies provided strong support for this explanation. In Study 1, ingroup stereotyping was found to fully mediate gender differences in relational self-construal. The results showed that the strong and reliable difference between men and women on relational self-construal disappeared completely when the perception of women and men on this relational dimension (ingroup stereotyping) was statistically controlled. In contrast, the relation between gender and ingroup stereotyping remained highly reliable, even when relational self-construal was statistically controlled. Three further experiments revealed that, consistent with Self-Categorization Theory, gender differences in relational self-construal were observed when participants were instructed to compare themselves with members of the opposite sex (inter-group context) but not when they were instructed to compare themselves with members of their own gender (intra-group context). In sum, and consistent with the reference group effect identified by Heine *et al.* (2002) in the cross-cultural domain, gender differences in self-construal appear to be a product of social comparison processes. When there are group-based comparisons across gender lines, strong differences in the self-concept of men and women are observed. But when intra-group comparisons are made, and people employ members of their own gender group as referent, no differences in the self-concept of men and women are found (see Guimond *et al.*, in press for more details). This means that if inter-group comparisons are seen as more appropriate and self-relevant in low power distance cultures compared to high power distance cultures, greater gender differences in self-construal should be observed in the former than in the latter cultures.

This is exactly the pattern of findings that Costa, Terracciano, and McCrae (2001) have reported, without however expecting such results. Using a sample of people from twenty-six cultures and assessing a broader range of dimensions (thirty specific traits from the five-factor model) than those studied by Kashima *et al.* (1995), Costa *et al.* (2001) found that the magnitude of gender differences did vary across cultures. More specifically, they report that gender differences in personality traits are stronger in European and American cultures (typically low in power distance) than in African and Asian cultures (typically higher in power distance). From the perspective of the five-factor model of personality, these findings were totally unexpected by Costa *et al.* (2001). Indeed, they are somewhat contradictory with their theory. In fact, Allick and McCrae (2004) who argued in favor of stable and enduring personality traits do not refer to these findings. The results of Costa *et al.* (2001) are important because a relatively large number of cultures were studied. But they are far from sufficient to confirm our analysis. Costa *et al.* (2001) do not, of course, have any data on the role of comparison processes in accounting for variations in gender differences. This is the contribution that our cross-cultural study was designed to offer. Thus, we used the same manipulation that was used by Guimond *et al.* (in press) but among participants from cultures varying on power distance.

Participants and cultures

The total number of participants is 1,342 with 785 women and 554 men (3 participants did not mention their gender). All are university students with the exception of Tunisia in which only a sample of high school students was obtained. This means that any difference in the findings involving Tunisia could be attributed to this difference in status and not to some other cultural factors. The mean age of the total sample is 20.38 years old with a range from 15 to 45 years. Age is statistically controlled in all analyses reported. More details about the method and the measures used in this study can be found in Guimond *et al.* (2005). Overall, unless indicated, the evidence suggests adequate and comparable reliability of the measures within each culture, supporting the assumption of conceptual equivalence across cultures (Schwartz, 1994).

The participants come from nations/cultures receiving different rankings on the power distance dimension identified by Hofstede (1980; Bollinger and Hofstede, 1987). More specifically, with a range from 0 (low power distance) to 104 (high power distance), the scores of the cultures selected are as follows: Switzerland = 34, UK = 35, Netherlands = 38, USA = 40, Belgium = 65, France = 68, and Malaysia = 104. Tunisia was not included in the study of Hofstede so its score is unknown. However, Hofstede (1980) reports that several countries grouped together as representing the Arab region have a score of 80. Tunisia would be expected to fall within that range (see Kabasakal and Bodur, 2002). These rankings are based on data gathered more than twenty-five years ago. Although not much change is expected (see Glick, this volume; Hofstede and McCrae, 2004), some variations may well have occurred over the years. To have some indication of how our participants can be ordered on power distance, a four-item scale of power distance beliefs adapted from Brockner *et al.* (2001) was included as Part 1 of the questionnaire (see Guimond *et al.*, 2005). A representative item is "There should be established ranks in society with everyone occupying their rightful place regardless of whether that place is high or low in the ranking." Scores on this scale can range from 1 to 7 with high scores reflecting the belief that inequalities are legitimate and desirable.

A 2 (participant's gender) × 8 (culture) ANOVA on this scale of power distance beliefs revealed a main effect of participant gender, $F(1, 1305) = 17.19$, $p < .001$, with males ($M = 3.75$) being more favorable toward status hierarchy than females ($M = 3.51$). The main effect of culture was also reliable, $F(7, 1305) = 36.67$, $p < .001$. As Figure 15.1 illustrates, Switzerland, which has the lowest score in Hofstede (1980), also has the lowest score on our measure of power distance beliefs, whereas Malaysia, found by Hofstede (1980) to have the highest ranking on power distance out of fifty-three countries, has the highest score on our measure.

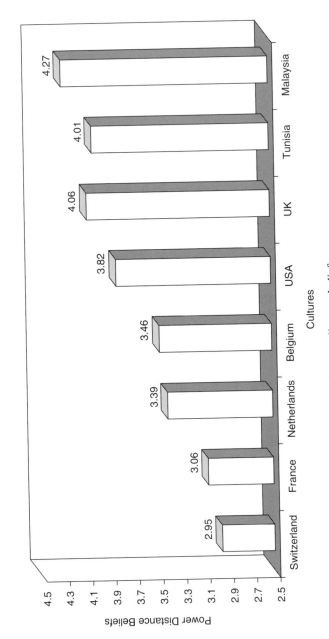

Figure 15.1. Mean scores on the measure of power distance beliefs

On the other hand, France and Belgium are lower on our measure of power distance beliefs than Hofstede would expect, whereas the USA and UK are higher than he would expect. In addition to these main effects, a significant gender by culture interaction was obtained on our power distance measure, $F(7, 1305) = 2.37$, $p < .05$. This interaction reflects the fact that there are no gender differences in Switzerland, Malaysia, and Tunisia on power distance, in contrast to the other cultures where males tend to score higher than females. However, this interaction does not change the overall ranking of the cultures on power distance beliefs shown in Figure 15.1.

Social comparison orientation Our first prediction relates to the propensity to engage in individual level social comparison, as measured by SCO. This scale consists of eleven items that assess the extent to which participants have a tendency to compare themselves with others using a five-point scale format (see Buunk and Gibbons, this volume). Because of our interest in gender-based comparison, we wanted to be sure that scores on the SCO reflect an intra-group or intra-gender orientation and not an inter-group orientation. For this reason, participants were also asked to indicate, on a five-point scale, how often they share their experiences and concerns with members of their own gender, and with members of the other gender. As expected, and consistent with Guimond *et al.* (2005), there is a significant and positive correlation between scores on the SCO and contact with members of one's own gender, $r(1295) = .17, p < .001$, whereas the predisposition to compare with others, as assessed by the SCO scale, is not related to having contact with members of the other gender group, $r(1300) = .04$, ns.

A 2 (participant's gender) × 8 (culture) ANOVA on SCO indicates a main effect of gender, $F(1, 1300) = 15.91, p < .001$, with females scoring higher ($M = 3.6$) than males ($M = 3.4$). The predicted main effect of culture is also reliable, $F(7, 1300) = 15.00$, $p < .001$, and explains 8 percent of the variance in SCO. As Figure 15.2 indicates, with the exception of Tunisia, the ordering of the cultures on SCO fits with our hypothesis. The culture with the highest power distance, Malaysia, also displays the strongest propensity to engage in interpersonal comparison, whereas the culture with the lowest power distance, Switzerland, also displays the lowest score on SCO.

As Buunk and Gibbons note in Chapter 1, SCO is related to an interdependent or relational self-construal. Because people from Malaysia are higher than others on relational self-construal (see Guimond *et al.*, 2005), the effect of culture on SCO may be confounded with self-construal. Analysis of covariance that control for our measure of relational

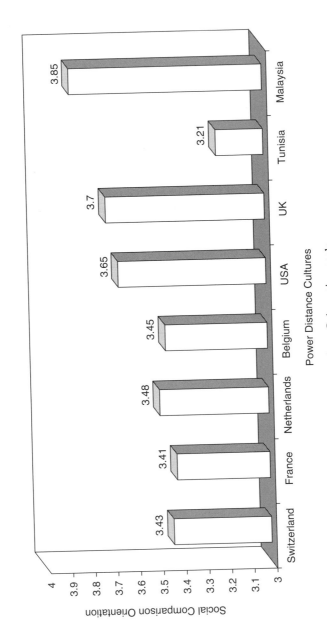

Figure 15.2. Mean scores on the Social Comparison Orientation scale

self-construal revealed however that this was not the case; the effect of culture on SCO remains reliable. Furthermore, regardless of culture, there is a significant and positive correlation between SCO and scores on the scale of power distance beliefs, $r(1276) = 0.14$, $p < .001$. This relation is a weak one, but it is nevertheless consistent with our theoretical framework suggesting that the more rigid and hierarchical a cultural system is, the more likely it is that people will restrict their social comparison activity to their own group and engage mainly in individual level social comparison. There is no interaction of sex and culture on SCO.

In terms of the potential for between-gender social comparisons, the measure of the frequency with which participants report sharing their experiences and concerns with members of the opposite sex is relevant. The higher this frequency, the more likely it is that participants have the opportunity to engage in between-gender comparisons. An ANOVA on this measure indicates a main effect of culture, $F(7, 1327) = 25.53$, $p < .001$. As expected, Malaysia ($M = 2.95$) and Tunisia ($M = 2.44$) have a mean score below the midpoint of the scale suggesting a low frequency of contact with the opposite sex whereas in all other cultures, the mean score is above 3.5 on a five-point scale suggesting a greater frequency of inter-gender interaction. Because contact is expected to increase the possibility of engaging in social comparison (Suls, 1977; Suls and Wheeler, 2000), this again supports our argument that people in high power distance cultures are less likely to feel that between-gender, group level, social comparisons are appropriate.

The effects of within- and between-gender comparisons on the self Section 2 of the questionnaire, the self-rating task, was used to manipulate within and between-gender social comparisons (see Guimond et al., in press). Male and female participants were randomly assigned to one of three conditions in which they were asked to rate themselves "personally" either in a standard no-referent control condition, an intra-group condition involving comparison with their own gender group, or an inter-group condition involving comparison with the other gender group. These ratings were made on seven-point scales ranging from "not at all" self-descriptive to "totally" self-descriptive. The only difference between the control condition and the other two conditions is that preceding each attribute in the self-rating task (e.g., "I am good at taking care of others"), male participants in the intra-group condition encountered the expression "Compared to most men, I am ..." or the expression "Compared to most women, I am ..." in the inter-group condition. The reverse was the case for female participants. The intra-group and inter-group conditions differed only by the substitution of the word "men" for "women."

Participants rated themselves on a total of fourteen attributes from which several measures of self-construal were derived (see Guimond *et al.*, 2005). Results obtained in the control condition allowed for a test of the cross-cultural invariance in gender differences hypothesis. Consistent with Heine *et al.* (2002), and following our first prediction about cultural variations in social comparison, we expected that even in a standard control condition, gender differences in self-construal would *not* be invariant across cultures. Rather, because in high power distance cultures between-gender comparisons are perceived as inappropriate, there should be few gender differences in self-construal. Conversely, because the propensity to engage in inter-group comparisons is expected to be greater in low power distance cultures, reliable gender differences in self-construal should be found in those cultures. Furthermore, we expected that our manipulation of intra- and inter-group social comparisons would provide additional experimental evidence relevant to our analysis. As Mussweiler, Rüter, and Epstude (2004) noted, "changes in self-evaluation can be used as an indicator of social comparison activities" (p. 690) because we know that comparison with others change the way we see ourselves. Thus, our inter-group comparison manipulation was expected to have little impact on the self-construal of people in high power distance cultures, reflecting their propensity not to engage in this form of social comparison. In contrast, and consistent with the results of Guimond *et al.* (in press), the inter-group comparison condition was expected to increase gender differences in self-construal among people in low power distance cultures.

Adding three new cultural groups to the five examined in Guimond *et al.* (2005) and using measures of self-construal as dependent variables in a 2 (participant's gender) × 8 (culture) × 3 (experimental condition) ANOVA does not change the findings reported previously in terms of gender differences in self-construal. Rather, the findings are confirmed and expanded further. The two key dependent variables here are a measure of relational self-construal based on self-ratings on four items (caring, family-oriented, affectionate, and value human relationships) and a measure of agentic self-construal also based on four items (boastful, selfish, dominant, and often use coarse language). We summarize below the main results for these two measures of self-construal.

Relational self. If we examine only the control condition, in order to have a direct bearing on previous research suggesting that gender differences in relational self-construal are invariant across cultures, we fail to replicate these findings. A 2 (participant's gender) × 8 (culture) ANOVA on relational self-construal within the control condition indicates a main effect of gender, $F(1, 427) = 39.40$, $p < .001$; a main effect of culture, $F(7, 427) = 10.49$, $p < .001$; and these main effects are qualified by a significant interaction, $F(7, 427) = 2.91$, $p < .005$. As Figure 15.3 indicates, this interaction is largely due to the fact that gender differences are strongest in Switzerland, the low power distance culture, and weakest in Malaysia, the high power distance culture. This pattern is strongly supportive of our hypothesis that social comparison, which is variable across cultures, underlies gender differences in relational self-construal. Furthermore, because we use only the control group in this analysis, our findings are directly comparable to those obtained in previous studies. These data then are not consistent with the claim that gender differences in relational self-construal are invariant across cultures.

Turning now to the effects of our manipulation of social comparison, our theoretical analysis is further confirmed. In the intra-group condition, when all participants compare themselves to other ingroup members, there is no main effect of sex on relational self-construal, $F(1, 408) = 1.74$, ns, even with a sample of 230 females and 178 males. There is no sex by culture interaction, $F(7, 408) = 0.82$, ns. Only a main effect of culture is observed, $F(7, 408) = 11.89$, $p < .001$. This effect indicates, consistent with Markus and Kitayama (1991), that Malaysia has the highest score on relational self-contrual ($M = 6.22$).

In contrast, within the inter-group condition, when all participants compare themselves to outgroup members, there is a strong main effect of gender on relational self-construal, $F(1, 467) = 35.34$, $p < .001$, a reliable main effect of culture, $F(7, 467) = 9.07$, $p < .001$, and a significant interaction, $F(7, 467) = 2.38$, $p < .05$. This interaction is similar to the one depicted in Figure 15.3. Because our manipulation of social comparison can erase or create gender differences and variations in those differences across cultures, this is compelling evidence for the thesis that a) social comparison processes underlie gender differences in self-construal and b) variations in social comparison processes across cultures account for the variations in gender differences across cultures.

Agentic self. The agentic self reflects a more assertive and independent concept of self which is typically ascribed to men (Conway et al., 1996). The findings on this measure generally replicate those obtained on the measure of relational self-construal although there are some differences. In the control condition, we find no interaction of gender and culture on agentic self ratings, only main effects of sex and culture. But in the

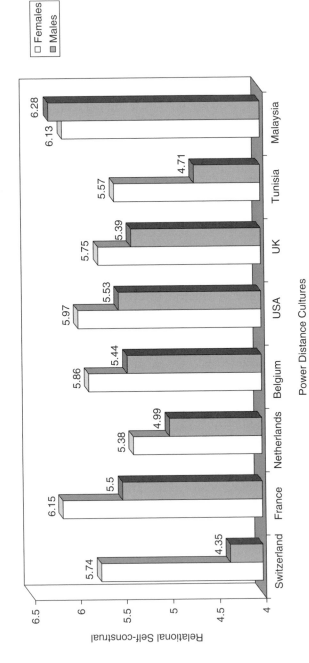

Figure 15.3. Gender by culture interaction on relational self-construal in the control condition

inter-group condition, the interaction is reliable, F (7, 466) = 2.92, $p = .005$. Figure 15.4 displays this interaction. Again, we see that there are no gender differences in self-construal in Malaysia whereas males define themselves as more agentic than females in all other cultures, and especially in low power distance cultures. This interaction disappears in the intra-group condition, when participants compare themselves with other ingroup members, F (7, 409) = 1.28, ns.

Moderators of the impact of outgroup comparison on self-construal The fact that there is a gender by culture interaction in the inter-group condition means that, as expected, the effect of outgroup comparison on the self varies across cultures. This manipulation has no impact whatsoever on self-ratings in the high power distance culture of Malaysia whereas it produces strong gender differences in low power distance cultures, as found in the initial set of experiments carried out by Guimond *et al.* (in press). These results support Tajfel's hypothesis. As we have outlined, Tajfel (1974, 1981) argued that inter-group comparisons will be perceived as relevant when the legitimacy of the inter-group structure is questioned, but not when it is accepted (see also Chapter 5, this volume). This hypothesis was tested above using power distance as a *cultural* dimension (Hofstede, 1980). However, it can also be tested at the psychological level by using two distinct instruments included in the study: the measure of power distance beliefs mentioned previously and the social dominance orientation scale (Sidanius and Pratto, 1999).

Power distance beliefs. This scale attempts to measure, at the psychological level, that is at the level of individual participants, the cultural dimension of power distance. This dimension refers to the tendency to perceive inequality as more or less desirable, normal, and legitimate. Thus, using this scale of power distance beliefs, instead of nations/cultures, allows for a test of Tajfel's hypothesis at the psychological level. More specifically, one can predict that outgroup comparison will have a greater impact among participants who score low on the scale of power distance beliefs (they perceive inequality as illegitimate) than among those who score high (they perceive inequality as legitimate).

Multiple regression analysis was used to examine the moderating effect of power distance beliefs on the impact of inter-group comparisons. The measure of relational self-construal was first used as a dependent variable and all variables entered into the equation were centered (Aiken and West, 1991). Participants' gender and age were entered in the first step, followed by power distance beliefs in the second step, and the interaction of gender and power distance beliefs in the last step. Using participants from the inter-group condition only, and based on Tajfel's analysis, our

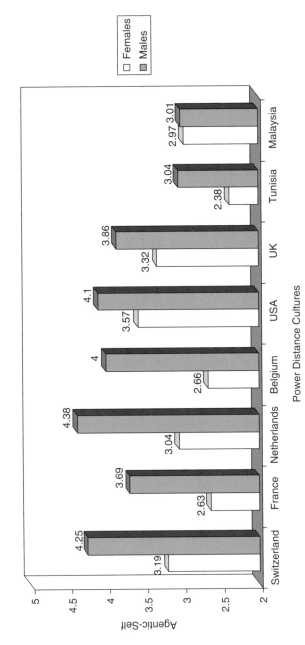

Figure 15.4. Sex by culture interaction on agency in the intergroup comparison condition

prediction is that a significant interaction of gender by PD beliefs should be observed, revealing the moderating role of PD beliefs (Baron and Kenny, 1986). Because in this condition, participants from all cultures are forced to engage in an inter-group comparison, whether this comparison has an impact on the self should depend on PD beliefs. More specifically, when PD beliefs are low (participants tend to question the legitimacy of the inter-group structure), group-based social comparison should be seen as relevant and have an impact on self-construal leading to a strong gender difference in self-definition. But when PD beliefs are high (participants believe that inequalities are legitimate), according to Tajfel (1981), group-based comparison should not be seen as relevant. Consequently, these comparisons should have little impact on the self.

The predicted interaction was found to be significant, $p < .01$, confirming the moderating role of PD beliefs. Inspection of this interaction revealed that there are no gender differences in relational self-construal among participants in the inter-group condition who score high on the scale of PD beliefs. For these participants, between-gender comparison does not lead men and women to define themselves in different ways. In contrast, for those who score low on PD beliefs, we find that women define themselves as significantly more relational than men, reflecting a strong impact of between-gender comparison on the self. Similar moderating effects of PD beliefs are found on the measure of agency in the inter-group condition. However, we find no such interaction within the control condition. Thus, the moderating role of PD beliefs is only observed when people are confronted with a group-based social comparison. Because nation/culture is not used in these analyses, these findings cannot be seen as dependent on the particular selection of some cultural groups.

Social Dominance Orientation. Our cross-cultural study included an additional measure that can be used to test Tajfel's hypothesis: the scale of Social Dominance Orientation (SDO, Pratto, Sidanius, Stallworth, and Malle, 1994). Previous research suggests that this scale does not measure a basic personality type but rather ideological beliefs about inequality and social hierarchy (Dambrun, Duarte, and Guimond, 2004; Duckitt, 2001; Guimond, Dambrun, Michinov, and Duarte, 2003; Jost and Burgess, 2000). For example, Jost and Burgess (2000) state that SDO refers to some "ideological tendencies to legitimize social arrangements." (p. 303) Consistent with this view, we find that the measure of PD beliefs is positively and significantly correlated with SDO, $r = .41$, $p < .001$ (excluding participants from Malaysia). Furthermore, whereas the reliability and validity of our measure of PD beliefs can be questioned, the SDO scale is known for its high reliability. Indeed, we find in all cultures very high reliability coefficients for a ten-item version of SDO with an average alpha of .80. There is one major exception however: Malaysia. Our Malay version of the SDO scale did not show adequate reliability, suggesting some problems with the back translation procedure. Thus, we excluded the sample from Malaysia and performed a test of the role of SDO as moderator of the effect of intergroup comparison on self-ratings with participants from all other cultures together. Using the same regression procedure as with power distance beliefs, we found a significant gender by SDO interaction on self-ratings for the measure of relational self, $p < .01$, and for the measure of agentic self, $p = .052$. These interactions show that when people strongly support inequality and social hierarchy (SDO is high), males and females rate themselves in a very similar manner – this means that the intergroup comparison has no effect on self-ratings. But, when people reject the existing hierarchical system and support equality (SDO is low), inter-group comparisons are perceived as self-relevant and lead to clear gender differences in self-ratings: women define themselves as more relational and less agentic then men.

Conclusion

Previous chapters in this volume illustrate the many and various ways in which comparison processes can contribute to a better understanding of human social behavior. Considered together, these contributions offer a strong tribute to Festinger (1954). However, today's research on social comparison has moved much beyond anything that Festinger wrote about. This, we believe, is an important sign of progress in social-psychological theory and research. In this chapter, following Heine *et al.*'s (2002) challenging analysis, we have examined social comparison processes across cultures. Despite the growing recognition that studying culture is of central importance for social psychology (see Fiske and Cuddy, this volume, Lehman *et al.*, 2004; Nisbett, 2003), the study of social comparison has remained up to this day a largely intra-cultural affair. The efforts presented here as a means of spurring things further in the direction of an inter-cultural analysis are modest, being based on a limited number of nations/cultures and samples of students. Nevertheless, the outcome gives substantial reasons to believe that much is to be learned by studying social comparison across cultures. First, on the methodological side, our design incorporated an experimental manipulation that allowed us to move beyond mere descriptions of co-occurrences. The fact that social comparison can be easily manipulated, even in cross-cultural investigations, suggests that it can rapidly become a very useful psychological tool in this domain.

Second, on the theoretical side, the chapters in the first part of this volume indicate that social and temporal comparisons are fundamental to an understanding of cognition and interpersonal relations. In relation to this individual level perspective, we show that there can be not only individual differences in social comparison orientation but also cultural differences. Of course, more research is needed to fully appreciate the true nature of this finding. Other cultures high in power distance need to be studied in order to sustain the hypothesis that such cultures tend to restrict social comparison to an intra-group form. For example, the reasons why young students from Tunisia score lower than others on SCO are not clear. Nevertheless, we were successful in bringing forward several indications that support the overall validity of our findings. For example, our correlational findings are supported by our experimental findings: the culture that is highest on SCO is also the culture in which we find no effect whatsoever of outgroup comparison on self-construal. Similarly, by identifying psychological constructs (i.e. power distance beliefs and SDO) as moderators of the effects of inter-group comparison on gender differences, the results support the generality of our analysis beyond the particular cultures that we have selected. In short, the findings reported appear to be quite robust.

The chapters in the second part of this volume suggest that studying social comparison at the group level of analysis brings additional explanatory power to social psychology. Different outcomes in terms of self-esteem (Chapter 6), social attitudes (Chapter 7), emotions (Chapter 8), prejudice (Chapter 9), and discrimination (Chapter 10) can arise when people shift to an inter-group comparative frame of reference. To this, our findings add that the effects of intra- and inter-group comparisons can differ across cultures. As such, they support the claims made in several chapters in the last section of this volume about the possibility that cultural similarities and differences in cognition and inter-group relations may be better understood by taking into account the role of social comparison processes. We hope that these preliminary results will stimulate further research on these issues in order to develop a cross-cultural social psychology that is even more exciting in the future.

References

Abeles, R. P. (1976). Relative deprivation, rising expectations and black militancy. *Journal of Social Issues, 32*, 119–137.

Aiken, L. S. and West, S. G. (1991). *Multiple regression: Testing and interpreting interactions*. Newbury Park, CA: Sage.

Allik, J. and McCrae, R. R. (2004). Toward a geography of personality traits: Patterns of profiles across 36 cultures. *Journal of Cross-Cultural Psychology, 35*, 13–28.

Baron, R. M. and Kenny, D. A. (1986). The moderator-mediator variable distinction in social psychological research: Conceptual, strategic, and statistical considerations. *Journal of Personality and Social Psychology*, *51*, 1173–1182.

Berry, J. W., Poortinga, Y. H., Segall, M. H., and Dasen, P. R. (1992). *Cross-cultural psychology*. Cambridge: Cambridge University Press.

Bollinger, D. and Hofstede, G. (1987). *Les différences culturelles dans le management: Comment chaque pays gèrent-ils ses hommes?* Paris: Les éditions d'organisation.

Brockner, J., Ackerman, G., Greenberg, J., Gelfand, M. J., Francesco, A.-M., Chen, Z. X., Leung, K., Birbrauer, G., Gomez, C., Kirkman, B. L., and Shapiro, D. (2001). Culture and procedural justice: The influence of power distance on reactions to voice. *Journal of Experimental Social Psychology*, *37*, 300–315.

Conway, M., Pizzamiglio, M. T., and Mount, L. (1996). Status, communality, and agency: Implications for stereotypes of gender and other groups. *Journal of Personality and Social Psychology*, *71*, 25–38.

Costa Jr., P. T., Terracciano, A., and McCrae, R. R. (2001). Gender differences in personality traits across cultures: Robust and surprising findings. *Journal of Personality and Social Psychology*, *81*, 322–331.

Crocker, J. and Blanton, H. (1999). Social inequality and self-esteem: The moderating effects of social comparison, legitimacy, and contingencies of self-esteem. In T. R. Tyler, R. M. Kramer, and O. P. John (ed.) (1999). *The psychology of the social self* (pp. 171–191). London: Lawrence Erlbaum.

Cross, S. E. and Madson, L. (1997). Models of the self: Self-construals and gender. *Psychological Bulletin*, *122*, 5–137.

Dambrun, M., Duarte, S., and Guimond, S. (2004). Why are men more likely to support group-based dominance than women? The mediating role of gender identification. *British Journal of Social Psychology*, *43*, 1–11.

Dambrun, M. and Guimond, S. (2001). La théorie de la privation relative et l'hostilité envers les Nord-Africains. [Relative deprivation theory and hostility toward North Africans] *International Review of Social Psychology*, *14*, 57–89.

Duckitt, J. (2001). A dual-process cognitive-motivational theory of ideology and prejudice. In M. P. Zanna (ed.). *Advances in experimental social psychology* (Vol. XXXIII, pp. 41–112). San Diego, CA: Academic Press.

Festinger, L. (1954). A theory of social comparison processes. *Human Relations*, *7*, 117–140.

Gabriel, S. and Gardner, W. L. (1999). Are there "His" and "Hers" types of interdependence? The implications of gender differences in collective versus relational interdependence for affect, behavior, and cognition. *Journal of Personality and Social Psychology*, *77*, 642–655.

Gastorf, J. W. and Suls, J. (1978). Performance evaluation via social comparison: Performance similarity versus related-attribute similarity. *Social Psychology*, *41*, 297–305.

Gibbons, F. X. and Buunk, B. P. (1999). Individual differences in social comparison: Development and validation of a measure of social comparison orientation. *Journal of Personality and Social Psychology*, *76*, 129–142.

Glick, P. and Fiske, S. T. (2001). An ambivalent alliance: Hostile and benevolent sexism as complementary justifications for gender inequality. *American Psychologist*, *56*, 109–118.

Guimond, S., Branscombe, N. R., Brunot, S., Buunk, B. P., Chatard, A., Désert, M., Garcia, D. M., Haque, S., Martinot, D., and Yzerbyt, V. (2005). Culture, gender, and the self: variations and impact of social comparison processes. *Manuscript submitted for publication.*

Guimond, S., Chatard, A., Martinot, D., Crisp, R., and Redersdorff, S. (in press). Social comparison, self-stereotyping, and gender differences in self-construal. *Journal of Personality and Social Psychology.*

Guimond, S., Dambrun, M., Michinov, N., and Duarte, S. (2003). Does social dominance generate prejudice? Integrating individual and contextual determinants of intergroup cognitions. *Journal of Personality and Social Psychology, 84*, 697–721.

Guimond, S., Dif, S., and Aupy, A. (2002). Social identity, relative group status, and intergroup attitudes: When favourable outcomes change intergroup relations ... for the worse. *European Journal of Social Psychology, 32*, 739–760.

Guimond, S. and Dubé-Simard, L. (1983). Relative deprivation theory and the Québec nationalist movement: The cognition-emotion distinction and the personal-group deprivation issue. *Journal of Personality and Social Psychology, 44*, 526–535.

Hafer, C. L. and Olson, J. M. (1993). Beliefs in a just world, discontent, and assertive actions by working women. *Personality and Social Psychology Bulletin, 19*, 30–38.

Helgeson, V. S. (1994). Relation of agency and communion to well-being: Evidence and potential explanations. *Psychological Bulletin, 116*, 412–428.

Heine, S. J., Lehman, D. R., Peng, K., and Greenholtz, J. (2002). What's wrong with cross-cultural comparisons of subjective Likert scales? The reference-group effect. *Journal of Personality and Social Psychology, 82*, 903–918.

Hofstede, G. (1980). *Culture's consequences: international differences in work-related values.* Beverly Hills: Sage.

Hofstede, G. and McCrae, R. R. (2004). Personality and culture revisited: Linking traits and dimensions of culture. *Cross-cultural Research, 38*, 52–88.

Josephs, R. A., Markus, H. R., and Tafarodi, R. W. (1992). Gender and self-esteem. *Journal of Personality and Social Psychology, 63*, 391–402.

Jost, J. T. and Burgess, D. (2000). Attitudinal ambivalence and the conflict between group and system justification motives in low status groups. *Personality and Social Psychology Bulletin, 26*, 293–305.

Kabasakal, H. and Bodur, M. (2002). Arabic cluster: A bridge between East and West. *Journal of World Business, 37*, 40–54.

Kashima, Y., Kokubo, T., Kashima, E. S., Boxall, D., Yamaguchi, and Macrae, K. (2004). Culture and self: Are there within-culture differences in self between metropolitan areas and regional cities? *Personality and Social Psychology Bulletin, 30*, 816–823.

Kashima, Y., Yamagushi, S., Kim, U., Choi, S.-C., Gelfand, M. J., and Yuki, M. (1995). Culture, gender, and self: A perspective from individualism-collectivism research. *Journal of Personality and Social Psychology, 69*, 925–937.

Kemmelmeier, M. and Oyserman, D. (2001). Gendered influence of downward social comparisons on current and possible selves. *Journal of Social Issues, 57*, 129–148.

Lehman, D. R., Chiu, C., and Schaller, M. (2004). Psychology and culture. *Annual Review of Psychology*, 55, 689–714.

Major, B. (1994). From social inequality to personal entitlement: the role of social comparisons, legitimacy appraisals, and group membership. In M. P. Zanna (eds.), *Advances in experimental social psychology* (pp. 293–355). San Diego, CA: Academic Press.

Major, B., Sciacchitano, A., and Crocker, J. (1993). Ingroup vs. outgroup comparisons and self-esteem. *Personality and Social Psychology Bulletin*, 9, 711–721.

Major, B., Testa, M., and Bylsma, W. H. (1991). Responses to upward and downward social comparisons: The impact of esteem-relevance and perceived control. In J. Suls and T. Wills (eds.), Social comparison: Contemporary theory and research (pp. 237–260). Hillsdale, NJ: Erlbaum.

Markus, H. and Kitayama, S. (1991). Culture and the self: Implications for cognition, emotion, and motivation. *Psychological Review*, 98, 224–252.

Markus, H., Kitayama, S., and Heiman, R. J. (1996). Culture and "basic" psychological principles. In E. T. Higgins and A. W. Kruglanski (eds.), *Social psychology: Handbook of basic principles* (pp. 857–913). New York: Guilford Press.

Miller, C. T. (1982). The role of performance-related similarity in social comparison of abilities: A test of the related attributes hypothesis. *Journal of Experimental Social Psychology*, 18, 513–523.

  (1984). Self-schemas, gender and social comparison: A clarification of the related attributes hypothesis. *Journal of Personality and Social Psychology*, 46, 1222–1229.

Moskowitz, D. S., Suh, E. J., and Desaulniers, J. (1994). Situational influences on gender differences in agency and communion. *Journal of Personality and Social Psychology*, 66, 753–761.

Mussweiler, T., Rüter, K., and Epstude, K. (2004). The man who wasn't there: Subliminal social comparison standards influence self-evaluation. *Journal of Experimental Social Psychology*, 40, 689–696.

Nisbett, R. E. (2003). *The geography of thought: How Asians and Westerners think differently and why*. London: Nicholas Brealey Publishing.

Onorato, R. S. and Turner, J. C. (2004). Fluidity in the self-concept: The shift from personal to social identity. *European Journal of Social Psychology*, 34, 257–278.

Pettigrew, T. F. and Meertens, R. W. (1995). Subtle and blatant prejudice in western Europe. *European Journal of Social Psychology*, 25, 57–75.

Pratto, F., Sidanius, J., Stallworth, L. M., and Malle, B. F. (1994). Social dominance orientation: A personality variable predicting social and political attitudes. *Journal of Personality and Social Psychology*, 67, 741–763.

Ryan, M. K., David, B., and Reynolds, K. J. (2003). Who cares? The effect of gender and context on the self and moral reasoning. *Psychology of Women Quarterly*, 28, 246–255.

Schwartz, S. H. (1994). Beyond individualism/collectivism – New cultural dimensions of values. In U. Kim, H. C. Triandis, C. Kâgitçibasi, S.-C. Choi, and G. Yoon (eds.), *Individualism and collectivism: Theory, method, and applications* (pp. 85–119). London: Sage.

Sedikides, C., Gaertner, L., and Toguchi, Y. (2003). Pancultural self-enhancement. *Journal of Personality and Social Psychology*, *84*, 60–79.

Shweder, R. A. and Bourne, E. J. (1984). Does the concept of the person vary cross-culturally? In R. A. Shweder and R. A. Levine (eds.), *Culture theory* (pp. 158–199). New York: Cambridge University Press.

Sidanius, J. and Pratto, F. (1999). *Social dominance: An intergroup theory of social hierarchy and oppression*. New York: Cambridge University Press.

Sidanius, J., Pratto, F., and Bobo, L. (1994). Social dominance orientation and the political psychology of gender: A case of invariance? *Journal of Personality and Social Psychology*, *67*, 998–1011.

Smith, P. B. and Bond, M. H. (1999). *Social psychology across cultures*. New York: Allyn and Bacon.

Smith, H. J. and Leach, C. W. (2004). Group membership and everyday social comparison experiences. *European Journal of Social Psychology*, *34*, 297–308.

Suls, J. M. (1977). Social comparison theory and research: An overview from 1954. In J. M. Suls and R. L. Miller (eds.), *Social comparison processes – Theoretical and empirical perspectives* (pp. 1–19). New York: Wiley and Sons.

Suls, J. and Wheeler, L. (eds.) (2000). *Handbook of social comparison: Theory and research*. New York: Kluwer Academic/Plenum Publishers.

Tajfel, H. (1974). Intergroup behavior, social comparison and social change. Katz-Newcomb Lectures, University of Michigan, Ann Arbor.

  (1981). *Human groups and social categories. Studies in social psychology*. Cambridge: Cambridge University Press.

Taylor, D. M. and McKirnan, D. J. (1984). A five-stage model of intergroup relations. *Bristish Journal of Social Psychology*, *23*, 291–300.

Triandis, H. C. (1989). The self and social behavior in differing cultural contexts. *Psychological Review*, *96*, 3, 506–520.

Turner, J. (1999). Some current issues in research on social identity and self-categorization theories. In N. Ellemers, R. Spears, and B. Doosje (eds.), *Social identity* (pp. 6–34). Oxford: Blackwell.

Turner, J. C. and Brown, R. J. (1978). Social status, cognitive alternatives and intergroup relations. In H. Tajfel (ed.), *Differentiation between social groups*. London: Academic Press.

Turner, J. C., Brown, R. J., and Tajfel, H. (1979). Social comparison and group interest in ingroup favouritism. *European Journal of Social Psychology*, *9*, 187–204.

Turner, J. C., Hogg, M. A., Oakes, P. J., Reicher, S. D., and Wetherell, M. S. (1987). *Rediscovering the social group: A self-categorization theory*. Oxford: Blackwell.

Turner, J. C., Oakes, P. J., Haslam, S. A., and McGarty, C. (1994). Self and collective: Cognition and social context. *Personality and Social Psychology Bulletin*, *20*, 454–463.

Turner, J. C. and Onorato, R. S. (1999). Social identity, personality, and the self-concept: A self-categorization perspective. In T. R. Tyler, R. M. Kramer, and O. P. John (eds.), *The psychology of the social self* (pp. 11–46). Mahwah, NJ: Lawrence Erlbaum.

Tyler, T. R. and Smith, H. J. (1999). Justice, social identity and group processes. In T. R. Tyler, R. M. Kramer, and O. P. John, (ed.). *The psychology of the social self* (pp. 223–264). London: Lawrence Erlbaum.

Walker, I. and Smith H., (eds.) (2002). *Relative deprivation: Specification, development, and integration.* Cambridge: Cambridge University Press.

Wood, W., Christensen, P. N., Hebl, M. R., and Rothgerber, H. (1997). Conformity to sex-typed norms, affect, and the self-concept. *Journal of Personality and Social Psychology, 73,* 523–535.

Wright, S. C. and Tropp, L. (2002). Collective action in response to disadvantage: Intergroup perceptions, social identification and social change. In I. Walker and H. Smith (eds.), *Relative deprivation: Specification, development, and integration* (pp. 200–236). Cambridge: Cambridge University Press.

Author index

Albert, S., 76
Allick, J., 324
Allport, G. W., 102
Aupy, A., 212, 320

Banaji, M. R., 310
Bargh, J. A., 35, 38, 41
Baumeister, R. F., 35
Biernat, M., 33, 130
Blanton, H., 131, 137, 230
Bless, H., 84
Bodenhausen, G. V., 218, 233
Branscombe, N. R., 191
Brenninkmeijer, V., 21
Brewer, M. B., 132, 133
Brickman, P., 16, 139
Brockner, J., 305
Brooke, R., 62
Brown, R. J., 80
Brunot, S., 63, 86, 87
Butler, R., 82, 83
Buunk, B. P., 19, 21, 23, 24, 25, 26, 27

Collins, R. L., 48, 64, 102, 128, 133, 239
Conway, M. A., 58, 84
Costa (Jr), P. T., 303, 326
Crocker, J., 88, 103, 130, 131, 132, 230
Crosby, F. J., 158
Crush, J., 215, 217

Dambrun, M., 208, 209, 210, 215, 217, 218, 220, 221
Darley, J. M., 35, 36, 39, 49, 64, 100
Deschamps, J.-C., 265
Désert, M., 274, 275, 314, 318
Desmarais, S., 156, 157, 158, 163
Devos, T., 177–179
Dif, S., 85–86, 89, 212, 231, 320
Dijksterhuis, A., 34, 38, 47
Dijkstra, P., 25
Doosje, B., 3, 188, 240
Dreu, K. W. de, 26

Dubé-Simard, L., 218
Dumont, M., 184, 186, 189, 191, 234
Dweck, C. S., 82

Eagly, A., 250, 270, 277, 283, 290, 303
Ellemers, N., 3, 240
Epstude, K., 37
Esses, V., 217

Festinger, L., 1, 4, 9, 11, 15, 22, 30, 35–36, 39, 43, 49, 50, 55, 64, 72, 76–77, 93, 100–101, 123, 127, 130, 147, 156–157, 171, 174, 200, 230, 244, 264, 274, 279, 320–321, 338, 340
Fiske, S. T., 305, 313
Fong, G. T., 63
Frye, N. E., 70

Gabriel, S., 130
Garcia, D., 163, 166, 167, 318
Gardner, W. L., 130
George, G., 230
Gergen, K. J., 48, 127, 231
Gerrard, M., 20, 27
Gibbons, F. X., 19, 20, 24, 27
Glick, P., 288, 289, 290, 296, 298, 305
Goethals, G. R., 35, 36, 39, 49, 64, 100
Gordijn, E. H., 182, 184, 186, 189
Green, S. M., 83
Greenholtz, J., 323
Gschneiger, E., 85
Guimond, S., 85–86, 90, 208, 209, 210, 212, 218, 220, 231, 286, 320, 325
Gurr, T., 89, 111, 174

Haslam, S., 3
Hecquet, C., 220
Heine, S. J., 323, 324, 325
Higgins, E. T., 69
Ho, C., 196
Hochschild, L., 130
Hofstede, G., 285–286, 304, 327

Hogg, M. A., 3, 155–156, 273
Holmes, E., 58
Hunyady, O., 312

Ipenburg, M. L., 24

Jackman, M. R., 288
Jost, J. T., 310, 312

Karney, B. R., 70
Kitayama, S., 318
Kramer, G. P., 218
Kruglanski, A. W., 35, 38, 260
Kunda, Z., 62, 63, 64, 66

Leach, C. W., 80, 320
Leggett, E. L., 82
Lehman, D. R., 323
Lemaine, G., 2
Lerner, M. J., 40, 180, 250, 251, 311
Levine, J. M., 83
Leyens, J.-P., 191, 275, 313, 314
Lockwood, P., 66
Lorenzi-Cioldi, F., 267, 268

McAdams, D. P., 60
McCrae, R. R., 303, 324, 326
McDonald, D., 215, 217
McFarland, C., 130
Mackie, D., 131, 177–179
McKirnan, D. J., 239, 322
Major, B., 88, 103, 130, 132, 133, 137
Markus, H., 60, 67, 68, 318
Martinot, D., 85–86, 134, 138, 231
Mathieu, B., 191
Mayer, D., 87
Meertens, R. W., 320
Middendorf, J., 80
Miller, D. T., 130, 131
Miller, R., 2
Monteil, J.-M., 102
Moya, M., 292, 305
Mullen, B., 79–80
Mummendey, A., 77, 92, 102, 104, 194, 229, 237, 265
Mussweiler, T., 37, 39, 40, 45, 46, 64, 81, 232, 233

Newby-Clark, I. R., 85
Nurius, P., 67

Oakes, P. J., 3
Oettingen, G., 87
Oldersma, F. L., 26, 27
Olson, J. M., 233–234

Ortiz, D. J., 195
Ouellette, J. A., 27

Peng, K., 323
Pettigrew, T. F., 320
Pleydell-Pearce, C. W., 58
Postmes, T., 229, 234, 241
Pratto, F., 209

Quinn, K. A., 233–234

Redersdorff, S., 85–86, 134, 231
Ross, M., 70, 80, 81, 82, 84, 85
Runciman, W. G., 88, 99, 100, 111, 113, 174, 193, 207, 284
Rüter, K., 39, 40
Ruvolo, A. P., 68

Sanitioso, R., 62, 63, 64
Schmitt, M. T., 134, 152, 154, 161, 167, 231
Schwarz, N., 84, 85
Sciacchitano, A., 132
Sedikides, C., 273, 319
Seron, E., 234
Sherif, M., 33, 217
Sidanius, J., 209
Simon, B., 34, 90, 127, 133, 161, 197, 277
Smith, E. R., 175, 176, 177–179, 196, 198
Smith, H. J., 80, 195, 320
Spears, R., 3, 240
Stapel, D. A., 18, 133, 259
Stock, M. L., 20
Strack, F., 85
Suls, J., 2, 79–80
Süsser, K., 218

Tajfel, H., 2, 156, 160, 285, 321–322, 335
Taylor, D. M., 215, 217, 239, 322
Taylor, S. E., 25
Terracciano, A., 303, 326
Tesser, A., 132
Tocqueville, A. de, 88
Tougas, F., 88, 92, 152, 156, 163, 164, 168, 194, 207, 218
Triandis, H. C., 265, 318
Tropp, L., 195, 237, 320
Turnbull, W., 130
Turner, J. C., 2, 3, 155–156, 273–274
Tyler, T., 102, 114, 121, 321

van der Zee, K. I., 19, 24
van Ypren, N. W., 24

Walker, I., 88, 174, 194, 197, 206, 240, 284, 320

Wänke, M., 84
Weber, J. G., 132, 133
Wheeler, L., 15, 34, 35, 36, 38, 49, 100,
    121, 174, 256, 321, 331
Wigboldus, D., 182, 184, 186, 189
Wills, T. A., 25
Wilson, A. E., 70, 80, 81, 82
Wohl, M. J. A., 191
Woike, B., 61

Wood, J. V., 16, 25, 35, 38, 47, 108, 130,
    231, 274, 277, 283
Woolf, V., 1
Wright, S. C., 195, 237, 238, 320

Ybema, J. F., 24
Yzerbyt, V. Y., 182, 184, 186, 189, 191, 234

Zagefka, H., 113, 114

Subject index

Page numbers in *italic type* refer to figures and tables.

absent-exempt effect, 20
accessibility, 40–48, *42*, 58, 60,
   81, 232
action tendencies, 177, 178, 184–186,
   190, 195
actual self, 62, 67, 69
affective components
   of RD, 207
   of RG, 218–219, *219*
affirmative action policies, 152, 155,
   163–167, *165*, *166*
agentic/independent gender stereotype,
   306, 308–309, *309*, 333–335, *336*
Ambivalence toward Men Inventory (AMI),
   287, 289–290, 291–294, 294–296
ambivalent gender ideologies, 287, 290,
   293, 299–300
   attitudes toward men, 289–290
   attitudes toward women, 287–289
   and gender equality, *294*, 294–296
   gendered attitudes to, 296–299, *298*
   and power distance, 291–294, *294*
Ambivalent Sexism Inventory (ASI), 287,
   287–289, 291–299
AMI *see* Ambivalence toward Men
   Inventory
anger, 177, 178, 185, 187, 192, 193
appraisal theories of emotion, 176, 177
ASI *see* Ambivalent Sexism Inventory
Asian settings, status/competence in,
   251–252
assimilation effect
   and group discrimination, 241–242
   and intragroup comparisons, 130, 131,
      132–137, *135*, 140
   and intrapersonal comparisons, 65,
      66–67, 68, 69, 81, 85
   and personal discrimination,
      232–236
   and similarity, 46, 48

attitudes
   impact of employment policies on,
      163–167, *165*, *166*, *167* see also
      ambivalent gender ideologies
autobiographical knowledge, 58–59, *59*,
   64–65
autobiographical memories, 56–60
   and motivated self-perception, 62–63
   as part of self, 55, 59–60, 61
   and temporal-self comparisons, 66–67,
      68, 69

behaviour, and group-based emotions,
   186–188
belief in just world *see* just world beliefs
benevolence toward men (BM), 289–290,
   296
benevolent sexism (BS), 287–289, 296,
   297–298
boundaries *see* group boundaries

category membership, and accessibility,
   43, 47
cognitive component of RG, 210, 218–219,
   219, 221
cognitive downward comparisons, 25–27
cognitive efficiency, 34–40
coherence of memories, 56–57
collective action, 195, 237, 320
collective guilt, 188–189, 191
collectivism, 266–267, 269–274, *272*, 277
communal stereotype *see* relational/
   interdependent gender stereotype
comparable worth policies, 152, 155,
   163–167, *165*, *167*
comparative information processing, 33
   cognitive efficiency in, 35–40
competence, 249–252, 312
complementary ideologies *see* ambivalent
   gender ideologies; power distance

conflict in organizations, 168
congruency of memories, 60–62
consensus, in emotional reaction, 191–193
contempt, 178
context
  of comparisons, 83
  and self-categorization, 155 *see also*
    employment context
contrast effect
  and dissimilarity, 46, 48
  and group discrimination, 241–242
  and intragroup comparisons, 131–132
  and intrapersonal comparisons, 65,
    66–67, 81, 85
  and personal discrimination, 232–236
cooperation in organizations, 169
correspondence of memories, 56, 57
cross-cultural differences, 338–339
  in concept of self, 318–319
  in gender stereotypes, 304–305,
    310–315
    method and results, 305–310
  in personality traits, 303, 324
  in power distance beliefs, 327–329, *328*
  self-construal and gender, 324–338
  and target selection, 323–324 *see also*
    ethnic minority groups; national
    differences; status-competence
    hypothesis
cross-gender comparisons, 283, 300
  and ambivalent gender ideologies,
    287–290
  inhibited by power distance, 286, 291
cultural targets, 323–324
cultural values, and group status, 264–267,
  269–274, *272*, 276–278
culture *see* cross-cultural differences

depersonalization process, 175
depression, 21–22
deprivation *see* relative deprivation
discrimination *see* gender discrimination;
  personal-group discrimination
  discrepancy
dispositional bias, 251, 273
dissimilarity hypothesis
  and group discrimination, 241–242
  and personal discrimination, 232–236
dissimilarity testing, 42–48, *45*, 65
distancing, 180, 183
downward comparison theory, 25
downward comparisons, 100, 108–111, 231
  negative impact of, 23–27
  and self-esteem, *129*, 131, *135*,
    136, 139

ecological validity, 214–216
economic status, 104, 209, 217–218
emotions *see* affective components;
  group-based emotions
empathy, 18
employment context, 22–23, 151–153,
  157–163
employment policies *see* gender-based
  redistributive employment policies
enhancement
  and group comparisons, 100, 107–111,
    113
  and individual comparisons, 70, 82, 273
entity intelligence theorists, 82–83
equal opportunity in organizations, 169
  see also gender-based redistributive
    employment policies
equality *see* gender equality
equity, 101, 107–108, 111, 112, 284 *see also*
  gender-based redistributive
  employment policies
ethnic identification, and RG, 222, *222*
ethnic minority groups
  and group-based emotion, 186–188,
    188–191
  intergroup comparisons, 104–107, *106*
  ingroup identification, 116–118, *117*
  motives, 107–108, *109*
  structural variables, 115
  target status/deprivation, *112*, 112–114
  intragroup comparisons, 131
ethnic prejudice, and RG, 209, 211, 215–216
evaluation
  and group comparisons, 107, 108–110,
    132
  and individual comparisons, 41–48, 81–83
expectations, 87, 220–221

fantasies of future, 87
fear, 177, 178, 186–188
five-stage model of intergroup relations, 322
future self, 67–69, 70, 84–90

gender
  and individualism, 268
  in intergroup comparisons, 237
  and intragroup comparisons, 134–137,
    135
  and relationships, 21
  and self-construal across cultures,
    324–338
  and status, 137–142, *141*, 255, 270–274,
    272
gender attitudes, and RG, 220
gender categorization, 283

gender discrimination, 151–153, 304
Gender Empowerment Measure (GEM),
    292
gender equality
    and ambivalent gender ideologies, 288,
        289, *293*, *294*, 294–296, 298, 299–300
    impact of comparisons on, 283
    and Power Distance, *293*, *294*, 294–296,
        298, 299–300
gender ideologies *see* ambivalent gender
    ideologies
gender stereotypes, 158, 303–304, 325
    cross-cultural differences, 310–315
        method and results, 305–310
        and Power Distance, 304–305 *see also*
            ambivalent gender ideologies
gender traits, 274–275, *276*, 278
gender-based redistributive employment
    policies, 155–156
    and employment context, 157–159
    impact on attitudes, 163–167, *165*,
        166, *167*
    impact on beliefs, 160–163, *162*
    and intergroup relations, 168–169
    resistance to, 152
generativity, 60
goal-oriented comparisons, 82 *see also*
    motivation for comparison
group boundaries, 100, 114–116, 120–121,
    160–161, 238–240
group discrimination, 229–230, 236–242
    see also personal-group discrimination
        discrepancy (PGDD)
group interests, 154–156
group level comparisons, 2–3, 319–321 *see
    also* intergroup comparisons;
        intragroup comparisons
group relative deprivation, 194, 207, 237,
    320, 321
group status, 137–139
    and assimilation effect, 132–137, *135*
    and comparative choice, 111–114, 120
    and comparative context, 274–275, *276*
    and cultural values, 264–267, 269–274,
        272, 276–278
    as deserved, 249
    and gender, 137–142, *141*, 255, 270–274,
        276
    and group interests, 154
    and individualism/collectivism, 269–274,
        272
    and RD, 237
    and self-esteem, 128, *129*, 134, *135*,
        140–144, *141 see also* status-
            competence hypothesis

group-based emotions, 175–184, 198–199
    action tendencies and identification,
        184–186
    emotions and consensus, 191–193
    and RD, 193–198
    victim or perpetrator identity, 188–191
guilt, 188–189, 191

happiness, 192, 193
health and illness, 20–21, 26, 79
hostile sexism (HS), 287–289, 296
hostility toward men (HM), 289–290, 296,
    297, 299
hypothesis-testing, 41–44

ideal self, 69
identification *see* ingroup identification
identity *see* social identity
immigrants, 215–216, *216*
improvement, 102, 218–219
incongruence approach, 81
incremental intelligence theorists, 82–83
independent self, 318 *see also* agentic/
    independent gender stereotype
individual level comparisons, 16, 319–321
    see also interpersonal comparisons;
        intrapersonal comparisons
individualism
    and group status, 264, 266–267,
        269–274, *272*, 277
    in Western cultures, 159–160, 168, 264,
        267–269, 270
information processing
    cognitive efficiency in, 34–36 *see also*
        comparative information processing
infra-humanization theory, 313
ingroup comparisons *see* intragroup
    comparisons
ingroup identification, 132–137, 240–241
    and comparison choice, 100, 116–119,
        117, 121
    and group-based emotions, 184–186, 197
    as mediator of RG effect, 221–223, *222*
    and self-esteem, 142
intelligence, 82–83, 210–214, *212*, *213*
interdependent/relational gender
    stereotype, 306, 307–308, *308*
interdependent/relational self, 319, 329,
    332–333, *334*
intergroup comparisons
    in employment context, 158
    and group discrimination, 236–242
    irrelevance of, 320
    and legitimacy, 322
    and RD, 113–114, 207–208

and RG *see* relative gratification
target choice, 99
    and ethnicity *see* ethnic minority groups
    ingroup identification, 116–119,
        117, 121
    motives, 101–102, 107–111, *109*,
        119–120
    primacy of ingroup, 102, 106
    and SIT, 99–101
    structural variables, 114–116,
        120–121
    target status/deprivation, 111–114,
        112, 120, 266–267
    temporal, 76–77, *78*
    types of, 102–104, 106 *see also* group
        status; ingroup identification
intergroup conflict, 168–169
internal standards of comparison
    see temporal-self comparisons
interpersonal comparisons, 319–321
    gender status and, 273–275, *276*, 278
    individualism, status and, 264, 266–267
    pervasiveness of, 267–269
    temporal, 76–77, *78 see also* intragroup
        comparisons; social cognition
        perspective; Social Comparison
        Orientation
interpersonal conflict, 168
interpersonal orientation, 18
intragroup comparison bias, 103, 107
intragroup comparisons, 102, 106
    assimilation effect, 130, 131, 132–137,
        135, 140
    contrast effect, 131–132
    in employment context,
        157–159
    and ingroup identification, 116–119
    and personal discrimination, 230–236
    and RD, 113–114
    role of status *see* group status
    temporal, 76–77, *78 see also* interpersonal
        comparisons
intrapersonal comparisons
    in employment context, 157, 158–159
    see also autobiographical memories;
        temporal-self comparisons
Iowa-Netherlands Comparison Orientation
    Measure (INCOM), 17

just-world beliefs, 251, 311
justice *see* equity; legitimacy

legitimacy, 114–116, 120–121, 290, 299,
    322–323 *see also* System Justification
    Theory (SJT)

legitimacy appraisals, 190
legitimizing ideologies *see* ambivalent
    gender ideologies; power distance
legitimizing myths, 209, 220
life-span model, 79–80

maths/science ability, 306, 309–310,
    310, 314
memories *see* autobiographical memories;
    self-congruent memories
men
    attitudes toward, 289–290
    impact of group status on self-esteem,
        140–142, *141 see also* gender
mobility, 100, 160–161, 238–240
motivated self-perception, 62–63
    and social comparison, 64–66
    and temporal-self comparisons,
        66–70
motivation, influence on memories, 61
motivation for comparison, 101–102
    comparison choice, 119–120
    comparison type, 70–71
    intergroup comparisons, 107–111, *109*,
        119–120
    self-protection, 234–236 *see also*
        enhancement; equity; evaluation

national differences
    and gender ideologies, 288, 289,
        290–299
    and group-based emotion, 186–191
    see also immigrants
Neosexism scale, 164, *165*
neuroticism, 18, 24

optimal distinctiveness model, 133
optimistic bias, 20
organizational cultures, 159–163
organizational identity, 169
organizations, conflict and cooperation in,
    168, 169

past selves, 66–67, 70, 84–88, 90
PD *see* Power Distance
perceived improvement, and RG, 218–219
Perceptions of Meritocracy Inventory
    (PMI), 163, 164, *165*
permeability of boundaries, 100, 114–116,
    120–121, 160–161, 238–240
perpetrator identity, 188–191
personal discrimination, 229–236
personal identity, 154
personal relative deprivation, 194,
    207, 320

personal-group discrimination discrepancy (PGDD), 180, 183, 228
  group discrimination, 236–242
  personal discrimination, 230–236
  sources of, 229–230
personality
  and SCO, 17–19
  and self-congruent memories, 61
personality traits, 325
  cross-cultural comparisons, 303, 324, 326 see also dispositional bias; gender traits; stereotypes
PGDD see personal-group discrimination discrepancy
political ideology, 214, 222, 222
possible self, 67–69
posttraumatic stress disorder (PTSD), 56
power distance (PD), 285–287, 304–305, 327–329, 335–337
  and ambivalent gender ideologies, 291–294, 293, 294, 297, 298, 299–300
  cultural differences, 322–323, 327–329, 328
  and gender equality, 293, 294, 294–296, 299–300
  in gender stereotypes research, 306, 307, 308, 308, 309, 309, 310, 310, 312
  and SCO, 331
prejudice
  and culture, 251
  and RD, 207–208
  and RG, 208–210, 216–223
  RG and immigrants, 215–216, 216
prestige, 267–268, 268
Protestant Work Ethic, 251
proximity of target, 100

RD see relative deprivation
reality, and memories, 56, 57
redistributive employment policies see gender-based redistributive employment policies
reference group see target choice
reference groups theory, 130
relational self-construal, 319, 329, 332–333, 334
relational/interdependent gender stereotype, 306, 307–308, 308
relationships, 21, 26, 27–28, 70
relative deprivation (RD)
  and attitudes toward immigrants, 215, 216, 216
  group RD, 194, 207, 237, 320, 321
  and group-based emotions, 193–198
  and intergroup attitudes, 207–208

personal RD, 194, 207, 320
  and social change, 237, 284
  and target choice, 111–114, 112, 120, 237
  and temporal-self comparisons, 85–86, 88–90
relative gratification (RG), 208–210
  and attitudes toward immigrants, 215–216, 216
  ecological validity of, 214–216
  and intelligence, 210–214, 212, 213
  mediators of, 218–223
  moderators of, 217–218
  and temporal-self comparisons, 85–86
  routine standard use, 38–40

sadness, 187, 192, 193
satisfaction, 218–219
science ability see maths/science ability
SCM see Stereotype Content Model
SCO see Social Comparison Orientation
SCT see Self-Categorization Theory
SDO see Social Dominance Orientation
selective accessibility, 40–48, 42, 81, 232
self
  actual and transitory, 62
  autobiographical memory as part of, 55, 59–60, 61
  comparison with see temporal-self comparisons
  cross-cultural comparisons, 318–319
  purpose of comparison for, 55
Self-Categorization Theory (SCT), 153, 155, 161, 174, 179, 325
self-coherent memories, 56–57
self-congruent memories, 60–62
self-consciousness, and SCO, 18
self-construal, 324–338
self-enhancement motive, 70, 82, 273
self-esteem
  and group comparisons, 128, 129, 144–146, 231–232
    group status, 137–139, 140–144, 141, 144
    upward intragroup comparisons, 128–132
  of men, 140–142, 141
  and SCO, 18
  and temporal-self comparisons, 70, 84–88
  of women, 140, 141
self-evaluation, 41–48, 81–83
self-evaluation maintenance model (SEM), 132
self-knowledge, 41–48, 233
Self-Memory-System (SMS), 58–59, 62

self-perception, 62–63, 64–70, 266
self-protective motivations, 234–236
SEM (self-evaluation maintenance model),
     132
similarity, 100
similarity hypothesis
     and group discrimination, 241–242
     and personal discrimination, 232–236
similarity testing, 42–48, 45, 64–65
SIT see Social Identity Theory
SJT (System Justification Theory), 251,
     310–315
SMS (Self-Memory-System), 58–59, 62
sociability, 312
social attribution, 272
social change, 160, 284, 285 see also
     collective action
social change orientation, 239
social cognition perspective, 33, 48
     accessibility, 40–48, 42
     cognitive efficiency, 34–40
social comparison
     across cultures see cross-cultural
          differences
     at group level see intergroup comparisons;
          intragroup comparisons
     at individual level see interpersonal
          comparisons; intrapersonal
          comparisons
     compared with temporal comparisons,
          77–81
     fundamental nature of, 15–16, 33,
          174, 318
     individual difference in use of, 16 see also
          Social Comparison Orientation
     levels of analysis, 127, 144–146,
          319–321
     motives for see motivation for comparison
     and social hierarchy, 284–285
     study of, 1, 2–3 see also cross-gender
          comparisons
Social Comparison Orientation (SCO), 16
     contexts of, 19–23
     cultural differences, 322–323, 329–338,
          330
     downward comparisons, 23–27
     measure of, 17
     and personality, 17–19
     upward comparisons, 27, 28
Social Dominance Orientation (SDO),
     219–220, 222, 222–223, 337–338
Social Dominance Theory, 209
social hierarchy, 284–285
     legitimizing ideologies see ambivalent
          gender ideologies; power distance

social identity, 154–156
     and group discrimination, 238
     and group status, 265
     identifying, 181–182
     impact on emotions see group-based
          emotions
     as victim or perpetrator, 188–191
Social Identity Theory (SIT), 99–101, 111,
     128, 160, 161, 311
social policies see gender-based
     redistributive employment policies
social psychology, 1–3
social status see group status
social stigma, 86, 88
socio-economic status, 104, 209, 217–218
socio-political attitudes, 88–90 see also
     political ideology
Southern African Migration Project
     (SAMP), 215
stability, 114–116, 120–121, 290, 299
standard extremity, 43, 46
standards
     judging similarity to, 42–48, 45, 64–65
     selection of, 33, 35–36, 38–40 see also
          target choice
status see group status
status boundaries, 160–161
status-competence hypothesis, 249–251,
     256–260
     in Asian settings, 251–252
     international studies, 252–255, 254, 256,
          257, 258
Stereotype Content Model (SCM), 249,
     257, 313
stereotype threats, 235
stereotypes
     of competence see status-competence
          hypothesis
     cultural and personal, 259–260
     of gender see ambivalent gender
          ideologies; gender stereotypes
     and RG, 209, 218
     and target choice, 158
Stigma theory, 88, 103, 107
stress, 25
structural variables, 114–116, 120–121
System Justification Theory (SJT), 251,
     310–315

target choice, 130–131
     cultural, 323–324
     and discrimination, 230–232, 236–241
     in employment context, 157–159
     ingroup identification, 116–119, 117, 121
     motives, 101–102, 107–111, 109, 119–120

target choice (cont.)
  primacy of ingroup, 102, 106
  and social identity theory, 99–101
  structural variables, 114–116, 120–121
  target status/deprivation, 111–114, *112*,
    120, 266–267 *see also* downward
    comparisons; standards; upward
    comparisons
target information, dismissal of, 142–144,
  144
temporal comparisons, 76–77, *78*, 90–91
temporal self-appraisal theory, 81
temporal-group comparisons, 76–77, *78*,
  80, 103, 106, 107, 116–119
temporal-self comparisons, 76
  choice of, 103, 106, 107, 116–119
  frequency of, 77–81
  motivation for, 70–71
  nature of, 77, *78*
  RD and socio-political attitudes, 88–90
  and RD/RG, 85–86
  self-esteem, well-being and, 84–88
  and self-evaluation, 81–83
  and self-perception, 66–70
threat, 234–236, *235*

tokenism, 238
traits *see* personality traits
transitory self, 62

unemployment, 86, 87
upward comparisons, 100, 108–111,
  231–232
  benefits of, 27, 28
  and mobility, 239
  and self-esteem, 128–132, *129*, 132–137,
    135, 138, 140, *141*, 143

V-curve, 215, *216*
victims, 188–193

warmth, 312
well-being, 84–88
women
  attitudes toward, 287–289
  impact of group status on self-esteem,
    140, *141*
  position in workforce, 151–153 *see also*
    gender
work *see* employment context
working self in SMS, 58–59, 60, 61